Idiocy

REPRESENTATIONS:
HEALTH, DISABILITY, CULTURE AND SOCIETY

Series Editor
Stuart Murray, University of Leeds

This series provides a ground-breaking and innovative selection of titles that showcase the newest interdisciplinary research on the cultural representations of health and disability in the contemporary social world. Bringing together both subjects and working methods from literary studies, film and cultural studies, medicine and sociology, 'Representations' is scholarly and accessible, addressed to researchers across a number of academic disciplines, and practitioners and members of the public with interests in issues of public health.

The key term in the series will be representations. Public interest in questions of health and disability has never been stronger, and as a consequence cultural forms across a range of media currently produce a never-ending stream of narratives and images that both reflect this interest and generate its forms. The crucial value of the series is that it brings the skilled study of cultural narratives and images to bear on such contemporary medical concerns. It offers and responds to new research paradigms that advance understanding at a scholarly level of the interaction between medicine, culture and society; it also has a strong commitment to public concerns surrounding such issues, and maintains a tone and point of address that seeks to engage a general audience.

Already published

Representing Autism. Culture, Narrative, Fascination
Stuart Murray

Idiocy

A Cultural History

Patrick McDonagh

LIVERPOOL UNIVERSITY PRESS

First published 2008 by
Liverpool University Press
4 Cambridge Street
Liverpool L69 7ZU

British Library Cataloguing-in-Publication data
A British Library CIP record is available

ISBN   978-1-84631-095-9 cased
ISBN   978-1-84631-096-6 limp

Typeset in Iowan Old Style by R. J. Footring Ltd, Derby
Printed in the European Union by Bell and Bain Ltd, Glasgow

To Gloria and Michael McDonagh

Contents

Preface and acknowledgements

In the middle of the 1980s, the provincial government of British Columbia, on the west coast of Canada, decided to shut down Woodlands, a large institution located in New Westminster, a suburb of Vancouver. Woodlands had been created in 1878 as the Provincial Lunatic Asylum, and in 1950 became a residential institution for several thousand people identified as 'mentally defective' (and, later, 'retarded'). By the 1980s, though, the community-living movement had been making effective cases against large institutions like Woodlands, and at any rate the growth of Vancouver meant that the institution's location was much more valuable as the future site of high-density living (a fate that also overtook Woodland's close neighbour, the BC Penitentiary). At the time, I had been working with the Dunbar Autistic Youth (DAY) programme for three or four years and, with my co-workers in this programme, including Susan (Stanfield) Kurliak and Ernie Baatz, had become aware that young adults diagnosed as autistic had few long-term community-living support options available to them. Eventually Susan, Ernie and I decided to form the Spectrum Association for Community Living, and enlisted co-workers and parents as early board members. We incorporated in April 1987, and quickly found that we were not going to be providing services for autistic youths as we had anticipated – the government contracts were simply not awarded according to such criteria. However, we appeared on the scene at a crucial stage in the deinstitutionalization movement in BC, and so it happened that shortly after incorporating we signed our first contract with the government to find a new home for two couples moving out of Woodlands. Part of our job – demanded by the housing commission, as I recall – was to canvas the area where we planned to establish this four-person home, in order to let the neighbours know what we were doing. One day, Susan reported to Ernie and I that she had met one elderly individual who had expressed a fear that the sort of people we were bringing into the neighbourhood would 'break through my screen door and kill my pets'. This response was too odd for us to be offended or outraged; we were simply bewildered and wrote it off as a bizarre anomaly (which, in the context of our canvassing, it was, and our attempt at providing supported living in a larger community seemed quite successful, especially for a first-time effort). But I could not shake this person's fear from my mind. Where would such an idea come from? What did it mean?

Of course, like most people, I had already witnessed some of the ambiguity around notions of intellectual competence. I began my formal education as a child at Sir William Osler Elementary School Annex in Vancouver, Canada. The annex was a small cluster of three or four portable buildings joined together on an empty lot that had been hastily tossed together a few years earlier to accommodate the city's growing number of children, and it was filled with pupils between grades 1 and 3. Our playground extended to a wire fence, and on the other side of that fence was a playground for another school, Oakridge, also new but in more permanent buildings. We had very little to do with the children at this school, but one day I remember standing near the dividing fence with a group of boys. On the other side was a girl, about the same age as we were – that is, somewhere between six and eight years old. 'Are you retarded?', one boy asked her through the wire. His tone had an accusatory ring to it, which may be why I remember this episode – because I doubt I had a sense of what the word meant. But I can still remember the words hanging in the air, and the offended look on the girl's face as she measured the question, responded 'No', and then turned and walked away. But the question was a fair one: she was in the 'special' school, after all, and children are curious.

I have no doubt that time has also affected and embellished these memories – neither Susan nor Ernie remembers quite so clearly the story of 'pet-killer fear' that caught my attention, and I have long since lost contact with everyone lingering at the edge of the fence when I was a child. But these episodes point to some important questions about intelligence and intellectual disability. What do these concepts mean? How do they come to be associated with certain values or qualities? And how do these concepts matter to us? I have thought about these incidents frequently over the years that I have been exploring the history of intellectual disability and its various conceptual cousins. Why would someone believe that this specific group of people would pose a danger to her well-being? And if that little girl insisted she was not retarded, then what did the term mean to her, and how could we reconcile her denial of this status to her place on the other side of the fence we were looking through? These questions lie at the core of this book.

Many people have contributed to this project, from its earliest incarnation as a doctoral dissertation to its current, much reworked state. This research began as a PhD thesis in the interdisciplinary humanities programme at Concordia University, and I have to credit my supervisors, Robert Martin, Graham Carr and Anthony Synnott, for its early formation, as well as the external examiners, John Miller and David Wright, whose comments helped shape the direction of this later project, and Marcie Frank, who helped me envision how to transform the thesis into a proper book.

Timothy Stainton and Chris Goodey both allowed me to read their own manuscripts exploring other aspects of the history of intellectual disability, and each has offered much commentary and productive criticism over the years. Both have been instrumental in helping me form the ideas expressed in this book, and if the reader finds points where the ideas are a bit fuzzy, it is entirely my own responsibility.

Some of the texts quoted are in translation, primarily from French. My strategy here has been to use translations that were contemporary – or close to it – with the original, such as the 1802 translation of Jean Itard's 1801 report on the 'wild boy of Aveyron'. But in those cases where there were no contemporary translations, I have chosen to provide new ones. Some of the translations from French sources are my own, but most – and certainly the longer passages – were made by Rhonda Mullins, for whose help I am greatly indebted. Chris Goodey also provided assistance with the odd Latin phrase. Thanks to both!

I also received helpful feedback from my copy-editor, Ralph Footring, and from Martin Halliwell; thanks are due to them for the invaluable work they put into making this a better book, as well as to Liverpool University Press's editor Anthony Cond and series editor Stuart Murray for their support and understanding, especially when I unilaterally altered deadlines. I would also like to acknowledge the very helpful librarians at Concordia University, McGill University (and especially at the Osler Medical History Library), the University of Manchester, the British Library and the Surrey Historical Centre in Woking.

Over the years I have solicited many other friends as readers and critics, including some of those who have been with me longest on this journey, most notably Susan Kurliak, Ernie Baatz, Aaron Johannes,

Joanne Thauli and Gulraj Thauli. All (with the exception of Aaron, who arrived a bit later, with Spectrum) were part of my first experiences working with people with autism and other intellectual differences; all helped form my early understandings and I have benefited from their exemplary generosity and goodness over the years.

I have also benefited from the commentaries of other readers who have encouraged me to produce something as readable and accessible as possible. Thanks to Lenore Alford, Wilson Blakely, Deborah Dunn, Rob McFadden and Tegan McFadden (these latter also for the audio book – there is nothing like having someone else read your work aloud and record it to make you realize that another draft might be needed).

I am a part-time faculty member at Concordia University, but I work primarily as a freelance writer; much of this work was discussed in weekly lunches with fellow freelancers Rhonda Mullins, Andrew Mullins and Maria Turner, to whom I owe thanks for consistent support and commiseration. In addition, much of this book was written and re-written at the New Navarino, under the benign supervision of Michelle Boulanger, Tony Sharkey, Peter Tsatoumis and others too numerous to name: thanks for the customized coffee, the odd embarrassing shout of encouragement and the bemused forbearance.

Over the past twenty years my association with the Spectrum Society for Community Living has kept me connected to the real lives of people identified as having intellectual disabilities: thanks (again!) to Aaron, Ernie, Gulraj and Susan, as well as to Shirley Birtwhistle, Diane Blackwood, Craig Blackwood, Sam Davison and Sarah Khan, and also to Sharon Baatz, Brenda and Ken Black, Mark Hamilton, Irene Holman, Michael McIntyre, Karen (Mah) Ostrom, Manuel Pickburn, Aki Takei, David Whelan and numerous others who have helped me learn through Spectrum and my previous work with PAAC and DAY.

Other people provided various forms of help along the way – a patient ear for when I felt the need to ramble on about my writing, or my own idiocy; a bed to sleep on while doing research on the road; flexible working arrangements and environments; and many happy and occasionally fruitful distractions: thanks are thus due to Diana Ayton, Patrick Baker, Malcolm Balk, Nuria Belastegui and Alan Roughley, Arnold Bennington, Carson and Amanda Bergstrom, Liana and Anthony Burgess, Iain Cooke, Stewart Cooke, John Cox, David Cronkite, Nathalie de Han, Helen Dyer, Owen Egan, Cornelius Fischer-Credo, Gordon Fletcher, Sylvia Franke, Lisa Godwin and Alistair Williamson, Sheldon Goldfarb, Trevor Gould, Linda Dawn Hammond, John Heward, Corinne Jetté, Linda Jordan, Kathy Kennedy, Catherine Kidd, Lyne Lanthier, Fabrice Laurent, Francine MacInnis,

Annette Mahon, Dean Makarenko, Kristine Markovic, Deborah Marks, Daniel McCabe, Fred McSherry, Katherine Morrow, Andrew Mullins, Tina Nielsen, Nadine Norman, Robyn Ouimet, Peter Park, Jamie Parker and Mim Pierce, Gary Rosenberg, Megan Roughley, Richard Rushton, Julian Samuel, The Shamefuls (including Jo-Anne Balcaen, Catharine Brown, Kurt Chaboyer, Chris Flower, Andrea Holtslander, Alan Kohl, Chris Roderick, Tracy Smee, Claude Theoret and Tod van Dyk), Cheryl Simon, Stuart Slind, Si Stainton, Kerri Strobl, Kristine Thelen, Jane Tingley, Terry Tobin, Cathy and Gary Tronrud, Nathalie Valiquette, Jennifer Westlake and Dawn Wiseman. And, of course, I have to credit my mother, Gloria, my sisters, Kathleen and Mary, my brother-in-law, Andy Hoppenrath, and nieces, Alicia and Helena Rose, for their consistent support and distractions over the years.

And, finally, thanks to Pasha and Manzie for taking me out for fresh air.

I have received necessary and much appreciated support to attend conferences from the Concordia University Part-Time Faculty Association, and a travel research grant from the Wellcome Trust that allowed me to explore the Earlswood archives.

Some of this work has been published in previous forms: Chapters 4 and 5 were once a short article appearing in the *British Journal of Learning Disabilities* (vol. 28, 2000); and Chapter 8 appeared in an earlier form in *Disability and Society* (vol. 21, 2006).

CHAPTER 1

Introduction: idiocy, culture and human relations

'I have to tell you a tale', said John Charles Bucknill to the governors of the newly formed Birmingham and Midland Counties Asylum for Idiots at their first annual meeting in 1873, at Birmingham town hall. 'Not, I trust, as Shakespeare says, "A tale told by an idiot full of sound and fury, signifying nothing", but, still, a tale of an idiot or of idiots. And I am warned by experience that I must trespass upon your patience so far as to describe what an idiot is' (Bucknill 1873: 169).

We might be surprised that Bucknill, onetime medical supervisor at Devon County Asylum, the Lord Chancellor's Visitor of Lunatics and the founder of the *Asylum Journal* (later the *Journal of Mental Science*), would assume that the governors of an idiot asylum would need to have an idiot described to them, but he was, as he says, relying on experience. Let us allow him to continue:

> On the occasion when it was decided by the Justices of the Peace for this County to establish the Asylum for Pauper Idiots, at Hatton, I well remember hearing an influential magistrate make the earnest inquiry – 'Who can tell me what an idiot really is?' I believe this question was not a vain and futile one, and that there are plenty of well-informed people who would have found it an exceedingly difficult one to answer well, and although I do know what an idiot is, I fear I shall not myself find this question an easy one to answer in this place. (Bucknill 1873: 169–70)

What is an idiot, and what is idiocy? We can imagine why Bucknill might be concerned – it was his job to know, after all – and why the governors of the Birmingham and Midland Counties Asylum for Idiots might need to know as well. But why might we care today? The idea of idiocy has not been the subject of much serious consideration over the years, yet the history of idiocy and related concepts has much to tell us – not only about class, gender and race relations, including social organization and political theory, but also about our assumptions concerning intelligence and those qualities that we believe ourselves to possess. The idiot has been transformed into a resilient contrast group, a category of people against whom we rational modern (and post-modern) folk can identify ourselves, to affirm our intelligence and to assert our claims to respect and justice. But to become this contrast group, idiots had to become stable and unidimensional. They had to be stripped of the numerous markers by which we understand ourselves and others, those qualities that accumulate to give us identities. People identified as idiots had to become *only* idiots, and nothing else. But this process occurred over time, over history, and developed according to the demands of a specific social environment. In Britain, the idea of 'idiocy' evolved in writings and social interactions, and through the physical segregation imposed by the asylum system of the late nineteenth and twentieth centuries. The formation of idiocy, the refinement of its symbolic and ideological functions, was also a part of the process by which we became the people we are, or believe ourselves to be: rational, reasonable, with a claim to rights and authority. Thus, idiocy is as much a socially and ideologically meaningful concept as it is a way of saying something about other people, and the study of idiocy is the study of a particular form of exile, through which some humans are removed in order to enable the remainder to believe in their own unalloyed intelligence. 'Idiocy' is thus a term to designate *other* people, or other groups of people. In sum, the idea of idiocy takes shape as part of a historical process, and this process is also that which creates the contemporary individual.

In 1823, fifty years before Bucknill stood before the asylum governors in the Birmingham town hall to tell them about idiocy, the physician and psychologist John Haslam had claimed that, while lunacy might be complex and subject to difficult interpretation, 'the state of idiocy is well understood, although cases of an intricate nature may occasionally occur' (Haslam 1823: 18). Clearly, things had changed by Bucknill's day, and the questions posed by idiocy seemed more challenging than they had been. One symptom of this growing complexity in the idea of idiocy can be seen in the attempts to delineate its various forms. Édouard Séguin, the French pioneer of pedagogy for people identified as 'idiots', had singled out only *l'idiotie profonde* and *l'idiotie superficielle* in 1846, and the American Samuel Gridley Howe in 1848 proposed three divisions, 'pure idiots', 'fools' and 'simpletons' (the last, he noted, were also known as 'imbeciles' in Britain). But in 1861, P. Martin Duncan and his colleagues elaborated a taxonomy that included six distinct forms of idiocy and another seven 'accessory cases', from 'imbeciles' to 'backward children'. In 1866, Duncan and William Millard simplified these classifications to an eight-part division of idiocy and imbecility, including both congenital and non-congenital forms; that same year, John Langdon Down, onetime superintendent at the National Asylum for Idiots in Earlswood, had identified six 'ethnic' classifications of idiocy, including his famous 'mongoloid idiot'. And in 1872, the year before Bucknill met the asylum governors, W. W. Ireland, medical supervisor of the Scottish National Institution for the Training of Imbecile Children, argued that 'idiocy and imbecility are purely mental classifications; in short ... they are other names for psychical deficiency commencing in early life' (Ireland 1872: 335). He then proposed his own ten classifications, among them hydrocephalic idiocy, epileptic idiocy, traumatic idiocy, congenital idiocy and idiocy by deprivation. No wonder, then, that defining idiocy should prove a challenge.

But in some ways the opposite was true as well, and Bucknill's consternation about describing idiocy does not diminish his certainty that he knows what idiocy is. Idiocy could be an ambiguous state, albeit at the same time, in Haslam's words, 'well understood'. In 1823, the same year that Haslam asserts the relatively uncomplicated nature of idiocy, John Galt's novel *The Entail* (discussed in Chapter 4) presented as a central character Walter (Watty) Walkinshaw, a 'Natural' who is worried about his inheritance (Galt 1822/23: 102). His father, Claud Walkinshaw, says of him that, 'haverel though it's like to be, is no sae ill as to be cognos't' (36), meaning that Watty may be something of a half-wit, but he still has enough wit left to avoid being declared an idiot judicially. Throughout the novel, other characters offer other assessments of Watty's prospects: Mr Keelevin, the family lawyer, suggests that 'Watty, not to speak disrespectful of his capacity, might never marry' (57), although the elder Walkinshaw disputes this claim and also rebuts Keelevin's later assertion that Watty 'should na be meddled wi'' but just left to wear out his time in the world, as little observed as possible' (59). Watty does eventually marry and receives the paternal estate in favour of his disinherited older brother, Charles, whose choice of wife has alienated him from his father. A scheming younger brother, George, realizes that Watty's capacity can be called into question, as the lawyer Keelevin had supposed, and eventually, despite Claud Walkinshaw's prediction, Watty is declared legally an idiot, his inheritance reverting to George. Shamed by the decision, Watty slowly withers and dies.

In contrast, Maria Fulmont in Charlotte Yonge's 1860 novel *Hopes and Fears, or Scenes From the Life of a Spinster* is eventually identified as being 'innocent' half way through the novel, at which point the character is in her early teens. Her family, including several close sisters, have not recognized her condition, although one sister, Phoebe, admits that she 'always knew [Maria] was not clever'; however, Phoebe credits this to Maria's isolation from society, saying of her, 'She is so good and kind! If only she could see a few things, and people, and learn to talk' (241). It is left to the governess to diagnose Maria as having 'not the usual amount of capacity', and she notes 'that she cannot be treated as otherwise than deficient' (242). For the remainder of the novel, Yonge makes it clearer through her descriptions and the statements of the other characters that Maria is indeed mentally deficient, but the revelation comes as a shock to the family (and in fact to me: I wasn't sure if it was Maria or Bertha, the stuttering rationalist, who was deficient until the 'outing', even though I knew one of them was). Once the label is applied and Maria is revealed as 'the poor innocent' (321) she always was, the descriptions of her before her diagnosis – such as her 'leav[ing] off trying to read a French book that had proved too hard for her' (121) – assume a new portentousness.

Watty Walkinshaw, the 'haverel' of *The Entail*, is legally declared an idiot, but for the reader (and in the world of the novel) this construction remains contingent upon the case elaborated by the prosecution: that Watty's grief at the deaths of his wife and daughter was excessive and took unconventional forms, and that he could not manage money responsibly. The reader can acknowledge the strength of the case before Watty and even accept Watty as *'fatuus'* (Galt 1823: 181) but at the same time must remain aware of the parameters of the label and the manner in which it is constructed and imposed: Watty clearly seems to meet the criteria in some areas, whereas in others he is an irreproachable gentleman. The legal designation carries authority, but of a restricted sort. Thirty-seven years later, though, the limits on this authority are fast disappearing. Maria Fulmont becomes fully the 'poor innocent' as soon as everyone realizes that this is her state; after Maria is fixed as being deficient, Yonge is able to refer to her walking with 'the shuffling gait of the imbecile' (372). Idiocy is at least in part a social role in the earlier novel, but it resides completely within the individual by the time of the latter. This distinction is not just a consequence of differing authorial whims on the parts of Galt and Yonge. The concept of idiocy alters in the time between these two novels, acquiring a significantly more formal status in medical, sociological and pedagogical discourses.

But this new status does not necessarily make idiocy any easier to nail down, as Bucknill's address to the Birmingham governors shows, and the question is still a poser: what, exactly, did the term 'idiot' mean to a mid-Victorian audience? As Martin Duncan had observed in 1861:

> It may readily be assumed, from the paucity of reliable and trustworthy information on idiocy, that hasty generalizations, baseless assertions, and captivating theories should abound; nor is it likely to be doubted that the first steps of the truthful inquirer, when brought into contact with the objects of his study, are retrogressive. To unlearn is to take a great step in this, as in many other pursuits. (233)

We shall come back to the latter portion of Duncan's observation; for now, let us consider those 'hasty generalizations' and 'baseless assertions' that muddied the idea of idiocy – and, for that matter, continue to muddy the contemporary concepts of intellectual disability, or mental retardation, or cognitive impairment, or developmental delay, or learning disability. Anyone wanting to understand the history of the idea of intellectual disability and its various genealogical precursors, such as idiocy, must contend with the slipperiness of the key terms. As Arthur Lovejoy noted in 1948, any history of ideas has to struggle with 'the rôle of semantic transitions and confusions, of shifts and of ambiguities in the meanings of terms, in the history of thought and of taste' (xii). With concepts as slippery as 'idiocy' and its kin, this task is imposing, but critical, especially as these terms relate to individual people. Certainly there are individuals so designated who need assistance in performing some – or even most – of the acts of daily life; others need occasional support services to facilitate some of the more complex elements of social life. But our interpretation of these needs has been heavily overdetermined, as have been our denials of our own similar needs in our assertions of independence and competence. Our broad cultural notions of intelligence (and its apparent lack) are laden with baggage packed with ideas and preconceptions about gender, class, ethnicity and religion, among others. Consequently, idiocy as a concept is nothing if not problematic, ambiguous and obscure – a shadow image (Stainton and McDonagh 2001) or, more prosaically (and at the very least), a social construction (Rapley 2004). Idiocy appears as a state of being when applied to an individual, but it is also a reification: an idea given flesh and embodied by (or imposed upon) specific individuals. All the same, many histories tend to accept a relatively uncomplicated reading of idiocy as something residing fully within the people so designated, with different historical approaches simply providing different lenses through which to view the same phenomenon.

This historiographic inclination misses some important questions. First of all, how do we know if the phenomenon designated by 'idiocy' or one of its many related terms is the same across the ages? And secondly, if 'idiocy' is not the same thing from one time or place to the next, what *is* it? We have no way of knowing for certain if someone called a 'fool' in the sixteenth century would, if transported through time, be called 'simple' in the eighteenth century, an 'imbecile' in the 1890s, or 'moderately or mildly retarded' in the 1960s; nor do we know if someone called an 'idiot' in 1760 would still be one in 1860, or 'severely retarded' in 1960. Even in their own days, these terms signified a remarkably wide range of characteristics: the sixteenth-century designation 'fool' could be applied to atheists, physically distinct people like dwarfs or hunchbacks, people who seemed lacking in wit,[1] professional performers and even those hapless amateurs who imitated professional performers. In the fourteenth century, the legal term 'idiot' meant exactly what it said in Greek: a private man. When the term was affixed to an individual by the Court of Chancery after an investigation into the defendant's ability to perform such tasks as handle money and identify lineage, it meant that person was no longer considered a 'public individual' capable of holding any degree of authority at the indulgence of the Crown; instead, he was demoted to the lowly status of an *idiota*, who does not hold a public office and is thus level with peasants and (most) women (Goodey 2008). The criteria for being identified as a 'fool' or even a fourteenth-century 'idiot' would not necessarily include those individuals diagnosed as 'idiots' in the nineteenth century. Even after the professionalization of the treatment of idiocy, there was no guarantee of constant diagnoses. Among his tales to the Birmingham governors, Bucknill recounts a story told by the medical officer of the Western Counties Asylum, one Dr Pycroft, who had noted that 'In the year 1864 the first patient was admitted, but as he was adjudged by the medical officer and by the committee generally to be a clever boy of much more than average intellect, he was returned to his parents'. Misdiagnoses such as these were, of course, 'wonderful and exceptional cases', Bucknill assured his listeners, and there was no danger of such errors taking place at the new Birmingham and Midlands Counties Asylum (Bucknill 1873: 180).[2] But 'idiocy' professionals were aware of the porosity of their taxonomies. Duncan and Millard (1866: 13) warned that 'there are no accurately distinctive symptoms which separate clearly the sub-divisions of congenital idiocy; there is a gradual progression in intellect and physical power from the lowest to the highest; yet the artificial and broad definitions will be found useful'. Not surprisingly, then, asylum records show individuals receiving different diagnoses at different times and from different physicians. When patient number 2762 at the Earlswood institution was admitted as an eight-year-old in 1891, he was described as a 'good laundry boy', amiable but unsuccessful in schooling; in later years he was diagnosed in case updates as an imbecile (May 1915, January 1919, May 1941, May 1946, May 1951) and, according to the last three entries, with a mental age of three, but also as an idiot (June 1931, August 1936); he died in the institution in 1952, after living sixty-one of his sixty-nine years within its walls.[3]

If such variation existed in one institutional reading of an individual, imagine the faith required to believe in the stability of 'idiocy' across decades. And across cultures – even closely related ones – the problems are magnified. The English physician Martin Duncan, summarizing an 1848 Massachusetts report on idiocy, concluded that 'it would appear that the statistics of one nation will not apply to the idiots of another, unless the social and climatic conditions are the same'; instead, the report's 'fairest conclusions become doubtful when they are examined and tested by our experience amongst our own countrymen' and 'in America there is hardly a case whose history does not bear upon its cause; here it is quite the opposite' (Duncan *et al.* 1861: 237) – an observation that anticipates the virulence of the American eugenics movement compared with the British version. So, when Samuel Gridley Howe (1848) claimed that his term 'simpleton' is the American equivalent to the British 'imbecile', we must ask if they are truly equivalent. Of course, this question needled mid-century observers as well as twenty-first-century historians. The anonymous writer of 'Cretins and Idiots' in the 1858 *Atlantic Monthly* noted that most residents of the Earlswood institution were not, in fact, 'idiots' as the term was understood in the United States, but rather 'the greater part of the admissions ... are from the pauper and poor laboring classes; and the simple substitution of wholesome and sufficient food for a meager and innutritious diet is alone sufficient to effect a marked change in them' (Anonymous 1858: 417). Thus, while agreeing that the asylum is a force for benevolence, the article claims that 'these youths are not idiots, and no such analogy exists between them and idiots as would enable us to infer with certainty the successful treatment of the latter from the comparatively rapid development of the former' (417). This slippage in terms is important for our understanding of idiocy's social-symbolic function. That is, if basic definitions are not harmonized across cultures, we should be asking if the concept does or does not perform the same functions across cultures. To the British writer, American 'idiocy' is rooted in a perverse familial lineage, whereas the American writer perceives a British 'idiocy' connected to class; surely this distinction is important.

Rather than being an insurmountable difficulty for historians, these shifting concepts, diverging associations and wide-ranging terminologies and diagnostic categories help us to track those historical processes shaping the concept of idiocy and its related terms, and form a subject of critical study in their own right. As the cultural historian Roger Chartier has noted, drawing on the work of the sociologist Pierre Bourdieu, 'the historian examining classifications and groupings is not ... straying from the social realm' but is rather 'identifying trouble-spots that are all the more conclusive for being less immediately material' (Chartier 1988: 5). While the history of the idea of idiocy and its related groupings has been grossly neglected, it is critical to our understanding of both contemporary and historical notions of intelligence – in addition to providing a necessary complement to social and institutional histories in developing an understanding of 'intellectual disability'. Indeed, the importance of stable notions of idiocy to our belief in intelligence – and, by extension, in our own intelligence – is probably the primary reason for this strenuous neglect of idiocy's history.

This book argues that ideas such as 'idiocy' and 'imbecility' are, as Ireland claimed, 'mental classifications' buttressed by a dynamic interplay of factors – but with a difference, of course. The history of idiocy as an idea must address the issues that arise when such 'mental classifications' are given flesh – that is, when they become part of the daily matter of the social life of specific individuals. Concepts are applied to individuals for a number of ideologically potent reasons that are laden with unexplored associations. One goal of this book is to look into these associations – what can they reveal about idiocy, about intelligence, about the people identified as idiots and about ourselves?

In describing a cultural history of the idea of idiocy as it has been applied to particular groups of people, this book is not presenting a history of 'idiocy' as an invective, an allegation tossed at others, as when Alexander Pope mocks his poetic competitors in *The Duncaid* (1742) by having them compete to win the approval of the goddess 'Dulnes', the 'fair Ideot', 'Daughter of Chaos and eternal Night', who 'rul'd, in native Anarchy, the mind' (from lines 11–16).[4] But these applications of the term are not entirely separate, and we could very easily see the bodily presence of people identified as idiots as a flesh-and-blood personification of this invective, rather than the opposite.

'Its considerable semantic shifts and dislocations not withstanding, everyone knows what it means to call someone an idiot', Avital Ronell points out in her playful (yet very cerebral) exploration of stupidity (Ronell 2002: 167). But do we insult people by calling them 'idiots' because we want to align them with those devalued individuals whose intellectual, social and moral capacities are considered subnormal, or do we diagnose people as 'intellectually disabled' (or 'idiotic') and assert a phalanx of restrictions and prohibitions over them because we wish to isolate a disturbing concept within a specific population rather than leave it loose to roam among 'normal' humans such as ourselves? Idiocy is a metonymic state: when it is a diagnostic label pasted onto a human, that human becomes defined by his or her capacity to embody the part of human nature called 'idiocy', which is also that part of our being receiving the invective. The 'idiot', in embodying for us our own flaws, our fears, our incapacities and our failures, becomes that part of ourselves we usually avert our eyes from. But this argument suggests that intelligence itself is a reification, a particularly malleable and squishy concept, open to conflicting definitions, that masquerades as a specific and identifiable quality or set of qualities that we can call our own. Perhaps our unwillingness to look directly at what a relatively slow cognitive process means to us has made idiocy (or intellectual disability – or, for that matter, intelligence) seem invisible as a category worthy of critical analysis; we have long assumed it to be an ideologically neutral designation, although nothing could be further from the truth.

Of course, from the early decades of the twentieth century the physical separation and isolation in institutions of those people who wore the 'idiocy' label made the historical processes shaping the concept even more invisible. That the history of ideas of idiocy and its flip side, intelligence, has been ignored as an appropriate subject of investigation and analysis, and that the relation of this history to other streams of thought, other realms of discussion, has been almost completely neglected, suggests just how effectively the idea has been absorbed within frameworks that shape its meaning. Now might be a good time to recall the latter portion of our earlier quotation from Martin Duncan on working with idiots: 'the first steps of the truthful inquirer, when brought into contact with the objects of his study, are retrogressive. To unlearn is to take a great step...' (Duncan 1861: 233). Learning the history of idiocy, or intellectual disability, or mental retardation, demands that we forget much of what we think we already know. As recent publications suggest, some of this 'unlearning' has already begun, at least provisionally.

The critical background

For years, the only available histories of idiocy and related concepts were works such as Leo Kanner's *A History of the Care and Study of the Mentally Retarded* (1964), Richard Scheerenberger's *A History of Mental Retardation* (1983) and Peter Tyor and Leland Bell's *Caring for the Retarded in America* (1984), all of which tracked the growth of the professional treatment of people bearing the relevant labels; a shorter and more politicized rendition of this history appeared in Ryan and Thomas's *The Politics of Mental Handicap* (1987). The past dozen years, however, have seen a flood of publications by historians, primarily in social and institutional history; most of the chapters in David Wright and Anne Digby's seminal edited collection *From Idiocy to Mental Deficiency* (1996) focus on these areas. Mathew Thomson's *The Problem of Mental Deficiency* (1998) examines the development and application of mental deficiency laws and their relation to movements in health care and eugenics, while Mark Jackson's *The Borderland of Imbecility* (2000) investigates the growth of the concept of feeble-mindedness through an analysis of Mary Dendy's Sandlebridge schools (see Chapter 12). David Wright's *Mental Disability in Victorian England* (2001) presents a social history based on his research on the archives of the Earlswood asylum, while James Trent's *Inventing the Feeble Mind* (1994) and Philip Ferguson's *Abandoned to Their Fate* (1994) track the asylum movement in the USA, and Steven Noll's *Feeble-Minded in Our Midst* (1995) documents the history of 'institutions for the mentally retarded' in the southern United States from 1900 to 1940.[5] Some of these works sustain a critical analysis of the categories used to define people; for example, Trent, Thomson and Jackson are concerned primarily with the creation of those categories – 'feeble-minded' in Britain, 'moron' in the USA – that rest on 'the borderland of imbecility' and they investigate some of the social currents, especially growing middle-class anxiety about urban poverty, economic competition and moral degeneracy, and, in the United States, race and miscegenation, that helped feed these concepts, as well as the political responses to them. Recently, Edward Shorter has written the political history *The Kennedy Family and the Story of Mental Retardation* (2000), focusing on the role played by the Kennedy administration and family in the reform of laws governing 'mental retardation' in the United States.

However, the core concept – idiocy – still remains largely untouched by critical historical analysis. There are exceptions, of course. Chris Goodey (1994, 1996, 2004) has contributed a series of provocative and challenging analyses of the ideological development and application of idiocy and related concepts by writers from John Locke to Thomas Willis and Paracelsus; Jonathan Andrews (1998a, 1998b) explores the social meaning of idiocy in a pair of wide-ranging and informative articles; Tim Stainton (2004) has analysed the representation of folly and disability in northern European Renaissance art; and Goodey and Stainton (2001) have challenged conventional thinking about the 'changeling' myth in the light of intellectual disability. Martin Halliwell's *Images of Idiocy* (2004), while not a history *per se* and concerned with textual images rather than the interaction of text and context, addresses the symbolic functions of 'idiot' characters in modern fiction and film, and thus provides insights into some of the symbolic resonances of the idea of idiocy; and Robert Bogdan's *Freak Show* (1988) approaches tangentially the display of people with intellectual (and other) disabilities in the late nineteenth and early twentieth centuries.[6] But these instances are few, and the history of idiocy is long and rich.

So what are we talking about when we discuss the history of idiocy? And how might we further unravel the strands that tie together the concept? Most historians have turned to archives to understand the history of idiocy, but these tell the story primarily from one perspective: that of the institution and its employees. Thus, Jackson's work relies heavily on the Sandlebridge archives and Wright's on Earlswood's; and Thomson is indebted to political records and related documents, as well as institutional archives. These histories, all offering critical insights into the social history of idiocy, often allude to broadly 'cultural' sources of historical evidence to support or illustrate their findings, but do not actively investigate these sources. Recently, autobiographical information and first-person oral histories have been made available by academic researchers working in conjunction with people who have been identified as having intellectual disabilities (e.g. Walmsley 2001; Atkinson and Walmsley 1999; Atkinson and Williams 1990; Dybwad and Bersani 1996), and groups such as People First[7] have set out to document the histories of their members. But these latter sources, despite their contemporary importance, are of limited use to the historian of periods before the 1950s, as few older autobiographical records have been left behind by people identified as idiots.

One challenge for the historian is to determine the whole range of factors that make some people more likely to bear the label than others. If we do not analyse the constituents of the idea of idiocy – if we are not trying to identify the forces that help shape it into being – then we are implicitly accepting idiocy as an objective category, without a pervasive metaphorical or symbolic function, and free from ideological taint. And this would be an error. All the evidence shows that idiocy performs symbolic and ideological tasks.

Names and naming

'The terms used in the literature of idiocy, complicate the first steps of practical inquiry greatly, and different writers, regardless of the necessity for unanimity, use the same words to describe various classes of idiots' wrote Duncan *et al.* in 1861:

> It soon becomes manifest, that a total revision is necessary, and that when the subject has been studied for years, and its theoretical portion becomes advanced, the word 'idiot' itself will have to give place to some other, more expressive of the cases to which it is now applied. (Duncan *et al.* 1861: 236)

This wide and fluid terminology that worries Duncan and his colleagues has often appeared as both an obstacle to understanding idiocy and as an indication of its universality: after all, everyone seems to have a word for it. Séguin opens his 1846 *Traitement moral, hygiène et éducation des idiots* with a multi-linguistic and cross-cultural list of synonyms for 'idiocy', a strategy he reprises in his English-language work twenty years later (Séguin 1866). But as Duncan points out, these words all too often do not signify the same thing.

People who are now designated 'mentally retarded', 'intellectually disabled', 'developmentally delayed', 'learning disabled' or 'cognitively impaired' have – as the multiplicity of current terms suggests – been subject to a staggering number of labels and epithets over the years, and the condition denoted by any one term may not be absolutely (or even remotely) identical to that denoted by another, especially as each term is the product of a specific social and cultural environment. Disability activists and theorists have elaborated a distinction between the concepts of 'impairment' and 'disability': the former denotes a physical condition whereas the latter is a social condition, a form of oppression, exclusion or constraint (Davis 1995; Oliver 1996; Gleeson 1997). Disability is thus a state that 'any society *might* produce in its transformation of first nature – the bodies and materials received from previous social formations', argues Brendan Gleeson (1997: 193). However, in the case of 'idiocy' this impairment is already ambiguous and unstable: where is it, precisely, and how do we know it exists in any other than a statistical sense, as a predetermined deviation from a mathematical mean? The people to whom terms such as 'intellectual disability' or 'idiocy' refer (or have in the past referred) may well have an impairment of some sort – but this is far from certain, as the 'impairment' may be no more substantial than the 'disability', and often remains indistinguishable from it.[8] However, my goal is not to evaluate the meaningfulness of some possible impairment or the accuracy of terms used to designate it, but rather to investigate the process by which a particular society reproduces and re-imagines this presumption of impairment within the culturally meaningful notion of idiocy.

On a fundamental level the labels and syntax used to identify disabilities reflect the speakers' positions. Certainly the label most favoured by the US disability civil rights movement, 'people with [intellectual] disabilities', is meant to denote a group whose members are determined to emphasize their humanity, with the disability assuming the status of a secondary characteristic, rather than being a primary designation. However, this label is not without its critics. Gleeson, following disability theorist Paul Abberley, argues that 'the endless tendency to reinvent titles for disabled people is characteristic of a vacuous humanism which seeks to emphasise a "human commonality" over the material reality of oppression', and denounces this formulation as 'a retrograde terminological change which effectively depoliticises the social discrimination that disabled people are subjected to' (Gleeson 1997: 182), a criticism shared by disability theorist Michael Oliver, a primary figure in the development of the social model of disability (see for example Oliver 1990). Gleeson, Oliver and the British disability movement in general have endorsed the use of the term 'disabled person' as a more politically direct designation that foregrounds social oppression.

Obviously, *some* term has to be used to designate the people who are implicated in the notion of intellectual disability. Throughout my work, I alternate between some variation of the 'people identified as having…' formulation when referring to the actual human beings judged 'idiotic' or diagnosed as 'intellectually disabled', and whatever designation – 'idiot', 'innocent', 'imbecile' – is used in the text being cited or the period being discussed. This terminological approach will foreground of the social position of those people identified as being 'idiots'; the tension between the terms is critical to our understanding of how concepts have shifted across time and space, and of what consequences these shifts have for people so identified. On a very basic level, I do not replace 'idiocy' and its historical brethren with terms more harmonious to contemporary sensibilities, such as 'intellectual disability', because they are not the same thing, even if they are conceptually related. The varying meanings of the different labels become much clearer when no single one is given priority as a more correct or accurate way of designating a particular state of being, impaired, disabled or otherwise. For this reason, I replicate the historical terms, as well as diagnoses, as I find them.

The cultural history of idiocy

'Amongst the abnormal conditions of humanity, imbecility, at first sight so repulsive, so barren of all suggestion, will appear when we come to look at it more closely, to be rich in analogical inference and full of tender poetry', wrote asylum advocate and poet Dora Greenwell in 1868 (76). True to her observation, poetry and analogical inference have played a major role in shaping the idea of idiocy and imbecility, but not everyone has been pleased by this state of affairs. In 1862, John Langdon Down lamented:

> The opinion which has been formed, both in and out of the [medical] profession, in reference to idiocy, has arisen more from the representations of poets and romance-writers than from the deductions of rigid observation. The popular novelist, in this as in other cases, seizes on the characteristics of some exaggerated specimen, portrays them by the aid of a vivid imagination, and henceforth the exaggeration becomes the type of a species in the mind of men. (See Down 1887: 92)

Clearly, literary and other cultural products are important to understanding the history of the idea of idiocy, even if the notions expressed in these sources do not always conform to those endorsed by medical practitioners and their allies.

When 'idiocy' appears in texts, whether they are novels, personal letters, medical reports or newspaper articles, it is laden with meanings from the explicit to the subtle and unacknowledged. Such evidence often makes metaphoric and symbolic use of the idea of idiocy and its conceptual cousins, even while making no assumption of objectivity. Literary works, for instance, play to popular notions and ideas, thus providing insights into the components of a concept like 'idiocy'. Of course, evidence gathered from cultural products has important limitations: it does not necessarily record how those people labelled as idiotic, imbecilic or feeble-minded were treated in society; nor does it provide a consistently reliable means of revealing social attitudes to these people, although some sources may contain these kinds of insights. However, by placing vernacular alongside other forms of evidence we can layer the symbolic function of idiocy, most explicit in cultural texts, over the more apparently objective renditions of the idea expressed in professional and institutional works; we can thus read more clearly the tensions and correlations that help define idiocy's cultural significance. Mary Poovey argues in respect of Victorian gender imagery 'that the construction and deployment of these images performed critical ideological work ... that they were intimately involved in the development of England's characteristic social institutions, the organization of its most basic economic and legal relations, and in the rationalization of its imperial ambitions' (Poovey 1988: 2). Representations of 'idiocy' also act in what Poovey (1988: 15) calls the 'symbolic economy' of texts: that is, within the relations of signs and symbols that constitute a work's meaning, the 'internal structure of ideology'. This approach has influenced my own attempts to make sense of 'idiocy' imagery, and to determine how and why these images are put to work in texts in the way that they are. The better we understand the ideological and symbolic labour performed by idiocy in the nineteenth century, for example, the easier it becomes to give shape and form to the ideas motivating and validating the concept.

By the nineteenth century in Britain, the once prevalent, theologically inspired reading of idiocy, which, depending on one's theological position, aligned the condition with either divine or demonic powers, was layered over (rather than replaced) by subsequent readings born of evolutionary theories, social concerns, political philosophies, economic policies, medical hypotheses and educational strategies, all functioning within the dynamic relations of that society. Maria Fulmont in Yonge's *Hopes and Fears* is presented as both a pathologized imbecile with her 'shuffling gait' and a Christian 'innocent', a fusion not easily maintained philosophically or scientifically, as expressing two distinct and often opposed positions, but one which was apparently much less challenging to support in daily life. Occasionally, older concepts of idiocy resurface within newer frameworks, or simply refuse to disappear. Indeed, these older concepts often determine the shape assumed by newer ideas, so that the demonic idiot shares significant features with the later pathological or degenerate idiot.

Cultural works foreground the symbolic functions of nineteenth-century notions of idiocy in a manner that is often repressed in forms of writing that presume objectivity – although not so often as we might expect, as many nineteenth-century physicians and related professionals were willing to engage in flights of metaphor and analogy in their writings. All the same, the symbolic or metaphorical uses of 'idiot' characters in literary works often express culturally charged beliefs about the subtexts or connotations of idiocy, which are less overtly explored in professional or institutional writings and rarely articulated in the same manner. In *Narrative Prosthesis*, David Mitchell and Sharon Snyder argue that 'disability pervades literary narrative, first, as a stock feature of characterization and, second, as an opportunistic metaphorical device' (Mitchell and Snyder 2000: 47). Disability images provide a means of 'complicating … representational universes' (2) and thus conveying meanings that otherwise would remain inexpressible or transgressive, with the result that disability becomes 'foundational to both cultural definition and to the literary narratives that challenge normalizing prescriptive ideals.... In short, disability characterization can be understood as a prosthetic contrivance upon which so many of our cultural and literary narratives rely' (51). Disability imagery fills a narrative void, acting as a bridge (or a prosthetic) to enable a metaphysical or symbolic reading that the text cannot articulate (or refuses to) explicitly. Mitchell and Snyder are writing almost exclusively about physical disability – hence their use of the 'prosthetic' metaphor – but the same notion often applies to narratives drawing on images of idiocy.

Critical analyses of the concept of idiocy allow us to ask 'What did idiocy *mean* to the people writing and reading these texts? And *why* did it mean what it did?' The goal of cultural history, as Mark Poster (1997: 10) defines it, is:

> the study of the construction of the subject, the extent through which and the mechanisms through which individuals are attached to identities, the shapes and characteristics of these identities, the role the process of self-constitution plays in the disruption or stabilization of political formations, and the relation of all these processes to distinctions of gender, ethnicity and class.

The challenge facing historians, then, becomes:

> to describe the mechanisms through which such people [as 'suffering workers' or 'victimized women'] were constituted as subjects in relation to the measure of stable, centered autonomy; to show how the discursive figure of the universal, free individual was paradoxically able to designate these groups and others as outside the universal and as unfree, to show that modern freedom has always only been possible through its exclusions. (11)

As Poster suggests, our objective is to obtain a fuller understanding of the various manifestations, articulations and parameters of the ideas of idiocy and their functions within different social spaces and contexts. In *The Archaeology of Knowledge*, Michel Foucault (1969: 32) writes that:

> It would certainly be a mistake to try to discover what could have been said about madness at a particular time by interrogating the being of madness itself, its secret content, its silent, self-enclosed truth; mental illness was constituted by all that was said in all the statements that named it, divided it up, described it, explained it, traced its developments, indicated its various correlations, judged it, and possibly gave it speech by articulating, in its name, discourses that were to be taken as its own. Moreover, this group of statements is far from referring to a single object, formed once and for all, and to preserving it indefinitely

as its horizon of inexhaustible ideality; the object presented as their correlative by medical statements of the seventeenth or eighteenth century is not identical with the object that emerges in legal sentences or police action; ... it is not the same illnesses that are at issue in each of these cases: we are not dealing with the same madmen.

To meet this problem, Foucault focuses on discursive formations, statements in which 'one can define a regularity (an order, correlations, positions and functionings, transformations)' (1969: 38). The critical concern becomes not whether we are referring to exactly the same physiological condition across the years, but whether the terms used to designate a condition are part of repeating, transforming and interconnected discourses. Our goal then shifts from describing a presumed objective condition – 'idiocy' in our case – to analysing the terms, the language and structures that articulate the cultural idea of that condition, and thus confer upon a concept such as 'idiocy' its status as an objective state.

The path from sixteenth-century folly to nineteenth-century idiocy does not follow a straight line; in fact, the path from early modern legal applications of 'idiocy' does not follow a straight line to nineteenth-century medical 'idiocy' either, even though the terms are the same. Idiocy, mental deficiency, folly, mental retardation, intellectual disability and learning disability are not all the same names for a trans-historically stable subject; instead, they designate different manifestations of a set of related ideas, which are then embodied in specific individuals (or perhaps not – 'folly' was often presented as a general characteristic of all humanity in sixteenth-century writings). The discourse of idiocy is connected to broader social and cultural discourses and, thus, must be considered in this context. The concept of idiocy may be dramatically different from one time and place to another. For instance, it would be very difficult to find a physician today who would state that idiocy could be caused by excessive masturbation – itself a difficult-to-quantify notion, for how much is too much? In the United States of the 1850s, however, those physicians were apparently quite common – substantially more so than in Britain.[9] This association between masturbation and idiocy is significant, even if, from a twenty-first-century perspective, clearly wrong. Why were US physicians so convinced of the connection between the two? And why were their British confrères more reticent about asserting these links? The questions tell us something about the different symbolic functions of, and the ideological work performed by, the idea of idiocy in US and British society.

As both time and geography exert strong forces on the concepts that mould idiocy, it is necessarily a culturally specific notion. This history focuses primarily upon British notions of idiocy, and thus British sources of evidence, although there are exceptions: the influential writings of Samuel Gridley Howe and other Americans are considered, but especially as they affect or illuminate British conceptions of idiocy. So too are the writings of Jean Marc Gaspard Itard and Édouard Séguin in France, as these works lay the foundation for later efforts and initiatives to educate idiots, and their ideas resonate throughout the nineteenth century – and, in many ways, to the current day.

To comprehend nineteenth-century idiocy and related concepts, then, demands that we delve into the discursive spaces in which the idea takes shape, and track the different lines of thought that express its points of cohesion, tensions and directions of development. This development is not linear and progressive, but rather the product of conflicting notions (and social applications) of the term. Thus, we have the innocent Christian idiot, the moral and, later, racial degenerate, the helpless and the dangerous, the drain on social resources and the exemplar of supportive community, the diminished male and the promiscuous female, and a plethora of other characterizations. Investigating these associations and exploring more fully their tensions and interrelations in cultural, social and political milieux may help us bring the history of idiocy out of its narrow readership to a larger audience, by demonstrating the importance of the concept to other realms of discourse and activity. Such a move would be informative as well as emancipatory. I like to think it would also be interesting, engaging, even pleasurable.

A tale told by an idiot

I have been calling this book a 'cultural history', but I am not wedded to that classification. Perhaps it is the social-cultural history of an idea; perhaps, following Bucknill (albeit at a distance) and Shakespeare's *Macbeth*, it is merely a tale told by an idiot:

> To-morrow, and to-morrow, and to-morrow,
> Creeps in this petty pace from day to day
> To the last syllable of recorded time;
> And all our yesterdays have lighted fools
> The way to dusty death. Out, out, brief candle!
> Life's but a walking shadow, a poor player,
> That struts and frets his hour upon the stage,
> And then is heard no more: it is a tale
> Told by an idiot, full of sound and fury,
> Signifying nothing.
> (*Macbeth*, act V, scene v, lines 18–27)

But there is more to this passage than is noted by those commentators, like Bucknill, common in the nineteenth century, who equated 'idiocy' with meaninglessness and offered to impose rationality where before none existed. Shakespeare, or Macbeth at any rate, proposes that *life* is that tale told by an idiot – at least, this is Macbeth's gloomy interpretation of life as he learns of his wife's suicide. Significantly, Shakespeare's idiots were part of life, and idiocy, like its cousin folly (and those fools whose travels to dusty deaths were lit by yesterdays), was something in which everyone shared ('Lord, what fools these mortals be!' Shakespeare's Puck observed, wonderingly). And Macbeth's 'idiot' is not our own (nor Bucknill's). His image draws on two prominent and concurrent meanings of the term: a person of lesser wit but also one whose language signifies nothing because he is a private person and has no public authority – unlike the king, who epitomizes this authority. Notably, the lead actor Richard Burbage, for whom Shakespeare writes these lines, also compares life to 'a poor player'. The juxtaposition should be clear, but generations of readers, playgoers and scholars have missed it, in large part because of a simplistic understanding of the term 'idiot': the renowned Burbage is to the 'poor player' what Macbeth, the king, is to 'the idiot', or private, powerless peasant. But life does not accept such elevation, and will ultimately level them, the stage star with the poor player, the king with the peasant idiot: all are fools on the road to dusty death. The sound and fury are that meaningless cacophony generated by all mortal beings, because all, ultimately, are idiots in that second sense of the term: before the unwavering power of mortality, no voice, not even the king's, can claim any authority. It is not intellectual capacity but social standing and power that are underscored by the term 'idiot' in this passage, in which all humans, as mortal beings, are peasant idiots. The 'nothing' signified by idiocy is Macbeth's own socio-existential crisis.

Idiocy involves interpretation, whether by physicians or psychologists performing a diagnosis, or historians and cultural analysts reading old documents. We ignore this process at our peril: we cannot pretend to understand the history of idiocy (or intellectual disability, or intelligence) if we forget to question and analyse what forces shape this concept and its precursors. How and why were they understood in the ways that they were? Without asking these questions, those other questions of asylum management, workhouse tenancy and community living become analyses of policy and implementation rather than of the underlying processes that define idiocy (or, later, intellectual disability) and those parameters that determine what position an individual so identified will occupy in a society.

What lies before us...

Ideas of idiocy and the social position and treatment of people identified as 'idiots' intersect with cultural and political notions in shaping a broad social understanding of human relations and human identities. This book looks at some of the ways idiocy took form and what functions – analogical and symbolic as well as social and political – it performed, primarily (although not exclusively) in nineteenth-century Britain. The period spanned by the book is primarily between the end of the eighteenth century and the start of the twentieth. Literary critics have long pointed to the 1798 publication of *Lyrical Ballads*, including William Wordsworth's poem 'The Idiot Boy', as a defining moment at the start of British romanticism, and it parallels philosophical investigations into idiocy. Looking back from a vantage point in 1904, the US physician Martin Barr wrote that the capture in 1800 and subsequent education of 'the savage of Aveyron' 'might be likened to a guide-post reading two ways':

> Standing at the beginning of the nineteenth century, a literal symbol of the parting of ways for his caste, in this uncouth figure is represented all the cruelty of the past and the beneficent influences of a new era. The last of those of whom history or tradition speaks as, either through neglect or through wilful desertion, driven from the haunts of men; he is also the first example recorded of an idiot reclaimed from the life of a mere animal to be trained to a human existence. (Barr 1904: 30–31)

These twin events – the publication of Wordsworth's renowned poem and the beginning of Itard's equally renowned pedagogical experiments – mark the start of a rise in social concern with idiocy, which also included the increasingly aggressive attention given to developing medical and scientific theories regarding idiocy's causes and, later, social policies meant to control it. These policies culminated in Britain in the 1913 Mental Deficiency Act, which might, to return to Barr's quote, mark the point at which the idiot was once again 'driven from the haunts of men'. In addition, while at the start of the nineteenth century 'idiocy' is often a general term applied to a number mental conditions, in 1913 'idiocy' is itself formally subsumed under the broader concept of 'mental deficiency' (as Duncan predicted) and no longer functions as the general denominator. The greater part of this effort at writing the cultural history of idiocy ends when 'idiocy' ceases to be the dominant term used to describe a form of mental difference.

The chapters that follow form essays, rather than a strictly linear narrative, that set out the history of the idea of idiocy, primarily through how it appears in cultural, scientific, philosophical, medical and sociological representations. The concept of idiocy acquires and sheds meanings, slipping in and out of different realms of understanding. There are dates in the history of idiocy, of course, even in the cultural or conceptual history. And many of the essays here are structured around events – the publication of a book, the capture of a feral child, the opening of an institution – that form a chronology. But the essays also attempt to describe how the idea of idiocy blends with other notions, concerns and understandings across decades and centuries, to see how it enters into these, and how it is in turn shaped by them.

To do this, we open *in medias res* and, in this instance, with a something akin to a firm date. Chapters 2 and 3 focus on William Wordsworth's poem 'The Idiot Boy', published in 1798 as part of *Lyrical Ballads*, a landmark text of English romanticism, and on the 'wild boy of Aveyron', who enters recorded history in 1797 (although he was not captured for good until 1800). The first of these focuses on Wordsworth's poem and the epistolary exchange it prompted between the poet and his young admirer John Wilson on what we might call the aesthetic value of idiocy, and the connection of this aesthetic value to actual human relations. The second considers the impact on these human relations of Jean Marc Gaspard Itard's pedagogical experiments with the *enfant sauvage*, eventually named Victor, who was considered by some to be an 'ineducable idiot' and others – such as Itard – to be an example of a *tabula rasa* through whom scientists could learn how humans acquire knowledge and awareness. This chapter also investigates some of Itard's aesthetic assumptions in his two case reports on the growth of Victor's mind and his social identity. These chapters share a common theme: they explore the uncertain relation of people considered 'idiots' to other people in their world at the start of the nineteenth century. Wordsworth's 'The Idiot Boy' and Itard's 1801 and 1806 reports on his progress with Victor would become key texts in the reconceptualization of idiocy later in the nineteenth century.

In the next four chapters we leap through time, travelling from the fourteenth to the nineteenth century, to consider the historical roots of some very resilient associations of idiocy and its conceptual cousins. The primary concerns in these chapters are thematic, and thus depart from chronology; however, they inform the more chronologically specific material covered later in the book. Chapter 4 focuses on the common associations of idiocy with financial incompetence and self-governance when it appears in men, following legal definitions of idiocy from the thirteenth-century *Prerogativa Regis* to nineteenth-century documents on 'manliness'; Chapter 5 looks at those points where ideas about women, and especially female sexuality and physical appetite, intersect with notions of intelligence and idiocy, from the sixteenth through to the nineteenth century. Similarly, Chapter 6 explores the lengthy history of associations of idiocy, through its discursive or conceptual precursor 'folly', with innocence and sin, reaching back to the early modern period and including the works of Sebastian Brant, Erasmus and Robert Armin, as well as the King James Bible. Chapter 7 continues this line of investigation by tracking the connection between these complex early modern representations of folly to nineteenth-century cultural expressions of the innocent, the trickster and the amoral fool.

This background material in place, Chapter 8 returns to a more specific time and geography – that is, England in 1841, the Chartist movement and Charles Dickens' novel *Barnaby Rudge* – to explore the relations between working-class agitation, political reforms, the debate over paternalism and the shifting understanding of the idea of idiocy amid all this social turmoil. The remaining chapters focus more chronologically on the latter half of the nineteenth century, although they are not organized in a strictly linear fashion. Chapter 9 looks at the growth of the asylum movement in the early 1840s until the 1860s, and also considers how this movement vigorously transformed the innocent idiot into an unreclaimed being who could be educated and woven into the Victorian social fabric; supporters of educational asylums drew upon traditional imagery to work upon the sentiments of readers (who were, notably, also important sources of funding), while at the same time portraying the uneducated idiot as a subhuman brute who could be reclaimed for humanity by the dedicated work of caring physicians and educators. Chapter 10 pairs the ambiguous representations of idiocy in the 1860s 'sensation novel' with ideas of physiological and moral education developed by Édouard Séguin and his many followers, also primarily in the 1860s, to argue that these new ways of constructing the reader as subject to 'sensation' take shape by juxtaposition to the concept of the uncertainly 'insensate' idiot. Chapter 11 considers the growth in the 1850s, '60s and '70s of degeneration theories that drew on both Lamarckian 'acquired characteristics' and Darwinian 'natural selection', often yoked uneasily together. These theories, as expressed in medical, scientific, sociological and literary writings, had profound consequences on the scientific construction of idiocy as a form of degeneracy of the familial line or, more worryingly, of the English race. Chapter 12 considers another consequence of degeneration theory: the reformulation of idiots as morally degenerate beings likely to commit crimes and to procreate with abandon. This fear is linked to the growing concern over the threat of the 'feeble-minded' and the consequent broadening of the notion of idiocy. In Chapter 13,

Joseph Conrad's 1907 novel *The Secret Agent* is set against the 1908 report from the Commission on the Feeble-Minded to explore the symbolic work of idiocy in this discourse, but the chronological focus ranges from the late 1860s up to the 1913 Mental Deficiency Act, which grew out of the recommendations of the 1908 report.

Notes

1   This opposition of folly and wit is further complicated by the fact that sixteenth-century 'wit' is not identical to our current notions of intelligence, although it is a precursor to contemporary intelligence.
2   Asylums would continue to make such 'errors', according to their criteria. Perhaps most famously, in 1957 Mayo Buckner, an inmate at the Iowa Home for the Feebleminded, where he had been originally entered as a 'medium-grade imbecile' fifty-nine years earlier, scored 120 on an IQ test; a 1958 *Life* magazine feature by Robert Wallace brought Buckner's story to an international audience and claimed that among the 130,000 people in the USA's ninety institutions, at least 5,000 were not, in fact, 'retarded' (Trent 1994: 253). But the question of misdiagnosis should not obscure the much more important issue: what quality, precisely, exists to be quantified, thus enabling a diagnosis in the first place?
3   Earlswood archive 6523/1/6 (case-book starting in 1891).
4   Pope, as a short, hunchbacked Catholic with an oddly shaped head, was no doubt aware that he fit many of the criteria of the traditional fool; his verbal assaults on other poets may also project his own anxieties regarding his provisional status in the English high society of the 1720s and 1730s.
5   There have also been several unpublished doctoral dissertations, notably by Michael Barrett (1986), Spencer Gelband (1979) and Lilian Zihni (1990).
6   There have also been some doctoral dissertations submitted in this area, including by Paul Marchbanks (2006a) and Gina Herring (1988).
7   People First, a self-advocacy group of people labelled as having intellectual disabilities, traces its history to the mid-1970s (Dybwad 1996). It is now an international organization, with chapters in Britain, the United States, Canada, Australia and elsewhere. The group's name reflects the desire of people so labelled to be recognized as human beings rather than pathologized entities such as 'retarded', 'handicapped' or 'disabled'; People First chapters lobby to promote this goal, while at the same time serving as 'consciousness-raising' or support groups for people identified as having intellectual disabilities.
8   To draw a blunt image, a person with one leg is clearly 'impaired' under this division, as people are biologically constructed to have two legs. However, an IQ of 75 simply designates a place on a statistically defined curve. No specific physiological impairment need be involved.
9   To elaborate upon this example, the supposed association of idiocy with masturbation (touched upon more fully in Chapter 11) arose from a set of beliefs drawn from a range of sources, including Christian morality as well as scientific theories regarding 'vital fluids' and what Barker-Benfield (1976: 181) calls the US fixation with the 'spermatic economy', in which the vitality of the individual labourer or businessman was deemed to be crucial to the economic vitality of the nation.

CHAPTER 2

'Stripping our own hearts naked': William Wordsworth and John Wilson read 'The Idiot Boy'

John Wilson would one day rank among Britain's leading cultural and literary critics; he would contribute regularly to *Blackwood's Edinburgh Magazine* under the pseudonym Christopher North and eventually assume the Chair of Moral Philosophy at the University of Edinburgh. But in May 1802 Wilson was a precocious seventeen-year-old writing a fan letter to poetry's bright new star, William Wordsworth. The epistle reads like an early exercise in Wilson's literary criticism, with his comments on *Lyrical Ballads* being part analysis and part adulation. '[T]hough I am not personally acquainted with you, I may almost venture to affirm, that the qualities of your soul are not unknown to me', he writes to Wordsworth. 'In your poems I discovered such marks of delicate feeling, such benevolence of disposition, and such knowledge of human nature as has made an impression on my mind that nothing will ever efface' (quoted in Brett and Jones 1991: 334). Wordsworth's poetry, he writes, is 'the language of nature', written 'not ... merely for the pleasure of philosophers and men of improved taste, but for all who think – for all who feel' (335). He claims further that the poems 'are of a very great advantage to the world', thanks to their 'system of philosophy' and 'morality of the purest kind', and praises how 'they represent the enjoyment resulting from the cultivation of the social affections of our nature' (336).

But while the letter is filled with the gushing devotion of a youthful admirer, its real substance comes after Wilson's effusive praise of *Lyrical Ballads* in general. Indeed, while lauding the collection, he writes in detail of the one poem he feels to be Wordsworth's failure, whose problem, he argues, can be found in the subject's inability to engage sympathy:

> no description can please, where the sympathies of our soul are not excited, and no narration interest, where we do not enter into the feelings of some of the parties concerned. On this principle, many feelings which are undoubtedly natural, are improper subjects of poetry, and many situations, no less natural, incapable of being described so as to produce the grand effect of poetical composition. To describe these in poetry would be improper. (337)

For Wilson, the poem 'The Idiot Boy' was profoundly guilty of this impropriety, and he dedicates much of the letter to setting forth his objections to this apparent anomaly in Wordsworth's *oeuvre*.

Wordsworth, in the Preface he added to the 1800 edition, writes that his objective with 'The Idiot Boy', as well as 'The Mad Mother', was to trace 'the maternal passion through many of its more subtle windings' (Brett and Jones 1991: 247). 'But sir', responds Wilson:

> the manner in which you have executed this plan has frustrated the end you intended to produce by it; the affection of Betty Foy [the eponymous boy's mother] has nothing in it to excite interest. It exhibits merely the effects of that instinctive feeling inherent in the constitution of every animal. The excessive fondness of the mother disgusts us, and prevents us from sympathizing with her. We are unable to enter into her feelings; we cannot conceive ourselves actuated by the same feelings, and consequently take little or no interest in her situation. The object of her affection is indeed her son, and in that relation much consists, but then he is represented as totally destitute of any attachment towards her; the state of his mind is represented as perfectly deplorable, and, in short, to me it appears almost unnatural that a person in a state of complete idiotism should excite the warmest feelings of attachment in the breast even of his mother. (337)

In fact, claims Wilson, none of his friends and acquaintances like the poem either, leading him to suggest that:

> The inability to receive pleasure from descriptions such as that of 'The Idiot Boy' is, I am convinced, founded upon established feelings of human nature, and the principle of it constitutes, as I daresay you recollect, the leading feature of Smith's *Theory of Moral Sentiments*. I therefore think that, in the choice of this subject, you have committed an error. (337–38)

After daring to criticize his hero so roundly, Wilson makes a concession:

> the fault, if there be one, lies in the plan, not in the execution.... In reading the 'Idiot Boy', all persons who allow themselves to think, must admire your talents, but they regret that they have been so employed, and while they esteem the author, they cannot help being displeased

with his performance. I have seen a most excellent painting of an idiot, but it created in me inexpressible disgust. I admired the talents of the artist, but I had no other source of pleasure. The poem of the 'Idiot Boy' produced upon me an effect in every respect similar. (338)

Perhaps feeling he had gone far enough in his criticisms of 'The Idiot Boy', or perhaps simply hoping to lure Wordsworth into continuing the correspondence, Wilson closes by noting that 'remarks on your other poems must be reserved for another letter' (338).

About two weeks later, in June 1802, Wordsworth penned his response, creating an exchange that is unique in the annals of the aesthetics of idiocy. After the requisite opening compliments – 'Had it not been for a very amiable modesty you would not have imagined that your letter could give me any offence', he writes (see *Early Letters*, De Selincourt 1935: 292) – and responses to some of Wilson's broader observations, he turns his attention to his poem, defending not only his choice of subject, but also the place of real 'idiots' in the human community. 'You begin what you say upon "The Idiot Boy" with this observation, that nothing is a fit subject for poetry which does not please. But here follows a question, Does not please whom?' (294). Wordsworth then lays out a catalogue of examples to demonstrate varieties and superficialities of taste, noting that they vary with knowledge, experience and even 'professional and national prejudices' (295); in response to Wilson's invocation of Adam Smith's *Theory of Moral Sentiments* (1759), Wordsworth alludes disdainfully to 'the instance of Adam Smith, who, we are told, could not endure the ballad of *Clym of the Clough*, because the author had not written like a gentleman' (294–95). Given the superficialities of taste, then, how can one judge the value of poetry? Wordsworth, like Wilson, refers to human nature as the arbiter of correct response. But what is this human nature? And how might we best measure and define this essence? Wordsworth's answer is emphatic:

> by stripping our own hearts naked, and by looking out of ourselves to[wards men] who lead the simplest lives, and those most according to nature; men who have never known false refinements, wayward and artificial desires, false criticisms, effeminate habits of thinking and feeling, or who, having known these things, have outgrown them.... People in our rank in life are perpetually falling into one sad mistake, namely, that of supposing that human nature and the persons they associate with are one and the same thing. (295)

One must travel beyond the limited social sphere that is the *beau monde* of gentlemen and intellectuals, counsels Wordsworth, who is clearly thinking in terms of both literary ambition and social environment:

few ever consider books but with reference to their power of pleasing these persons and men of a higher rank; few descend lower, among the cottages and fields, and among children. A man must have done this habitually before his judgment upon 'The Idiot Boy' would be in any way decisive with me. I *know* I have done this myself habitually. (295, original emphasis)

Moreover, writes Wordsworth, the poet's objective should not simply be to reflect human feeling, but 'to rectify men's feelings, to give them new compositions of feeling, to render their feelings more sane, pure, and permanent, in short, more consonant to nature, that is, to eternal nature, and the great moving spirit of things' (295–96). Ultimately, he notes:

> the loathing and disgust which many people have at the sight of an idiot, is a feeling which, though having some foundation in human nature, is not necessarily attached to it in any virtuous degree, but is owing in a great measure to a false delicacy, and, if I may say it without rudeness, a certain want of comprehensiveness of thinking and feeling. (296)

In effect, Wordsworth has flipped the accusation: the 'loathing and disgust' spring from the stupidity and narrow-mindedness of the viewer, and not the idiot being observed. As for his own response, he explains,

> I have often applied to idiots, in my own mind, that sublime expression of scripture, that *their life is hidden with God*. They are worshipped, probably from a feeling of this sort, in several parts of the East. Among the Alps, where they are numerous, they are considered, I believe, as a blessing to the family to which they belong. I have, indeed, often, looked upon the conduct of fathers and mothers of the lower classes of society towards idiots as the great triumph of the human heart. It is there that we see the strength, disinterestedness, and grandeur of love; nor have I ever been able to contemplate an object that calls out so many excellent and virtuous sentiments without finding it hallowed thereby, and having something in me which bears down before it, like a deluge, every feeble sensation of disgust and aversion. (297, original emphasis)

But even Wordsworth qualifies his endorsement of idiots as a poetic subject, noting that 'my "idiot" is not one of those who cannot articulate, or of those that are unusually disgusting in their persons' (297). Ultimately, his rebuttal comes down to this conclusion:

> There are, in my opinion, several important mistakes in the latter part of your letter which I could have wished to notice; but I find myself much fatigued.... I must content myself simply with observing that it is probable that the principle [*sic*] cause of your dislike to this particular poem

lies in the *word* Idiot. If there had been any such word in our language *to which we had attached passion*, as lack-wit, half-wit, witless, etc, I should have certainly employed it in preference; but there is no such word. (297, original emphasis)

The opposing positions are clear. For Wilson, 'idiocy' is something that well cultivated minds should not wish to consider, and a condition with which it is impossible to experience sympathy. Wordsworth, on the other hand, argues that Wilson has essentially failed to recognize the people to whom the word 'idiocy' is applied, being misdirected by the social and cultural connotations of the word itself. The idea of idiocy and the 'false delicacy' surrounding it (as well as his 'want of comprehensiveness of thinking and feeling') have barred him from recognizing the human experience of fellow creatures. Underpinning this exchange are powerful notions of human nature, sympathy and delicacy of taste, especially those developed by Adam Smith and his friend and mentor David Hume. But before we consider these ideas, let us turn to the poem itself.

Johnny Foy's night ride to poetry

Wordsworth's 'The Idiot Boy', published in 1798, was a centrepiece of the *Lyrical Ballads* collaboration with Samuel Taylor Coleridge. The original plan, as Coleridge recalls in his *Biographia Literaria* (1817), was to create a volume that combined poems by Coleridge in which 'the incidents and agents were to be, at least in part, supernatural' with others by Wordsworth, to be drawn from 'the characters and incidents … such as will be found in every village' (Engell and Bate 1983: 6–7). As already noted, in the Preface to the 1800 second, expanded edition of *Lyrical Ballads*, Wordsworth describes 'The Idiot Boy' as 'tracing the maternal passion through many of its more subtle windings' (Brett and Jones 1991: 247). Indeed, in the second edition, the poem is given priority as one of only two (along with Coleridge's 'Rime of the Ancient Mariner') to have its own title page – a sign of Wordsworth's estimation of its importance to his overall poetic project.

In this comic poem, Betty Foy (the surname conjures both the French *foi* – 'faith' – and *fol* – 'fool') sends 'him whom she loves, her idiot boy' (line 11), Johnny, on a quest to fetch a doctor for her ailing neighbour Susan Gale, thus trusting him with both her neighbour's life and his own well-being – and, the narrator makes clear, she also trusts to the instinctive intelligence of the pony, a 'horse that thinks' (line 122). Betty waits at Susan's bedside and, although Johnny does not reappear in person until the final stanzas of the poem, he occupies his mother's thoughts as she awaits his return with growing anxiety – a feeling the narrator presumes to be universal:

> There's not a mother, no not one
> But when she hears what you have done,
> Oh! Betty she'll be in a fright
> (lines 24–26)

Johnny is described as both joyful and idle as he sets off on his quest:

> For joy he cannot hold the bridle
> For joy his head and heels are idle,
> He's idle all for very joy.
> (lines 84–86)

But Betty also feels a mother's pride in her son:

> And Betty's standing at the door,
> And Betty's face with joy o'erflows,
> Proud of herself, and proud of him,
> She sees him in his travelling trim;
> How quietly her Johnny goes.
> (lines 97–101)

While Johnny sets off in silence, eventually he starts to 'make the noise he loves' (line 110): his 'lips they burr, burr, burr,/And on he goes beneath the moon' (lines 115–16). And thus he disappears, and Betty returns to waiting at Susan's bedside, telling her sick friend of

> What comfort Johnny soon will bring,
> With many a most diverting thing,
> Of Johnny's wit and Johnny's glory.
> (lines 134–36)

But Johnny does not return when expected, and the remainder of the poem narrates Betty's growing fears and her attempts to find her son, along with the narrator's hypotheses of what fates or adventures may have waylaid him. Initially, the ailing Susan

> ... begins to fear
> Of sad mischances not a few,
> That Johnny may perhaps be drown'd,
> Or lost perhaps, and never found.
> (lines 187–90)

Finally Betty, her anxieties stoked, abandons Susan's bedside to search for her wayward son, while

... the thought torments her sore,
Johnny perhaps his horse forsook,
To hunt the moon that's in the brook,
And never will be heard of more.
(lines 223–26)

The anxious mother goes herself to find the doctor, that paragon of rational thought; were we to construct a spectrum of rationality in this poem, the doctor and Johnny Foy would be at opposite ends. But there is no news (nor sympathy, for that matter) to be found from the doctor, who brushes aside Betty's concerns: "'What, woman, should I know of him?"/And grumbling he went back to bed' (lines 270–71). Soon, more exotic fears present themselves to Betty's imagination:

'Oh saints! What is become of him?
Perhaps he's climbed into an oak,
Where he will stay till he is dead;
Or sadly he has been misled,
And joined the wandering gypsey-folk.

Or him that wicked pony's carried
To the dark cave, the goblins' hall,
Or in the castle he's pursuing,
Among the ghosts, his own undoing;
Or playing with the waterfall.'
(lines 232–41)

The narrator, a comic character in his own right, also speculates on Johnny's

adventures, imagining him roaming:
the cliffs and peaks so high that are,
To lay his hand upon a star,
And in his pocket bring it home
(lines 329–31)

or

Perhaps, with head and heels on fire,
And like the very soul of evil
He's galloping away, away,
And so he'll gallop on for aye,
The bane of all that dread the devil.
(lines 342–46)

But these remain imaginative hypotheses, and we are also led to doubt the narrator's capacity to tell this tale. He has been bound to the 'gentle muses' for fourteen years 'by strong indentures' (line 348), which is twice the standard seven years allotted to apprenticeship and raises the possibility that the narrator is himself a sluggish learner (Ronell 2002: 273). As the narrator cannot convince his muses to provide details of Johnny's midnight ride, the idiot boy remains obscure, a repository of unknown possibilities. And just as the narrator returns from his flawed hypotheses and failed supplications to the muses, Betty Foy finds her son, sitting still on the pony, which has wandered into a field to graze.

> She screams – she cannot move for joy;
> She darts as with a torrent's force,
> She almost has o'erturned the horse,
> And fast she holds her idiot boy.
> (lines 383–86)

Meanwhile, Susan Gale's anxiety over Betty and Johnny Foy overwhelms her own disease and sends her into the night in search of her friends, so that Johnny's disappearance works as a cure as strong any doctor's medicine. The links that Wordsworth draws in this poem between Johnny, the natural world, the pony, maternal love and the rural village suggest the curative powers of sympathy are not governed by the rational, but by those forces to be found in nature, love and community. The poem ends as 'our four travellers homeward wend' (line 443), a line that unites the natural world (as the pony is one of the four), maternal love (with Betty Foy) and the notion of community (the neighbour Susan Gale and the act of wending homeward), in opposition to the rational, urban and notably unsympathetic world of the doctor. Significantly, 'The Idiot Boy' endorses art as curative and non-rational. While Johnny Foy is an idiot boy, he is also, by the end of the poem, a version of Wordsworth's solitary poet (Bewell 1989): his final lines transform his evening hours spent listening to owls hooting in the moonlight into a world existing in the imagination:

> The cocks did crow to-whoo, to-whoo,
> And the sun did shine so cold.
> (lines 460–61)

In the poem's insistent reversal of rational and irrational, Johnny's words find a resonance that lends him an odd credibility; by finding meaning and art in nature, he becomes a comic representative of the transcendental nature that Jerome McGann sees as characteristically Wordworthian (McGann 1985: 300). In Avital Ronell's analysis, Johnny 'functions as the refusal of loss, as the very opposite of the experience of deprivation for which he [as an idiot] has been made to stand' (Ronell 2002: 260) and 'poetry, as the tremor of existence that draws a blank – poetry is the idiot boy' (276).

Nature's primary laws and the poetic environment

In his 1800 Preface, Wordsworth sets out his poetic project as being 'to make the incidents of common life interesting by tracing in them, truly though not ostentatiously, the primary laws of our nature' (Brett and Jones 1991: 245). And these 'primary laws of our [human] nature', he asserts, are more evident in humble subject matter:

> Low and rustic life was generally chosen because in that situation the essential passions of the heart find a better soil in which they can attain their maturity, are under less restraint, and speak a plainer and more emphatic language; because in that situation our elementary feelings exist in a state of greater simplicity and consequently may be more accurately contemplated and more forcibly communicated; because the manners of rural life germinate from those elementary feelings; and from the necessary character of rural occupations are more easily comprehended; and are more durable; and lastly, because in that situation the passions of men are incorporated with the beautiful and permanent forms of nature. (245)

Wordsworth's Preface suggests a political project: recuperating the status of the despised rural labourers, conferring upon them a dignity they were commonly denied, in both poetry and real life. A radical political notion indeed, but still well within the tradition of pastoral poetry. The poems in *Lyrical Ballads* owe as much (and more) to aesthetic tradition as they do to social fact. William Empson (1966: 18) notes that, in the pastoral, 'the simple man becomes a clumsy fool who yet has better "sense" than his betters and can say things more fundamentally true; ... he is in contact with the mysterious forces of our own nature, so that the clown has the wit of the Unconscious; he can speak the truth because he has nothing to lose'. The image was well entrenched in literary form: the 'fool' was often credited with a unique form of grace, or an intangible affinity with the divine (notions which will be explored more extensively in Chapter 6). Johnny Foy is part of this tradition, a descendant of the 'holy fool', the 'natural' and the 'innocent'. As a figure with this historical lineage, Johnny Foy also refers to a passing world, an England where the forests are still so large that one could get lost in them (at least according to the imagination of a worried mother). Writing of *Lyrical Ballads* in general, Marilyn Butler (1981: 58) observes that 'Wordsworth's experiments with subjects from among the lower orders of society ... follow thirty years of public interest in this matter ... and are thus characteristic of the culture of the Enlightenment', especially the primitivist concerns with noble savages (and their local equivalent, noble rural labourers).

In constructing his poetic vision, Wordsworth was developing within a tradition rather than making a radical break with the past, and Mary Jacobus (1970) suggests that 'The Idiot Boy' parodies the popular ballads of Gottfried Bürger, such as the best-selling 'Lenore', which had been translated into English from the German in 1796; indeed, Wordsworth's 1800 Preface condemns 'frantic novels, sickly and stupid German Tragedies, and deluges of idle and extravagant stories in verse' as cultivating the public's 'degrading thirst in outrageous stimulation' (Brett and Jones 1991: 249). So the ballad form's marketability was not lost on Wordsworth and Coleridge, who collaborated on *Lyrical Ballads* not simply because they shared some ideas about how poetry should be written, but also because they planned a visit to Germany in the autumn of 1798 and Wordsworth needed money to finance the excursion. The collection of poems was to provide those funds, and when the publishers finally settled on a price for the volume, Wordsworth was ready to set sail. In short, then, while *Lyrical Ballads* marked a new stage in the development of English romanticism, it was working within an established tradition with both an audience and, significantly for Wordsworth's travel plans, an interested market.

Thus 'The Idiot Boy' draws on a cultural store of images and conventions – heroic ballads, pastoral verse, comic tales – as well as on conventional notions of the idiot as a 'natural' and a 'holy innocent'. Each of these contexts is important when we try to figure out what an idiot boy is doing in a poem – keeping in mind that 'idiot boys' were not commonly poetic subjects and that critics like the young John Wilson were strongly opposed to the idea that they might enter that repertoire. The way the image of idiocy functions in this literary environment indicates something of what idiocy could signify to Wordsworth and his readers, and it implies certain possibilities about nature (human and otherwise), sympathy and communities.

Interestingly, 'The Idiot Boy' was not Wordsworth's first attempt to represent idiocy in a poem; that distinction goes to 'The Somersetshire Tragedy', probably composed in 1797 and based on a story told to Wordsworth by his friend Thomas Poole. As Poole recounted in a narrative published in *The Bath and Bristol Magazine* many years later (in 1833), John Walford was a labourer who had married Jenny, a poor 'near-idiot by whom he had had two illegitimate children' (quoted in Jonathan Wordsworth 1966: 642). But, short-tempered and desiring another woman, Walford constantly beats his wife and eventually kills her by cutting her throat. He is then executed for the crime. Only two fragments remain of Wordsworth's poem based on this real-life episode, but they contain enough material to give us some sense of its direction.[1] We are told that:

> Her face bespake a weak and witless soul
> Which none could think worth while to teach or to controul

Wordsworth also describes her fearful existence with her husband:

> Ill fared it now with his poor wife I ween,
> That in her hut she could no more remain;
> Oft in the early morning she was seen
> Ere Robert to his work had crossed the green.
> She roam'd from house to house the weary day,
> And when the housewife's evening hearth was clean
> She linger'd still, and if you chanc'd to say
> 'Robert his supper needs,' her colour pass'd away.
> (Jonathan Wordsworth 1966: 642)

While Poole retains sympathy for Walford in his own narrative, from which the idiot wife all but disappears, Wordsworth's extant fragments suggest that she seems to have assumed a much greater importance as a personage in the poem.

David Hume, Adam Smith and Wordsworth's anxious readers

In his criticism of 'The Idiot Boy', John Wilson is frustrated by the poem's inability to create sympathy because it opposes 'established feelings of human nature', which he then identifies as a 'leading feature' of Smith's *Theory of Moral Sentiments*, published in 1759. Smith and his friend and teacher David Hume had both elaborated influential theories of human nature and the role of sympathy in developing subjectivity and social relations, and both Wilson and Wordsworth respond to these theories to buttress their arguments for and against the poetic representation of idiocy. Smith's work builds on ideas of sympathy and morality that Hume first presented in his *Treatise of Human Nature* (1739/40) and developed throughout his career, and Wilson is especially dependent upon Smith's ideas to give shape to his anti-'Idiot Boy' argument.

In his *Theory of Moral Sentiments*, Smith attempts to account for the growth of human compassion and sentiment, arguing that we enter into the emotions of others via acts of sympathetic imagination. 'As we have no immediate experience of what other men feel, we can form no idea of the manner in which they are affected, but by conceiving what we ourselves should feel in the like situation', writes Smith at the start of this work.

Though our brother is upon the rack, as long as we ourselves are at our ease, our senses will never inform us of what he suffers. They never did, and never can, carry us beyond our own person, and it is by the imagination only that we can form any conception of what are his sensations.... By the imagination we place ourselves in his situation.... (9)

The imagination allows us to experience sympathy, compassion or pity for one another. And the imagination – but especially the well cultivated imagination – is attracted by the beautiful.

David Hume argued in his *Treatise of Human Nature* that '*beauty* of all kinds gives us a peculiar delight and satisfaction; as *deformity* produces pain, upon whatever subject it may be plac'd, and whether surveyed in an animate or inanimate object' (298, original emphasis). Individuals also embody this beauty or deformity, which has consequences for one's social comportment. 'If the beauty or deformity, therefore, be placed upon our own bodies', writes Hume, 'this pleasure or uneasiness must be converted into pride or humility' (298). Beauty, he clarifies, is something of

> such an order and construction of parts, as either by the *primary constitution* of our nature, by *custom*, or by *caprice*, is fitted to give pleasure and satisfaction to the soul. This is the distinguishing character of beauty, and forms all difference betwixt it and deformity, whose natural tendency is to produce uneasiness. Pleasure and pain, therefore, are not only necessary attendants of beauty and deformity, but constitute their very essence. (299, original emphasis)

The pain associated with deformity is experienced as disgust, unease and humility. Notably, Hume identifies our sense of beauty as springing from a '*primary constitution* of our nature, by *custom*, or by *caprice*'; only the first source, though, is to be trusted. So how does one separate the sense of beauty that is innate from those lesser ones sanctioned by custom or guided by mere caprice?

Smith, drawing upon Hume's ideas as he defines beauty and deformity, suggests that whether something is beautiful is best determined by its apparent similarity to others of its species:

> in each species of creatures, what is most beautiful bears the strongest resemblance to the general fabric of the species, and has the strongest resemblance to the greater part of the individuals with which it is classed. Monsters, on the contrary, or what is perfectly deformed, are always singular and odd, and have the least resemblance to the generality of the species to which they belong. And thus the beauty of each species, though in one sense the rarest of all things, because few individuals hit this middle form exactly, yet in another, is the most common, because all the deviations from it resemble it more than they resemble each other. (198–99)

This conception of beauty, he argues, is entirely natural, being closely related to something we might anachronistically call 'social statistics', or deviations from a mathematical norm.

The question of how to define beauty is linked closely to concepts of taste and sympathy, as Wordsworth and Wilson both imply in their correspondence. In one of his *Essays Moral, Political and Literary* (1777), 'Of the Standard of Taste', Hume writes:

> amidst all the variety and caprice of taste, there are certain general principles of approbation or blame, whose influence a careful eye may trace in all operations of the mind. Some particular forms or qualities, from the original structure of the internal fabric, are calculated to please, and others to displease; and if they fail of their effect in any particular instance, it is from some apparent defect or imperfection in the organ. A man in a fever would not insist on his palate as able to decide concerning flavours; nor would one, affected with jaundice, pretend to give a verdict with regard to colours. In each creature, there is a sound and a defective state; and the former alone can be supposed to afford us a true standard of taste and sentiment. (233–34)

The cultivated man is responsible for nurturing his capacity to judge. In the same essay Hume writes:

> [A] quick and acute perception of beauty and deformity must be the perfection of our mental taste; nor can a man be satisfied with himself while he suspects, that any excellence or blemish in a discourse has passed him unobserved. In this case, the perfection of the man, and the perception of the sense or feeling, are found to be united. (236)

But this capacity cannot be assumed to exist innately, he continues. It demands both training and experience:

> A man, who has had no opportunity of comparing the different kinds of beauty, is indeed totally unqualified to pronounce an opinion with regard to any object presented to him. By comparison alone we fix the epithets of praise or blame, and learn how to assign the due degree of each. (238)

While the principles of taste, then, are intrinsic, differences in taste reflect varying capacities to recognize and judge true beauty or deformity:

> the general principles of taste are uniform in human nature: Where men vary in their judgments, some defect or perversion in the faculties may commonly be remarked; proceeding either from prejudice, from want of practice, or want of delicacy; and there is just reason for approving one taste, and condemning another. (243)

Hume also insists that refined taste does not necessarily exalt all that is natural, but seeks for the 'beautiful' within the natural, discarding the dross. As he writes in elsewhere in his *Essays*, in 'Of Simplicity and Refinement in Writing':

> Sentiments, which are merely natural, affect not the mind with any pleasure, and seem not worthy of our attention. The pleasantries of a waterman, the observations of a peasant, the ribaldry of a porter or hackney coachman, all of these are natural, and disagreeable. (191)

Wilson adopts this point of view wholeheartedly in his correspondence when he notes that 'many feelings which are undoubtedly natural, are improper subjects of poetry' (Brett and Jones 1991: 337). Robert Southey, in his negative review of the poem in *The Critical Review* of October 1798, makes a similar point:

> Upon this subject [i.e. 'The Idiot Boy'] the author has written nearly 500 lines.... No tale less deserved the labour that appears to have been bestowed upon this. It resembles a Flemish picture in the worthlessness of its design and the excellence of its execution. From Flemish artists we are satisfied with such pieces: who would not have lamented, if Corregio or Rafaelle had wasted their talents in painting Dutch boors or the humours of a Flemish wake. (Brett and Jones 1991: 322)

Each stresses that Wordsworth's technique is exemplary but that his subject is lamentable.[2] Wordsworth, in responding to Wilson, asserts with Hume that perception must be cultivated, but, as quoted above, he employs a distinctly non-Humean criterion for human nature to reprimand Wilson when he writes that 'few descend ... among the cottages and fields, and among children. A man must have done this habitually before his judgment upon "The Idiot Boy" would be in any way decisive with me' (Brett and Jones 1991: 295).[3] In other words, Wordsworth has honed his capacity for recognizing true human nature and beauty; his critics have not. It seems, then, that Hume, Smith, Wordsworth and Wilson agree: objective criteria can distinguish between the purely natural and the beautiful. However, Wordsworth and the others diverge on the exact nature of these criteria, the difference lying in Wordsworth's belief that the 'essential passions of the heart' that guide human nature are to be found among the humble rather than the elevated, as he argues both in his Preface and in the letter to Wilson.

Clearly, judgements of beauty, deformity and the natural are not confined to the realm of aesthetics but also influence human relations. Hume claims in the *Treatise* that:

> We are ashamed of such maladies as affect others, and are either dangerous or disagreeable to them. Of the epilepsy; because it gives a horror to

everyone present: Of the itch; because it is infectious: Of the king's-evil; because it commonly goes to posterity. Men also consider the sentiment of others in the judgment of themselves. (303)[4]

Hume does not mention idiocy here, but no doubt would class it among these disagreeable maladies or conditions that repel observers. Smith notes in an intriguing passage in *The Theory of Moral Sentiments* that a consideration of the judgement of others may also be an exacerbating factor in cases of idiocy. He writes:

Those unfortunate persons whom nature has formed a good deal below the common level, seem sometimes to rate themselves still more below it than they really are. This humility appears sometimes to sink them into idiotism. Whoever has taken the trouble to examine idiots will find that, in many of them, the faculties of the understanding are by no means weaker than in several other people, who, though acknowledged to be dull and stupid, are not, by any body, accounted idiots. Many idiots, with no more than ordinary education, have been taught to read, write, and account tolerably well. Many persons, never accounted idiots, notwithstanding the most careful education, and notwithstanding that, in their advanced age, they have had spirit enough to attempt to learn what their early education had not taught them, have never been able to acquire, in any tolerable degree, any one of those three accomplishments. By an instinct of pride, however, they set themselves upon a level with their equals in age and situation; and, with courage and firmness, maintain their proper station among their companions. By an opposite instinct, the idiot feels himself below every company into which you can introduce him. Ill-usage, to which he is extremely liable, is capable of throwing him into the most violent fits of rage and fury. But no good usage, no kindness or indulgence, can ever raise him to converse with you as your equal. If you can bring him to converse with you at all, however, you will frequently find his answers sufficiently pertinent, and even sensible. But they are always stamped with a distinct consciousness of his own great inferiority. He seems to shrink and, as it were, to retire from your look and conversation; and to feel, when he places himself in your situation, that, notwithstanding your apparent condescension, you cannot help considering him as immensely below you. Some idiots, perhaps the greater part, seem to be so, chiefly or altogether, from a certain numbness or torpidity in the faculties of the understanding. But there are others, in whom those faculties do not appear more torpid or benumbed than in many other people who are not accounted idiots. But that instinct of pride, necessary to support them upon an equality with their brethren, seems totally wanting in the former and not in the latter. (260–61)

This commentary stresses the impact of humility as a sort of pity, disgust or uneasiness that the individual turns inward because of 'a distinct consciousness of his own great inferiority'. Smith seems to be contemplating the possibility that some forms of idiocy – not those characterized by 'numbness' or 'torpidity' of the faculties but those stemming from lack of pride – are amplified, if not actually created, through the dynamics of social interactions. Although he does not expand upon this point, his analysis of some forms of idiocy as a deficit of pride as much as of intelligence bears some affinities with Édouard Séguin's notion that 'idiots' were deficient in sensitivity and will, which could though be strengthened through the educational process (see Chapter 9).

Wordsworth was also sensitive to these questions of physical beauty and deformity. As he writes at the end of his letter to Smith:

> my 'idiot' is not one of those who cannot articulate, or of those that are unusually disgusting in their persons.... The boy whom I had in my mind was by no means disgusting in his appearance, quite the contrary; and I have known several with imperfect faculties who are handsome in their persons and features. There is one, at present, within a mile of my own house, remarkably so, though [he has something] of a stare and vacancy in his countenance. A friend of mine knowing that some persons had a dislike to the poem, advised me to add a stanza, describing the person of the boy [so as] entirely to separate him from that class of idiots who are disgusting in their persons; but the narration in the poem is so rapid and impassioned, that I could not find a place in which to insert the stanza without checking the progress of the poem and [so leaving] a deadness upon the feeling. (De Selincourt 1935: 297–98)

The critical friend was probably Coleridge, who had two complaints with the poem:

> The one is, that the author has not, in the poem itself, taken sufficient care to preclude from the reader's fancy the disgusting images of *ordinary, morbid idiocy*, which yet it is by no means his intention to represent. He has even by the 'burr, burr, burr,' uncounteracted by any preceding description of the boy's beauty, assisted in recalling them. The other is, that the idiocy of the *boy* is so evenly balanced by the folly of the *mother*, as to present to the general reader rather a laughable burlesque on the blindness of anile dotage, than an analytic display of maternal affection in its ordinary workings. (Engell and Bate 1983: book II, 48–49, original emphasis)

Indeed, Coleridge suggests,

> the mother's character is not so much a real and native product of a 'situation where the essential passions of the heart find a better soil, in which they can attain their maturity and speak a plainer and more emphatic language', [quoting Wordsworth's 'Preface'] as it is an impersonation of an instinct abandoned by judgment. (48)

But Coleridge's objections are to those very parts of the poem that Wordsworth seems to delight in, including the mother's affections and Johnny's joyful burring.

So Wordsworth was happier disregarding Coleridge's advice, choosing to risk that his readers would judge a character 'disgusting in his appearance' rather than insert a digression that would rein in the poem's bounding energy – and as his exchange with Wilson makes clear, this risk is also an explicit challenge to readers. Ronell proposes that the letter to Wilson is 'in a sense meant for Coleridge but sent to his proxy Wilson' and argues that lurking in the letter's subtext is Wordsworth's recognition that 'the insertion of Coleridge would be death; it would spread a deadness of feeling, strike a castrative blow against the poem: his addition would amount to a subtraction' (Ronell 2002: 261). For the poet, the vital beauty of the poem's integrity trumps those defects that Coleridge and Wilson imagine in the idiot boy.[5]

Most of the disputed philosophical territory in the Wilson–Wordsworth exchange was already mapped in the works of Hume and Smith: queries into human nature and the growth of sympathy, the refinement of sentiment and delicacy of taste, as well as questions of beauty and deformity. These philosophical and aesthetic concerns could affect how one reads Wordsworth's poem, as the idea of idiocy – that image conjured up by 'the *word* "idiot"' as Wordsworth stresses to Wilson – certainly is shaped by their impact. But as Wordsworth and Smith explicitly state, and Hume implies, the way people understand the idea of idiocy also influences the roles played by individuals identified as 'idiots' in more quotidian life.

The idiot in society, c. 1798

Poetic decorum has its analogues in the world outside of books, the world where one could find real people who had been identified as 'idiots' – or could not find them, depending on one's social class. Of the 'false delicacy' that underlies the 'loathing and disgust which many people have at the sight of an idiot' (De Selincourt 1935: 296), Wordsworth explains that

> Persons of the lower classes of society have little or nothing of this: if an idiot is born in a poor man's house, it must be taken care of, and cannot be boarded out, as it would be by gentlefolks, or sent to a public or private asylum for such unfortunate beings. [Poor people,] seeing frequently among their neighbours such objects, easily [forget] whatever there is of natural disgust about them, and have [therefore] a sane state, so that without pain or suffering they [perform] their duties towards them. I could with pleasure pursue this subject.... (296–27)

Significantly, idiocy and sanity are here conjoined: the poor are sane in how they accept idiocy. With their attitudes unburdened with 'false delicacy' or a 'want of comprehensiveness of feeling', and with necessity compelling them to overcome what traces of 'natural disgust' they might harbour (296), Wordsworth's poor people approach the practical dilemmas posed by idiocy in order to mitigate its disadvantages, at least to the family and often to the idiot as well. Because idiot children cannot be sent away from poor homes, they must be integrated, and these families do not seem to experience the 'pain or suffering' that the theories of Smith and Hume might predict as a result of their proximity to deformity.

Wordsworth's version of social realities (at least in his letter, if not in the poem) is certainly accurate in noting that the poor must care for their own idiot family members (a reality given a considerably less romantic gloss in the writings of Wordsworth's contemporary George Crabbe, among others, as we shall see in Chapter 4). The presence of an idiot child would entail extra labour, as the primary responsibility in maintaining idiot members of communities fell to their families, according to the Elizabethan Poor Laws (established in 1601 and, with amendments over the years, still largely in effect until 1834). Under these laws, parents and children were responsible for each other; thus if a family member fell into poverty, the rest of the family was bound to provide whatever help was needed to support their impoverished kin. Idiocy worked within this same context: if someone's mental incapacity reduced his ability to work within the local economy, he would thus become poor and, by law, dependent upon his family.

Should the family be unable to provide the necessary support, owing to their own ill health or poverty, then, according to the Poor Law, responsibility fell to the parish. Under these circumstances, the parish might provide funds to help the family support the individual, or, less often, might pay for the individual's care in the home of a neighbour (Rushton 1988). In London, parish nurses were also likely to be called upon to ensure basic care was provided to 'simple-minded parishioners' (Andrews 1996: 82). In 1800 – and before – asylums rarely accepted people identified as idiots, although sometimes individuals who were capable and reliable workers were accepted. For the same reason, idiot inmates were not uncommon in workhouses, especially in London (Andrews 1996; Rushton 1996). Overall, then, there seems to have been a general recognition that people identified as idiots formed part of the community mix, albeit as a group particularly vulnerable to poverty. As Rushton writes of his study of archives in north-east England, 'the striking feature of early modern discussions … is that, at the local level at least, little public notice was paid to "idiots" outside the official structures of the Poor Law and magistrates courts' (1996: 58).

The social reality of idiocy may have been characterized by a rough sort of community care, but precisely what sort would depend on the community in question. If the family had the financial resources, they might hire a caretaker, or board their 'idiot' member with another individual or family, thus diminishing the immediate experience of idiocy in the middle and upper classes. This option was adopted by the family of the writer Jane Austen for her brother George, ten years her elder. Around 1780, when he was about fifteen years old, George was taken in by the Culham family some distance away; the same family was also to look after Austen's uncle, Thomas Leigh, suggesting that they earned at least some portion of their income in this manner. George lived with the Culhams to his death in 1838, with the Austen family continuing to pay for his care; his death certificate identified him as a 'Gentleman' but, because of his disability, George 'remained unmentionable' for the Austens (Tomasin 1997: 8). On the other hand, as Wordsworth observed, the less affluent had a much more direct experience of idiocy, and they were required to perform those tasks that for the poet expressed 'the greatest triumph of the human heart' and demonstrated 'the strength, disinterestedness, and grandeur of love' (De Selincourt 1935: 297).

Thus idiocy becomes a part of Wordsworth's broad inclusivity project in *Lyrical Ballads,* and the fact that the poem's subject matter attracts criticism renders it all the more important as an exercise in enlightenment. Alan Richardson (2001: 167) observes that 'Wordsworth dares the reader to see Johnny as less than human, all the while hinting at the intensity of Johnny's perceptions and emotions'. Not all readers were up to the challenge, but some were. As Wordsworth concludes in his letter to Wilson:

> This poem has, I know, frequently produced the same effect as it did upon you and your friends; but there are many also to whom it affords exquisite delight, and who, indeed, prefer it to any other of my poems. This proves that the feelings there delineated are such as men *may* sympathise with. This is enough for my purpose. It is not enough for me as a Poet, to delineate merely such feelings as all men *do* sympathise with; but it is also highly desirable to add to these others, such as all men *may* sympathise with, and such as there is reason to believe they would be better and more moral beings if they did sympathise with. (De Selincourt 1935: 298, original emphasis)

According to the poet, bringing readers to the active exercise of compassion and sympathy becomes a primary objective of poetic expression. A wider social movement dedicated to the cultivation and exercise of compassion and pity for those people categorized as 'idiots' would take political, educational and even architectural form by mid-century. But these developments were fifty years away, and, while 'The Idiot Boy' would be alluded to frequently during the fund-raising activities of asylum promoters, the context would dissipate the poem's disruptive energy, making Johnny Foy little more than an object of pity.

Another version: Southey's macabre idiot son

The *Morning Post* of 30 June 1798 contained another 'idiot son' poem, two months before the publication of *Lyrical Ballads*. The poem was unsigned, and it was only in 1955 that B. R. McElderry traced it to another of Wordsworth's circle, Robert Southey (it still does not appear in standard collections of Southey's works). Like Wordsworth's poem, Southey's 'The Idiot' employs a ballad format; it also includes a disingenuous note that 'The Circumstances Related in the Following Ballad Happened Some Years Since in Herefordshire'. In Southey's poem, the title character, Ned, is clearly a figure within the 'innocent' tradition (to be discussed further in Chapter 6):

It had pleased God to form poor Ned,
A thing of idiot mind.
Yet to the poor, unreasoning man
God hath not been unkind.
(lines 1–4)

God's kindness is evident in the fact that Ned's mother, Sarah, with whom he lives, 'lov'd her helpless child' so that 'life was happiness for him / Who had no hope nor fear' (lines 5, 7–8). But when Sarah dies, Ned is not only bereft: he is incapable of understanding mortality, so that although 'They told him she was dead – the sound / To him no import bore' (lines 19–20). He attends her funeral, but later that night returns to her grave, digs up her body and takes it home with him to place in its accustomed chair; then he gazes at his mother and asks 'Why, mother, do you look so pale, / And why are you so cold?' (lines 55–56). Soon, however, the benevolent Deity calls the son to join his mother in eternal bliss.

As this brief summary makes clear, the poem is a blend of pathos and the macabre. Over fifty years later, Harriet Martineau in the periodical *Household Words* recalls the gist of Southey's narrative (although apparently forgetting its poetic source):

How many elderly people now remember how aghast they were, as children, at the story of the idiot youth, not being able to do without his

mother, who had never left him while he lived: and how, when everybody
supposed him asleep, and the neighbours themselves were asleep, he
went out and got the body, and set it up in the fireside chair, and made a
roaring fire, and heated some broth, and was found, restlessly moaning
with distress, while trying to feed the corpse. (Martineau 1854: 199)

While emphasizing the idiot's status as one to whom God is kind,
Southey also presents him as a grotesque figure who transgresses the
sanctity of the graveyard in retrieving his mother. The fundamental
ambivalence of the character is a startling contrast to Wordsworth's
Johnny, and hints at a deep anxiety about the nature of idiocy, an
anxiety akin to that expressed by many of Wordsworth's other critics.
Elizabeth Duthie suggests that, in having Ned called to God at the end
of the poem, Southey 'includes a consolation for the feelings of pity it
evokes, and so nullifies them', while at the same time 'reassur[ing] the
reader that he is kind and benevolent (and therefore morally superior)'
(Duthie 1978: 219–20); Geoffrey Carnell suggests that the poem 'shows
that [Southey] was able to appreciate the pathos of the idiot's condition,
but one suspects that he could not enter into the intense joy and pain of
mother-love, the exultant idiocy, which is the strength of Wordsworth's
poem' and concludes that 'Southey's idiot ... was a deserving object of
pity; Wordsworth's boy was not' (Carnell 1956: 81, 82).

Southey's idiot adult exhibits qualities distinct from Wordsworth's
'exultant' idiot boy, yet both are informed by an aesthetic tradition that
locates in idiocy a divine naïveté. Ned, however, exists on the fringes
of human society in a perfect and conflict-free world with his mother,
and is fully isolated from it upon his mother's death; while he can be
read as a symbol of divine benevolence and pity, he has no relation to
any human community. Southey's Ned is innocent but bestial, an aber-
ration from the human whose sole connection to human society is his
mother, whereas Johnny Foy, as a participant in his rural world, is also
a part of the range of human possibilities. Indeed, Johnny is a variant
of the Wordsworthian poet, the idiot as artist and everyman, through
whom Wordsworth sought to engage a depth of sympathy well beyond
that slight portion of pity that Southey allots for his own idiot boy.

Framing idiocy

Theories of sympathy were hardly the only factors involved in
shaping either the idea of idiocy or the way in which people
identified as idiots were treated at the end of the eighteenth century.
A number of these discourses make short appearances – or prolonged

ones, for that matter – in 'The Idiot Boy'; they include the distinct but interwoven notions of gender, class, rurality and the natural world, and while I discuss these in greater detail in later chapters, I want to allude briefly to their presence here as well.

Wordsworth's association of the female community of Betty Foy and Susan Gale with Johnny Foy, and his location of them as part of a natural rural world opposed to the rational domain of the doctor, is significant, although hardly surprising. Many writers have noted an ongoing association of women, the mentally disabled and the poor with 'beasts' in early modern England (e.g. Salisbury 1994; Thomas 1984) – indeed, Southey stresses the same bond between the idiot son, Ned, and his devoted mother, Sarah. These associations lingered under various guises into the nineteenth century, although at the time Wordsworth was writing the primary emphasis had already shifted from bestiality to irrationality. The rational, masculine, urban world of the doctor, the man of science, is opposed by the poet to an alternative world of nature, art and feeling, pervaded by the maternal passion of Betty Foy, the neighbourly sympathy of Susan Gale, the magical reinterpretations of Johnny Foy and even the equine intelligence of the pony. Significantly, Johnny's father, while alive and providing for his family, is absent from the poem; there is no male presence other than the 'idiot boy' in this rural world. Johnny resides in this feminized environment because of his idiocy; he has no access to the rational world of other men. But the doctor's world is narrow, unsympathetic and deadening: true humanity is exiled by an insistent rationality, but prospers among Betty, Susan and Johnny. In a more restrained and conventional reading endorsed by later writers on asylums and pedagogy, women – less logical, but as a consequence slightly more natural – provide the link, or perhaps the transition, between the world of idiot boys and that of rational adult men.

By the time of the *Lyrical Ballads*, the pragmatism that Wordsworth describes as characterizing the attitudes of the 'humble' towards people identified as idiots is also being challenged by the fact that the rural world playfully depicted in 'The Idiot Boy' is dying away, thanks to rising populations, growing urbanization and the invention of machines that were revolutionizing industrial production. This changing landscape helps create some of the poem's tensions. As Marilyn Butler has argued, the rising interest in pastoral themes at the end of the eighteenth century was a consequence of increasing urbanism, and she suggests that 'enthusiasms for the remote past are all aspects of primitivism, and have their roots in a more general principle still, a revulsion against sophisticated urban life in favour of a dream of the pastoral' (Butler

1981: 20). The pastoral dream was largely an elegiac one. Wordsworth's 'nature' is experienced by solitary observers, by 'the dispossessed, the lonely wanderer, the vagabond', writes Raymond Williams (1973: 130), who argues that the 'lost community' of the natural world finds its human agent in the 'wandering, challenging if passive, embodiment [of] the beggar' (131) – or, we might add, the idiot boy.

But while the inhabitants of the natural world, the members of the 'lost community', are ever decreasing in number, the English population itself exploded from around five million in 1700 to eight million in 1800 (Wrigley and Schofield 1981); to Wordsworth's contemporaries, population growth with limited space for agricultural development threatened disaster. 'Population, when unchecked, increases in a geometrical ratio. Subsistence increases only in an arithmetic ratio. A slight acquaintance with numbers will show the immensity of the first power in comparison of the second', wrote an anxious Thomas Malthus in his *Essay on the Principle of Population* (1798: 20), published in the same year as *Lyrical Ballads*. As Malthus's fears suggested, agricultural lands in Britain were already heavily exploited and were under continual development to increase productivity. Forests were cleared for cultivation; swamps and marshes were drained. The economy shifted with this population growth, first to an 'advanced organic economy', dependent upon land for economic growth, a period which formed the first stage of Britain's industrial revolution and which lasted into the early nineteenth century (Wrigley 1988: 17). The expanding population and agricultural production placed hefty demands upon land, and even poorer soil was pressed into service to feed the populace. This changing world also touches 'The Idiot Boy'. Betty Foy's absent husband is 'at the wood, / Where by the week he doth abide, / A woodman in the distant vale' (lines 37–39): Johnny's father is felling trees, altering the face of the British countryside, and signalling to the reader the disappearing forest world of Johnny Foy's midnight ride.

The association of the 'natural' idiot with the natural world is not unusual, and from the sixteenth century the term 'natural' (as a noun) was used synonymously with 'idiot' and 'fool'. In *The Natural History of Selborne*, published in 1789, Gilbert White describes an 'idiot boy' who, 'from a child, shewed a strong propensity to bees; they were his food, his amusement, his sole object' (170). He is so adept at his apiary indulgence that he can remove the stingers from his victims and suck out their honey, according to White, who also observes that 'He was a very *merops apiaster*, or bee-bird' (171). Over fifty years later, in 1841, Charles Dickens's description of Barnaby Rudge at the end of the novel of the same name reiterates the theme: 'He was known to every bird and beast about the place, and had a name for every one. Never was there a lighter-hearted husbandman, a creature more popular with young and old' (737). There are pragmatic explanations for these ongoing associations; for instance, in a rural environment, the natural world provides a large and unstructured site of interest and stimulation and would be a realm easily accessible to relatively unsupervised children, 'idiot' and otherwise. Writers (and other people) can then reinterpret this association as they will, applying the appropriate symbolic meaning.

Joyful creation

Wordsworth recalled the creation of 'The Idiot Boy' in his commentary dictated to Isabella Fenwick in 1843:

> The last stanza – 'The Cocks did crow to-whoo, to-whoo, And the sun did shine so cold' – was the foundation of the whole. The words were reported to me by my dear friend, Thomas Poole; but I have since heard the same repeated of other Idiots. Let me add that this long poem was composed in the groves of Alfoxden, almost extempore; not a word, I believe, being corrected, though one stanza was omitted. I mention this in gratitude to those happy moments, for, in truth, I never wrote anything with so much glee. (Brett and Jones 1991: note 292)

While the poem's comic narrator may have been rebuffed by the muses, Wordsworth himself, even after forty-five years of poetic accomplishments and acclaim, recollects this poem's composition as among his most 'happy moments' with those same muses. His 'glee' in composing this poem must have at least partially motivated his rejection of Coleridge's proposed additions, and his vigorous defence against Wilson's objections to it.[6] For Wordsworth, poetry is fulfilled in 'The Idiot Boy'.

Yet Wordsworth's affection for the poem has often baffled critics. Interestingly, Geoffrey Hartman observes that while 'The Idiot Boy' appears to be 'both a minor *poem* and a considerable *text*' (original emphasis), in time 'the distinction may prove false'. As he suggests (with disarming modesty):

> We may have to conclude either that such poems are weak, and are redeemed only by the responsive interpreter, or that they have the sort of strength that we are not yet fit to perceive: that our present image of great poetry stands in the way of their peculiar textual quality. Eventually there might be a new convergence, and certain of Wordsworth's minor poems might be seen for what they are.... (Hartman 1987: 116)

Perhaps, as Wordsworth advises the young John Wilson, the 'principal cause' of critical disdain or confusion lies 'in the *word* Idiot', and readers today, like those of 1798, simply need to examine more clearly what we understand, and *how* we understand what we understand, by that word.

We have read 'The Idiot Boy' primarily in the context of Wordsworth's exchange with John Wilson, but Alan Bewell has identified another factor that might have informed the poem's creation, arguing that Wordsworth patterned it on 'the role that lost idiots played in the Enlightenment' (Bewell 1989: 69). For Enlightenment philosophers, he writes: 'the idiot was a "blank page" in more than one sense, for he provided the crude material upon which was inscribed the language of the philosophers' (64). However, he argues, Wordsworth substituted the Enlightenment emphasis on rational comprehension with the notion of nature as an instructive force, an instruction reflected in Johnny's poetic observation in the poem's final lines. Whether or not Bewell's assessment of Wordsworth's engagement with Enlightenment theories of language acquisition is accurate, his argument provides an interesting gloss on the work of Jean Marc Gaspard Itard with Victor, the 'wild boy of Aveyron' – the subject of the next chapter.

Notes

1 Seven pages of one of Wordsworth's notebooks – those pages containing 'The Somersetshire Tragedy' – were destroyed in 1931 by Gordon Wordsworth, grandson of the poet, who justified his act by writing that 'As Wordsworth never published this poem, and did not even keep a copy of it among his M.S.S., it seemed to me he had no desire for its preservation, and I accordingly cut out and destroyed the leaves on which it was written. It was in no way calculated to add to his reputation, and had even less poetical merit than 'The Convict', the only one of his published poems to which it bears resemblance' (quoted in Jonathan Wordsworth 1966: 642). One wonders if Gordon Wordsworth was motivated by objections similar to those expressed by Wilson in his criticism of 'The Idiot Boy'. Of course, these objections would have taken on a much different hue by 1931, especially given the rise of eugenics. Sympathy for 'near-idiots' bearing illegitimate children would have been very much out of favour, aesthetically, politically and scientifically (see Chapter 11 for more on degeneration and eugenics).
2 Lord Byron was both dismissive and satirical. In his 1809 poem 'English Bards and Scotch Reviewers' he conflates 'The simple Wordsworth' (line 236) with the narrator and Johnny Foy, writing:
    Thus, when he tells the tale of Betty Foy,
    The idiot mother of 'an idiot boy';
    A moon-struck silly lad, who lost his way,
    And, like his bard, confounded night with day;
    So close on each pathetic part he dwells,

And each adventure so sublimely tells,
That all who view the 'idiot in his glory',
Conceive the bard the hero of the story.
(lines 247–54, quoted from McGann 1980: vol. I, 227–64)

3 Wordsworth's response to Southey's review is pragmatic: in fulminating to his publisher, Joseph Cottle, he grumbled that Southey knew 'that I published those poems for money and money alone. He knew that money was important to me ... I care little for the praise of any other professional critic, but as it may help me to pudding' (De Selincourt 1935: 267–68). B. R. McElderry (1955: 490) may be right in identifying the root of Southey's dismissal of the poem when he claims that 'Southey's opinion was much influenced by his having himself published a poem called "The Idiot" in *The Morning Post* for 30 June 1798, two months before *Lyrical Ballads* appeared'. The poem, like an unloved bastard child, was never acknowledged by Southey in his lifetime, an indication that while he was interested in writing on such a subject, he perhaps felt it unbecoming of a proper poet.

4 'King's-evil' refers to scrofula, or tuberculosis; the 'itch' probably refers to sexually transmitted diseases.

5 Coleridge also objected to Wordsworth's concept of a 'real' language of common men, as presented in the 1800 Preface, where Wordsworth noted that, in effect, that which is noble in the language of such men is that which they share with all other men. Instead, Coleridge argues in his *Biographia Literaria* that 'language is the armoury of the human mind' (Engell and Bate 1983: book II, 31) and that 'The best part of human language ... is derived from reflection on the acts of the mind itself' (54); indeed, attempts to imitate 'real' or common language are apt to misfire, as 'the poet, who uses an illogical diction, or a style fitted to excite only the low and changeable pleasure of wonder by means of groundless novelty, substitutes a language of *folly* and *vanity*, not for that of the *rustic*, but for that of *good sense* and *natural feeling*' (55, original emphasis). Drawing on 'the sort and order of words which [the poet] hears in the market, wake, high-road or plough-field' (81) is not the act of a true poet but 'rather of a fool or madman: or at best of a vain or ignorant phantast' (81). Instead, he argues, the poet must weed out these degrading influences: 'it is the prerogative of poetic genius to distinguish by parental instinct its proper offspring from the changelings, which the gnomes of vanity or the fairies of fashion may have laid in its cradle or called by its names' (83). The bad poem thus becomes like a changeling – a folkloric figure, the fairy child exchanged for the human, but also a term used by John Locke to designate people whose intellectual capacity placed them between man and brute (see Chapter 3). Coleridge favours the folkloric definition of 'changeling', but the newer, post-Lockean interpretation allows a subtext: a bad poem is like an idiot boy, lurking in the place of proper offspring.

6 In her stimulating reading of 'The Idiot Boy', Avital Ronell (2002: 259) suggests that the increasing 'conservative constriction' of Wordsworth's later years (a conservatism she associates with the influence of Coleridge and other theorists of poetic form and decorum) marks this poem as his 'last wild ride on poetic license'.

CHAPTER 3

A 'pupil of innocent Nature!' The wild boy of Aveyron goes to Paris

In March 1797, a boy, about twelve years old and apparently feral, was caught by woodsmen in the fields around the town of Lacaune, in the rolling hills of southern France. He escaped after being on show briefly, was apprehended again in summer 1798, and again fled to the woods after several days. He was caught yet again by three hunters in mid-July of 1799, and was left with a peasant, who fed him on potatoes and nuts, the only food he accepted; he escaped – yet again – after eight days. Finally, he reappeared for good on 8 January 1800, in the village of Saint-Sernin in the district of Aveyron, where, perhaps motivated by hunger and remembering the kindness of the peasant, he approached the workshop of a dyer named Vidal, who took him in and called the appropriate authorities.

The wild boy was a sensation. Crowds gathered to see him in Saint-Affrique, where he was first placed in an orphanage; in Rodez, where he was transferred for observation to the custody of Abbé Pierre-Joseph Bonnaterre, professor of natural history at the École Centrale de l'Aveyron; and then in Paris, when, six months after entering Vidal's atelier, he first arrived at the Institution Impériale des Sourds-Muets (the Imperial Institute for Deaf-Mutes), headed by Abbé Roche-Ambroise Sicard. 'L'enfant sauvage de l'Aveyron', as he quickly became known, was a nine-day wonder in French media and society. As Joseph-Marie de Gérando wrote, 'this news, which has been featured in the papers for some time now, has occupied the idle, attracted the curious and provided fodder for many discussions, at the very least premature, as they are founded purely on conjecture' (de Gérando 1848: 110–11).[1] The much anticipated and widely discussed arrival of this 'natural man' in the national capital entranced the Parisian intelligentsia and distracted regular citizens from more quotidian concerns.

The appearance of a genuine feral boy provided material not only for newspaper and journal articles but also poems, plays and at least one novel. Among the contemporary works exploiting the wild boy's appearance was a vaudeville piece by Dupaty, Maurice and Chazet entitled *Le Sauvage du departement de l'Aveyron ou Il ne faut jurer rien* (*The Wild Boy of Aveyron, or You Never Can Tell*). In a preview of the play from *Le Journal de Paris* of 28 March 1800, we are told that a young Russian officer and prisoner of war, Polinski, falls in love with Mme Nina de Senanges, and discovers that the way to impress her would be to bring her the boy caught in the woods of Aveyron. After tracking down the hunters, Polinksi disguises himself in the costume of the wild boy (presumably not naked) and eventually uses this stratagem to win Nina's love (Gineste 2004: 181). In an excerpt published in *Le Journal de Paris* two days later, the faux 'wild boy' is examined by a physician, who sings

> I shall now contribute to
> Medicine and physics
> Bear with me while I perform
> A few anatomical studies on him,
> Does he believe that I have ill designs?
> His face shows his terror!
> Could he fear a physician?
> (Gineste 2004: 183)[2]

In addition, J. A. Neyer's novel *Rodolph ou le sauvage de l'Aveyron* was announced in advertisements that appeared in the *Journal général de la literature français* for 2 October 1800, although the book itself remains elusive and may never have been published (Gineste 2004). Most of these works are profoundly ephemeral, and not overly concerned with reconstructing anything like a factually accurate history (see Gineste 2004: 41–43; 181–83). But, for a time, the wild boy made a convenient premise upon which to launch a narrative.[3]

That is what the English poet Mary Robinson did in one of the few pieces of wild-boy ephemera to be recovered intact from history's dustbin – although she stays closer than most to the real narrative. Robinson, in the midst of losing the battle with what would be her final illness, composed 'The Savage of Aveyron' in December 1800 (quotes here taken from Pascoe 2000). Her 'wild boy' is not an abandoned child but rather one who had been witness to the murder of his mother and had survived attempts on his own life (the latter point has some factual grounding – the boy had scars suggesting that he may also have been an intended murder victim). The poem's narrator, wandering in 'The lonely wood of AVEYRON' (line 2), overhears a 'melancholy tone' and freezes in terror. The narrator, too, has a melancholy temperament – 'I thought no living thing could be, / So weary of the world as me' (lines 13–14) – and forms a bond with the wild boy, who nimbly climbs trees and shrieks the only word in his vocabulary: 'alone'. The boy eventually leads the narrator to his sleeping place, where there is a rag that had belonged to his murdered mother. The narrator brings the poem to a close with the realization that she is not the most abandoned of all creatures, but that the savage boy may well be:

> And could a wretch more wretched be,
> More wild, or fancy-fraught than he,
> Whose melancholy tale would pierce AN HEART
> OF STONE.
> (lines 172–75)

Robinson's poem is affecting and melodramatic, stressing the sympathetic connection – born of melancholy and solitude – between the wild boy and the narrator.[4] These themes, interestingly, are also prominent in some of the more formal and scientific descriptions of the boy and case studies of his treatment. J.-J. Virey and Jean Marc Gaspard Itard, for instance, were not averse to drawing on stock romantic imagery to describe the wild boy, as we shall see.

The early flurry of cultural products – journal articles as well as songs, novels, poems and plays – documenting and exploiting the wild boy's discovery was overshadowed eventually by those most famous and influential documents, the 1801 and 1806 reports published by Jean Itard, the boy's guardian and teacher. This chapter explores some of the main recurring themes in the reports written on the boy, including his shifting status as, among other things, *Homo ferus*, ineducable idiot and *tabula rasa* who is simply awaiting the teacher with his chalk. In addition to Itard's reports, we shall also consider the descriptions by the naturalists Bonnaterre and Virey, and the assessment of the boy presented by Philippe Pinel to the Société des Observateurs de l'Homme (Society of the Observers of Man). The writings about the wild boy condense certain fascinating elements of eighteenth-century thought concerning the boundaries of the human and questions about the virtue of the 'natural man', in a fusion of Enlightenment rationality and romantic desire for a pre-civilized state.

Searching for the natural man

Philosophers as distinct as Jean-Jacques Rousseau and Étienne Bonnot de Condillac, struggling to understand the nature of human cognition, had hypothesized a sort of unadorned man, a pre-societal figure who, if found and observed, could resolve the debates over exactly how humans came to think. Taxonomical concerns also ranked high among the intellectual issues of the day; from the mid-eighteenth century, philosophers and natural historians worked to distinguish humans from animals, with savages, *Homo feri* and great apes (especially, it seems, orang-utans) occupying a transitional or shifting position. These two lines of inquiry – the philosophical and the taxonomical – led to the same questions. What constituted a human being? Did humans exist on a continuum with beasts, or were they a separate entity? Where did savages rest on this hierarchy? And where were idiots? The questions were not without difficulties.

The capture of the wild boy promised answers to at least some of these intellectual conundrums, and the timing was serendipitous. The Société des Observateurs de l'Homme – a group of about sixty physicians, philosophers and naturalists – had been formed in December 1799, in the aftermath of Napoleon's consolidation of power and the apparent end of the bloodshed of the revolution (Shattuck 1980). Members of the group included the renowned psychologist Philippe Pinel, who, upon being named *médecin-chef* of the Bicêtre hospital in Paris in 1793, began his policy of releasing the mad from their physical chains and replacing this restraint with 'moral treatment', and Abbé Roche-Ambroise Sicard, director of the Institution Impériale des Sourds-Muets, who had developed innovative strategies for teaching language to the deaf. The calming of revolutionary violence also made it possible for people to pay attention to something so extraneous to daily demands as the presence of a wild boy. As Roger Shattuck observes, 'Because of the timing, people all over France took notice of him…. He had come on stage just as the eye of the storm passed over' (Shattuck 1980: 50).

When Lucien Bonaparte, Minister of the Interior, became aware of the wild boy's final capture, it was almost a month after the fact; on 1 February 1800, he requested that the child be brought to Paris, but Bonnaterre requested more time to complete his observations. Eventually, though, on 20 July 1800, the boy began his eighteen-day journey to Paris, accompanied by Bonnaterre and Clair Saussol, the gardener from the École Centrale who had been serving as his caregiver (Gineste 2004). When he arrived in Paris, where he was to be placed in the Institution Impériale des Sourds-Muets, the Société des Observateurs de l'Homme assigned a committee of five members to investigate him: Sicard, as keeper of the Institute; Pinel; Georges Cuvier, the renowned anatomist and taxonomist; Joseph-Marie de Gérando, a moral philosopher and naturalist; and Louis-François Jauffret, naturalist and co-founder of the Société (Lane 1976; Shattuck 1980).

Almost immediately after his capture, the boy was transformed into a subject for learned papers. Bonnaterre published his 'Notice historique sur le sauvage de l'Aveyron' in August 1800; this was followed a couple of months later by J.-J. Virey's 'Histoire naturelle du genre humain (avec une dissertation sur le sauvage de l'Aveyron)'. Philippe Pinel presented a paper on the wild boy at a December 1800 conference of the Société des Observateurs de l'Homme. Most famous, though, are the accounts of the boy written by Jean Itard, *De l'Education d'un homme sauvage ou des premiers développements physiques et moraux du jeune sauvage de l'Aveyron* in 1801 and his later report in 1806.[5]

These writings were informed by a number of philosophical traditions, most clearly those associated with John Locke and Jean-Jacques Rousseau. In his *Essay Concerning Human Understanding*, completed in 1689, Locke theorizes that the human mind is like a *tabula rasa*, a blank slate, which acquires knowledge as the memory records experience. Based upon this knowledge, the mind eventually learns to reason and to make abstractions. France's most prominent advocate of Locke's system, Étienne Bonnot, Abbé de Condillac, extended Locke's theories in his *Essai sur l'origine des connaissances humaines* (1746), most notably by elaborating on the link between sensory data and intellectual development (a distinction that greatly influenced Itard's instruction of the wild boy, and later Édouard Séguin's educational methods). The arrival of a wild child, untutored by humans and without the language that enables one to formalize thought, provided a means for philosophers to examine the empiricist ideas of Locke and Condillac. But there were opposing schools as well. What if the wild child, acquiring language, were able to recognize and present the innate ideas hypothesized by Cartesian thought? What shape might these ideas take when in pre-linguistic form? Or could the wild boy resolve the questions posed by Rousseau regarding the fundamental nature of man and its transformation by social life and civilization? Was Rousseau correct in arguing that socialized man is a degraded man, and that the ambivalent morality of civilized life spoils that which, in its more primitive, wild form, is noble? The wild boy would have an eager audience, when – and if – he learned to speak.

These questions extended beyond asking 'What is the nature of human understanding?' to the much more fundamental 'What is a human?' In his *Systema Naturae* of 1758, the Swedish naturalist Carl von Linné – better known as Linnaeus – proposed that the family of man, *Homo*, be divided into *sapiens*, or *Homo diurnus*, and *troglodyte*, or *Homo nocturnus*. *Homo diurnus* he then further divided into six groups: *Homo ferus, americanus, europaeus, asiaticus, afer* and, as a final catch-all category, *monstrosus*. *Homo nocturnus* was represented by the orang-utan, a creature whose status baffled philosophers and taxonomists; the orang-utan had in fact been christened *Homo sylvestris* by the seventeenth-century Dutch physician Jakob de Bondt, or Bontius as cited by Linnaeus (1758: 24).[6] The wild boy was clearly an example of *Homo ferus*, according to the Linnaean categories and to commentators such as Bonnaterre and Virey. Linnaeus identifies a number of feral precedents to support his taxonomy, noting that these feral humans were characterized by being 'tetrapus, mutus, hirsutus' – that is, they moved on all four limbs, did not speak and were hairy.

What is the relation between natural man and idiots, though? Unlike *Homo feri*, 'idiots' did not form any distinct taxonomical categories. However, some writers – most notably Locke – treated the problems posed by 'idiocy' as being both philosophical and taxonomical. As Locke's influence shows heavily in the thought of Condillac and Pinel, and in the treatment that Itard developed for the wild boy, we will take a detour through some of his writings on idiocy. One question looms prominently: why were Locke and Pinel so insistent that idiots were not only incurable but also ineducable? How did this idea take hold?

In book II of his *Essay Concerning Human Understanding*, Locke argues that the ability to reason distinguishes men from brute animals.[7] Immediately after making this argument, he establishes a distinction between idiots (or 'naturals', as he terms them) and madmen based upon their apparent reasoning processes:

> In fine, the defect in naturals seems to proceed from want of quickness, activity and motion in the intellectual faculties, whereby they are deprived of reason; whereas madmen, on the other side, seem to suffer by the other extreme: for they do not appear to me to have lost the faculty of reasoning; but having joined together some ideas very wrongly, they mistake them for truths, and they err as men do that argue right from wrong principles.... In short, herein seems to lie the difference between idiots and madmen, that madmen put wrong ideas together, and so make wrong propositions, but argue and reason right from them; but idiots make very few or no propositions, and reason scarce at all. (11, 12–13)

As Chris Goodey argues, Locke is proposing a subtle division in the 'Great Chain of Being' hierarchy, arguing that while madmen are human, idiots veer towards the bestial because of their failure to achieve rationality. Idiots, incapable of reasoning (or of reasoning very little, and poorly at that) rest somewhere below the fully human as defined by rational capacity. In book III, Locke develops the human/idiot distinction more emphatically (he uses the terms 'natural' and 'changeling' in this passage[8]):

There are creatures in the world that have shapes like ours, but are hairy, and want language and reason. There are naturals amongst us that have perfectly our shape, but want reason, and some of them language too. There are creatures, as it is said ... that, with reason and language, and a shape in other things agreeing with ours, have hairy tails; others where the males have no beards, and others where the females have. If it can be asked, whether these be all men or no, all of human species? it is plain, the question refers only to the nominal essence: for those of them to whom the definition of the word man, or the complex idea signified by that name, agrees, are men, and the other not. But if the inquiry be made concerning the supposed real essence, and whether the internal constitution and frame of these several creatures be specifically different, it is wholly impossible for us to answer, no part of that going into our specific idea; only we have reason to think, that where the faculties or outward frame so much differs, the internal constitution is not exactly the same. But what difference in the internal real constitution makes a specific difference, it is in vain to inquire; whilst our measures of species be, as they are, only our abstract ideas, which we know; and not that internal constitution, which makes no part of them. Shall the difference of hair only on the skin, be a mark of a different internal specific constitution between a changeling and a drill, when they agree in shape, and want of reason and speech? And shall not the want of reason and speech be a sign to us of different real constitutions and species between a changeling and a reasonable man? And so of the rest, if we pretend that distinction of species or sorts is fixedly established by the real frame and secret constitutions of things. (6, 22)

Locke's concern is with the nature of the human and he argues that, in the absence of a clear sense of internal workings of the mind, we have to judge the human according to that which we can perceive with our own senses. And our senses should suggest that 'idiots' do not operate like other humans and thus are quite probably not like other humans. To address the problem posed by the apparently ambivalent humanity of the idiot, Locke suggests a new taxonomical position:

It would possibly be thought a bold Paradox, if not a very dangerous Falsehood, if I should say, that some Changelings, who have lived forty years together, without any appearance of Reason, are something between a Man and a Beast.... Here every body will be ready to ask, if Changelings may be supposed to be something between Man and Beast, 'Pray what are they?' I answer, Changelings, which is as good a word to signify something different from the signification of MAN or BEAST, as the names Man and Beast are to have significations from one another. (book IV, 13–14)

Locke's psychological presentation of human nature in the *Essay* has a powerful political dimension: if individuals begin as blank slates and acquire knowledge through sensory experience, then they are autonomous individuals, and pose a challenge to established church and government authorities. Individual autonomy leads to all sorts of theological and political notions, including the idea that individuals are responsible for their own moral destiny – an important religious precept for a dissenter with a Calvinist upbringing like Locke, and one which has implications for the exercise (or limitation) of both royal and ecclesiastical authority. But what of humans who do not seem to acquire the knowledge and rationality necessary to take this responsibility? What of those humans for whom sense impressions leave only a temporary mark, rather than translating into experience and knowledge? Locke's idiots are enlisted to form a contrast group, the exception proving the rule that humans are rational, autonomous beings.

Of course, to serve this function, the idiot must also be a stable figure – that is, he must be neither curable nor educable, because if he were either, Locke would need to find another contrast group, and so 'in Locke's hands the concept of idiocy looks more like a desperate remedy, a few pieces of sticking plaster for fissures in the law of nature', writes Goodey (1994: 242), who stresses that 'Locke had no unified theory of idiocy as a component of his psychology' (1994: 222). Locke's thesis around idiocy seems to be adapted to his needs on an *ad hoc* basis – he is making it up as he goes along. And instead of simply reiterating a set of established precepts, he draws on a specific set of sources on idiocy (medical and jurisprudential notions, as opposed to class notions concerning the idiocy of illiterate labourers or gender-based ideas on the inherent irrationality of women) and transforms them to hypothesize his own particular figure of the idiot. Locke's idiot is theological rather than sociological (Goodey 1996), used to score philosophical points rather than to inform social policy. However, 'posterity has picked from [Locke's] idiocy what it has found convenient', writes Goodey (1994: 248); the philosopher's influence at the birth of the discipline of psychology is such that his notion of idiocy, drafted to support an argument, eventually becomes incorporated as a professional truism. Thus Pinel, examining the wild boy of Aveyron 120 years after Locke's essay, asserts that 'there is no hope whatever of obtaining some measure of success through systematic and continued instruction' (quoted in Lane 1976: 69). '[T]o be an ideot', writes Pinel in his *Traité médico-philosophique sur l'aleniation mentale; ou la manie* (1801), translated into English as *A Treatise on Insanity* (1806), 'is to be almost levelled with an automaton'. People so afflicted 'seldom admit of redress.... Humane attention to their physical wants and comforts, is in general the utmost that can be devised or done for these unfortunate beings' (quotations here and below are from Robinson 1977: 202).

Pinel's *Treatise on Insanity* describes in detail various forms of mental degeneration, including idiocy, and while he does transform the condition significantly from Locke's conception of it, there are also important continuities. According to Pinel, 'Ideotism ... is a partial or total abolition of the intellectual and active faculties'. Several possible causes are listed:

> excessive and enervating pleasures; the abuse of spirituous liquors; violent blows on the head; deeply impressed terror; profound sorrow; intense study; tumours within the cavity of the cranium; apoplexy; [or] excessive use of the lancet in the treatment of active mania. The greatest number of ideots are either destitute of speech or are confined to the utterance of some inarticulate sounds. Their looks are without animation; their senses stupefied; and their motions heavy and mechanical. (Robinson 1977: 165)

The condition thus described by Pinel was not unusual; indeed, he noted, 'Ideots constitute the greatest number of patients at lunatic hospitals; and their pitiable condition, has in too many instances, originated in severity of treatment experienced at other places' (Robinson 1977: 166). He goes on to observe that 'At Bicêtre [idiocy] constitutes one fourth of the whole number of patients', in large part, he claims, because the hospital is considered a repository for the untreatable (168). The idiocy Pinel describes in these passages is not congenital but acquired; congenital idiocy, he suggests, is most often caused by 'a malformation of the cranium' (166), and he later gives as evidence of this claim the 'state of degradation and nihility' that one can observe in 'the Cretins of Switzerland ... [who] exhibit, from their earliest years, unequivocal indications of their future destiny' (169). Pinel understands idiocy as a condition that, while not necessarily congenital, is certainly permanent and incurable. It is also remarkably fluid, resulting from a wide variety of distinct causes that share a common consequence: an apparent lack of physical and intellectual will.

Over the years, Locke's philosophical gambit transformed into a psychological truth, and the doctrine of idiot ineducability clung aggressively to the canons of received psychological knowledge, despite observations to the contrary. Even Pinel wrote that

> The natural indolence and stupidity of ideots, might in some degree be obviated, by engaging them in manual occupations, suitable to their respective capacities. With an able active man at their head, ideots are capable of being drilled into any sort of service where bodily strength alone is requisite. The new plantation at Bicêtre was made almost altogether at their expense. (Robinson 1977: 203)

Here we might question precisely what writers like Pinel mean when they refer to the ineducability of idiots. They may simply be indicating that idiots could not attain advanced philosophical knowledge, such as that exhibited by the members of the Société des Observateurs de l'Homme. The much more general notion of 'idiocy' as something shared by certain groups of people – the lower classes, women, children and savage peoples, most notably – would perhaps have muddled distinctions further and obscured the fact that individual people identified as 'idiots' did indeed show signs of learning things, because, even in learning, they would elevate themselves only from their specific idiocy to the more general idiocy of the mass of humanity – the types of people who build edifices but do not administrate them. This might explain Pinel's apparently contradictory assertions that people diagnosed as idiots can be directed to perform certain complex tasks, such as building a plantation, yet they cannot be taught.

John Locke's notions of a stable, unchanging idiocy reverberated through the development of psychology and, indeed, democratic society. 'Locke's view of what it is to be human emerged upon forfeit of a sacrifice; … a concept of "man" is generated only by excluding from that concept certain "men"', Goodey argues (1994: 249). Lockean natural law as it applies to species distinction is based on the belief that humans are distinguished from animals by rational processes. Otherwise, without this distinction, humans would lapse into a dangerous zone where they could be understood as simply another form of animal. Locke's conception of the human and of human understanding requires the idiot as a sort of 'buffer zone' between man and beast, as he negotiates the 'abyss' created when reason is identified as the defining human characteristic (Goodey 1994: 248).

Taxonomies grow out of philosophical and political as well as biological propositions.[9] For Locke, idiots or changelings pose problems because they are apparently human yet are also without the rational faculties that he uses to define humanity, and they must somehow be turned to useful account. Thus, the theory of rational consent fundamental to liberal democracy necessitates the construction of a contrast group, those incapable of rational consent. As Goodey notes, 'at the strange birth of liberal England there are some other anomalous offspring emerging. Totally determined inhuman idiots, at the opposite end from liberty, are necessary to the theory of consent' (Goody 1996: 114).

In France, Locke's work was continued by Etienne Bonnot, the Abbé de Condillac, who had proposed as a thought experiment a statue that is given sentience through the awakening of each of its senses. In his 1754 work *Traité des sensations* (translated in English as *Treatise on the*

Sensations), Condillac hypothesizes what sort of being would result if the sense of touch is first developed; then, what would result from awakening the sense of hearing exclusively; and so forth, finally bringing them all together to argue, following from Locke, that human experience and knowledge are a consequence of accumulated sense impressions. While statues that could be awakened in such a manner were an impossible-to-find resource, limited to the realm of philosophical fantasy, *Homo feri*, although rare, were possibly the next best thing.

Thus, wild children assumed an increasingly important status in Enlightenment thought as subjects upon whom philosophers could test theories of human nature, innate ideas, the acquisition of knowledge and language, and the role of civilization in forming or transforming the true nature of humans. Ironically, many of these 'feral children' were likely to have been abandoned idiots, who would have been well beyond the pale of psychological and philosophical consideration had they been found in a peasant's hovel (Bewell 1989). Still, avid students of human consciousness flocked to examine each feral human pulled from the shrinking forests of Europe[10] and there was limited but sufficient opportunity to do so, with twelve cases being reported between 1661 and 1797 (Douthwaite 1994/95).[11] As Douthwaite (1997: 176) notes: 'Enlightenment writers turned children found in the wild into the basis of zoological taxonomies, tales of sin and redemption, schemas of primitive society, or proof of human degradation'.

Taxonomizing the wild boy

The various taxonomical and moral functions ascribed to allegedly wild children are evident in the first two major reports on the wild boy of Aveyron, those by Bonnaterre and Virey. In their works, they itemize his various characteristics, beginning with a description of his physical qualities, then discussing the boy's lack of speech, the development of instincts (including such things as personal attachment), his eating habits and the daily regimen. Both agreed that the boy seemed to straddle the gap between human and beast. 'The child's manner of living has provided less contact with man than with animals', notes Bonnaterre (see Gineste 2004: 265). As a result, he behaves more like an animal than a human. 'Endowed only with instinct by nature, this child performs purely animal functions: he has no knowledge of feigned passions or conventional needs, which become as present as natural needs. His desires do not go beyond his physical needs', according to Bonnaterre (268). However, he concedes, the child's 'constant need for nourishment increases his connection with the objects around him and develops in him a certain measure of intelligence' (270). Bonnaterre places the boy solidly as one of Linnaeus' *Homo feri* in his comparisons with other feral children:

> He has pale skin, a pleasing physiognomy and is slender, like the savages of Lithuania and Ireland and the girl from Châlons.
>
> Only with great effort can he be accustomed to ordinary food, like the child of Lithuania.
>
> He chooses the foods that he likes by smell, like the children of Ireland, Hanover and Jean of Liège.
>
> When he was captured and during our voyage, when he saw a fountain or a stream, he lay down on his stomach and drank, putting his chin in the water up to his mouth, like the girl from Châlons. And like her, he disdains any form of clothing and constantly attempts to escape.
>
> When tired, he was seen to walk on all fours, like the savages of Hesse, Ireland and Bamberg.
>
> He defends himself by biting, like the children of Lithuania and Bamberg.
>
> He shows only feeble signs of reason, like the child of Lithuania found in 1661.
>
> He has no articulated language and may have the same difficulty speaking as the children found in Ireland, Lithuania and Hanover. He is gentle, compliant and allows himself to be caressed, like the child from Hanover and the girl from Over-Yssel.
> (Gineste 2004: 278)

Despite the fact that early in his report Bonnaterre identifies the boy as a 'being who is limited or verging on an imbecile' (266), at its conclusion he sounds a cautiously hopeful note:

> Such an astounding phenomenon will provide philosophy and natural history with important ideas regarding the primitive nature of man and the development of his intellectual faculties, provided that the state of imbecility, which we have seen in this child, is no obstacle to his instruction: but every success may be expected from this teacher of philosophy [Sicard] who has worked such miracles in this type of education; and one must hope that the child entrusted to his care may one day become the equal of Massieu, Fontaine and Mathieu [deaf students of Sicard's].
> (Gineste 2004: 279)

Virey also emphasizes those characteristics that identify the boy as *Homo ferus*, but counterpoints these passages with theological and philosophical observations. 'How could he know the existence of God, for example? Let him be shown the skies, green fields, earth's vast expanse, Nature's creations; he is aware of nothing if there is nothing to eat', Virey writes. 'One could believe that his mind is in his stomach, that it is the centre of his life. The scientist and the philosopher, on the contrary, live exclusively in their heads' (see Gineste 2004: 317). However, despite the boy's limitations, Virey asserts 'I have detected no clear sign of idiocy in the young man; I have seen only the profound, dark ignorance of a simple soul, who undoubtedly seems quite stupid compared to well-raised and sharp-witted Parisians of the same age'. But this 'profound, dark ignorance', he suggests, may render it impossible, 'even for the renowned Sicard, to completely drive the inertia from the mind of the boy from Aveyron' (299–300). Virey identifies the boy as both a 'child of nature' (314) and 'purely an animal, limited to simple physical sensations' (323). All the same, the boy's entry into civilized European society prompts Virey's closing eulogy on his loss of natural innocence:

> Go forth, young one, into this unhappy world; lose your primitive and simple crudeness in civil society. You lived in ancient forests; you found nourishment at the base of oaks and beeches; you quenched your thirst in clear spring waters; and, content with your destiny, limited to simple desires, satisfied with a life beyond which you know nothing, the usufruct of the earth was your sole domain. Now you have nothing except through the charity of man; you are at his mercy, without property, without power, and you have gone from freedom to dependence. Thus are born poor three quarters of humanity: what bitterness was prepared for you, in tearing you from the dryads who saw to your protection! You had but one need: to nourish yourself; how many others that you fail to satisfy will now dog you relentlessly? How many desires shall sprout under your feet and grow with the tree of your knowledge, with your social ties? How completely you shall lose your independence to the political shackles of our civil institutions! The tears you shall shed! The road to your education will be sprinkled by your weeping: and when your new soul once again rises toward the blue canopy of the skies, when you will distinguish order from beauty in this vast universe, what new thoughts will germinate in your young mind! When love finally opens the doors to a new existence, how many new and delicious sensations and unknown passions will stir in your sensitive heart! May you live happily among your compatriots! May you, simple man, display the sublime virtues of a generous soul and pass on to future generations this honourable example, as eternal evidence of what can be accomplished by a pupil of innocent Nature! (Gineste 2004: 323–24)

Virey's wild boy rests upon the borders of knowledge, and will soon cross over into the land of the civilized, with its heightened sensibilities, complex desires and emotions, and wrenching social inequalities; he is, like Adam, poised to leave his prelapsarian paradise. Yet, he trusts, the boy's heritage – guarded by protective dryads and nourished at the roots of the beech and the oak – should provide him with the necessary moral strength to resist the corrupting aspects of social life and become a true Enlightenment man, his soul expanded by knowledge, love and generosity.

But Virey's projection of the wild boy's future as an educated citizen of the new republic was a Rousseauian anomaly. More common was the position taken by Pinel in his presentation to the Société des Observateurs de l'Homme, given two days before Itard took responsibility for the boy at the end of 1800. Pinel moved away from general arguments about *Homo feri* to the specific observation that all attempts to teach the boy must fail for the simple reason that this particular *Homo ferus* was an ineducable idiot, and his 'wildness' a consequence of a fundamental inability to learn. Wrote Pinel in 1800, 'The child seems to have no notion of anything that does not have a bearing on his subsistence or his means of escape; or, lacking attention, he has only fleeting ideas, which disappear as quickly as they appear' (see Gineste 2004: 329). To support his case, he juxtaposed the wild boy's physical and intellectual characteristics against those of individuals residing in the city's asylums, whose status as 'idiots' was already established. While in some cases he had advanced skills, especially those needed to survive in nature, Pinel argued in 1801 that most often the wild boy fell behind the standards set by these institutionalized idiots, and concludes that:

> inhuman or impoverished parents abandoned the child as incapable of being educated, around the age of nine or ten, some distance from their home, and that the thorn of need drove him to nourish himself with unrefined food that nature put at his disposal, with no other means of judging their health-giving or harmful properties than impressions gained first through the sense of smell and then taste. He seems to have remained a wanderer and a vagabond in the woods, or in the hamlets in the years that followed, constantly reduced to purely animal instinct and occupied solely by the means of finding sustenance and escaping the dangers that threatened him. (Gineste 2004: 356–60)

His final judgement, as already noted, was that the boy 'must be classed among children suffering from idiocy and dementia, and … there is no real hope for success from continued systematic instruction' (360).[12]

Despite Pinel's assessment (and Pinel was the established authority), Jean Itard and Joseph-Marie de Gérando persisted in believing that Condillac's system could enlighten the wild boy and awaken his intellect. De Gérando's interest in the boy was an extension of his interest in non-European cultures. As a member of the Société des Observateurs de l'Homme, de Gérando had presented 'Considérations sur les diverses methods à suivre dans l'observation des peoples sauvages' (published in English as *The Observation of Savage Peoples*), a proto-anthropological guide prepared for Captain Nicolas-Thomas Baudin and François

Levaillant in advance of their 1800 expedition to Africa; in it, he had entreated that the explorers 'become particularly acquainted with the methodical signs used so successfully by citizen Sicard to establish his first communication with deaf-mutes. For the deaf-mute is also a savage, and Nature is the only interpreter to translate for him the first lessons of his masters' (de Gérando 1800: 72). Later, de Gérando notes that important observations could be carried out in Paris, if the right subjects were brought back: 'We should not finish without recommending to the travellers to bring back for us if they can Savages of both sexes, some adolescent and some infant', concluding that 'it would be desirable if a whole family could be persuaded to come back with them. In that case, the individuals composing it, less restricted in their habits and saddened by their losses, would better present their natural character' (100–1). Such studies would be an exploration of human evolution, argued de Gérando: 'The philosophical traveller, sailing to the ends of the earth, is in fact travelling in time; he is exploring the past; every step he makes is the passage of an age' (63). Noting that 'our ideas are nothing more than elaborated sensations', he urged the travellers to pay special attention to what ideas *peuples sauvages* expressed and how they formed them. The study of 'primitive' cultures was meant to shed light on the infancy of 'advanced' cultures, just as the study of primitive individuals would illuminate understanding of fully encultured and civilized man. Itard's proposal for the study of the wild boy reflects de Gérando's interest in the extensive observation of other peoples and cultures, foregrounding the link between study of the *enfant sauvage* and that of *peuples sauvages*.

Itard, who had studied under Pinel, was in 1800 an ambitious twenty-six-year-old who had served on occasion as the physician for students at Sicard's Institution, where he first came into contact with the wild boy. He insisted the child's apparent idiocy was the consequence of intellectual deprivation, as is clear in the Preface to his first report:

If it was proposed to resolve the following metaphysical problem, viz. *'to determine what would be the degree of understanding, and the nature of the ideas of a youth who, deprived, from his infancy, of all education, should have lived entirely separated from individuals of his species'*: I am strangely deceived, or the solution of the problem would give to this individual an understanding connected only with a small number of his wants, and deprived, by his insulated condition, of all those simple and complex ideas which we receive from education, and which are combined in our minds in so many different ways, by means only of our knowledge of signs. Well! the moral picture of this youth would be that of the Savage of Aveyron, and the solution of the problem would give the measure and the cause of his intellectual state. (Itard 1801: 99, original emphasis)

The Société decided to give Itard a chance to test his theory, despite Pinel's gloomy prediction that 'there seems to be no evidence for a more happy outcome in the future' even with training. On 31 December 1800, the Société formally gave Itard responsibility for the boy, and Sicard created for him the post of resident physician at the Institution Impériale des Sourds-Muets.

Jean Itard and Victor of Aveyron

The debate around the wild boy was not concerned with whether or not it was worthwhile to educate an idiot, as both Pinel and Itard, following Locke, Condillac and the dominant beliefs of their profession, agreed it was not, but rather with the source of the boy's apparent incapacity. The opening paragraph of Itard's first report gives a good sense of his perspective:

> Cast on this globe, without physical powers, and without innate ideas; unable by himself to obey the constitutional laws of his organization, which call him to the first rank in the system of being; MAN can only find in the bosom of society the eminent station that was destined for him in nature, and would be, without the aid of civilization, one of the most feeble and least intelligent of animals; – a truth which, although it has often been insisted upon, has not as yet been rigorously demonstrated. (Itard 1801: 91)

This truth Itard intended to demonstrate by educating the boy, whom he named Victor.

Itard based his training programme on the ideas of Condillac, the techniques used by Sicard at L'Institution Impériale des Sourds-Muets, and the concept of 'moral medicine' (Itard 1801: 101). He defines five goals for the wild boy's training programme (102):

> 1. To attach him to social life, by rendering it more pleasant to him than that which he was then leading, and, above all, more analogous to the mode of existence that he was about to quit.
> 2. To awaken the nervous sensibility by the most energetic stimulants, and sometimes by lively affections of the mind.
> 3. To extend the sphere of his ideas, by giving him new wants, and by increasing the number of his relations to the objects surrounding him.
> 4. To lead him to the use of speech by subjecting him to the necessity of imitation.
> 5. To exercise frequently the most simple operations of the mind upon the objects of his physical wants; and, at length, by inducing the application of them to objects of instruction.

This programme included a series of activities to train Victor's senses – to develop his responses to hot and cold, for instance; to refine his hearing and visual discrimination; to develop his capacity to receive direction; and, ultimately, to enable him to speak. While Victor never learned to communicate in the way Itard desired, it is clear from the two reports, and from Harlan Lane's comprehensive and insightful analysis of Itard's training regimen, that Victor learned a great deal.

Lane has already done an admirable job of describing and assessing Itard's training programme, so I will not concern myself with this task. My interest lies instead in looking at how Victor, his *gouvernante* Mme Guérin and Itard himself are developed as characters in a history composed for an audience of professional people – physicians and philosophers, administrators and politicians – whose approval Itard required for the support of both his training programme and his professional reputation. Itard's narrative rests upon his professional commitment to experiment and observation, and is perhaps best characterized as a form of case history. His first report, *De l'Éducation d'un homme sauvage ou des premiers développements physiques et moraux du jeune sauvage de l'Aveyron*, published in 1801, is organized around his initial attempts to solve the riddles of the human intellect posed by the wild boy. Each of the project's five pedagogical objectives is treated separately, and in increasing detail: while Itard's description of the work carried out to meet the first objective comprises only four paragraphs, the summary of his effort to achieve his fifth and final objective stretches to seventeen paragraphs of considerably longer and more detailed descriptions. Because he had been working with Victor for less than a year when the report was written, he draws only preliminary conclusions: notable among them are the observations that 'man is inferior to a great number of animals in a pure state of nature' and that the 'moral superiority ... said to be *natural* to man, is merely the result of civilization' (138, original emphasis). He also proposes that 'the progress of teaching may, and ought to be aided by the lights of modern medicine, which of all the natural sciences can co-operate the most effectually towards the amelioration of the human species, by appreciating the organical and intellectual peculiarities of each individual' (139). From the very beginnings of what would become 'special education', pedagogy and medicine were united.

As a physician, Itard brought the professional concerns of his time to his analysis, and the narrative – essentially a case history – records his various successes and failures in his pedagogical and intellectual quest. The case history format is inherently descriptive and documentary: it describes a problem, a process of treatment and the results of this treatment. But the form also involves a heroic, humanitarian quest narrative, as the physician struggles to solve a mystery – that is, the nature of a disease or affliction – and to bring some form of salvation to the patient.[13] The objective is not only to provide information but also to elicit sympathy for the physician on his quest – as well as for the focus of his attention, the patient-subject.

Within his narrative, Itard describes not only his training programme but also the more personal intimacies of his relationship to Victor. He plays with Victor; he caresses the boy; throughout the text he displays a deep attachment to his charge. Notably, however, he is also an authority figure, a role that requires distance on his part, especially when compared with Mme Guérin. This household of Victor, Itard and Mme Guérin (M Guérin dies part way through the period covered by Itard's reports) has clear divisions of labour, and these affect Victor's relationship to his tutor:

> The friendship he displays for me is much weaker [than for Mme Guérin], as might naturally have been expected. The attentions which Mme Guérin pays him are of such a nature, that their value may be appreciated at the moment; those cares, on the contrary, which I devote to him, are of distant and insensible utility. (Itard 1801: 115)

Itard is quick to point out that the large majority of the time he spends with Victor is linked directly to his goal of education, but that those 'hours of favourable reception' – the time with him that Victor actually seems to enjoy – are those 'which I have never dedicated to his improvement' (116).

Itard as pedagogue becomes the embodiment of law and rationality. One instance from the second report provides a clear illustration of this role. When Victor runs away and is lost for two weeks, his reunion with Mme Guérin is 'most touching':

> Victor had barely seen his gouvernante before he turned pale and briefly lost consciousness; but sensing her embrace ... he suddenly revived and expressed his joy by shrill cries, convulsive grasping of his hands and a beaming, radiant face. He presented the image, to the eyes of all around, less of a fugitive returned by force to the supervision of his guardian than a loving son who, of his own desire, was throwing himself into the arms of she who had given him life. (Itard 1806: 103)

The anecdote appeals to the sympathetic faculties of Itard's readers with this touching image of the broken family reunited. Of course, Victor is neither a criminal fugitive nor an affectionate son, but rather a ward of the state and the subject of an experiment in philosophy and pedagogy. While the reclaimed Victor is also happy to see Itard, his tutor is careful to instil in the boy a sense of his transgression:

Victor was still in bed. As soon as he saw me, he sat up quickly and, leaning forward, offered me his arms. But, seeing that instead of approaching him I remained still, immobile before him, with a cold demeanour and an angry countenance, he hid himself in his bed and, from beneath his covers, began to cry. I heightened his emotions by my reproaches, given in a loud, scolding voice; his tears doubled, accompanying by loud, deep sobs. When I had carried his emotions to their furthest point, I placed myself on the bed of my unhappy penitent. That was always the sign of my forgiveness. Victor understood me, made the first steps toward our reconciliation, and all was forgotten. (Itard 1806: 103)

The point, of course, is that through this self-conscious display of authoritarian wrath, Itard was careful to ensure that, even if all was forgiven, it would not be readily forgotten. The text is replete with other examples of Itard's performative embodiment of the law. On one occasion, he threatens to throw Victor out of a window in order to get the boy to attend to lessons, after several days of trying less dramatic options (Itard 1801: 131–33).

While Itard maintains an authoritative, professorial distance from Victor, Mme Guérin slips into a more conventionally bourgeois maternal role. Her contributions to Victor's education were no doubt many; certainly with regard to the first pedagogical objective, to awaken in Victor a pleasure for the company of people, her importance is paramount. As Itard writes, their strategy is to

treat [Victor] kindly, and to yield a ready compliance to his taste and inclinations. Mme Guérin, to whose particular care the administration [of the Institution] had entrusted this child, acquitted herself, and still discharges this arduous task, with all the patience of a mother, and the intelligence of an enlightened instructor. So far from directly opposing his habits, she knew how, in some measure, to comply with them; and thus to answer the object proposed in our first general head. (Itard 1801: 103)

Itard's four paragraphs in the first report on the boy's growing attachment to the company of others do not relate the specific manner in which Mme Guérin achieves this goal, but rather the bouts of joy and melancholy that characterize Victor. At one point in the section treating the process of developing the boy's socialization with other people, Itard notes how the 'grand phenomena of Nature' induce in Victor 'the quiet expression of sorrow and melancholy':

I have often stopped for whole hours together, and, with unspeakable pleasure, to examine him in this situation; to observe how all his convulsive motions, and that continual rocking of his whole body diminished, and by degrees subsided, to give place to a more tranquil attitude; and how insensibly his face, insignificant or distorted as it might be, took the well-defined character of sorrow, or melancholy reverie, in proportion as his eyes were steadily fixed on the surface of the water, and when he threw into it, from time to time, some remains of withered leaves. When, in a moon-light night, the rays of that luminary penetrated into his room, he seldom failed to awake out of his sleep, and to place himself before the window. There he remained, during a part of the night, standing motionless, his neck extended, his eyes fixed toward the country illuminated by the moon, and carried away in a sort of contemplative extasy, the silence of which was interrupted only by deep-drawn inspirations, after considerable intervals, and which were always accompanied with a feeble and plaintive sound. (Itard 1801: 104)

Itard goes on to note that 'it would have been as useless, as inhuman, to oppose these habits': instead, he allows Victor to continue them in order to 'associate them with his new existence, and thus render it more agreeable to him' (Itard 1801: 104). It is presumably this longing for the forest which stands in the way of Victor's socialization unless it is transformed into the more acceptable (and even desirable) form of melancholy, thus leading to Itard's inclusion of this passage in his description of the treatment for rendering social life more acceptable and pleasant to Victor. Itard's characterization of Victor here finds some common ground with the solitude and melancholy of Mary Robinson's 'The Savage of Aveyron', discussed above, in that Victor is also apparently longing for a lost world, his life before capture. Itard's interpretations are strikingly distinct from those Virey makes regarding the boy's inability to see beauty or God in nature. In his second report, Itard reiterates this type of observation. For example, as Victor drinks his water 'like an exquisite liqueur' at the end of a meal, he

stands by the window, eyes turned toward the countryside, as if, in this delectable instant, he seeks to reunite the two pleasures which alone survive the loss of his freedom: a drink of pure water and the vision of the sun and the countryside. (Itard 1806: 76)

There is also a certain slippage of scientific explanation that becomes clear when we look at the role played by gender in giving shape to socialized man. 'Civilization, in multiplying his sorrows, also necessarily elevates his joy', writes Itard, citing as evidence 'the zeal he demonstrates and the pleasure he finds in doing things for the people he loves and even in anticipating their desires with those small services he is capable of. One can see this especially in his relations with Madame Guérin' (Itard 1806: 104–5). Victor's much underplayed relationship with Mme Guérin is not treated in any depth by Itard, seemingly because of its lack of critical and philosophical interest. However, this omission belies another belief: that the bonds of woman and child are natural, while those of man and child are rational.

Presumably Victor already has the capacity to form links with the housekeeper because his natural state would not exclude it. The skills that Itard seeks to instil are of a different order. Civilization, it would seem, is a masculine condition.

The assumption that the natural child forms an automatic bond with his female 'keeper' reasserts the link between femininity and idiocy evident in Wordsworth's 'The Idiot Boy' (Chapter 2). Victor's assimilation into the world of Mme Guérin requires no analysis, according to the young physician; her success with her component of his education is, in Itard's representation, not due to pedagogical strategies or specific modes of interaction so much as to an innate capacity, an understanding of Victor's needs. Mme Guérin's official role in Victor's education is restricted to awakening in him a pleasure in human company, a project which would seem, according to Itard's narrative, to require the development of feeling but not necessarily of rational intellect. Thus, she does not arouse Victor's intelligence but renders him friendlier and more pliable: like Johnny Foy or, later, Dickens' Barnaby Rudge. Intellect, on the other hand, is a masculine responsibility. Thus, Itard's role is as progenitor of rationality, of the law of civilized man; a child without such influence in his life risks becoming tractable but irrational.

The melancholic wild boy

There is more going on in Itard's reports than detached scientific observation, and I suspect it is connected to the sense of solitude and melancholy that Mary Robinson develops in 'The Savage of Aveyron' – a romantic nostalgia, glancing back upon an abandoned world. Robinson's 'savage' recalls, if only dimly, his existence before his mother was slain in the woods, and his tragic melancholy stems from his longing for that distant and obscure time. Victor's melancholia, as Itard understands it, is rooted in a desire for his lost existence in the forest, which is becoming an increasingly faint memory.[14] In both cases, though, the writer develops a sentimental framework that would be easily understood according to the literary conventions of the day. In a very important sense, Itard's version of Victor is a literary creation as well as a psychological and philosophical one.

One of the most notable expressions of this literary impulse can be found in the name the teacher gives his charge. Itard writes that he named the boy 'Victor' because the child responded happily to the 'O' sound at the end of that word (Itard 1801: 119). However, as

Thierry Gineste has pointed out, 'in reality, the origin of the name is more simple, more poetic, even more eloquent' (Gineste 2004: 52). François-Guillaume Ducray-Duminil had published a novel entitled *Victor, l'enfant de la forêt* in 1796, a circumstance of which Itard could hardly have been ignorant, especially as the novel was turned into a play by Guibert and Pixerécourt and had been playing to full houses in three Parisian theatres simultaneously at the time the wild boy of Aveyron was brought to Paris. It was among the biggest theatrical hits of the day. The success of the play had even spawned a popular song, 'La romance de l'enfant de la forêt, au moment où il quitte Clémence', in which the narrator, Victor the forest child himself, leaves behind the woman he loves.[15] The novel, and the play based on it, tell the story of a child, found in a cradle in the forest by the Baron Fritzierne, who grows up with the Baron's family and falls in love with Clémence, the Baron's daughter, whom he believes to be his sister. As the story opens, the young protagonist Victor is contemplating leaving the chalet where he has been raised in order to avoid the pangs of his incestuous desires, but very soon he will learn that he and Clémence are not siblings, that the feelings he must repress are in fact legitimate before morality and law, that Clémence feels the same way and that, indeed, the Baron has hoped to promote a union between his daughter and the child he had found in the forest. Much of the story is told in narrative flashbacks, with characters recounting their histories, and Victor and his stepfather eventually learn that the boy's natural father is Roger, the leader of a group of outlaws living in the forest whom Victor had come close to slaying. The Baron demands that Victor earn the hand of Clémence by converting Roger from his life of crime to an honest but obscure existence; Roger proves immovable, however, and eventually Victor leaves in despair. Clémence, too, runs away, to become a nun, and the Baron grows heartsick, searching for his daughter, regretting the demands he had placed on Victor, and finally dying before he meets either again. In the end, of course, Victor and Clémence are reunited, but not before Victor has a moving reunion with Roger just before the execution of the latter, when both are in prison (Victor under suspicion as the son of the dangerous bandit): 'You will be free, Victor', Roger reassures his son. 'You will set out again on your road, on which you have laboured with so much toil. Don't forget my example' (Ducray-Duminil 1796: vol. III, 86). At the novel's conclusion, we are told that 'the misfortunes of Victor, his birth, and all his adventures' had been trumpeted through the land, and were impossible for him to put aside; there were still those who dismissed him as the son of an outlaw (vol. III, 105), but in the end Victor and Clémence live long and happily.

The story thus contains plenty of crowd-pleasing familial drama of the incestuous and oedipal sort. Gineste (2004: 52) suggests that at the root of the story's success one could find:

> the stories around the fate of the young Louis XVII, said to have escaped death by fleeing his imprisonment in the Temple and to be living hidden in the forest, awaiting better days and his eventual return to the throne. These rumours were witness to a collective guilt over the murder of a royal infant, a representative of God, which explains in large part the subject and popularity of the play and, in fact, the wild boy himself.

Thus, the young Louis, a lost child of exalted lineage, via the fictional Victor, becomes the historical Victor, the wild boy of Aveyron, for whom Itard also hoped to reclaim the full splendour of patrimony: that is, rationality and full inclusion in human society. Itard's responsibility with his wild boy is much the same as that of those loyal retainers rumoured to be raising the infant king in the woods of France.[16]

We can add to Gineste's reading by noting that in Ducray-Duminil's novel, Victor is merely the son of a bandit but, significantly, his upbringing has raised him far above the state of his father. The portrayal of Victor in the novel expresses the belief that education is all; his father may have been a criminal, but he, thanks to his tutelage under his faithful instructor Valentine in the chalet of Baron Fritzierne, is an honourable man, one who earns the respect of others by his honesty, candour and courage. It is not difficult to see in this aspect of the fictional Victor's makeup the outcome Itard must have desired for his own forest child. The fictional Victor overcomes his inauspicious parenthood because of his education, which then prepares him to face continual adversity throughout the course of the novel, much as Itard hoped to see Victor of Aveyron overcome his blighted youth and take on the role and responsibilities of a rational man. But this trajectory Itard imagined for his pupil is formed around a profoundly romantic, sentimental narrative. The intellectual problems posed by Victor – and the challenges of understanding and delineating that slippery concept 'human nature' – seem, on occasion, too immense to be contained by the theories employed by Itard and his compatriots, even in their official reports, and on these occasions Victor slips into the realm of poetry and romance.[17]

Itard's fruitful failure

By the time of his second report, *Rapport fait à son Excellence le Ministre de l'Intérieur, sur les nouveaux développements et l'état actuel du sauvage de l'Aveyron*, written in 1806 at the request of the Minister of the Interior,

Itard is uncomfortably aware of what he viewed as his failure. 'My Lord', he opens the second report, 'To speak to you of the Wild Boy of Aveyron is to utter a name that no longer inspires any interest; it is to recall a being forgotten by those who saw him for a time only, and disdained by those who thought to judge him' (Itard 1806: 63). He goes on to claim that he 'would have wrapped in a profound silence and condemned to eternal oblivion an undertaking that is less the story of the student's progress than that of the teacher's failure' (63–64) – a profoundly different tone from that pervading the first report and, interestingly, a marked opposition to the 'glee' with which Wordsworth wrote of his own composition of 'The Idiot Boy'. While Itard does include the proviso that 'to appreciate the current state of the young man, it is necessary to recall his former state' (64), his second narrative is marked by greater hesitation, a distraught sense of his own ambivalent accomplishments. Victor is not only an 'disgraced being' and the 'refuse of nature' (64) but also a failed experiment, a being whom society could not fully embrace, and Itard divides the share of blame between his own failings and Victor's initial deprivations. Itard's goal had been to reproduce Condillac's thought experiment, replacing the statue with the wild boy, and to lead the boy from mute ignorance to reflective, contemplative language – much as Sicard had apparently done with his deaf students. He is also, in some sense, seeking to re-create Ducray-Dumenil's *Victor, l'enfant de la fôret* in his efforts to build a romantic narrative leading not to the joyous reunion of the protagonist with his beloved, but to an even more profound reconciliation of the wild boy with humanity and civilization. But Victor's needs and abilities are not aligned with Itard's ambition, and the forms of communication that the boy does learn to use – signs, sounds and gestures – are not those that his tutor sought to develop. The heroic quest implicit in a case history would make Victor either the beneficiary of his patron's talents, had Itard fulfilled his objectives, or, as in this opposite case, reconstruct Victor as an object of compassion, who remains blighted by intellectual darkness despite the best efforts of the struggling yet valiant physician. Such a reading, although not necessarily intended by the author, is an inevitable outcome of the narrative form employed; it is also a narrative trajectory that repeats itself throughout professional writings on idiocy in the nineteenth century.

Describing a particularly difficult training session with his charge, he writes 'I was ready to renounce my self-imposed task and look on the time I had spent on it as lost, to regret having known this child, and to condemn the cold and inhuman curiosity of the men who uprooted him from an innocent, happy life!' (Itard 1806: 170–71). He concludes

ambivalently that 'many of the facts indicate that he could be improved, while others suggest the contrary' (113). He then enumerates
his findings: first of all, 'because of the nearly complete incapacity
of the organs of hearing and speech, the young man's education will
remain incomplete'; further, 'because of a long period of inactivity, his
intellectual faculties are developing slowly and with great difficulty'.
The emotions, too, are 'emerging with the same sluggishness from
their long period of sleep', which Itard suggests 'seems only to prove
that, if there exists a relationship between the needs of his senses and
the affections of his heart, this sympathetic harmony is, as with most
grand and generous passions, the fortunate fruit of his education'
(Itard 1806: 113–14). On the more favourable side, though, he notes:

> 1. that the improvement of sight and touch, and the new enjoyment
> of taste, have, in multiplying the sensations and ideas of our Savage,
> contributed powerfully to the development of his intellectual facul-
> ties; 2. that, in considering his general development, we find, among
> other happy changes, improvements in the knowledge of conventional
> meaning of symbols of thought, the ability to apply this knowledge
> to designating objects and describing their qualities and actions, from
> whence the range of relationships of the student with the people around
> him, his faculty of expressing his needs, receiving orders and engaging
> in a free and ongoing exchange of thought; 3. that, in spite of his im-
> moderate taste for the freedom of fields and his indifference for most
> of the pleasures of social life, Victor shows himself to be grateful for
> the care taken of him, responsive to affectionate friendship, sensitive to
> the pleasure of doing well, ashamed of his errors, and repentant of his
> outbursts.... (Itard 1806: 114–15)

Then, in the last clause of this long list of Victor's accomplishments
at the end of the second report, Itard argues his charge's claim to continued support from the state:

> 4. finally, my Lord, from whatever perspective one views this long ex-
> periment, whether one considers it the systematic education of a wild
> man or the physical and moral treatment of a being disgraced by nature,
> rejected by society, and abandoned by medicine, the care that has been
> taken of him, the care still to come, the voice of humanity, the interest
> aroused by so complete a desertion and so bizarre a destiny, all recom-
> mend this extraordinary young man to the attention of scientists, to the
> solicitude of our administrators and the protection of the Government.
> (Itard 1806: 115)

Itard's call for compassion – the voice of humanity – and his claim for
support are made more complex and startling by a concession: against
his earlier assertions of Victor's latent abilities, he accepts that Victor
may have been 'disgraced by nature' – that is, born without the full

range of potential allotted to most beings. This admission has pro-found implications for the treatment of idiots, as it runs counter to the psychological truism that idiots – those 'disgraced by nature' – could not learn. Itard's experiments may not have yielded the fully reclaimed social and moral being that the pedagogue had desired, but they still transformed the *enfant sauvage* into a young man with the ability to communicate basic ideas and desires and to form friendships. While Itard does not go so far as to designate Victor an 'idiot', he does allow the possibility. Itard eventually abandoned his efforts to educate Victor, who continued to live with Mme Guérin until his death in 1828, when he was probably in his forties; Itard died ten years later, in 1838.

Despite the fact that he considered his pedagogical attempts to be failures, Itard's experiments with Victor were to initiate a slow alteration in the meaning of idiocy, transforming it into a condition that might be relieved. But this change in the understanding of idiocy also subverted some long-held notions. Into the Edenic innocence of the idiot's mind Itard and Victor had brought the fruit of knowledge. And if idiocy is a state that can and thus should be overcome, how can 'innocence' be ascribed to the condition?

Before examining the transformation of the concept of idiocy in the nineteenth century, though, we must digress through the broader issue of gender and intellectual disability. In Wordsworth's 'The Idiot Boy' and in Itard's reports, the 'idiot' or 'wild' boy exists primarily in relation to a family environment. In the poem, this family is natural, although fatherless; in Victor's case, the natural family is replaced by a surrogate family formed by Itard and Mme Guérin. Victor's family is investigative, experimental; it is part of a project ultimately seeking to redress the weaknesses apparent in the natural family described by Wordsworth, where the maternal dominates over patriarchal rational-ity. This relation of idiocy to gender will be explored more fully in the next two chapters.

Notes

1 De Gérando's article, presented before the Société des Observateurs de l'Homme in 1801 (Gineste 2004: 418), was discovered among his papers after his death and published posthumously in 1848.
2 Je veux enricher aujourd'hui
La médecine et la physique
Souffrez que je fasse sur lui
Quelque recherche anatomique,
Me croirait-il mauvais dessein?
L'effroi se peint sur sa figure!
Aurait-il peur d'un médecin?

3 In more recent years, narratives have moved closer to the historical record. The most famous, of course, is François Truffaut's 1970 film *L'Enfant Sauvage*, in which Truffaut himself plays the role of Jean Itard. The film plays upon the union of wild and civilized man; but with the director in a lead role, we can also read the relation between Itard and his charge as being a metaphor of artistic creation – the teacher/artist crafting a civilized human from raw materials.

4 Robinson employs a metrical structure reminiscent of Coleridge's 'Kubla Khan' (which, as a friend of Coleridge, she was familiar with) and it is not too far a stretch to imagine that she is striving after the same uncanny, mystical romanticism achieved by that poem.

5 Itard's first report was translated into English and published in London in 1802 as *An Historical Account of the Discovery and Education of a Savage Man, or of the First Developments, Physical and Moral, of the Young Savage Caught in the Woods near Aveyron in the year 1798*. Quotations from the first report are from this 1802 translation, while those from the 1806 report have been translated here by Rhonda Mullins; the 1802 translation was republished by NLB in 1972 in a volume with Lucien Malson's *Wolf Children and the Problem of Human Nature* (1964).

6 The orang-utan was formed in the European mind by a mixture of travellers' tales of exotic men and the occasional specimen brought back by explorers. George-Louis Leclerc, Comte du Buffon, suggested that orang-utans, while apes (*singes*), were 'a more perfect species and even closer to the human species' (Buffon 1855: 24). The figures illustrating his description of the orang-utan show both large and small (*pongo* and *jocko*) versions standing upright and leaning on staffs, looking like especially hirsute shepherds. James Burnet, Lord Monboddo, went further, suggesting that the Pope should do for the orang-utan what he had done 'for the humanity of the poor Americans' and issue a papal bull decreeing that 'the Orang Outangs are men' (Monboddo 1774: 347). That Linnaeus called them 'troglodytes' – or cave dwellers – and Bontius designated them '*Homo sylvestris*' – men of the forest – suggests just how little consensus existed about these primates.

7 My analysis of Locke owes a great deal to Chris Goodey's writings on Locke and idiocy. See especially 'John Locke's idiots', 'The psychopolitics of learning and disability' and 'From natural disability to the moral man' (Goodey 1994, 1996, 2001); I have attempted to condense Goodey's arguments, although anyone interested in the history of rationality and idiocy should seek out these articles for themselves.

8 'Natural' was an established synonym for 'idiot', with its first recorded reference dating to 1533, according to the *Oxford English Dictionary*; 'changeling' was a term used both in common and in professional parlance to refer to an 'idiot' born to normal parents (Goodey 1994: 230; for more on the history of the idea of the changeling, see Goodey and Stainton 2001). The 'drill' referred to is *Mandrillus leucophaeus*, a close relation to the baboon.

9 Other examples can be used to supplement the Lockean instance. Linnaeus admitted that the category '*Homo*' should probably be subsumed under that of 'Primate', but had them as parallel categories all the same. Monboddo's orang-utans are human because he needed a non-lingual human community to support his theory of language acquisition. He had never actually seen an orang-utan, although he had seen a stuffed ape (most likely a chimpanzee); he relied on the notoriously unreliable tales of travellers for his information.

10 The retreating natural world so influential to romantic evocations of nature may also have heightened the desire to find a 'natural man', as feral children

would be seen as a vanishing resource in a Europe where the forests were disappearing. The loss of nature could also threaten the loss of *Homo feri*.

11 The most famous feral human before the wild boy of Aveyron was Marie-Angélique Memmie LeBlanc, or, as she was originally known, the wild girl of Champagne. Caught in 1731, the girl attracted the attention of writers and scientists across Europe; she eventually learned language, was christened by her domesticators, met with Lord Monboddo, and was miraculously transformed into a Catholic nun, before eventually leaving the convent. Her final years are obscure, as is her date of death; some sources have her alive for only forty years, while others give her sixty (Douthwaite 1994/95: 166; Newton 2002). 'Wild children' have continued to appear sporadically since the arrival of Victor; see Douglas Candland's *Feral Children and Clever Animals* (1993) for an overview of the phenomenon into the twentieth century.

12 Many readers have supplied their own diagnoses of Victor's state. Most notably in recent years, Uta Frith (1989: 16–26) has argued in detail that he was autistic; Nicolas Pethes (2003) tosses off the same diagnosis – simply referring to the boy as 'autistic' – as if it were an established truth. Lane (1976: 179) has suggested that 'Victor's symptoms ... may overlap with those of congenital retardation or autism, but are explained by neither; instead they are the result of his isolation in the wild, as Itard maintained all along'. Of course, Lane's book, published in 1976, predates autism's transformation into a spectrum disorder, and thus he is working with a much more restrictive definition of the term than that available to Frith. Lucien Malson, writing in 1964, stresses that Victor's supposedly 'innate idiocy cannot be proved' and concludes that 'there is no reason to suggest that he suffered from some defect at birth and indeed all the evidence points to the contrary' (79); however, Malson does not summarize this evidence.

13 As Rita Charon observes in her analysis of modern case histories, 'medicine, committed to recapturing a lost ideal state [that of complete health and wholeness], is ... a heroic and conservative undertaking' (Charon 1992: 119), a 'platonic longing for well-proportioned truth and beauty' (120) that is destined to be unrequited; thus there is an apologetic or melancholic note to many case histories. 'The response being sought from the readers of the case is not so often praise as forgiveness' (121). In the eighteenth century, argues Thomas Laqueur, 'a particular cluster of humanitarian narratives', including the novel as well as the case history, 'created "sympathetic passions"' that 'bridged the gap between facts, compassion, and action' (Laqueur 1990: 179). Some of these narratives were intended specifically to elicit compassion or stimulate reform, but that consequence was linked not solely to content but also to form: 'certain sorts of stories, whatever their purpose, have the capacity to engender the kind of moral concern that arose in the late eighteenth century' (197). Just as Wordsworth had sought to engage sympathy for the story of Johnny and Betty Foy (Chapter 2), so does Itard try to elicit readers' compassion for Victor and for his own role in attempting to educate his *enfant sauvage*.

14 Itard's 'nature' assumes the same position as Robinson's 'mother' in their versions of a wild boy's melancholic desires, a point which is significant for our understanding of the gender associations common to representations of idiocy (to be discussed in Chapters 4 and 5).

15 This song was directly referred to by the contemporary journalist Feydel in the fifth of his series of articles on *l'enfant sauvage*, 'Qu'est-ce que le sauvage de l'Aveyron', published on 14 October 1800 (see Gineste 2004: 53).

16 Similar suspicions abound in the case of Kaspar Hauser, who appeared in Nuremberg in 1828, and was thought by some to be connected to the royal

house of Baden. For more information, see *Kaspar Hauser: Europe's Child*, by
Martin Kitchen (2001).

17 Victor was not the only wild child to have a literary alter ego. Julie Douthwaite
(1994/95: 173) recounts a passage from Jean-Claude Gorjy's 1789 novel
Victorine, in which the eponymous heroine meets a 'wild woman' in a scene
reminiscent of that in which the wild girl of Champagne, Marie-Angelique
LeBlanc, was discovered; LeBlanc was also the subject of an anonymously
penned biography, *Histoire d'une jeune fille sauvage trouvée dans les bois à l'âge de
dix ans*, and of Louis Racine's 'Eclaircissement sur la fille sauvage'. And, of
course, Kaspar Hauser has been the subject of much literary treatment, most
notably Werner Herzog's 1974 film *The Enigma of Kaspar Hauser*, but also Jakob
Wassermann's 1908 novel *Caspar Hauser or the Inertia of the Heart*.

CHAPTER 4

Diminished men: masculinity and idiocy

In letter XVIII, 'The Poor and Their Dwellings', of George Crabbe's long poem *The Borough* (1810), the narrator describes an 'antient Widow' who lives with her idiot son:

> With her an harmless Idiot we behold,
> Who hoards up Silver Shells for shining Gold;
> These he preserves, with unremitted care,
> To buy a Seat, and reign the Borough's Mayor:
> Alas! – what could th'ambitious Changeling tell,
> That what he sought our Rulers dar'd to sell?
> (lines 40–45)[1]

The introductory header at the start of letter XVIII forecasts the section's contents, including 'Some Characters of the Poor' and then (in order) 'The School-mistress, when aged', 'The Idiot', 'The poor Sailor' and 'The declined Tradesman and his Companion'. As a result, even before we reach the passage quoted above, Crabbe's 'harmless Idiot' is presented as a feature of the Borough's social landscape, whose presence signified poverty in 1810, the year of the poem's publication. He collects shells, imagining them to be money, and plots to use these shells to acquire political power. The passage condenses some key recurring characteristics associated with representations of male 'idiots': dependence on a female caregiver, an incapacity for handling financial or business affairs, and a sort of mental inconstancy implied by the term 'changeling'. And the 'ambitious Changeling' also serves as a vehicle for satire or critique, in this case of those rulers who would sell access to political power by accepting bribes.

Crabbe is following some well established precedents in representing a male idiot character as being incapable of managing money, and

thus being either impoverished or in danger of becoming so. The brag-
gart and would-be rapist Cloten, in Shakespeare's *Cymbeline*, probably
written around 1610, is a fool who 'Cannot take two from twenty …
/And leave eighteen' (act II, scene i, lines 57–58), and when Guiderius
decapitates him in a battle offstage and returns brandishing the head,
the association with financial incompetence is reiterated:

> This Cloten was a fool, an empty purse,
> There was no money in't; not Hercules
> Could have knock'd out his brains, for he had none.
> (act IV, scene ii, lines 113–15)

Conversely, in George Peele's play from the early 1590s, *The Old
Wives Tale*, the bumpkin Corebus is first wished, and then receives,
'wealth to mend [his] wit' (lines 349, 830). Even 'Simple Simon',
of the eighteenth-century Mother Goose nursery rhyme, is quickly
defined as 'simple' because of his lack of financial resources, not
having the necessary penny to pay the pieman he meets on the way
to the fair. And, for a brief illustration to which we will return later in
this chapter, at Henry Roberts' 1744 idiocy trial, the inquest chairman
instructs the jury 'that *a Man may have Sense enough to manage* 300 £ *per
An. tho' not* 3000' (Anonymous 1747: 4, original emphasis). Not surprisingly, the notion also made its way into medical discourse as well.
As Étienne Esquirol noted in his profoundly influential *Des Maladies
mentales*, published in 1838 and translated into English in 1845 as
Mental Maladies: A Treatise on Insanity, 'A man in a state of dementia is
deprived of advantages which he formerly enjoyed; he was a rich man,
who has become poor. The idiot, on the contrary, has always been in a
state of want and misery' (441).

This chapter explores the history of some of the common features
of representations of male idiocy, in order to ask what functions male
idiots serve when they appear in texts, fictional or otherwise. What does
it *mean* to represent a male idiot? We will ask the same of representations of female idiots in the next chapter, but here we will inquire first
into the legal history of the concept of idiocy and its relation to feudal
political structures and patrilineage, before considering some prominent representations, both historical and literary, as case studies. We
conclude by considering how ideas of masculinity and manliness shift in
the middle of the nineteenth century, and how these changing notions
of masculinity are also evident in representations of male idiots.

In recent years, the ideological structure of masculinity has been
explored from a number of perspectives. In literary criticism, Kaja
Silverman's psychoanalytic approach has proven extremely influential.

Silverman, focusing primarily on twentieth-century texts, argues that notions of gender are ideological expressions that conform to a 'dominant fiction', an 'ideological reality' which 'solicits our faith above all else in the unity of the family and the adequacy of the male subject' (Silverman 1992: 15–16). Following Silverman's work, both literary and historical analyses have explored the ideological roots and expressions of dominant notions of masculinity, and have found a certain fluidity in the concept across geography and history. In the Middle Ages and, to a diminished degree, even into the eighteenth century, the fullest expression of masculinity was dependent upon how close one stood to the centre of power – that is, the throne. Masculinity was an expression of one's alliance to the king rather than of a particular strain of heterosexual desire; masculine status was something that rose or fell according to one's 'publicness' and proximity to that most public of bodies, the sovereign (Greenblatt 1980; King 2004), a notion that makes sense given the etymology of the term 'idiot' – a private individual, one lacking any public status (see Chapter 1). So, in very practical terms, the nature and responsibilities of alliances between the king and his men, his 'knight-tenants', were also critical to early modern formulations of 'idiocy'.

The king's men

In Britain, the concern with an individual's ability to manage his estate in accordance with the demands of the age can be traced back as far as the *Prerogitiva Regis*, a thirteenth-century document – possibly a clerical memo of sorts – which sets forth the crown's interest in administering wards and liveries.[2] The need to define certain parameters of mental aptitude is directly linked to the social and political parameters defining land occupancy and ownership. When the *Prerogativa Regis* was drafted, 'knight-tenants' did not own land outright but held their lands by dispensation of the crown, as a form of feudal tenure, and they repaid the king through both rents directed to the throne and military service. However, if the tenant died before his heirs had come of age, those heirs still had to be provided for until they reached their majority, at the age of twenty; in addition, the estate had to be properly managed. Both heir and estate then became the custody of the crown, which would, through its various offices, maintain and nurture both. So the under-age heirs became wards of the state, which then, through committees representing the Court of Chancery and later the Court of Wards and Liveries, granted (for a fee) custody of the ward to a guardian, who would become responsible for the upbringing, including the education and often the marriage, of the ward. The arrangement was far from flawless, and the role of guardian offered opportunities that could be easily exploited by the unscrupulous, as suggested by the thriving black market in wards, who could be bought and sold (Bell 1953). Eventually, if he survived, the ward would come of age, at which point he could assume control of his estate by suing for livery – that is, purchasing from the crown the claim to the lands formerly held by his parent. The selling of wards and liveries (as well as the rights to marriage, which, among knight-tenants, also had to be approved by the crown) generated tremendous revenues, so the Court of Wards and Liveries proved an important tool for keeping the crown finan-cially solvent. The process of buying, selling and managing wards also turned profits for the committee members representing the Chancery and later the Court of Wards and Liveries, and for the guardians themselves. At the same time, the Court was perceived to serve an im-portant societal function. For some time the Court's seal included the figures of two young children beneath the royal arms, bearing a scroll that read 'Pupillus Orphanis et Vidius Adiutor', loosely translatable as 'Learn from the orphan and help the bereaved'; and as Sir George Carew noted in the early 1600s, the role of the king, enacted through the Court, was 'to imitate and approach as neere as may be, the offices and duties of a naturall father' (quoted in Bell 1953: 112).

However, as the primary objective of the administration of wards and liveries was to harvest money for the crown, those individuals thought likely to do a poor job of maintaining their lands and paying rents, or to be disinclined to meet these responsibilities, posed a threat to the king's financial health. Thus, the Chancery, and later the Court of Wards and Liveries, also assumed custody of those individuals deemed incapable of managing their lands because of either natural folly or lunacy. Section 11 of the *Prerogativa Regis* notes that 'the king shall have the custody of the lands of natural fools, taking the profits of them without waste or destruction, and shall find them their necess-aries … and after the death of such idiots he shall render the same to the right heirs, so that such idiots shall not alien, nor their heirs shall be disinherited' (quoted in Neugebauer 1978: 159). In other words, in the cases of people identified as idiots or natural fools, the crown assumed custody of the individuals, their estates and all the profits generated by these estates. Then, upon the death of the ward, the estate passed to the next heir in line.

As for those thought to have lucid intervals between bouts of failing wit, section 12 of the *Prerogativa Regis* asserts that:

the king shall provide when any that before time hath had his wit and memory, happen to fail of his wit, as there are many *per lucida intervalla,* that their lands and tenements shall be safely kept without waste and destruction, and that they and their household shall live and be maintained competently with the profits of the same, and the residue besides their sustentation shall be kept to their use, to be delivered unto them when they come to right mind; so that such lands and tenements shall in no wise be aliened; and the king shall take nothing to his own use. (Quoted in Neugebauer 1978: 159)

Thus, in the case of someone who had happened 'to fail of his wit', the king took custody of the lands, but then passed the responsibility for this custody, as well as the care of the individual, along to the family or guardian of the individual, for so long as he was considered out of his wits, and the profits of the estate were directed to the upkeep of the individual and his family. Should the afflicted individual regain his wits, he also regained authority for his estate. Findings of 'idiocy' were thus much more lucrative to the crown, which would garner all profits of the estate for the entire lifespan of the 'idiot' in question.

The terms of the *Prerogativa Regis* were further entrenched in law with the 1540 and 1542 statutes establishing the Court of Wards and Liveries. Section 26 of the 1540 statute asserts that the Master of the Court:

[shall] have authority by this act to survey, govern and order all and singular idiots and natural fools now being in the king's hands or that hereafter shall come and be in the king's hands. And also to survey and order all the manors, lands, tenements and other hereditaments whatsoever now being in the king's hands or ... shall come and be in the king's hands, his heirs and successors. (Quoted in Neugebauer 1978: 163)

If the crown learned of a potential 'idiot' – the term enters the English language as a part of this early legal discourse – then writs of *Idiota inquirenda vel examinanda* were issued, and a committee established to interrogate the suspected individual and interview witnesses to his (or, less frequently, her) behaviour (if lunacy was suspected, a different writ, of *Dum non fuis compos mentis,* was issued, although the process followed was similar). Sir Anthony Fitzherbert's *Nouvelle Natura Brevium* (1534)[3] provides a sample writ from the king to the escheator concerning an individual known as 'I. of B.', preparing the process for an investigation of the alleged idiot's capacity for managing his estate:

Because we have received, that I. of B. a Fool and Idiot is, so that to the Government of his Lands, and Tenements, Goods, and Chattels, he is not sufficient; and that he in his foolishness a great part of his

Lands and Tenements hath aliened, and also a great part of his Goods
and Chattels dissipated to his disheris. and our manifest prejudice; we
willing to provide for his indemnity in this plaint, command you, that
in your proper person to him I. you go, and him by the ways and means,
by which of his Estate you may be better informed, circumspectly ye
examine; and nevertheless, by the Oath of honest and legal men of the
Bail, by whom the truth of the matter may be better known, diligently
inquire, if the same I. be a Fool or Idiot, as aforesaid is, or not; and if
he be, then whether from his birth or from another time; and if from
another time, then from what time, and in what manner, and how; and if
his Lucid intervalles he hath; and if the same I. in the same state being,
any Lands or Tenements hath aliened, or not; and if so, then what Lands
and Tenements, and where, and to whom, and in whose hands the Lands
and Tenements so aliened are, and in what manner, and how; and what
Lands and Tenements remain to him yet; and of whom, as well the Lands
and Tenements so aliened, as the Lands and Tenements retained to him,
are held, and by what service, and in what manner, and how; and what
the yearly value of them is in all issues; and who his next Heir is, and of
what age.... (Fitzherbert 1652: 581)

This writ, then, demands a personal visit from the king's representative to determine the individual's capacity and to reacquire, in the
king's name, any lands the individual may have lost, either through
debt or mismanagement, should he in fact prove, under examination,
to be an idiot. Of course, the crown has an interest in defining individuals as 'idiots', both in terms of the money that will consequently
be directed to the court and the 'aliened' lands that will be reclaimed.
A further writ might be issued from the king to the local sheriff, inquiring whether the individual in question 'from his birth hitherto a pure
Idiot hath been, for which the custody of his Lands and Tenements
in C. to us ought to belong' (582). Fitzherbert also reports that 'if an
Ideot doth Release all his right by Deed; yet if it be afterwards found
by Office, that he is an Ideot, the King shall seize the Land, and that
release shall not bind' (505).

Given the importance attached to declarations of idiocy, there had
to be some clear means of appeal, and any man declared an idiot also
had the right to appeal the decision. As Fitzherbert writes, 'he who is
found Idiot, may in person, or by his friends, come into the Chancery,
before the Chancelor, and the Kings Council, and shew the matter, and
pray that he may be examined before the Chancelor, and the Kings
Council, whether he be Idiot or not' (582). Should this final court of
appeal prove sympathetic, then all previous findings would be over-
ruled, and the individual regain control of his estate – and of his status
as a complete man. But any individual found to be an idiot would
lose all authority and would be formally consigned to a guardian. He

would become a ward of the Court, as if he were a child, but without the prospect of ever reaching his majority. The finding of idiocy would remove the individual from the world of men, relegating him to that of children, at least in a legal sense.

Later authorities reiterate Fitzherbert's description of the process. John Cowell's 1607 legal dictionary *The Interpreter: or Booke Containing the Signification of Words*, notes that:

> *Idiota inquirenda vel examinanda*, is a writ that is directed to the excheatour or the Shyreeve of any county, where the king hath understanding that there is an Idiot, naturally borne so weake of understanding, that he cannot govern or mannage his inheritance, to call before him the party suspected of Idiocie, & examin him: And also to inquire by the oaths of twelve men, whether he be sufficiently witted to dispose of his owne lands with discretion or not, and to certifie accordingly into the Chauncery: For the king hath the protection of his subjects, & by his prerogative the government of their lands and substance, that are naturally defective in their owne discretion.

Cowell's observation that the idiot cannot, by reason of his defective discretion, govern or manage his inheritance underscores the importance of patrimony in considerations of idiocy. As a legal entity (and 'idiocy' as such existed in no other form at this time) the condition exists entirely as a consequence of the need to maintain inheritances, as patrimony not only provided finances to the crown but also stabilized the social order and kept elevated families from falling in the social strata – a circumstance which, in its own right, would raise doubts about whether or not the social order was ordained by God and natural law. There would have been no point in identifying a peasant as an idiot, as peasants and labourers were already assumed to be incapable of managing the responsibilities that rested upon the shoulders of members of the landed classes. Indeed, Thomas Blount's *Nomolexikon*, first published in 1670, reiterates many of Cowell's main points, but adds the etymological note that 'Ideot is a Greek work, properly signifying a private man, who has no publick Office; Among the Latins it is taken for *illiteratus, imperitus*, and in our Law for *non compos mentis*, vulgarly, a natural fool'. The peasant, like the idiot, is a man without 'publick Office' and in a very real sense the association between the two remained strong: in English law, the declared 'idiot' was simply a man stripped of the status of public office, and removed a further distance from the king, while the peasant had never enjoyed the status that comes from living in proximity to the crown.

Cowell's dictionary remained the dominant text of its sort in England until it was supplanted by Giles Jacob's *New Law Dictionary*, first published in 1729. Jacob's work contains no radical revisions to Cowell's definition for this particular entry – aside from the significant observations of 'ideots' that 'such a one ought not to be prosecuted for any Crime, because he wants Knowledge to distinguish Good from Evil' and that 'Ideots shall not appear to any Action by Attorney, but in proper Person, and the Suit must be carried out in their Names, tho' followed by others'. This first addition asserts the essential innocence, in both moral and legal senses of the term, of 'idiots'; the second requires that in any suit involving an alleged 'idiot' the individual in question would appear in person, thus ensuring that the court could itself witness this alleged idiocy and also, so far as possible, could guard against the exploitation of 'idiots' by devious attorneys. Fundamentally, however, the associations of idiocy with the mismanagement of crucial financial resources, and the role of the crown in addressing this threat, remained consistent from the time a thirteenth-century royal scribe drafted the *Prerogativa Regis* into the eighteenth century.

The criteria for establishing idiocy also stayed remarkably consistent. As Fitzherbert spells out in the *Nouvelle Natura Brevium*:

> he who shall be said to be a Sot and Idiot from birth, is such a person, who cannot count to number twenty, nor can tell who was his Father, or Mother, nor how old he is, &c. so as it may appear, that he hath no understanding or reason what shall be for his profit, or what for his loss: But if he have such understanding, that he know and understand his letters, and to read by teaching or information of another man, then it seemeth his is not a Sot, nor a natural idiot. (Fitzherbert 1652: 583)

Similarly, John Rastell, a contemporary of Fitzherbert, wrote in his *Exposition of Certaine Difficulte and Obscure Words and Termes*, a legal dictionary originally written in French and first appearing in English in 1527 (and republished in the seventeenth century as *Les Termes de la ley*), that:

> Idiot is he that is a foole naturally from hys birth and knoweth not how to accompt of number 20 pence nor cannot name hys father, or mother, nor of what age hymselfe is, or such like easie and common matters; soe that it appereth he has no manner of understanding of reason, nor gouvernement of himselfe, what is for his profit or disprofit, etc. But if hee have soe much knowledge that he can reade, or lerne to reade by instruction and informatyon of others, or can measure an elle of cloth, or name the daies in the weeke, or begette a childe, sonne or daughter, or such lyke, whereby it may appere that he hath some light of reason, then such a one is noe Ideot naturallye.

The most notable difference between these two definitions is Rastell's identification of the individual's capacity to beget children as proof against idiocy, although, according to Bell (1953), this form of evidence dates from the fourteenth-century reign of Edward III. Later works, including those by Cowell and Jacob, offer no substantial changes but rather simply repeat these criteria. At the examination of Thomas Pope in 1615, investigators noted that he was 'very well able to discern and know the difference of all pieces of silver of the Queen's coin and the perfect value of them from xiid to an half-penny'; the examiners of German Bradshaw in 1597 noted that he 'numbered 20 forwards and backwards and counted money and divided and discerned the same' (quoted in Neugebauer 1996: 29).

So, while the motivations for conceiving of and identifying idiocy were found in the need to preserve patrimony and to keep the money flowing to the crown, the criteria for defining it was rooted in the capacity for performing what would be mundane activities, at least for someone of the settled classes. Notably, the ability to name one's age or to count to twenty would not be universal, and would be considered unnecessary, perhaps even presumptuous, accomplishments for peasants and labourers. The committees inquiring into the state of an individual's mental faculties also accepted the anecdotal evidence of witnesses concerning the mental strength or weakness of the individual under investigation. But the foundation of the legal diagnosis of idiocy remained an inability to handle finances, to name one's parents and to beget children – all essential elements for maintaining both patrimony, as a sum total of resources to be passed from one generation to the next, and patrilineage, as an actual hereditary line. The qualities that make a good man – financial competence, an exalted lineage and the capacity and inclination to continue that lineage – are simply inverted to define an idiot.

Because the Court of Wards and Liveries was intended to generate money, only individuals with personal wealth or real estate were brought to its attention. Not surprisingly, then, according to the records of this Court (and the less comprehensive Chancery records), the majority of those declared idiots were men, although 20 per cent of the cases in these records refer to women who, as widows or heiresses, could hold property. In addition, while 40 per cent of the cases brought to the Court of Wards and Liveries belonged to the families of the landed classes – gentry and aristocracy – the remainder were primarily from the families of merchants, small tradesmen and, occasionally, yeomen (Neugebauer 1996). All of these, of course, are holders of small amounts of property. The number of inquests focused on individuals who were not landed gentry suggests that the management of resources and inheritance along a patrilinear line were important for these families as well. These inquests also point to a breakdown of the 'honour' mode of defining status, as claimants to the trappings of patrilineage emerge in the lower orders (Goodey 2008).

The relatively generic use of the term 'idiot' in writs *de idiota inquirendo* meant that a wide range of possible conditions might fall under the rubric of idiocy, thus gathering to the crown's coffers more funds than narrower definitions might have netted (Neugebauer 1996). As income from the estate would go to the crown, the wardship of an idiot was considered less profitable than that of an under-age heir (Bell 1953). However, rents upon the lands owned by people judged to be idiots seem to have been eliminated at some point in the mid-sixteenth century, to the benefit of both the family estate and the guardian (Holdsworth 1966; Neugebauer 1978). In addition, a dramatic shift occurs in the balance of 'idiot' and 'lunatic' grants between 1540 and 1640: in 1540, almost 80 per cent of all grants for wardship involved cases of idiocy; by 1640, the proportion had dropped to a mere 30 per cent. As definitions of idiocy did not change, this shift is most likely a consequence of families seeking to retain greater control over estate finances by avoiding 'idiocy' verdicts (Neugebauer 1996). Wardships for under-age heirs usually, although not always, stayed in the family; the same seems most likely to have held true for those people found to be idiots, especially given the low margins of profit associated with the care of 'idiot' wards, compared with under-age heirs (Bell 1953). Many arrangements were probably similar to those of the renowned physician Sir William Harvey, who in 1637 went to the Court of Wards and Liveries to gain custody of his nephew William Fowke, whom he presented as an idiot; however, after gaining custody, Harvey assigned his nephew to the care of a niece (Neugebauer 1989, 1996).

In sum, then, while legal investigations into cases of alleged idiocy also included anecdotal evidence from witnesses and judgement calls on behalf of the examiners, at their heart lay the need to ensure that the individual's estate would continue to produce money. A man's claim to masculine authority was demolished upon being found an idiot and subordinated to a guardian. As the dominant social-economic structure moved from feudalism to agricultural capitalism, the individual's ability to understand and profit from the circulation of capital became a new way of defining masculine authority. Thus the legal concerns with the proper management of resources and the transmission of property would continue to shape the idea of idiocy into the eighteenth and even the nineteenth century, long after the crown's rights articulated in the *Prerogativa Regis* had passed into history. The apparent incapacity of the 'idiot' to function within feudal or capitalist society is reflected in both cases in his inability to handle finances. Some examples, both historical and literary, will help to illustrate how these associations with the idea of idiocy have been culturally expressed.

The sad case of Henry Roberts, Esquire

In 1747 a broadsheet, authored anonymously, entitled *The Case of Henry Roberts, Esq, a Gentleman, who, by unparalleled Cruelty was deprived of his Estate, under the Pretence of Idiocy*, offers a partisan narrative of the 1744 idiocy trial of Henry Roberts. The narrative opens by asserting the august lineage of Roberts' family, noting that he was 'last Heir of a Family whose Ancestors often represented [the] County in Parliament; by the Mother's Side lineally descended from Bishop Ridley, who suffered Martyrdom in 1555' (Anonymous 1747: 3); the father died in 1718, a year after his son's birth, and thus Henry became a ward of one Dr John Finney. In 1739, after reaching his majority, Roberts allegedly 'called his Trustees to account for the mesne profits of the Estate during his Minority, which they evaded by suggesting Casualties that affected it during that Interval, such as the Failure of Bankers, Losses at Sea, and the Difference of Exchange betwixt London and Barbadoes' (3). The trustees then brought the case of idiocy against Roberts, which the author implies was motivated by their attempts to cover their deceits. At the inquest, the writer reports that the chairman:

> opened the Court with a long and elaborate Speech to the Jury, purporting, 'That, Indeed the Laws of *England* confined their Inquiry to *Idiocy* or *Lunacy*, but that now, for wise and good Purposes, it was thought fit to *Extend the Laws*, and that they were to enquire, whether Mr. Roberts's Understanding was *Adequate* to his Fortune, and if he could be imposed upon in the Management thereof, adding, that *a Man may have Sense enough to manage* 300 £ per An. tho' not 3000 and that the Jury were at Liberty *by all Methods* to try the *Extent of his Capacity*; besides, without taking Notice of *Lunacy* or *Idiocy*, they might find him of *unsound Mind*, which being a Term of great Latitude, would *save their Consciences* as to the Oath. (4–5)

The sliding scale of capacity and intelligence is aligned here to levels of economic engagement, a precursor of how professional literature would in later years see a strengthening of the metaphorical and conceptual link between psychological and economic development (Goodey 2008). In the process of the trial, the 'Witnesses of low Degree' who formed part of the prosecution's case

> swore they had seen him shoot with a Bow and Arrow, and that when he was about 13 Years old, they had seen him blow Feathers; others

swore they had seen him toss up his Hat, and catch it with his Hands, and that he used to kick about Pebble-stones. Others, that when he was on Horseback, he could not open a Gate. One fellow swore that Mr. Roberts could not write his Name, but that he must be directed Letter by Letter. (9)

The litany of charges against Roberts seems frivolous, although the source is not necessarily reliable. Roberts' own account of the trial, as reported by confidantes, suggests that the goal of interrogations was to fluster the subject into giving confused answers, rather than to measure any levels of mental competence. In recounting his interrogation to a sympathetic listener, Roberts is reported to have said that his questioners

came around me and asked their Questions together, without giving me Time to answer. They asked me what a *Lamb*, and what a *Calf* was called at one, two and three Years old. They gave me a Sum of Money to tell, which I miscounted; and then I heard them say, he is not capable of managing his Affairs, *we will return him Incapable*. (11–12)

At the end of the proceedings, Roberts was found of unsound mind and one of his prosecutors, Dr Lynch, Dean of Canterbury, for whom Roberts had 'the greatest dislike … got the custody of his Person, with an Allowance of 400 Pound a Year, and thirty Pounds for Cloaths' (13). Roberts died a year later, in 1745, allegedly from illness brought on by his close confinement after he was found an 'idiot'. The author concludes by noting that 'The Prosecutors, who now by [Roberts'] Death, enjoy his whole Estate, under old Entails, to the amount of near 3000 Pound a Year, were in no way related to him: His Heirs at Law and Relations are quite excluded from all Benefit' (15). Indeed, even Roberts' old guardian Dr Finney had lost his estate owing to the expense of supporting Roberts through the prosecution.

While the narrative's primary objective is to reveal the devious machinations of the trustees and prosecutors, it also foregrounds the relationship between Roberts' apparent incapacity and the amount of money he was expected to manage. In this case, the prosecution held out for the application of those terms – 'unsound Mind' – with which they might best convince the jury, but which constituted neither idiocy nor lunacy. Henry Roberts' wit was not equal to his fortune of £3,000 per year, although it may have been sufficient for a smaller estate.

The story illustrates the fact that trials of idiocy were not simply a means for determining mental competence, but also a way of asserting degrees of masculinity and patriarchal authority within a socio-economic system based on both the circulation of capital (Roberts owned a sugar plantation in the West Indies) and the maintenance of patrimony. Masculine authority and intelligence are here understood as related qualities that predict or define how well one prospers in this new economy. The ultimate measure of this success is, of course, money: profitable ventures lend one authority and provide evidence of intelligence. The definition is notably circular: one becomes wealthy because one is intelligent, and one's financial success enables one to be recognized as intelligent.

Masculinity, idiocy and *The Entail*

The Henry Roberts tale finds an interesting literary parallel in John Galt's 1822/23 *The Entail*, a novel of embattled versions of masculinity, especially in the case of Walter (or Watty) Walkinshaw, the 'fatuous' second son of the novel's patriarch. Given the novel's concern with paternal lineage and the proper ordering of patriarchy, it is a rich site for investigating how idiocy intersects with masculinity in the early nineteenth century.

A selective plot summary is in order. The importance of patrilineage and inheritance is signalled in the novel's first line: 'Claud Walkinshaw was the sole surviving heir of the Walkinshaws of Kittlestonheugh' (3). His predecessors have squandered the family estate, but through a successful career as a pedlar along the borders, Claud earns enough money to buy the farm of Grippy, once part of his patrimony. From this stone he steps to the next, marrying Grizy Hypel, daughter of the Laird of Plealands, whose land was also formerly part of the Kittlestonheugh estate. But Grizy's father, without a male heir, is concerned with the survival of his name and so entails his estate on Walkinshaw's second (or, should the second die, his third) son, on the condition that the boy take the Laird's surname, Hypel, and thus ensure patrilineal progression. Through these complicated negotiations Watty comes into line for an estate, despite being a second son. Watty's chances of full patrimony are greatly increased, however, when lawyers discover that Plealands' entail is only partly binding; thus Watty inherits the estate at the death of the old Laird, but, thanks to a legal loophole, need not give up the Walkinshaw name. This circumstance leads to Claud's plan to spuriously disinherit his first son, Charles, in order to pass the entire, reunified estate to Watty, despite the fact that, as Claud notes, Watty's mental capacity is 'meted by a sma' measure' (25). Charles, disinherited and with scant resources, then dies, leaving a widow and two children, James and Mary. Claud, in despair over the loss of his beloved son, whose future he had blighted because of an obsessive concern with reacquiring the familial heritage, also dies, just before he can put his name to a document that would have passed the Grippy estate to its proper heir, Charles's son James.

The first half of *The Entail* tells the story of Watty's increasing isolation from the 'dominant fiction' of masculinity. He is wrongly invested with authority by his father, with only his close alliances to his mother and later his wife enabling him to pass as a complete man. But the novel does not present Watty as being devoid of valuable qualities. The first mention of his character is his mother's assessment that he is 'a weel-tempered laddie' (24) and clearly the reader is expected to believe in Watty's innate goodness. His union with the attractive, lively and unconventional (indeed, almost masculine) gamekeeper's daughter, Betty Bodle, reinforces this perception. The narrator anticipates readers questioning Betty's interest in Watty:

> Such a woman, it may be supposed, could not but look with the most thorough contempt on Walter Walkinshaw; and yet, from the accidental circumstance of being often his playmate in childhood, and making him, in the frolic of their juvenile amusements, her butt and toy, she had contracted something like an habitual affection for the creature; in so much, that, when her father ... proposed Walter for her husband, she made no serious objection to the match; on the contrary, she laughed, and amused herself with the idea of making him fetch and carry as whimsically as of old, and do her hests and biddings as implicitly as when they were children. (79–80)

So, seeing no danger of having to play the role of a submissive wife, Betty accepts Watty. The novel plays with the possibility of a structure in which Betty and Walter can thrive, with Betty as the 'head' of the family – appropriate, given her intellectual superiority to Watty. Galt experiments with an alternative subjectivity, allowing it, for a brief space, credence and authority within the world of the novel.

But this state of affairs does not last. Betty dies in childbirth, and Watty's despair over his wife's death, followed soon by that of his infant daughter, prompts him to kidnap (briefly) his niece Mary, Charles's orphaned daughter, and to rechristen her Betty Bodle, after his dead wife. However, he quickly invites Charles's widow and son to join him, and he shares the house and the entire wealth of the estate with them. Indeed, he plans to settle his estate on his niece, redirecting his patrimony to a female line. At the same time, though, he becomes reluctant to give his mother sufficient funds to maintain their household, because he unaware of exactly how much money he has to pass to his adopted daughter. This circumstance alienates Watty from his mother's protective goodwill, and gives the scheming younger brother George his chance to seize the family estate by initiating hearings to prove Watty's fatuity. In the world of *The Entail*, Watty's crimes are neither moral nor legal, but symbolic: he sins against his patrilineage in mishandling his name, his authority and his money. Galt's satire progresses, and as the lawyer Keelevin observes, 'it's a terrible thing to think o' proving a man *non compos mentis* for the only sensible action he ever did in his life' (183).

As John Tosh, a historian of concepts of masculinity, argues, 'dominant masculinity is constructed in opposition to a number of subordinate masculinities whose crime is that they undermine patriarchy from within or discredit it in the eyes of women' (Tosh 2005: 191). Watty is fatuous[4] precisely because he does not fulfil his responsibilities within the patriarchal structure of *The Entail*'s world, but rather threatens that structure. While Galt does briefly consider a state of affairs in which Watty can prosper as Betty's husband, Watty must ultimately be removed from the novel so that the Kittlestonheugh patrimony can wend its way to the rightful heir, and patriarchy can be reaffirmed as the dominant fiction.

Watty is defined in large part through his relationships with women: his mother, his wife, Betty Bodle, his daughter of the same name, and then his niece, to whom he also gives that name after his daughter has died. Indeed, the novel's women function to justify the dominant status of patriarchy, in part through association with Watty, who is clearly not a conventional patriarch. His inability to manage without assistance denies him the privileges of a man, and the jury's verdict of 'fatuity' is a symbolic castration. When the prosecuting lawyer, Mr Threeper, asks 'What are you, Mr. Walkinshaw?', he responds 'A man, Sir. – My mother and brother want to mak me a daft ane' (197) – clearly recognizing the diminished status in store for him. George and his mother succeed at their task, and Watty ceases to become relevant in the battle for the patrimony; as a 'daft' man, he no longer has any authority within the dominant fiction. One cannot be a man and a *fatuus* simultaneously, and the declaration of fatuity is a visible, public unmanning of Watty Walkinshaw.

The burden of idiocy not only denies Watty full masculinity, but also infantilizes him. In a telling exchange with his brother, Watty says 'I dinna like big folk.... Cause ye ken, Geordie, the law's made only for them; and if you and me had ay been twa wee brotherly laddies, playing on the gowany brae, as we used to do, ye would ne'er hae thought o' bringing yon Cluty's claw frae Enbro' to prove me guilty o' daftness' (211). Galt's construction of his idiot character draws on the tradition of the holy innocent as a truth-speaking critic of society, while simultaneously sentimentalizing this notion and making Watty the object of pathos.

We should also glance briefly at the relationship between Watty and his mother, anticipating some points to be presented in more detail in the next chapter. The initial portrayal of Grizy recalls Coleridge's assessment of Wordsworth's Betty Foy as a study in 'anile dotage': but in the world established in this novel, one cannot rationally love an idiot son. When Watty is declared fatuous, and soon after dies (several years later in the time-scale of the novel, but several pages in the text), Grizy Walkinshaw's comic role is transformed, and she becomes a determined matriarch who struggles to maintain her family, promote the claims of the rightful heir, James, and resist her scheming son George.

The well tempered man

As a general rule, idiot men appear with 'protectors', usually women. However, the idea of masculinity alters over the course of the nineteenth century. In the Victorian period, discussion of the idea of 'manliness' occupied many volumes of text, making it a 'high profile ideology of masculinity, if there ever was one' (Tosh 2005: 180). Much of this discussion focused on defining notions of proper 'manliness', as opposed to simple 'maleness', and in much writing – both fictional and non-fictional – the dominant aesthetic governing Victorian notions of masculinity and the middle-class gentleman (that paradigmatic expression of the Victorian man) invokes the idea of self-control. This sense of self-control is hardly exclusive to the Victorian era, of course; in the Tudor court, noblemen were expected to exert a certain amount of 'self-policing', subordinating their own interests to those of the crown (Goodey 2008; King 2004). In the nineteenth century, though, this self-regulation was enacted primarily within the domestic sphere, and from there translated to commercial and public activities. Herbert Sussman (1995) has suggested that 'the formations of Victorian manhood may be set along a continuum of degrees of self-regulation' (3) and that this construction of masculinity was 'threatened at one extreme by emasculation and at the other by social eruption and individual dissolution' (25). This dominant masculinity is also practically embodied in traditional patriarchal authority of the type described by David Roberts as rooted in the nuclear family but extending beyond it to render 'paternal authority generalized, impersonal, and hierarchical', forming a 'pattern of authority that was repeated in the public schools and universities, in the army and navy, and in the Church and local government' (Roberts 1978: 76).

The increasingly dominant middle-class aesthetic of masculine self-regulation, and its female counterpart, the image of the 'angel of the hearth', recreate relations between idiot or 'simple' characters and their patrons. In both fictional and non-fictional writings, 'idiots' increasingly become a measure of the goodness of their patrons; they are the objects of charitable acts that define the actors as responsible and morally worthy citizens. So, as notions of masculinity began to emphasize traditionally female qualities of compassion and generosity, male characters also assumed the guardian role: the relationship between Smike and Nicholas in Charles Dickens's *Nicholas Nickleby* (1839) provides an example of this phenomenon. Nicholas serves as a benevolent, loving patron to the simple-minded and helpless Smike, the unacknowledged son of Nicholas's money-grubbing, exploitative uncle Ralph Nickleby.

Dickens's 1850 novel *David Copperfield* provides an interesting variation on the usual relations, as the weak-minded Mr Dick lives under the protection of Betsy Trotwood in a state of affairs that recalls that of Watty Walkinshaw and Betty Bodle. Betsy Trotwood both rejects and appropriates male authority: she resumes her maiden name after her marriage fails and, indeed, renames Copperfield 'Trotwood' when he arrives in her household, in a clear denial of patriarchal possession and lineage. Mr Dick also dispenses with his surname, Babley, which he 'can't bear' (257). Thus, both Betsy Trotwood and Mr Dick effectively deny patrilinealage in their refusal to accept their legal surnames; while 'Babley' itself has connotations of 'babble', that is, nonsense language, we are also led to believe that Mr Dick's family had behaved abusively towards him, and had attempted to consign him to an asylum, when Betsy Trotwood stepped in to take care of him. Thus, his denial of his surname also expresses his resentment of those who would have him incarcerated for his weak mind. At the same time, his first name is also a common slang term for the penis, a connotation Dickens could hardly have overlooked (especially given the proximity of 'Dick' to 'Dickens'). The use of the name here seems primarily comic: Mr Dick carries his name precisely because his claim to male authority – the Lacanian phallus – is so minimal and circumscribed. While Mr Dick's good nature is consistently noted, he remains a man whose potential is hidden to all but his female patron; eventually, however, he performs the act that Betsy had long predicted would vindicate her belief in his abilities by reconciling Dr Strong and his wife Annie, and thus consolidates his claim to a limited sort of authority. Notably, he succeeds by his ability to reopen communication between the doctor and his wife, which then allows understanding to grow between them; Dick distinguishes himself by his capacity to promote sympathy, a social skill more traditionally associated with women.[5]

As a number of critics have noted, *David Copperfield* marks an attempt by Dickens to restructure masculine identity by incorporating what would be considered 'female' characteristics into the male protagonist (Houston 1993; Poovey 1988; Tosh 1999). Mr Dick cannot exist as a hero, as that is the role occupied by David Copperfield, but rather as a figure whose innate decency is not compromised by his lack of rational thought. The differences between Mr Dick and Watty Walkinshaw illustrate this shift in the construction of the 'weak-minded' male character. Like Watty, Mr Dick is not financially responsible, and thus is forbidden to spend money without Betsy Trotwood's approval. However, in order to spare him mortification, she permits him to have coins to jingle in his pocket, and these coins enable him to pass as a man of some resources in society. They also publicly express his claim to a degree of masculine authority, although the claim is exercised under the control of his patroness. Thus, Mr Dick is rendered superficially valid, incorporated within the patriarchal structure as the recipient of benevolence and charity, although without the ability to exercise power independently.

These associations of masculine idiocy with financial mismanagement and poverty had specific consequences in the way idiocy was dealt with, as men were much more likely than women to be identified as 'idiots' or 'fatuous'. R. A. Houston (2000), drawing on court records, notes that in eighteenth-century Scotland the ratio of men to women cognosced for fatuity was four to one. David Wright (2001) has observed that male admissions to the Earlswood asylum outnumbered female admissions two to one and that in the censuses of 1871 and 1881 'congenital idiocy' appeared in males 30 per cent more often than in females. These numbers puzzled Victorian commentators, some of whom hypothesized that men must be more inclined towards idiocy than women; others, such as Duncan and Millard (1866: 89), suggested that the difference 'may arise from the greater trouble caused at home by imbecile boys than imbecile girls'. Both Wright (2001) and Houston (2000) suggest that the differences may be attributed to the greater consequences of mental weakness for men, whose social role demanded participation in the world of work and commerce. As a result, those activities in which they were deemed incapable would be more public and the effects of their difficulties in these areas more dramatic, making it both easier and more important to identify them as idiots.

Elizabeth Gaskell's idiot boy
and his sister

The image of the male idiot was flexible and could be applied to a range of symbolic tasks; for instance, Elizabeth Gaskell adapts the notion to perform a feminist critique of patriarchal authority. In the 1855 short story 'Half a Life-Time Ago', the protagonist, Susan Dixon, honours her mother's deathbed request to look after her younger brother Willie, but this forces Susan to choose between her brother and her lover, Michael Hurst, who wishes to place Willie in the Lancaster Asylum. After refusing to commit Willie, Susan is abandoned by Michael and isolates herself from all society, living with a servant and caring for her brother while running her farm; even after Willie's death, Susan rebuffs suitors and remains in solitude. John Kucich has observed that:

> one of the more curious patterns in Gaskell's work is her frequent inversion of her protagonists' sexual identity. In many of these characters, gender is not blurred or revised; it is flatly reversed. Women are rigidly masculinized, and men rigidly feminized, in static and stereotypical ways. (Kucich 1990: 188)

Certainly, one can argue that Susan Dixon is 'masculinized' and perhaps Willie is 'feminized'. Michael Hurst is emphatically not feminized, however; indeed, given Gaskell's descriptions of the men populating the world of this short story, Hurst may be excessively male. The men of the Westmoreland district, writes Gaskell, are especially distinguished by a pleasure in 'drinking for days together, and having to be hunted up by anxious wives, who dared not leave their husbands to the chances of the wild precipitous roads, but walked miles and miles, lantern in hand, in the dead of night, to discover and guide the solemnly-drunken husband home' (4). In the world Gaskell describes, manliness is enacted through drunkenness and violence (Wright 1995). But the qualities Susan acquires over the course of the story are those of a steady farmer and manager, one who knows not only the 'butter and chicken that every farmer's wife about had to sell' but also those items that fall on 'the man's side' – livestock, grain, produce – so that her financial savings become the object of speculation among townspeople (Gaskell 1855: 50). Susan Dixon's apparent masculine qualities are expressed in her commercial activities.

Many commentators, when examining Susan's relationship with Willie, find the influence of Wordsworth at work in the story (Wright 1995; Easson 1979), but the tone of 'Half a Life-Time Ago' is considerably more sombre than that of 'The Idiot Boy' and, at points, Gaskell even presents Susan as mirroring Willie's idiocy. Susan tends Willie through fits, but afterwards:

> when he was laid down, she would sally out to taste the fresh air, and to work off her wild sorrow in cries and mutterings to herself. The early labourers saw her gestures at a distance, and thought her as crazed as the idiot-brother who made the neighbourhood a haunted place. (48)

The idiot brother acts as a symbolic double for Susan, his incapacity both the cause and the expression of her own isolation in the male world of the Westmorelands. However, while Willie acts to some degree as a double for Susan, he is more meaningful when seen in conjunction with Michael Hurst, whom he supplants in Susan's life. Although Willie is less than a man in terms that are immediately accessible to the tale's readers, as well as to the characters within it, Michael hardly prospers in comparison.

In acceding to her mother's deathbed request that she care for Willie, Susan defers to a matriarchal authority rather than take the more expected route of marrying Hurst and assuming his name. While Susan cares for the declining Willie, Hurst marries another woman and proves to be an incapable husband. Susan glimpses her possible 'other' life when she witnesses a drunken Hurst beating a horse (46) and hears reports of his dissipation and improvidence (51). Hurst's death in a snowstorm leaves his widow and children in worse poverty than Willie had caused for Susan, a disjunction that would have been significant to Gaskell's readers. Indeed, having an 'idiot' family member was at this time a legitimate cause by which poor families could justify their poverty and receive special Poor Law benefits (Rushton 1988). Thus, Susan's wealth and competence are all the more dramatically opposed to Michael's poverty and incompetence. Michael is similar to Willie in his inability to be responsible for himself and those around him. Willie's idiocy provides a critique of masculine folly – the drunkenness, violence and wastefulness foregrounded by Gaskell throughout the story – that condemns women to subservience and poverty; Susan's 'cries and mutterings' outside her cottage thus signify not only the oppressive character of her immediate fate, but in a larger sense the oppression of women in general.

Willie Dixon is no Wordsworthian idiot boy, but rather a tool Gaskell uses to critique masculine power while valorizing female strength. The conclusion of the story bears out this reading: Susan's adoption of Michael's widow and orphans, after they nurse her back to health from a stroke, is possible because of the skills she has developed and the money she has earned and saved. Anne Mellor, writing about female romanticism, argues that the idea of an all-female community, which occurs in much fiction by Victorian women, not only offers a model of 'personal fulfillment' but, more significantly, contests 'the patriarchal doctrine of the separate spheres by articulating a very different domestic ideology' (Mellor 1993: 84). Gaskell's conclusion not only sees Susan Dixon happy, but also locates her in a community notable for its independence from masculine authority and the behaviours that, for proto-feminist writers such as Gaskell, render this authority unjust.

Idiocy and male sexuality: nature makes amends?

Interestingly, and oddly, sexual activity and expressions of sexuality are missing in most early accounts of male 'idiots'. Indeed, they seem precluded from the world of sexual activity by the fact that, since the time of Edward III, 'begetting a child' had served as proof that an individual was not an idiot. One of the more poignant moments in the narrative of the ordeal of Henry Roberts comes when the author cites a letter in which Roberts writes 'I am hurried to death, and am resolved to marry very soon, for they tell me, if I should have a Child, they cannot hurt me' (Anonymous 1747: 21). Certainly, this legal requirement is compatible with the argument that maintaining the paternal line is a critical masculine responsibility. But there are, of course, exceptions. In *The Entail*, Watty Walkinshaw fathers a child, although both mother and child die quickly and Watty is cognosced as *fatuus* all the same. And in John Cleland's erotic novel *Memoirs of a Woman of Pleasure* (1748/49), more commonly known as *Fanny Hill*, the prostitute Louisa seduces a 'perfect changeling, or idiot' tellingly nicknamed 'Good-natured Dick' (much like Dickens's Mr Dick), because she had 'conceived a strange longing to be satisfied, whether the general rule held good with regard to this changeling, and how far nature had made him amends in her best bodily gifts for her denial of the sublimer intellectual ones' (197–98). Indeed, when Fanny and Louisa undo their victim's breeches, they discover

> the idiot's standard of distinction, erect, in full pride and display: but such a one! it was positively of so tremendous a size that, prepared as we were to see something extraordinary, it still, out of measure, surpassed our expectation, and astonished even me, who had not been used to trade in trifles … its enormous head seemed, in hue and size, not unlike a common sheep's heart. (198)

Fanny retires from the activity after satisfying her curiosity, but Louisa continues the experiment, discovering that nature had indeed fully compensated the 'purely sensitive idiot' (202). But Cleland's literary imagining of 'idiot' sexuality is unusual, and likely an expression of the broad but largely underground cultural interest in the sex lives of 'deviant' characters in general rather than idiots in particular (Wagner 1988). 'Good-natured Dick' is initially a passive participant in the sexual process, as he is seduced by Louisa, rather than the other way around. But once the social exchange involved in seduction has been completed, Dick becomes sexually dominant – indeed, extraordinarily so, as befits someone whose being is 'purely sensitive'. In fact, the focus is not so much on the fool's capacity in lovemaking as on the physical size of his penis – a consideration which does have precedents, dating back at least to the late sixteenth or early seventeenth century, as in this parody of a female aristocrat's inclinations:

> Missa will needsly marry with a foole
> Her reason:
> O sir, because he hath an excellent ——
> (Quoted in Goodey 2008)

But while the notion of the well endowed idiot existed, the physical feature did not seem to translate into increased sexual activity, and there are relatively few examples of or commentaries on the sexual capacity of male 'idiots'. This state of affairs continues through the first half of the nineteenth century, where 'idiot' men are presented, at least in literary works, as relatively benign versions of adult children. They offer little threat and their sexual identity is muted. More ominous associations with sexuality will not come to the surface until later in the nineteenth century, when a number of factors, including the rise of the urban poor and fears of racial degeneration, will prompt some people to imagine the male idiot as a sexual threat. By the later decades of the nineteenth century, and especially with the creation of the category of 'feeble-mindedness', the fecundity of idiots becomes a major social concern. For female idiots, however, the association of intellectual incapacity with an undisciplined sexuality is as fundamental, and almost as historically resilient, as that link of idiocy and financial mismanagement for male idiots.

We will treat the association of female idiocy and sexuality in the next chapter. In this chapter, I have tracked idiocy and masculinity over a broad historical period not to argue that all male characters are portrayed in the same manner and for the same reasons – as clearly they are not – but rather to stress that in any representation of idiocy, gender identity is significant. There are, broadly speaking, consistent associations made in representations of idiocy and gender, and, in association with men, idiocy is often identified as a lack, frequently expressed through an inability to deal with money. The idiot male, in his incapacity to exercise the authority of patriarchy and to manage the wealth of patrimony, is a profoundly diminished man.

Notes

1 Quotations from Crabbe here and below are taken from Ward (1907).
2 These interests were the responsibility of the Court of Chancery until two statutes, in 1540 and 1542, created an independent Court of Wards and Liveries, which took over these concerns until its dissolution in 1660, at which point they reverted to the Chancery.
3 The authoritative and tremendously popular *Nouvelle Natura Brevium* was originally published in French with legal Latin in 1534, and reprinted many times before the first English translation appeared; I quote from the 1652 English version, which is a faithful reproduction of what Fitzherbert had written over a century earlier.
4 According to Robert Houston (2000), 'fatuous' and 'furious' were the terms most frequently used in Scottish trials of mental capacity.
5 Consider, in this context, the role played by Mme Guérin in the education of Victor of Aveyron (Chapter 3): her job was to awaken in the boy a pleasure in the company of others, and a sympathy for his fellow humans.

CHAPTER 5

Essential women:
femininity and idiocy

Eugenia Tyrold, fifteen years old, is small, limps from a childhood accident and is scarred by smallpox. Among the many female characters populating Fanny Burney's 1796 novel *Camilla*, Eugenia is distinct in her physical unattractiveness, although she is equally distinguished by her intelligence and generosity. Sheltered by her loving family, she does not realize the disadvantages of her appearance until one day, on a public outing, she is singled out and abused by a vulgar crowd. Mortified, Eugenia tries to isolate herself from the world, until one day her father insists on taking her and her sister Camilla on an outing. They travel to meet a young woman, a 'beautiful figure' who, not seeing her visitors, 'sits down upon the grass, which she plucked up by hands full, and then strewed over her fine flowing hair'; Eugenia compels herself to watch, with subdued envy, the 'object before her, who was young, fair, of a tall and striking figure, with features delicately regular' (308). Soon it becomes clear, though, that something is amiss with the beautiful young woman: she sobs violently, bursts into a 'fit of loud, shrill, and discordant laughter' and then spins on the grass 'with a velocity that no machine could have exceeded' (309). When the girl finally realizes she has visitors, she greets them enthusiastically, 'while the slaver drivelled unrestrained from her mouth, rendering utterly disgusting a chin that a statuary might have wished to model' (309). The girl proceeds to latch upon her cat, 'wholly unresisting the scratches which tore at her fine skin', and then ties her handkerchief over her face and begins to hit herself in the head with both hands. Eugenia, shocked, absorbs her father's lesson, exclaiming 'how dread a reproof you have given to my repining spirit!' (310) and her father then reveals the truth: he had previously learned that the girl, of an 'uncommon beauty' but 'born an idiot, and therefore, having never known brighter days … insensible to her sorry state', was being cared for at this estate, and had arranged to have her appear in the window and then be released upon the lawn when he arrived with his daughters. 'Poor, ill-fated creature! it has been, indeed, a melancholy sight', he concludes (310), before underlining the moral of the encounter to his physically ill-favoured Eugenia: 'You have seen, here, the value of intellects in viewing the horror of their loss; and you have witnessed, that beauty, without mind, is more dreadful than any deformity' (311). The repentant Eugenia embraces her father, and then Camilla, 'throwing her arms about them both, bathed each with the tears of joy and admiration, which this soothing conclusion to an adventure so severe excited' (311).

Burney's *Camilla* provides a comprehensive exploration of the interconnections between beauty, desirability and intelligence in its treatment of the Tyrold sisters, Camilla, Eugenia and Lavinia, as well as their beautiful cousin Indiana Lynmere – who, unlike the Tyrold girls, 'promises to turn out rather dull' (15). Eugenia is studious, Lavinia thoughtful and Camilla high-spirited; all are intelligent and generous. In contrast, the 'fair Indiana' exhibits an 'aversion unconquerable by her teacher' to any notion of study (44) as a child, but remains a much-admired enchantress all the same. Burney describes her as having a

> beauty of so regular a cast, that her face had no feature, no look to which criticism could point as susceptible of improvement, or on which admiration could dwell with more delight than the rest. No statuary could have modelled her form with more exquisite symmetry; no painter have harmonized her complexion with greater brilliancy of colouring. But here ended the liberality of nature, which, in not sullying this fair workmanship by inclosing in it what was bad, contentedly left it vacant of whatever was noble or desirable. (84)

Melmond, a 'young Oxian' friend of her cousin Lionel, exclaims upon first seeing Indiana that she is 'all I ever read of! all I ever conceived! she is beauty in its very essence! she is elegance, delicacy, and sensibility personified!' When Lionel demands how his friend 'should know anything of her besides her beauty', he responds (with great enthusiasm) 'How? by looking at her! Can you view that countenance and ask me how? Are not those eyes all soul? Does not that mouth promise every thing that is intelligent? Can those lips ever move but to diffuse sweetness and smiles? I must not look at her again! another glance might set me raving' (103–4). But Melmond is already bewitched, and eventually becomes engaged to his idol, only to find himself regretting her 'mental and intellectual littleness' (813); the eyes that once enthralled him 'have lost all their illusory charm', as he perceives in them only 'their vacancy of the soul's intelligence' (813); fortunately for him, she later elopes with another man, and he is given the chance to court Eugenia.

Burney's analysis of gender relations and the value of female intelligence was replicated by later writers. 'A woman ... if she have the misfortune of knowing any thing, should conceal it as well as she can', wrote Jane Austen in her 1818 novel *Northanger Abbey*, before referring explicitly to Burney's precedent:

> The advantages of natural folly in a beautiful girl have already been set forth by the capital pen of a sister author; – and to her treatment of the subject I will add only in justice to men, that though to the larger and more trifling part of the sex, imbecility in females is a great enhancement of their personal charms, there is a portion of them too reasonable and too well informed themselves to desire any thing more in woman than ignorance. (125)

Burney and Austen lob satirical darts at the male tendency to fear women with lively and astute intellects, but in playing with associations of imbecility with women, and especially with women's sexuality, these authors have a historical legacy of religious, philosophical, scientific, legal and social thought upon which to draw.

History offers numerous instances where writers (usually male but sometimes female) denigrate the intellectual capacities of women, who were regularly presented as (and almost as often perceived to be) weak-minded and irrational. At the same time, that most anxiety-provoking quality associated with women – that is, their sexual nature, with its attendant demands on men – is the subject of much commentary and speculation, as well as many concerted efforts – social, legal, ecclesiastical, medical and scientific – to control it. When the women in question were thought to be even more mentally deficient than most women, these questions of guidance and control became even more pressing. The ongoing threat, of course, was that without careful strictures, women would descend quickly to a debased form of sexual, irrational humanity, dragging civilized men with them. Natural folly was the lot of all women, it seemed to many (mainly male) observers; careful male guidance was necessary if women were to remain chaste and rational. Or as rational as possible.

This rationality was becoming increasingly important by the eighteenth century, which saw the growing circulation of arguments that women should be educated to be helpmates to men; after all, they were responsible for running a stabilizing domestic environment that would balance masculine activity in the world of commerce and enterprise. At the same time, there were limits to what education could be expected to achieve, and women's apparently less profound or less robust intellect would come to provide one rationale for a guiding and protecting male authority. These ideas developed through the nineteenth century, culminating in the notion of the idealized domestic goddess, those 'angels of the hearth' so familiar to readers of Victorian fiction. But this domestic goddess was increasingly desexualized, at the same time as expectations of her level of intelligence were being elevated, at least within a specific (i.e. domestic) sphere of influence. This relation between the sexual woman and the intelligent domestic helpmate is an inverse one, and during the eighteenth and nineteenth centuries, as women were increasingly perceived to be intellectual beings, the explicit emphasis laid upon their sexual nature was diminished. At the same time, concern over female sexuality remained ever-present. After all, not all women were domestic angels, and many, especially those among the disreputable poor and the degenerate aristocracy, came to be associated with an undisciplined, threatening sexuality. Certainly for every ideal Victorian heroine one can find parallel examples of debased women. The one was consistently balanced with a cautionary example of her opposite(s), as Dickens does with the angelic 'more-than-sister' bride Agnes, the fallen woman Emily and the silly child-bride Dora in *David Copperfield* (1850). Not surprisingly, women perceived as having intellectual disabilities were also incorporated into this group of threatening females, and representations of female 'idiots' consistently emphasize sexual or other physical appetites. This association is durable, although, as we will see, it performs different functions, according to context.

John Fletcher's 1621 drama *The Pilgrim* contains a bedlam scene featuring a 'she-fool', who is described as being 'as lecherous as a she-ferret' and is separated from the madmen because, as one of her keepers points out, 'If any of the madmen take her, she is pepper'd; They'll bounce her loins' (act III, scene vi). Sure enough, upon her first appearance the she-fool immediately invites the keeper to join her in the coal house, asking 'Will you buss me, and tickle me and make me laugh?' But this licentiousness is not isolated in the fool. Instead, the she-fool is blurred with the virtuous female heroine Alinda, who disguises herself as the fool so that even her father, Alphonso, is taken in. Female identity is remarkably malleable in this play, as Alinda also conceals herself as a young boy, an elderly woman and a shepherdess; furthermore, the 'she-fool' reappears towards the end of the play in the boy's garb with which Alinda had previously disguised herself, and which she had traded for the fool's motley. The fool's qualities are thus not confined within one individual; rather, her erotic inclinations are also associated with Alinda, who, despite her apparent virtue, disguises herself in order to avoid marrying one man and to pursue another. Not surprisingly, folly is a general attribute in *The Pilgrim*, as in much early modern drama: the term 'fool' is applied, at various times, to Alinda (even when she is not in her 'fool' disguise), her serving maid, Juletta, her father, her beloved Pedro, and the villainous Roderigo, among others. But despite its status as a general quality, folly is also becoming the more formal and contained 'idiocy' at this time and Alinda's she-fool disguise emphasizes the specific gender associations of idiocy, femininity and undisciplined sexuality. Eventually, Alinda appears as her clever and resourceful self, her erotic designs fulfilled as she marries the 'Pilgrim' of the title in a comic denouement that sees the cantankerous Alphonso forced to accede to his daughter's will.

But female sexuality, while fodder for comedy on-stage, was, when off-stage, no laughing matter. Nor was apparent idiocy proof against punishment for sexual misconduct: when Elizabeth Stewart, described as 'almost an idiot', was accused of fornication in Scotland in 1702, she was recommended to the magistrate for deportation because of her 'very bad fame' (quoted in Mitchison and Leneman 1989: 192). And in George Crabbe's 1810 poem *The Borough*, the narrative of Ellen Orford and her 'idiot daughter' clearly links the daughter's idiocy to her mother's 'erring wish' in accepting the advances of a rake. Indeed, by the end of the nineteenth century, the presumed sexual promiscuity of 'feeble-minded' women would feed the growing fears of racial degeneracy, and these women would soon be identified as the prime culprits in the supposed decline of the nation's racial health (Cox 1996; Gladstone 1996). The Mental Deficiency Act 1913 specifically focuses on women suspected of mental weakness who give birth out of wedlock, and provides the state with the ability to institutionalize them as a danger to the eugenic health of the nation. This chapter will track the associations of sexuality, intelligence and idiocy in women.

Dangerous sexuality

In early modern England, the status of a woman was closely connected to that of her household, led by its masculine head; in effect, masculine honour – that abstract mode through which one measured status – was transferable to women according to their relation to men (Goodey 2008). The daughter or wife of a man of honour would be a woman of honour, although her claim was most often dependent upon that of her male patron – if his status fell or rose, so, most likely, would hers. And, of course, she had to maintain the recognized outward signs of female honour: virginity for the unwed, fidelity for married women. Sexual conduct formed the recognizable external expression of honour or grace for women, just as the proper management of lands and finances was an expression of male competence. Sexual promiscuity is necessarily understood in this structure as dishonourable or disgraceful, analogous to a man squandering his lands and fortune.

In 1523, the Spanish nobleman Juan Luis Vives, living in the court of Henry VIII, wrote *Instruction of a Christian Woman* for the young Mary Tudor (allegedly at the request of Mary's mother, Catherine of Aragon). The work, intended as a moral guide for women, was translated by Richard Hynde from Latin into English in 1529, and had appeared in nine editions by 1592; eventually translated into French, Spanish and German, among other languages, it became sixteenth-century Europe's most influential behaviour guide for young women. Vives stresses the importance of chastity in both body and mind, noting that 'the maid herself ... hath within her a treasure without comparison, that is, the pureness both of body and mind' (quoted in Klein 1992: 103); for a maid to lose her virginity before marriage was a foul crime, violently punished in both this world and the next. While the need to protect chastity applied to both men and women, failure to do so was more consequential to women, he notes, as 'their offenses be reckoned fouler ... and doubtless ... women be worthy these punishments [of eternal damnation] and much worse that keep not their honesty diligently' (Klein 1992: 106). The loss of chastity in a woman, wrote Vives, 'is like as in a man, if he lacks all that he should have. For in a woman, the honest is in stead of all' – that is to say, chastity is the treasure of women, as lands, riches, fame and lineage are the treasure of men. Without her chastity, a woman becomes like an impoverished man, excluded from the life of the state. And as a man who 'lacks all that he should have' is in danger of being found an idiot, so also a woman without chastity becomes a woman without value or status: she, too, becomes like an idiot.

The virginal, chaste maid may have represented the feminine ideal, but many observers feared that this ideal was rarely approached in reality. Indeed, they worried, women's essential nature seemed to be found at quite the opposite extreme of sexual behaviour. In 1615, the appearance of *The Araignment of Lewde, Idle, Froward and Unconstant Women*, signed by Thomas Tell-Troth but soon identified with one Joseph Swetnam, sparked a pamphlet war that supported ten editions of this work by 1637, and prompted at least three responses (see Henderson and McManus 1985), demonstrating a ready market for tracts and counter-tracts on the lewdness and folly of women. In Swetnam's diatribe, women appear as lust-driven deceivers:

> For women have a thousand ways to entice thee and ten thousand ways to deceive thee and all such fools as are suitors unto them.... They lay out the folds of their hair to entangle men into their love; betwixt their breasts is the vale of destruction; and in their beds there is hell, sorrow and repentance. (Quoted in Henderson and McManus 1985: 201)

Such lurid imagery was not solely the province of satirical pamphleteers. In his *Description anatomique des parties de la femme qui servent à la génération*, published in 1708, the French physician Jean Palfyn set out to describe:

> those parts of the body which cause women a thousand miseries, that irritate men in a thousand ways, that have allowed women – themselves weak and defenseless – to triumph over the strongest of men, overthrow several very powerful Kings, undo august Emperors, make fools out of wisemen, trick the learned, seduce the prudent, drive the healthy to loathsome ailments, strip the rich of their wealth, and strike down the most celebrated heroes. (Quoted in Huet 1993: 57)

Notably, for both Swetnam and Palfyn the dangerous and cunning sexuality of women made fools of those men who pursued them. Such diatribes denouncing female sexuality were countered with the more exuberant reams of pornography that exploded onto the marketplace in the early eighteenth century (Harvey 2004). These works, ranging from full-length books to short pamphlets and engravings, conventionally portrayed women as either sexually passive or insatiable, either innocents to be educated in the arts of carnal love or pedagogues themselves in this discipline; more often, it was the latter, reflecting a dominant belief in an 'essential female lasciviousness', stemming from women's supposed connection to nature (Peakman 2003: 189).

So while women were often counselled and exhorted to be chaste and honest, there was little belief that they would be so of their own accord. Much effort, both masculine and feminine, went into trying to ensure chastity among (some) women, either by encouragement or by imposition; and a comparable effort went towards penning tortured laments on the lewdness and cunning deceits of the female sex.

The irrational woman

Male anxiety about female sexuality finds a parallel in the association of femininity with irrationality and ignorance, an association with a very long lineage in European history. Aristotle, in his *Politics*, notes that:

rule of free over slave, male over female, man over boy, are all natural, but they are also different, because, while parts of the soul are present in each case, the distribution is different. Thus the deliberative faculty of the soul [i.e., the rational soul] is not present at all in a slave; in a female it is inoperative, in a child undeveloped. (Book I, 13)

As Robert Mayhew glosses Aristotle's position:

man is to woman as soul is to body or as reason is to appetite, the woman possesses the deliberative part of the soul, but lacks authority; the intellectual virtues are different for men and women – most significantly, whereas men can possess practical intelligence, the most a woman can attain is true opinion. (Mayhew 2004: 92)

Aristotle's views would find echoes in the influential seventeenth- and eighteenth-century writings of English philosophers John Locke and David Hume. Locke's position on the rationality of women is ambivalent; he suggests in *The Reasonableness of Christianity* (1695) that both those whose 'hand is used to the plough and the spade' as well as 'the other sex' are restricted in their understanding to 'plain propositions, and a short reasoning about things familiar to their minds, and nearly allied to their daily experience' (76), although he stresses that these intellectual limitations form a general feature of most humanity. And in the second of his *Two Treatises of Government* (1689) he proposes that man and woman share parental government within the home, while at the same time qualifying the position with the observation that 'it ... being necessary that the last determination (i.e., the rule) should be placed somewhere, it naturally falls to the man's share as the abler and the stronger' (157). This superior ability and strength is intellectual and moral as well as physical. Following Locke, David Hume, in his *Essays Moral, Political and Literary* (1777), would simply present as an apparent truism that 'nature has given *man* the superiority over *woman*, by endowing him with greater strength both of mind and body'; however, it then becomes the man's responsibility to 'alleviate that superiority, as much as possible, by the generosity of his behaviour' (133, original emphasis).

These broadly held notions of female intellectual inferiority had wide-reaching social consequences. Even child-raising, that most fundamental of traditional female responsibilities, was not exempt from concerns that it was dominated by the ignorant and unlearned. As William Cadogan observes in the opening lines of his 1748 *Essay Upon Nursing and the Management of Children*,

It is with great Pleasure I see at last the Preservation of Children become the Care of Men of Sense: It is certainly a Matter that well deserves their

> Attention.... In my Opinion, this Business has been too long fatally left
> to the Management of Women, who cannot be supposed to have proper
> Knowledge to fit them for such a Task, notwithstanding they look upon
> it to be their own Province. (3)

The author, a physician, then defines the knowledge necessary to
the job at hand: 'a Philosophic Knowledge of Nature, to be acquired
only by learned Observation and Experience, and which therefore
the Unlearned must be incapable of'. Cadogan's concept of learning
puts the responsibility for such tasks as raising children permanently
out of reach of women – the knowledge that develops from 'learned
Observation and Experience' is a form of understanding of which they
are simply 'incapable'.

Such an argument points not only to a particular understanding of
women's intellectual powers but also to their capacity for improvement: that is, their powers are low and not likely to be raised much by
study. Those exceptions, when they could be found, were simply taken
as proof of the rule. 'Sir, a woman preaching is like a dog's walking
on his hind legs', Samuel Johnson famously wrote in a letter to Lord
Chesterfield on 31 July 1763. 'It is not done well; but you are surprised
to find it done at all'. Johnson was unleashing a witticism, of course,
but no doubt he and Chesterfield could share a chuckle because they
believed in the validity of the comparison. Even in the nineteenth
century, the fact that Harriet Martineau could write an extended series
of works on political economy – not traditionally an area of female
expertise – would provoke wonder and mockery (Pichanick 1980).

Many authors (male and female) hypothesized that intellectual dis-
parities were rooted in the differences thought to define women's
nervous constitution. This supposed female sensitivity – the consequence of a nervous system thought to be notably different from that
of men – also had an impact on mental stability, rendering women
delicate, both physically and intellectually. As the physician and pamphleteer Bernard de Mandeville wrote in his *Treatise of the Hypochondriak
and Hysterick Diseases* (1711),

> Their immortal substance is without doubt the same with ours, and it
> is only within body that we differ: We are of a stronger, but they of a
> more Elegant composure, and Beauty is their attribute as Strength is
> ours: Their frame, tho less firm is more delicate, and themselves more
> capable both of Pleasure and Pain, tho' endued with less constancy of
> bearing the excess of either. This delicacy as well as imbecillity [*sic*]
> of the Spirits in Women is Conspicuous in all their actions, those of
> the Brain not excepted: They are unfit both for abstruse and elaborate
> Thoughts, all studies of Depth, Coherence and Solidity that fatigue the

Spirits, and require a Steadiness and Assiduity of thinking; but where the Advantages of Education and Knowledge are equal, they exceed the Men in Sprightliness of Fancy, quickness of Thought and off-hand Wit; as much as they out-do them in sweetness of Voice, and Volubility of Tongue. (174–75)

Thanks to the 'imbecillity of the Contexture of Spirits in Women' (176), Mandeville writes, 'One Hours intense Thinking wastes the Spirits more in a Woman, than six in a Man' (177).

Mandeville assigns the mental weakness of women to a delicacy of physical constitution. But other theories shifted the responsibility from female physiology to social organization. From at least the mid-seventeenth century, proto-feminist writers – described by historian Hilda Smith (1982: 66) as 'mavericks, operating in a largely hostile environment' – had argued against the prevailing belief that women were the intellectual inferiors of men and had opposed the exclusion of women from educational and social institutions. As the anonymous author (most likely Mary Astell) argued in the 1696 *Essay in Defence of the Female Sex*, men were loath to admit the fact that the gap between male and female intellectual achievement was due to the differences in the education each received: 'it does not serve their Pride; there is no Honour to be gained by it', she observes, pointing out that 'a Man ought no more to value himself upon being Wiser than a Woman, if he owe his Advantage to a better Education, and greater means of Information, than he ought to boast of his Courage, for beating a Man, when his hands were bound' (20). Masculine honour is garnered through martial success, but only in equal combat; the notion of male intellectual superiority over women is another expression of that honour but, as women were rarely allowed education to the same degree as men, it was an honour won without the equality of resources demanded upon the field of battle. So ran the convincing counter-argument, but the notion of the intellectually inferior woman was well entrenched and not easily discredited.

These apparent differences became representative of all-embracing dichotomies, because, through the eighteenth and nineteenth centuries, sexual difference acted as a model for a range of other distinctions. 'Women versus men, nature versus culture, became key terms in … conflicts of the period', writes Ludmilla Jordanova of the realms of science and medicine (Jordanova 1989: 30). While she does not list here female 'feeling' and male 'intelligence' among these dichotomies, they would not be out of place. Theories of gender become entwined with those of nature, and of man's (specifically male) relation to nature; in representational art, nature appears persistently in a female form, with rational science a masculine viewer or investigator. Nature is embodied in women, poor labourers and savage peoples, while educated, rational men – *cultivated* men – rise beyond its borders.

Nineteenth-century society and the place of women

'From the time of adolescence up to the time of marriage, the law of England supposes a perfect capacity on the part of the adult woman as well as of the adult man', wrote William Thompson in his 1825 *Appeal of One Half the Human Race*. 'But as soon as adult daughters become wives, their civil rights disappear; they fall back again, and remain all their lives – should their owners and directors live so long – into the state of children or idiots, the passive property of their owners' (quoted in Helsinger *et al.*, 1983: vol. I, 28). Women's presumed intellectual inferiority and isolation from economic activity helped to identify them with children and idiots – at least in relation to men. In addition, as women were barred from public life – like the Greek 'idiot' or private individual – their status was equivalent to those other groups not participating in the public realms of politics and, increasingly, commerce and the arts (Hall 1992). Over forty years after Thompson, Frances Power Cobb, in her 1868 essay 'Criminals, Idiots, Women and Minors', noted that her essay title designated 'the four categories under which persons are now excluded from many civil, and all political rights in England', which had been 'complacently quoted this year by the *Times* as every way fit and proper exceptions; but yet it has appeared to not a few, that the place assigned to Woman is hardly any longer suitable' (Cobb 1868: 110).

Cobb's essay, like Thompson's, was arguing for the legislative change that would eventually result in the Married Women's Property Act 1870. By the middle decades of the nineteenth century, the 'woman question' was being debated across Britain – in legal, medical, scientific, economic and religious texts, as well as through direct political engagement and literary expression.[1] The second half of the century was marked by burgeoning, politically focused feminist thought, with the oppression of married women the primary focus of concern. The greatest portion of energy in this stage of the feminist struggle went to countering dominant notions (and the laws that expressed those notions) of masculine property, which included wives and children in addition to the property brought into marriage or earned by a woman. In practical terms, the claims to property and its transmission over generations – that is, patrimony – lay at the heart of economic distinctions between men and women, so claims to equality in this realm challenged fundamental, long-held notions of what it meant to be male or female. Eventually, the Custody of Infants Act 1839 allowed women to petition the courts for custody of children under seven and for visitation rights to older children; the Matrimonial Causes Act 1857 allowed women to divorce a husband who was consistently adulterous and abusive, although a husband was still permitted to sue for divorce if his wife had a single adulterous episode; and the Married Woman's Property Act 1870 allowed women to claim certain private property within a marriage, whereas previously all the woman's property became her husband's upon marriage (an 1882 revision of this Act extended further rights to women). While the Matrimonial Causes Act of 1884 extended the rights of women with respect to divorce, the passing of more equal divorce laws would have to wait until the 1920s.

While Cobb could point out the unsuitability of linking women with idiots, the association proved pervasive, and was hardly confined to the realms of law and politics. In a letter of 2 June 1893, the author George Gissing noted that 'half the misery of life is due to the ignorance and childishness of women. The average woman pretty closely resembles, in all intellectual considerations, the average male *idiot* – I speak medically.' However, he continues:

> That state of affairs is traceable to the lack of education, in all senses of the word. Among our English emancipated women there is a majority of admirable persons; they have lost no single good quality of their sex, and have gained enormously on the intellectual (and even on the moral) side by the process of enlightenment, that is to say, of brain-development. (Quoted in Young 1961: 117)

But these women are in the minority, and a concern with what he calls 'the crass imbecility of the typical woman' (Young 1961: 117) is counter-pointed throughout his works with concerns over the poor education provided to women (Schmidt 2005), still an issue almost two centuries after the *Essay in Defence of the Female Sex* attacked the inequality of educational opportunities. That women have uneducated and thus under-developed brains is not merely unfortunate for them, depriving them of the pleasures of intellectual exercise; by the time Gissing is writing, 'imbecility' and 'feeble-mindedness' were read as degenerative traits that threatened the health of the entire nation. Gissing's notion of this degeneration (like that of many of his contemporaries) allows for both social causes (such as poor education and abominably unhealthy environments) and biological heredity.

The idea of the intellectually inferior woman was clearly well entrenched, even when this woman was admitted to have other qualities. In 1871, Charles Darwin observed in *The Descent of Man* that the 'chief distinction in the intellectual powers of the two sexes is shewn by man attaining to a higher eminence, in whatever he takes up, than woman can attain – whether requiring deep thought, reason or imagination, or merely the use of the senses and hands'. He then notes that this superiority suggests that 'the average standard of mental power in man must be above that of woman' (327), while conceding that 'Woman seems to differ from man in mental disposition, chiefly in her greater tenderness and less selfishness' (326). As for the source of these differences, Darwin hypothesizes that 'it is probable that sexual selection has played a very important part' (326), thus returning us to the satirical observations of Burney and Austen that opened this chapter: men prefer their women to be imbecilic, or, failing that, merely ignorant. Or, perhaps, as stereotypes also suggested, that less intelligent, more 'feeling' women were simply more sexually available.

Ellen Orford's 'erring Wish'

The associations of female sexuality and idiocy that permeate social and scientific writings are also prominent in literature, and nowhere more explicitly than in George Crabbe's *The Borough* (1810), a long poem depicting village life. In letter XX, 'The Poor of the Borough. Ellen Orford', Ellen is seduced by a wealthy, unfaithful lover and gives birth to a daughter who is both beautiful and an idiot. Ellen eventually marries another man, but he is worked upon by religious zealots and condemns the sins of his wife and stepdaughter until, finally despairing, he kills himself. With him Ellen has had five sons, but at her husband's suicide the Parish takes four of them, leaving her with her 'Idiot-Maid, and one unhealthy Boy' (line 258).

'Ellen Orford' is very much a poetic kin to sociological case history, and as such runs counter to the romantic aesthetic that, at least in hindsight, seems to have dominated this period (McGann 1985). The opening epigram of letter XX parodies the rhythm and imagery of gothic romances, and most of its first 120 lines dwell upon 'prouder Sorrows' – that is, those trials of heroes and heroines that form the improbable plots of gothic romances and poems, much as Wordsworth parodies German gothic narratives in 'The Idiot Boy'. However, Crabbe's response to this gothic romanticizing is considerably darker than Wordsworth's. 'Ellen Orford' is a story of poverty and sorrows without relief except that distant recompense promised by religious faith: what 'Ellen Orford knows' is that 'we should humbly take what Heav'n bestows' (lines 124–25). Letter XX ends with her saying 'my Mind looks cheerful to my End, / I love Mankind and call God my friend' (lines 336–37) – a stunning conclusion, given the relentless misery that has preceded this assertion.

As Jerome McGann (1985) observes, Crabbe wrote a 'poetry of … empirical research' (306) and the story of Ellen Orford 'vigorously forbids any solution that is grounded in the Romantic Imagination' (301). Rather than presenting a form of salvation through transcendent notions of art or nature, as Wordsworth might, Crabbe locates his characters in a social world where Ellen can conclude her story by reaffirming her faith in man and God, even though there is no apparent earthly reward for such faith. Crabbe's opposition to romantic transcendence did not endear him to many of his contemporaries. William Hazlitt judged Crabbe to be 'a repulsive writer', whose 'morbid feelings droop and cling to the earth, grovel where they should soar, and throw a dead weight on every aspiration of the soul after the good and beautiful' (quoted in Pollard 1972: 272); Francis Jeffrey's favourable review of *The Borough* in the April 1810 *Edinburgh Review* conceded that Crabbe's critics often charged the poet with 'frequently excit[ing] disgust, instead of pity or indignation, in the breasts of his readers' (Pollard 1972: 89). And, indeed, an unsigned review in the *Monthly Mirror* suggests that 'the misery of Ellen Orford … is worked up only to torture, without medicating our feelings…. A poet may be allowed to excite our pity for the pain of others, with a view to purge our own passions; but he should never put us to real pain ourselves, with no view besides' (Pollard 1972: 114–15). As a tangential observation on the aesthetic value of idiocy, it is interesting to see the similarities in these comments and those John Wilson and others applied to Wordsworth's 'The Idiot Boy', although in other respects Wordsworth and Crabbe employed vastly different approaches to their poetic renditions of rural life. Yet, like Wordsworth, Crabbe, in compiling his relentless social documentary, also constructs his struggling characters according to powerful and resilient stereotypes. Ellen Orford's daughter is a case in point.

The association of Ellen's daughter with transgressive sexual activity is difficult to miss. The daughter, who is born as the result of a premarital affair in which a gullible Ellen is seduced by a rake, dies in childbirth after having been raped. In *The Borough*, the daughter's condition is the expression, the punishment and the reminder of the mother's transgression. While Crabbe is careful to identify Ellen's faithless lover as the primary cause of her predicament, he also emphasizes the idiot girl's role as a symbolic reprimand which keeps Ellen from making the same mistake. As Ellen recounts her story:

Four Years were past; I might again have found
Some erring Wish, but for another Wound:
Lovely my Daughter grew, her Face was fair,
But no Expression ever brighten'd there;
I doubted long, and vainly strove to make
Some certain Meaning of the Words she spake;
But Meaning there was none, and I survey'd
With dread the Beauties of my Idiot-Maid.
(lines 210–17)

Ellen explicitly identifies her daughter's condition as a warning to caution her from taking another lover. For both the narrator and the reader, the idiot girl is linked with Ellen's sexual activity, her 'erring Wish'. At the same time, the daughter is so physically attractive that Ellen 'survey'd / With dread the Beauties of [her] Idiot-Maid', whose identity comes to be defined by and expressed through the twin characteristics of her idiocy and her sexuality.

The narrative then follows Ellen's marriage and the deaths of her husband and sons, but these sorrows are followed by yet another:

Alas! I needed such Reliance more:–
My Idiot-Girl, so simply gay before,
Now wept in pain; some Wretch had found a time,
Deprav'd and wicked, for that Coward-crime;
I had indeed my doubt, but I supprest
The thought that day and night disturbed my rest;
She and that sick-pale Brother – but why strive
To keep the Terrors of that time alive?

The Hour arriv'd, the new, th'undreaded Pain,
That came with violence and yet came in vain.
I saw her die: her Brother too is dead;
Nor own'd such Crime – what is it that I dread?
(lines 308–19)

Of course, she dreads admitting the possibility that her sickly son has raped or seduced her idiot daughter, who dies in childbirth – an accumulation of the sorrows and punishments following upon her 'erring Wish'. Ellen eventually becomes a schoolteacher in the village, and in her old age goes blind.

Throughout, the daughter remains morally innocent, and her association with sexuality is largely passive, as a woman more easily exploited than others. This passive, innocent 'idiot' sexuality points to an important distinction: whereas intellectual disability in men is defined as a lack, in women it is seen rather as a reduction to a fundamental characteristic – female sexuality. The danger faced by Ellen's daughter is increased by her beauty, which is not supplemented with those qualities that would make it valuable; it may serve to attract suitors, but it cannot gauge their worthiness or protect her from unscrupulous promises. Indeed, Ellen also proved unable to judge the honesty of her own seducer: the deficiencies of the idiot daughter are simply those of the mother writ large.

Women, idiocy and representation

Ellen's 'erring Wish' haunts representations of 'idiot' women, who are frequently portrayed as being sexually unstable, incapable of guarding virginity and rationing sexual favours solely to a deserving husband according to the conventional marriage contract. As such, they become a threat to idealized notions of 'woman' and, in addition, their sexual availability poses a danger to the ideal of a rational and well regulated masculinity. However, women identified as idiots also embody a paradox in that, like Ellen Orford's daughter, they are often represented as sexual innocents. The notion of the sexual innocence of the idiot maid seems related to the belief that the individual was in fact incapable of committing sin owing to an incapability for rational thought. As Erasmus's Stultitia observes of idiots and fools in *Praise of Folly* (1511), 'they can't even sin' (117); and in the legal context, Giles Jacob's *New Law Dictionary* (1729) observed early in the eighteenth century that 'such a one [i.e., an 'idiot' or 'natural fool'] ought not to be prosecuted for any Crime, because he wants Knowledge to distinguish Good from Evil'. But this state of innocence was tenuous at best, and in eighteenth-century Scotland punishment was considered an appropriate response to female promiscuity, regardless of apparent intellectual capacity (Mitchison and Leneman 1989).

The specific representations of 'idiot maids' in nineteenth-century literature also owe much to changing notions of 'the female', especially in Victorian culture. Mary Poovey has observed that as late as the mid-eighteenth century, 'woman was consistently represented as the site of willful sexuality and bodily appetite' (Poovey 1988: 9). Julia Douthwaite, writing on Marie-Angélique Memmie Leblanc, the 'wild girl of Champagne', who was captured in 1731, writes that 'images of woman's unruly appetite were widespread in eighteenth-century texts' and notes that the wild girl's sexuality, which was of prime interest to her contemporaries, reinforced the 'apprehension in political theory that female nature threatened the social order, and in medical discourse that it was the site of miasmic disorders' (Douthwaite 1997: 187).

But in much Victorian fiction, the innocent female idiot appears as a character who is notable for a resolute asexuality, or at the very best a repressed sexuality. Interestingly, this feature parallels many representations of able-minded Victorian heroines, whose relations are defined in a context that is increasingly domestic rather than erotic (Barickman *et al*. 1982: 8). Early Victorian heroines, like their fictional idiot girl counterparts, shed their erotic features in favour of domestic ones. Maggy in Dickens's *Little Dorrit* (1857) (discussed below), Ariel in Wilkie Collins's *The Law and the Lady* (1875) and Mrs Wragge in Collins's *No Name* (1862) are all notable for the vagueness of their shape and the obvious lack of femininity in their appearance, rendering them sexually non-threatening. Collins's narrator describes Ariel as having a 'round, fleshy, inexpressive face', with 'rayless and colourless eyes'. She has 'nothing but an old red flannel petticoat, and a broken comb in her frowsy flaxen hair, to tell us that she was a woman' (210). Similarly, Collins describes Mrs Wragge as having 'a large, smooth, white round face – like a moon – ... dimly irradiated by eyes of mild and faded blue, which looked straightforward into vacancy' (202). Interestingly, Collins's characters are also domestically incompetent, despite the fact that their ostensible responsibilities lie within that sphere (Collins's works are discussed in more detail in Chapter 10).

As might be expected, the repressed physicality of Victorian heroines resurfaces elsewhere. Maggy, of Dickens's novel *Little Dorrit*, first appears as 'an excited figure of a strange kind' crying out 'Little mother, little mother!' after Amy Dorrit, who in turn calls Maggy a 'clumsy child' when she bumps into Dorrit and Arthur Clennam and then falls down, spilling her basket of potatoes in the mud (140). Dorrit explains Maggy to Clennam: '"When Maggy was ten years old," said Little Dorrit, watching her face as she spoke, "she had a bad fever, sir, and she has never grown any older since"' (143). A ten-year-old who in reality has eight-and-twenty years, Maggy is intellectually like a child and physically like a large, bald, good-humoured baby, 'with large bones, large features, large feet and hands, large eyes and no hair' (142).

Dickens's portrayal of Maggy continues:

> Her large eyes were limpid and almost colourless; they seemed to be very little affected by light, and to stand unnaturally still. There was also that attentive listening expression in her face, which is seen in the faces of the blind; but she was not blind, having one tolerably serviceable eye. Her face was not exceedingly ugly, though it was only redeemed from being so by a smile; a good-humoured smile, and pleasant in itself, but

rendered pitiable by being constantly there. A great white cap, with a quantity of opaque frilling that was always flapping about, apologised for Maggy's baldness, and made it so very difficult for her old black bonnet to retain its place upon her head, that it held on around her neck like a gipsy's baby. A commission of haberdashers could alone have reported what the rest of her poor dress was made of; but it had a strong general resemblance to seaweed, with here and there a gigantic tea-leaf. Her shawl looked particularly like a tea-leaf after a long infusion. (142)

But while Maggy is comparable to a large infant (an impression furthered by the accompanying drawing by Halbot K. Browne), she also expresses the needs denied by Amy.

Maggy is presented as a large child, but Amy Dorrit is not so different. Her 'diminutive figure, small features, and slight spare dress, gave her the appearance of being much younger than she was. A woman, probably of not less than two-and-twenty, she might have been passed in the street for little more than half that age', Dickens tells us (93). Thus, despite her adulthood, Little Dorrit, like Maggy, is childlike – a circumstance frequently commented upon in the novel, which constantly plays with child/adult oppositions. 'Little' Amy Dorrit is also known as the Child of the Marshalsea, the debtors' prison where she is born, and Arthur Clennam tries (unsuccessfully) to check the impulse to call her a 'poor child' (137). When he agrees to call Amy by the name 'Little Dorrit', Maggy suggests 'Little Mother' as another alternative (210). The accumulation of designators for Amy Dorrit underscores the various (occasionally conflicting) elements of her identity – she is both child and mother, both sexually innocent and maternal. While Amy appears childlike, and is treated by the others with condescension, she is also responsible for their comfort and security. At one point, Amy and Maggy return too late to the Marshalsea, whose gates have been locked for the night, and must wander the streets of London until dawn. In order to avoid trouble from the 'brawling and prowling figures' they meet, Amy pretends to be Maggy's child – an inversion of their daytime relationship that reinforces the symbolic association between the two (217). While on their midnight travels, they meet a young woman who is preparing to jump to her death from London Bridge. The woman reprimands Maggy for having her child out at such a late hour, only to express shock when she realizes that Amy is an adult. At this point, the woman, 'with a strange, wild, cry, ... went away' (218). We are not told if she simply runs away or jumps from the bridge: both readings are possible. In either case, though, the passage points to the tenuous status of young women in the world portrayed by the novel, without actually broaching the reason for the young woman's despair. Dorrit and Maggy, both apparently children – one intellectually, the other in physical stature – are comparatively safe from threats of seduction and ruin, yet remain in need of protection; the young adult woman presents a possible outcome for women without the guidance that Amy offers Maggy, or the self-discipline with which Amy carries herself. She is the vulnerable woman, destroyed by her sexuality and her subsequent defencelessness in the face of worldly vanity and deceit. Little Dorrit's sexuality is also expressed through deflected maternal imagery, as when Dickens compares Amy to that 'classical heroine' who 'ministered to her father in prison as her mother had ministered to her', noting that Amy 'did much more, in comforting her father's wasted heart upon her innocent breast, and turning it into a fountain of love and fidelity that never ran dry or waned through all his years of famine' (273–74). This form of love is a combination of maternal care fused with a daughterly fidelity to the father, and rendered innocent and apparently asexual – despite the erotic and incestuous imagery evoked by that 'classical heroine' whose father survives by sucking at her breast.[2]

Maggy, like Amy, is resolutely asexual; however, as Elaine Showalter notes, Maggy is also a 'shadow' for Amy Dorrit, an expression of 'Little Dorrit's physical, aggressive and uninhibited self', who 'betrays the appetite and the competitiveness which Amy has struggled to extinguish' (Showalter 1979: 35). If Amy is marked by her stunted growth, a consequence of early malnourishment and, later, sacrificing her meals for her father, Maggy is characterized by her lust for food and her general policy of self-indulgence, constantly singing the praise of roast 'chicking'. She is a comic Victorian rendition of the woman with a powerful bodily appetite, a repository of desires and impulses controlled by more proper women. But while Maggy is an 'innocent', she is also physically unattractive, unlike Ellen Orford's beautiful 'Idiot-Maid' daughter. Instead, she is aggressively rendered childlike, as Dickens's description of her suggests, and her insatiable appetite for food remains an infantilizing substitution for sexual appetite. In this, Maggy also parallels Amy, who is physically infantilized by malnutrition and self-denial, and who recreates a father–child relationship with Clennam in the novel. That is not to say that sexual desire is absent. When Amy tells Maggy the story of the princess and the spinning-woman who hides her 'shadow', or her unexpressed love for another, the tale is an expression of Amy's desire for Clennam. When Maggy later recounts the story to Clennam, she garbles it so that its subtext is incomprehensible. But, of course, Maggy still recognizes the desire for what it is and, unlike Amy, directs the story to its proper recipient.

Maggy is present throughout Amy's most significant meetings with Clennam, not as her charge but rather as an embodied appetite, a character expressing that quality denied by Little Dorrit herself. Their relationship goes even further, though: Amy Dorrit is a 'holy fool' in her own right, and none of Dickens's novels is so explicitly concerned with the relation of idiocy, imbecility and folly to intelligence and cleverness. This aspect of the novel will be discussed further in Chapter 7.

Feminist revisions of the idiot girl

Not surprisingly, the image of female idiocy performs different functions in different contexts and, especially in the second half of the nineteenth century, feminist writers use notions of female idiocy to critique the inequities of Victorian society. For Gilbert and Gubar (1979), the image of *Jane Eyre*'s madwoman in the attic becomes a cipher of the Victorian woman writer: a repressed creative figure, one simultaneously threatening and desirable, who is an expression of the writer's shadow self. Images of the idiot partake of some of the same symbolism as those of the madwoman, but the idiot character is less a creative-destructive force struggling for expression than it is an oppressed and manipulated identity.

In Charlotte Brontë's 1853 novel *Villette*, the protagonist, Lucy Snowe, finds work as a teacher in a school in Belgium, much as Brontë herself had done. Lucy, an 'unobtrusive shadow', suffers from 'low spirits' that are exacerbated when she is left alone in the school during a vacation period, with only one student remaining in her care: Marie Broc, 'a poor deformed and imbecile pupil, a sort of crétin whom her stepmother in a distant province would not allow to return home' (218). Lucy's solitude weighs heavily:

> Even to look forward was not to hope: the dumb future spoke no comfort, offered no promise, gave no inducement to bear present evil in reliance on future good. A sorrowful indifference to existence often pressed on me – a despairing resignation to reach betimes the end of all things earthly. (218)

On the other hand, as Lucy narrates:

> the crétin did not seem unhappy. I did my best to feed her well and keep her warm, and she only asked food and sunshine, or when that lacked, fire. Her weak facilities approved of inertion: her brain, her eyes, her ears, her heart slept content; they could not wake to work, so lethargy was their paradise. (219)

But at the same time as being committed to inertia, Marie is also a source of trouble and a burdensome responsibility:

> The hapless creature had been at times a heavy charge: I could not take her out beyond the garden, and I could not leave her a minute alone; for her poor mind, like her body, was warped: its propensity was to evil. A vague bent to mischief, an aimless malevolence made constant vigilance indispensable. As she very rarely spoke, and would sit for hours together mopping and mowing and distorting her features with indescribable grimaces, it was more like being imprisoned with some strange tameless animal, than associating with a human being. (220)

Eventually, Marie's aunt, 'a kind old woman' (220), arrives to take the girl away for the remainder of the vacation. As Gilbert and Gubar (1979: 414) write, Marie is 'a nightmare version of [Lucy] herself – unwanted, lethargic, silent, warped in mind and body, slothful, indolent, and angry'; similarly, Showalter observes (1985: 71) that the Marie is 'an external-ized representation of Lucy's own primal but now stunted desires'.

Marie Broc serves as not only an expression of Lucy's sense of despair and frustration, but also as a gauge of her capacity as a woman. Shortly after her experience tending the 'crétin', Lucy is met acci-dentally in an art gallery by Dr Emmanuel Paul, a fellow teacher for whom she develops an ambiguous romantic regard. She has been gazing critically at a painting of Cleopatra, which she dismisses as 'an enormous piece of claptrap' (285). However, Paul is shocked at her lack of decorum – 'How dare you, a young person, sit coolly down, with the self-possession of a garçon, and look at that picture?', he exclaims (287) – and instead directs her to contemplate four dreary paintings showing the stages of a woman's life: young girlhood, marriage, mother-hood and widowhood. As their discussion turns to her vacation, she tells him of her misery in attending to Marie Broc, whom, she notes, 'was well known to M. Paul' and inevitably created 'antagonist im-pressions' for him. On the one hand, Paul would be irritated by Marie's 'personal appearance, repulsive manners, her often unmanageable dis-position', but on the other 'her misfortunes constituted a strong claim on his forbearance and compassion' (289). When Lucy admits that she has found caring for Marie too onerous, he reprimands her by asserting that 'Women who are worthy the name ought infinitely to surpass our coarse, fallible, self-indulgent sex, in the power to perform such duties' (290). That Lucy has failed to do so debases her claim to the mantle of womanhood. Thus, Marie becomes not only a projection of Lucy's own despair, but also a means of assessing her failure to meet the expectations of her imposed by those social conventions expressed by Paul's judgement, the four images of womanhood, and the painting of

Cleopatra. Somewhere between these absurd extremes, suggests Lucy (and Brontë), women must be able to find other options. When Lucy recounts her episode with Marie, she stresses the tedium and relentlessness of the responsibility of surveillance, which eventually wore her down and left her bed-ridden. Lucy's attempts to control Marie are displaced efforts to control her own wayward desires and compulsions, which result in her mental and physical collapse. Following the lead of Brontë's friend and biographer Elizabeth Gaskell, many readers have noted the relation between the author and her fictional creation Lucy. And, as Gaskell also notes, Brontë was certainly aware of the symbolic qualities of names, having vacillated between calling her protagonist Lucy Snowe and Lucy Frost, but stressing that 'a cold name she must have' (Gaskell 1857: 441). Interestingly, Brontë chose for her 'crétin' the very uncommon surname 'Broc', which shares the same initial letters as her own name – and because the final 'c' would be muted in French pronunciation, the aural similarity would be even closer.[3] Presumably, the choice of 'Broc', sounding like an abbreviated 'Brontë', is also not coincidental.

Victorian feminist writers also used female 'idiot' characters to embody sexual exploitation, or the threat of it. In George Eliot's 1862/63 novel *Romola*, the title character, the intelligent, beautiful and sensitive daughter of an elderly blind scholar, marries the unscrupulous egotist Tito Melema. One of Tito's betrayals involves Tessa, a 'simpleton' (27) whom Romola perceives as having 'a child's mind in a woman's body' (438). Tessa bears Tito's children while wrongly believing herself married to him, and her 'ignorant lovingness' (287) doubles Romola's trusting simplicity: the intellectual Romola is seduced and betrayed as surely as the childlike Tessa is. It is worth noting that as the heroine of a Victorian novel, Romola could not be allowed to suffer her double's fate without alienating the novel's readership. Instead, Eliot gives the illegitimate children to Tessa, who represents not so much Romola's sexually active and potentially disruptive side (as she would from a patriarchal viewpoint), but rather her exploitation. As in Elizabeth Gaskell's 'Half a Life-Time Ago' (discussed in Chapter 4), the novel ends with an all-female community that provides an alternative to masculine notions of the separate spheres (Mellor 1993). Romola eventually lives with Tessa and helps to raise her children, creating a matriarchal environment that rejects the self-interested philosophy embodied by Tito and his fellow Florentines.

Like *Romola*, Margaret Oliphant's *Salem Chapel* was published in 1863 and also presents an idiot character as an expression of an aspect of female sexuality. Alice Mildmay is described as 'a beautiful girl – more beautiful than anything mortal' (405), and her beauty combined with her idiocy makes her especially vulnerable. Alice is kidnapped by her father, a degenerate aristocrat, who, as one character suggests, plans to 'make a decoy of her, and sell her somehow, either to be married, or worse –' (253). While the reader is left to interpret the possible motives for the kidnapping, sexual exploitation is high on the list of likelihoods. The plot is complicated by the fact that the kidnapped Alice is being cared for by Susan Vincent, sister of the novel's protagonist Arthur Vincent, the dissenting minister of Salem Chapel. Susan has become engaged to a man who is later discovered to be Alice's unscrupulous father under an assumed name, who, in abducting his daughter, simultaneously deceives Susan. Thus, the kidnapping of Alice also threatens to become the desecration of the virginal Susan, the exploitation of the idiot woman mirroring threats to the sexual integrity and independence of women in general (*Salem Chapel* will be discussed further in Chapter 10). Oliphant returns to this problem in *Innocent: A Tale of Modern Life* (1873), where the title character is endangered by her lack of experience borne of educational deprivation. Interestingly, Barbara Thaden (1997) notes certain feral characteristics in the heroine Innocent: she has only one dress and is also very much a *tabula rasa*.

When portraying female 'idiots' or 'simpletons', Brontë, Eliot and Oliphant depart from the prevailing tendency to construct the idiot characters as expressions of unregulated female appetites (sexual, but also, as in the case of Maggy, gustatory). The female idiot is still associated with sexuality, but instead the emphasis shifts onto her vulnerability. She is no longer threatening and undisciplined, but rather oppressed and exploited.

Maternal impressions and daily guardians

The link between women and idiocy expressed itself in many forms, with one of the most powerful being the resilient theory of maternal impressions: that is, the belief that the imagination of the pregnant woman, fed by desires and fear, often expressed itself upon the body of the unborn infant, leaving everything from birthmarks to womanish boys to damaged intellects. These maternal impressions asserted themselves over the masculine intellect, so that 'the maternal imagination erased the legitimate father's image from his offspring and thus created a monster', as Marie-Hélène Huet (1993: 8) argues. Renaissance theories had deviant births resulting from the 'mother's desiring imagination' (Huet 1993: 37) and although this particular formulation of the maternal impressions theory was altered dramatically over the years, the idea that a mental or physical shock to the mother could influence the both the shape and the intellect of her child remained common currency. In Charles Dickens's 1853 article 'Idiots', he notes that idiocy 'would seem to be generally associated with mental suffering, fright or anxiety, or with a latent want of power, in the mother' (see Stone 1968: 499), and in his novel *Barnaby Rudge* maternal impressions are the primary cause given for Barnaby's idiocy as well as for his blood-smear birthmark (of course, these impressions are caused by the appearance of Barnaby's murderous father, and form part of the interplay of symbols in the novel).

As late as 1904, the American physician Martin Barr stresses the role of the mother's imagination in deviant births, noting that 'Paget cites a case of a girl with a thick harsh crop of brown hair on back and arms who bore a striking resemblance to a monkey. The mother had received a sudden shock caused by the monkey of an organ-grinder springing upon her back' (Barr 1904: 96). This he follows with two instances from his own patients. One was a boy 'born a veritable Esau, with a thick growth of reddish hair on back and chest', whose 'mother during pregnancy was chased by a cow'; in the other, 'a woman three months pregnant attending a circus was much frightened by a "freak" exhibited under the name of "What is it?" Her child – an idiot girl – born at full term, presented a most extraordinary Calibanish appearance' (96). Barr explains these anomalous births scientifically by noting that:

> researches into the effect of environment, of emotional life, and of what is termed 'use heredity' go far to prove that these influences prolonged and acting and reacting upon unstable nerve centers throughout the period of parturition, tend to create a condition in the mother so abnormal so as to constitute direct transmission by her to her offspring of weakness – mental, moral or physical – singly or associated, just in proportion to the character and to the pressure of the influence, and also to the character of any neurosis latent, but waiting 'on call' to arouse to what may be only temporary, and for that reason unrecognized, activity in the mother, and to become evident in the enfeebled constitution of the child. (97)

Despite the rational justification and professional terminology (such as 'neurosis latent, but waiting...'), Barr's explanation is little more than an instance of the traditional 'maternal impressions' theory keeping its firm grip on the scientific imagination.

The feminine association with idiocy is further deepened by the fact that, in most literary texts, the guardians or caretakers of 'idiots' are usually women, and most often mothers, who also risk being perceived as deviant. Walter Scott plays with this notion in his 1814 novel *Waverley* (discussed in Chapter 7), when Rose Bradwardine explains the family history of the 'fool' David Gellatley:

> Once upon a time there lived an old woman, called Janet Gellatley, who was suspected to be a witch, on the infallible grounds that she was very old, very ugly, very poor, and had two sons, one of whom was a poet, and the other a fool, which visitation, all the neighbourhood agreed, had come to her for the sin of witchcraft. (114)

Rose presents this tale ironically (and we cannot help but catch the literary joke of associating poetry with folly), while Scott himself footnotes the episode for a brief authorial intrusion, describing a real-world historical precedent and noting that 'The accounts of the trials for witchcraft form one of the most deplorable chapters in Scottish story' (*sic*) (115).

Scott resisted the easy association of 'idiot' son with 'idiot' (or at least deviant) mother, at least partially – Janet Gellatley does first appear, after all, as an 'old wretched-looking woman' (437). Other writers, though, were happy to point out such connections, especially in critiques of Wordsworth's 'The Idiot Boy'. As we have seen Chapter 2, Coleridge observes that 'the idiocy of the *boy* is so evenly balanced by the folly of the *mother*, as to present to the general reader rather a laughable burlesque on the blindness of anile dotage, than an analytic display of maternal affection in its ordinary workings', while Lord Byron, in 'English Bards and Scotch Reviewers', writes of 'simple Wordsworth' who 'tells the tale of Betty Foy, / The idiot mother of "an idiot boy"' (see Chapter 2, note 2). Such criticisms are not restricted to Wordsworth's contemporaries: the twentieth-century literary critic V. G. Kiernan (1989) condemns the 1798 *Lyrical Ballads* in general, dismissing what he calls its 'idiot style' and 'the two unbearable gossips of "The Idiot Boy"' (102), but praises Wordsworth's additions to the 1800 edition, noting that 'hardly anything of the "idiot" style survives' and that 'Wordsworth has got away from his helpless weaklings to real men, men like old Michael of the "stern and unbending mind"' (107).

Literature abounds with examples of female caregivers to 'idiot' characters. As we saw in Chapter 4, Watty Walkinshaw is cared for by both his mother and his wife in *The Entail*, and Grizy Walkinshaw is also portrayed as very much a fond old woman, although Betty Bodle is not; in Gaskell's 'Half a Life-Time Ago' Susan wails outside her cottage, much as her weak-minded brother Willie does; and in Robert Southey's poem 'The Idiot' (Chapter 2) the son dies shortly after the death of the mother (whose corpse he retrieves from her grave, incapable of understanding why she does not remain in her chair).

Dickens has Betsy Trotwood looking after Mr Dick in *David Copperfield*, in addition to Amy Dorrit caring for Maggy in *Little Dorrit*.

In social life, too, the care of 'idiots' fell often, although certainly not exclusively, to women. Most often, female caregivers had male supervisors, so that female support was provided within the framework of rational masculinity. In early modern London, female nurses were often hired by the parish as attendants for 'idiots' (Andrews 1996); Victor of Aveyron lives with Mme Guérin for many years after Itard abandons his pedagogical efforts and his state ceases to be of interest; he becomes simply another idiot boy living with his female guardian (Chapter 3). The physician Sir William Harvey, after gaining custody of his nephew William Fowke, consigned him to the care of a niece (Neugebauer 1989, 1996). And upon her capture, Marie-Angélique Memmie LeBlanc, the wild girl of Champagne, is moved into a convent – the exemplary female community within a patriarchal structure headed by a male (Douthwaite 1994/95). Given the weight of these precedents, it is not surprising that Duncan and Millard, writing in 1866, note that in idiot asylums 'the youngest children require a middle-aged woman as the responsible nurse, and her assistants had better be young' (83) – although as they grow older they require male attendants. In these instances, art and life are not so distinct.

The notion of 'idiocy' exists in a complex relation with ideas of the feminine. While, clearly, not all female 'idiot' characters are identical, there are striking consistencies in representation in both literary and non-literary writings. As this chapter and the previous one have stressed, in any representation of idiocy, gender is significant. In literary representations there is no such thing as an idiot beyond gender; even the amorphous Maggy in *Little Dorrit* is rendered meaningful as a woman through her doubling with Amy. At the same time, the historical record shows a markedly different set of concerns surrounding female idiocy than its male counterpart: while idiocy is identified as a lack in men, when it appears in women it is more often seen as a 'stripping down' to an essential element of female nature, a representational consistency that seems aligned with the common association of men with culture and women with nature (Jordanova 1989; Shuttleworth 1996). Thus, women with intellectual disabilities serve to validate the sovereignty of the masculine over the feminine in the binary opposition that structures understanding of gender over much of recorded Western history. This association of female sexuality with female idiocy will also play an important role later in the nineteenth century, especially as anxieties concerning genetic recapitulation and racial degeneration create debates around the regulation of the dangerously fertile wombs of women feared to be intellectually subnormal.

Notes

1 See the three-volume collection *The Woman Question*, by Helsinger *et al.* (1983) for a comprehensive treatment of the issues invoked by the term 'the woman question' in the middle of the nineteenth century.
2 Dickens refers to the story of Pero and her father Cimon, often known as 'Roman Charity'. The father, an old man incarcerated in a Roman prison, is saved from starvation by suckling at his daughter's breast. The scene was depicted by painters such as Peter Paul Rubens and Jean-Baptiste Greuze.
3 The French word *broc* denotes a pitcher, or other vessel with a handle.

CHAPTER 6

Holy fools, witty fools, depraved fools: folly, innocence and sin

'Doesn't the happiest group of people comprise those popularly called idiots, fools, nitwits, simpletons, all splendid names to my way of thinking?' demands Stultitia, the goddess Folly, midway through Eramus's *Moriae Encomium*, or *Praise of Folly* (Erasum 1511: 116). Not only are they freed from both the mundane and the spiritual crises facing others but also, as she observes, 'if they come still closer to dumb animals in their lack of reasoning power, the theologians tell us they can't even sin.... They are indeed under the protection of the gods, and most of all, under mine; and for this reason they are rightly held in honour by all' (117). Furthermore, she claims, 'They're the only ones who speak frankly and tell the truth', which has a 'genuine power to please if it manages not to give offence, but this is something the gods have granted only to fools' (118–19). Earlier, she argues that folly is distinguished by an attachment to emotion rather than to reason: 'this is what marks the wise man off from the fool: he is ruled by reason, and the fool by his emotions. That is why the Stoics segregate all passions from the wise man, as if they were diseases' (105–6). Not surprisingly, the boundaries dividing the wise from the foolish are porous and shift with context: 'Nothing is so foolish as mistimed wisdom, and nothing less sensible than misplaced sense' (105), Stultitia argues, while 'to play the fool in season is the height of reason' (186). Confounding notions of wisdom and folly, Erasmus's Stultitia/Folly stresses that her gifts are universal, noting that 'the entire world is my temple ... and I'll never lack priests to serve it as long as there are men' (141). The overriding implication of Stultitia's argument is that all humans, even (or especially) those proclaiming their own wisdom, are fools.

Erasmus's satirical articulation conflates folly as a concept with those people actually known as 'fooles, doltes, ideotes and paches' (in the phrase of Erasmus's first English translator, Sir Thomas Chaloner, who rendered the work as *The Praise of Folie* in 1549).[1] While Erasmus draws on both literary notions of the fool and the folk tradition expressed through the fool festivals that existed across medieval and early modern Europe (see Billington 1984; Davis 1975; Welsford 1935; Zjiderveld 1982), his innovations are profound; according to Walter Kaiser (1963), Erasmus was the first writer to allow Folly to speak, and thus to satirize scholastic philosophers and theologians, degenerate monks, religious hypocrites, obsequious courtiers and bloodthirsty military leaders. Not surprisingly, despite cloaking these criticisms in the garb of Folly, Erasmus's 'little book', as he styled it in his letter to Martin Dorp, still gave offence. While mock encomia were a staple of classical rhetoric before Erasmus took hold of the form, the *Moraie Encomium* transformed the genre: 'The simplest statement of his strategy – that Folly praises folly – propounds an insoluble dilemma of permanent uncertainty', writes Kaiser (1963: 36); that is, Erasmus has created a new and more complex form of irony than had hitherto existed. Erasmus 'exploited paradox to confound logic itself', suggests Marjorie O'Rourke Boyle, thus 'render[ing] dialectic itself ridiculous' (Boyle 1985: 187). Folly speaks truth, because she is a fool, and mistakes truth, also because she is a fool, and readers are left to their own devices to discern the wisdom implicit in this Erasmian formulation. Of course, this wisdom is evident only after one accepts the judgement of Folly: that all men are fools and had best recognize the fact.

Erasmus (and his readers) take pleasure in the reign of Stultitia, but often the image of the fool represents sin and depravity. The Biblical prototype for this understanding of folly can be found in the very similar opening lines of Psalms 14 and 53, with the latter reading: 'The fool hath said in his heart, There is no God. Corrupt are they, and have done abominable iniquity: there is none that doeth good.' These God-rejecting fools, who reappear in other passages of the King James Bible's Old Testament, are similar to those fools aboard Sebastian Brant's satirical *Narrenschiff*, or *The Ship of Fools*, published less than two decades before Erasmus's masterwork, in 1494, and translated into English in 1509 in two competing versions, by Alexander Barclay and Henry Watson. Brant's morally depraved fools are reprimanded in book 22 by Wisdom (shown as an angel in the accompanying woodcut): 'who hates me, suffers harsh damnation', claims Wisdom, making clear that much of the world is headed for eternal perdition. In English, Brant's work is itself preceded by Nigel Wireker's twelfth-century *Speculum Stultorum* and John Lydgate's fifteenth-century *Order of Fools*, among others, and it later influenced such works as John Skelton's *Boke of Three Fooles* and *The XXV Orders of Fools*, attributed to Timothy Granger around 1570. In the 112 distinct pieces, each with an accompanying woodcut, that comprise *The Ship of Fools*, Brant satirizes various sins and follies, from 'Greed', 'Adultery' and 'Insolence toward God' to 'Bad Marksmanship', 'the Lewdness of Women', 'Useless Wishing' and, in a self-mocking barb, 'Useless Books'. While Erasmus knew, admired and was influenced by Brant's satire, their tones are strikingly differ-ent (Zeydel 1962); Brant is, in Zeydel's words, 'the scholasticist at the threshold of humanism' (43), for whom 'what was bad, in his eyes, was not bad *per se*, but because the authorities – the Bible, the canoni-cal writers, the ancients – said so' (7). In addition, Brant's use of folly is metaphorical rather than representational: as Stainton (2004: 229) demonstrates, 'the "natural fool" never appears as a subject [on *The Ship of Fools*]. Although the image of folly is certainly one of depravity and moral degeneracy, it is also purely allegorical'. Erasmus's concept of folly, on the other hand, is at least part of the time embodied in natural fools, in what Stainton identifies as a metaphorical shift in 'natural folly' also evident in the paintings of Hieronymus Bosch (who created his own 'Ship of Fools') and Pieter Bruegel the Elder, as the condition is more frequently used to represent a sort of moral depravity or degeneracy. There is, Stainton (2004: 240) concludes, a 'transition from the more general medieval view of folly, an attribute of Everyman and represented by the fool in cap and bells, with no direct representation to intellectual or other disability, to a direct representa-tion and association between disability and depravity'.

   This relation of folly or idiocy to depravity and the devil has prece-dents in both literature and society. For instance, in 1383, the officials examining Emma de Beston for idiocy determined that her mental in-capacity resulted from 'the snares of evil spirits' (quoted in Neugebauer 1996: 31), although this does not seem to have been a common diag-nosis. Martin Luther is also attributed with associating idiocy with the devil; describing a 'twelve-year-old boy ... [who] devoured as much as four farmers did, and he did nothing else than eat and excrete', Luther suggested that the boy was 'simply a mass of flesh without a soul' and that 'the devil himself is in his soul'(quoted in Goodey and Stainton 2001: 230).[2] In another passage, Luther is quoted as saying that 'Changelings' are 'Divels' switched by Satan:

it oftentimes falleth out, that the Children of women in Childe-bed are changed, and Divels are laid in their stead; one of which more fowleth it self in the Excrements, then ten other Children do, so that the parents are much therewith disquieted, and the mothers in such sort are sucked out, that afterwards they are able to give such no more. Such Changelings (said Luther) are also Baptized, in regard that they cannot bee known in the first year; but are known onely by sucking the mothers drie. (Quoted in Goodey and Stainton 2004: 230)

As Goodey and Stainton note, the markers of these 'Changelings' do not concern the level of intellectual ability but rather excrement production and milk consumption; however, the use of the term 'Changeling' in the 1652 English translation hints at an association with 'natural folly', without dictating that association.[3]

As the examples of Brant, Erasmus and Luther demonstrate, folly in the late medieval and early modern period presents a vibrant, complex image, capable of signifying holiness and innocence as well as depravity. And from each of these positions folly also offers an analogical or symbolic tool for critiquing society and power. Further, folly forms a broad tent. It is not simply an intellectual or moral attribute but is also signified by a wide range of physical differences: hunched backs, dwarfishness, ugliness and so forth. Medieval and early modern folly is difference or deviance, but not exclusively, or even necessarily, an intellectual condition.

Holy folly and humanist folly

Erasmus's *Encomium* builds upon the long tradition of 'holy folly', usually traced back to the epistles of Paul to the Corinthians (Saward 1980). There, Paul poses the rhetorical question 'Hath not God made foolish the wisdom of this world?' (1 Cor 1: 20) to argue that 'the foolishness of God is wiser than men; and the weakness of God is stronger than men' (1 Cor 1: 25); further, 'God hath chosen the foolish things of the world to confound the wise' (1 Cor 1: 27). 'Let no man deceive himself', Paul continues. 'If any man among you seemeth to be wise in this world, let him become a fool, that he may be wise' (1 Cor 3: 18). But Paul's crucial passage, at least in terms of the concept of the holy fool, comes later in his first letter to the Corinthians, when he writes that 'God hath set forth us the apostles last, as it were appointed to death: for we are made a spectacle of unto the world, and to angels, and to men. We are fools for Christ's sake, but ye are wise in Christ; we are weak, but ye are strong; ye are honourable, but we are despised' (1 Cor 4: 9–10). The apostles, in their state of poverty and persecution, commit the foolish act of renouncing worldly power and wealth in preaching the word of Christ, but in so doing reveal something greater: their 'wisdom of the cross' expresses a faith in God that promises ultimate redemption. When the wisdom of God confronts the wisdom of the world, it appears as folly; thus, if Christians follow the wisdom of God, they will appear as fools according to the wisdom of the world (Saward 1980). This judgement seems to have befallen Paul, who, likely responding to accusations of his own folly, ironically reiterates his fool status in his second letter to the Corinthians:

> Let no man think me a fool; if otherwise, yet as a fool receive me, that I may boast myself a little. That which I speak, I speak it not after the Lord, but as it were foolishly, in this confidence of boasting. Seeing that many glory after the flesh, I will glory also. For ye suffer fools gladly, seeing ye yourselves are wise. (2 Cor 11: 16–19)

Paul employs folly to license his impertinence in the cause of the Lord and at the same time avoid accusations of spiritual pride:

> I speak as concerning reproach, as though we had been weak. Howbeit, whereinsoever any is bold, (I speak foolishly,) I am bold also. Are they Hebrews? so am I. Are they Israelites? so am I. Are they the seed of Abraham? so am I. Are they ministers of Christ? (I speak as a fool) I am more. (2 Cor 11: 21–23)

Paul's folly becomes here the condition that qualifies him to speak freely, and thus to denounce the sins of the people of Corinth. It also provides a model that will later be used to license medieval fools to speak without reprisal.[4]

Erasmus would have experienced more immediate influences than Paul during his student years at Deventer between 1475 and 1484 (Huizinga 1952), where he absorbed the local strain of anti-scholastic humanism; the school also produced two other fifteenth-century humanist thinkers whose work valued Christian folly as a path to redemption, in Thomas à Kempis and Nicholas de Cusa (Billington 1984). De Cusa's *Idiota* (1450) – something of an abstract of or primer to his more complex *Doctor of Ignorance* (1440) – expounds the fundamental wisdom of the idiot; while his use of the term draws primarily on the classical sense of an untutored or ignorant private man, the term is ambiguous and veers towards something akin to the satirical or truth-speaking fool (Billington 1984). The first English translation, by John Everard in 1650, renders de Cusa's Latin *idiota* – an ignorant or unlettered man – as 'idiot', even though the primary English sense of this word was as a legal definition of a person unable to manage his own affairs (see Chapter 4); as Stainton (2004: 228) notes, 'While Everard may not be intending to evoke this legal usage, it is interesting that he sees no need to adopt some other term, thus suggesting a conflation of the two meanings'. The book's opening exchange recalls the Pauline notion of Christian folly, as the Idiot reprimands the Orator:

> I marvel at thy pride, that being wearied with continuall reading of innumerable bookes, thou are not yet led to humility: without doubt this proceeds from nothing else, but that the knowledge of this world, (wherein thou thinkest thou excellest all other) is a certaine foolishnesse before God, and thereupon puffes men up, whereas true knowledge humbles them. (1–2)

The Orator then wonders at the 'presumption' of this 'poore Idiot & utterly ignorant' (2), and the rest of de Cusa's work develops the wisdom of this 'poore Idiot' in a series of exchanges with the Orator and, later, a Philosopher.

The epitome of Christian folly is, of course, Christ himself, whose crucifixion becomes simultaneously the ultimate act of human foolishness and the embodiment of divine wisdom (Saward 1980). As Stultitia concludes Erasmus's *Encomium*, 'All mortals all fools, even the pious. Christ too, though he is the wisdom of the Father, was made something of a fool himself in order to help the folly of mankind, when he assumed the nature of man and was seen in man's form' (198–99). Ultimately, she argues, 'the Christian religion has a kind of kinship with folly in some form, though it has none at all with wisdom' (201); it is a religion of emotion, of the Passion of Christ, and thus of folly (Boyle 1985). Indeed, building upon the Pauline notion of 'holy folly', some medieval morality plays – notably the Wakefield *Coliphizacio* or *Buffeting* of Christ, and the York cycle's *Lytsteres* and *Tyllemakers* – draw upon popular 'fool games' to form the dramatic basis of the trial and torture of Christ, who fills the place of the seasonal yuletide fool; these plays thus ironically reference the Christmas celebrations and the success of Christianity, which 'overthrows worldly power represented by the torturers' (Billington 1984: 18).

Folly becomes 'holy' at the same time as it becomes a subversive strategy for social commentary, with Paul's self-presentation as a 'fool for Christ's sake' (1 Cor 4: 9–10). Thus, the legal and moral innocence of people identified as fools becomes a means for social critique. In late medieval and early modern Europe, including England, the fool enjoyed preeminent status as a 'symbolic actor' (Kaiser 1963: 3) and popular festivals employed the image of the 'natural fool' in parodies that both subverted and affirmed ecclesiastic authority, thus providing Erasmus with a convenient model for his own critique of knowledge and ethics in his *Praise of Folly*. Later, in the seventeenth century, the literary fool yields the stage to other vehicles for satire, but never completely vanishes, and the notion of a divinely inspired folly which unwittingly reveals truths continues to resonate, as does the parallel notion of the fool as a sort of agent of both divine and demonic chaos. Thus, the image of the fool as an exemplar of the world – or at least the greater part of it – forms a powerful and venerable literary conceit. From Erasmus, More and later Elizabethan and Jacobean writers like Shakespeare, Middleton and Armin, into nineteenth century works by the likes of Scott, Dickens and Eliot, and to the present day, the holy fool, the innocent natural, and the depraved sinner fool have occupied front-line positions in the literary armoury of satirists and social critics. The image of the fool evoked awe and fear, even if the 'fool' in person did not.

As this overview suggests, the early modern fool encompasses the innocent, the trickster and the demon, associations still evident in early- and mid-nineteenth-century literature, from the idiosyncrasies of David Gellatley in *Waverley*, to the pervasive 'idiocy' imagery of *Little Dorrit* and the fateful persistence of Jacob in George Eliot's *Brother Jacob* (all to be discussed in the next chapter). This chapter examines how these notions of folly are expressed in the early modern period, with an emphasis on the social and political parameters that help give shape to the image of the fool.

Festive fools and the legitimacy of folly

The phenomenon of fool festivals and the social function of the medieval and early modern fool have been ably explored by a number of historians and literary critics,[5] who have described how the fool works as a subversive critic (intentional or not) of the world he inhabits and a conservative element ultimately reinforcing the values of this world. In the late medieval and early modern period, 'folly' is also an activity, usually seasonal and connected to holy days, performed as part of celebrations of misrule. Fool festivals were especially vigorous in France, although evidence shows they also flourished in England, Germany and other parts of Europe (Bakhtin 1984; Billington 1984; Davis 1975; Welsford 1935). The central image of the festival was the natural fool, even if such an individual was not personally involved. Rather, the festival 'fool' was, according to his detractors, a knavish man, although also often a member of the minor clergy. As Bakhtin (1984: 74–75) writes, 'Nearly all the rituals of the feast of fools are a grotesque degradation of various church rituals and symbols and their transfer to the material bodily level: gluttony and drunken orgies on the altar table, indecent gestures, disrobing'. The folly of these knavish fools and their claims to the privileges of that state are inspired by natural fools or idiots and the theological claims that as innocents they were incapable of committing sin – or, more secularly, of being found legally responsible for crimes they may have committed. As one French apologist, associated with the Paris School of Theology, wrote in 1444, the fool festivals were necessary

> so that foolishness, which is our second nature and seems to be inherent in man, might spend itself at least once a year. Wine barrels burst if from time to time we do not open them and let in some air. All of us men are barrels poorly put together, which should burst from the wine of wisdom, if this wine remains in a state of constant fermentation of piousness and fear of God. We must give it air in order not to let it spoil. This is why we permit folly on certain days so that we may later return with greater zeal to the service of God. (Quoted in Bakhtin 1984: 75)

Not all authorities were as understanding, and ecclesiastical powers continually struggled, albeit with little success, to repress the festivals; the first recorded prohibition was issued by the Council of Toledo in the first half of the seventh century, while the final judicial prohibition in France, of the Parliament of Dijon in 1552, came more that 900 years later (Bakhtin 1984). Welsford (1935: 203) cites what must have been a reluctant compromise from the Chapter of Sens in 1444, whose 'instructions for reform of the Feast laid down the regulation that "not more than three buckets of water at most must be poured over the precentor stultorum at Vespers"'; indeed, most evidence and information about these festivals comes from records of attempts to suppress or control them. In England, holy-day festivities involved groups of people – primarily young men – who played 'fool games', sang and generally caroused throughout the evening, in the field or on the church grounds; official restraints were imposed upon these activities in 1536 (Billington 1984). The individuals involved in such (usually rural) fool games took as their mascot the 'natural' fool, and in doing so imposed upon him the role of popular critic-satirist.

Up into the seventeenth century, fools were also frequent dwellers within the confines of grand houses and courts. These fools could be either 'natural' or 'artificial', the latter adopting and adapting the persona of the former. According to Welsford (1935: 195), the court fool, as a political or social critic, fits a world order that rests on divine authority, 'human inadequacy, and efficacious ritual'; the fool can survive only in a society with sacraments. In order to be a fool, one must run counter to an established order, one that is not recognized as arbitrary and secular.

Zijderveld (1982) also hypothesizes that one of the functions of the licensed court fool was to exhibit the monarch's power. The fool could speak without fear of abuse – at least in theory – whereas courtier-knights were compelled to subordinate themselves and their wills to the acknowledged centre of authority. The monarch's or lord's indulgence raises the fool above the other courtiers as a constant reminder of both the courtier's worth and the ruler's power, an instance of the highly theatrical, testostrionic expression of power in this period.

The relation between apparently natural fools and those who, as 'artificial' fools, assumed the privileges of folly was fraught with theological and philosophical tension. According to much medieval theology, while the innocent natural fool is a part of God's creation, the artificial fool is a knave performing the devil's work and thus condemned to the eternal flames of hell; but it was not always easy to tell them apart. In the prologue of the fourteenth-century dream-vision poem *Piers Plowman*, William Langland distinguishes the moral state of artificial fools, in the C-text version condemning as agents of the devil those who

> Fyndeth out foule fantasyes and foles hem maketh
> And [han] wytt at wille to worche yf thei wolde.
> [Devise false tales and make themselves fools
> But have wit and strength to work if they wished].[6]

As Billington (1984) notes, the B-text version of *Piers Plowman* is especially vigorous in its condemnation of these feigned fools:

> But thoo that feynen hem foolis, and with faityng libbeth
> Ayein the lawe of oure lord, and lyen on hemselue,
> Spitten and spuen and speke foule wordes,
> Drynken and dreuelen and do men for to gape,
> Likne men and lye on hem that leneth him no [g]iftes
> Thei konne na moore mynstralcie ne Musik men to glade
> Than Munde the Millere of *Multa fecit dues*.
> (vol. X, lines 39–45)

> [But those that pose as fools and perform frauds
> Against the laws of our lord, and lie about themselves
> Spitting and spewing and speaking foul words
> Drinking and drooling and making men gape
> Mocking and slandering those who give them no gifts
> They can no more make music to please men
> Than Munde the Miller can speak Latin]

The A-text version of *Piers Ploughman*, on the other hand, makes the clearest distinctions between the devil's lack of power against the innocence of 'yonge fauntes [and] folis, with hem failith Inwyt' (vol. X, line 58) – that is, 'children and fools, and those whose wit fails' – from his authority over those 'sottis thou might se, that sitten at the nale' (vol. X, line 60), or those 'drunks you might see in the ale-house':

> Thei helde ale in here hed til Inwyt be drenchit,
> And ben braynwood as bestis so herre blood wexith.
> Thane hath the pouk power, sire *princeps huius mundi*,
> Over suche maner of men might in herre soulis.
> Ac in fauntis ne in folis the [fend] hath no might
> For no werk that thei werche, wykkide other ellis.
> (vol. X, lines 60–65)

> [They hold ale in their head until their wit is drowned
> And become like beasts as their blood waxes.
> Then the devil, the ruler in their world, has power
> Over the souls of such men.
> But with children and fools the fiend has no power
> Over any acts they perform, which might otherwise be wicked]

A similar distinction is made by John Heywood in his court interlude *A Play of Wytty and Wyttles* (c. 1530), which examines the relationship between and relative worth of folly and rationality, in both secular and theological terms. According to Heywood's disputation, the rational man goes to Heaven as a result of exercising his will wisely and properly; he must make choices, perform deeds, act and think faithfully. The natural fool, on the other hand, goes to heaven because of what he is. His soul's state of being is constant, forever like that of an infant child; it cannot be altered, as he is incapable of rational choice. As for artificial fools, Heywood, following Langland, condemns them to perdition, but much of the vigour of his damnation may have arisen from the fact that, as an entertainer in the court of Henry VIII, he was also a rival of the renowned 'artificial' fool Will Somers.

Not everyone saw a rigid boundary between natural and artificial folly. Erasmus blends the two freely, as does his friend Thomas More, to whom Erasmus had dedicated *Praise of Folly*. In *Utopia* (1516), More recognizes a difference between natural and artificial folly, but then conflates the two categories:

> There chanced to stand by a certain jesting parasite or scoffer, who would seem to resemble and counterfeit the fool. But he did in such wise counterfeit, that he was almost the very same indeed that he laboured to represent: he so studied with words and sayings brought forth so out of time and place to make sport and move laughter, that he himself was oftener laughed at than his jests were. Yet the foolish fellow brought out now and then such indifferent and reasonable stuff, that he made the proverb true, which saith, 'he that shooteth oft, at the last shall hit the mark'. (More 1516: 31)

More's rhetorical turn here is in part a strategy to mock practitioners of artificial folly, but at the same time a means of asserting that folly is, after all, the lot of man.[7] Thus, the 'counterfeit' fool transforms, in the next sentence, into a truly 'foolish fellow'.

Robert Armin and the fool's profession

'Madmen and fools are a staple commodity', observed Isabella, wife of the mad-house doctor Alibius in Thomas Middleton and William Rowley's 1622 play *The Changeling*. The lines apply well to the dramatis personae of the Elizabethan and Jacobean stage (Gentili 1988; Reed 1952), but also point to a shift that was taking place in representations of folly over the fifteenth and sixteenth centuries. Where once folly was perceived as a quality of 'everyman', it becomes increasingly identified with particular individuals, especially those known as natural fools, and frequently with depravity (Stainton 2004). At the same time, the role of 'fool' is becoming professionalized and commodified, as court jesters and actors assert their status as witty fools and public entertainers (Johnson 2003; Zijderveld 1982). These tendencies are not incompatible, and both are clearly evident in the writings of English actor, author and playwright Robert Armin, who wrote about professional 'natural' fools and blurred boundaries further by performing the roles of both John of the Hospital, based on a recognized London 'natural fool', and the 'witty fool' Tutch in his play *The Two Maids of More-Clacke* (1609). In addition, his jest book *Foole Upon Foole* (1600) documents tales of 'six sortes of sottes' (according to its subtitle), all reputedly based on real individuals.

Armin's reputation today rests upon his membership with the Lord Chamberlain's Men, and later the King's Men, where Shakespeare's later fool characters, notably Feste, Touchstone, Lear's fool and perhaps even Caliban, were written for his particular talents (Felver 1961; Hotson 1952; Wiles 1987). As a professional clown, he also enjoyed renown as the heir to the famed Elizabethan clown Richard Tarlton; according to a story recounted in the anonymous *Tarlton's Jests* (1613), Tarlton witnessed a witty sally launched by Armin, then a goldsmith's apprentice, against a debtor, and duly impressed, made him his 'adopted sonne' (17), effectively apprenticing the young Armin to refine his comic talents. The model of master and apprentice here follows those of the established professions – Armin was, after all, already an apprentice goldsmith – and reflects the growing professionalization of the fool in the late sixteenth century.

Armin was 'as well attuned to Renaissance notions of folly as to the English folk tradition', writes David Wiles (1987: 136), and his various depictions of natural fools enable a number of possible readings: the fool as Christian innocent; the fool as moral degenerate; the fool as vehicle of satire and misrule; the fool as rustic clown; the fool as professional entertainer. His jest book *Foole Upon Foole* appeared in two editions, in 1600 and again in 1605, building upon his fame as a comic performer, and a much-reworked 1608 issue of the book appeared as *A Nest of Ninnies*. This publication also contains new material in the form of a dialogue between a 'Cinnick' philosopher and the World, forming the book's introduction and conclusion and providing commentary between the six segments. *A Nest of Ninnies* develops a clear tension between the tales as entertainments and instructive moral tales warning readers against degeneracy. While Armin's literary 'fools' are based explicitly on real-life counterparts, these fool characters also assume a status as universal exemplars, less vehicles of satire than embodiments of the broad human comedy. However, Armin's fools are still agents of misrule in a traditional sense, provoking laughter, inflicting (and suffering) pain, dealing out (and receiving) humiliation and generally poking at the vanities and hypocrisies of power and authority.

Armin's first edition of *Foole Upon Foole* presents 'six sortes of sottes' (including John of the Hospital, who also appears in his play *The Two Maids of More-Clacke*, and Henry VIII's court fool Will Somers) and all are natural idiots, according to the writer. The book's originality is striking, as, while most jest books simply recycled old material, most of Armin's tales appear for the first time in his works (Lippincott 1979); further, he implies that his tales are true, and links his fools to specific places and people, to claim a degree of historical verisimilitude. Whether or not he is a reliable reporter of actual deeds performed by known fools is not as relevant as his claim to be doing so, and the fact that people were (and still are, judging from what few critical responses exist) willing to believe that there was at least a kernel of truth to the tales. History has generally accepted that Will Somers was an artificial fool (Ettin 1998), and the same may be true of at least some of Armin's alleged 'naturals', but, again, the claim that the individuals portrayed are 'idiots' (a term Armin applies to most of his characters, although not to Somers) is as significant as any faithfulness to biographical reality. The fact that Will Somers is a 'natural' fool but not an 'idiot' should prompt us to ask about Armin's classifications: does he see these as distinct categories? Is the assessment of Somers as an 'artificial' fool a retrospective reading based on Somers' reputation as a 'witty' fool?

Armin leavens this apparent historical truth with a sort of moral truth as well. The foolish protagonists are treated with an amused condescension and, according to Felver, illustrate 'the humane concern of Robert Armin for his fellow men' (Felver 1961: 80). Their follies parody the competitive world of the courtier, such as when Jack Oates and Will Somers (in separate tales) confront rival fools; they poke fun at the delusions of folly, as in the tale of Jemy Camber, the 'fat fool', who outraced a footman over forty miles (or so he thought), and that of Lean Leonard, who, hearing how his master's hawk was a fine bird, ate it and afterwards, feeling ill, insisted he had consumed better; they illustrate the affections of folly, such as Jack Miller's delight at meeting Grumball and John of the Hospital tolling the bell upon the death of his nurse's chicken; and generally they recount pranks from the absurd to the malicious. Throughout, Armin maintains a sympathetic tone, and in his writings on John of the Hospital, both in *Foole Upon Foole* and in the Preface to *The Two Maids of More-Clacke*, he expresses what seems to be a genuine affection for the character, and perhaps even for the individual upon whom his character was based.

In one tale about Jack Miller, 'a cleane foole', the Lord Chandos's Men, a group of travelling players, visit Jack's home town of Esom in Worcestershire. Jack is especially enthralled by the troop's clown, 'whom he would embrace with a joyfull spirit, and call him grumball (for so he [i.e., the clown] called himself in Gentlemens houses, where he would imitate playes doing all himselfe, King, Clowne, Gentlemen and all)' (112). Jack, the village fool, swears that 'he would goe all the world over with Grumball' and so, to save the townspeople from losing a favourite character, the innkeeper locks him in a back room. But from a window Jack sees the players departing and he escapes after them, crossing over the newly frozen Severn River in his pursuit. At this point, Armin slips into an uncharacteristic first-person narration. As Jack runs across the ice, he writes,

> my heart aked to see it, and my earres heard the ize cracke al the way: when he came unto me, I was amazed, and tooke up a brickbat (which lay there by) and threwe it, which no sooner fell upon the Ize but it burst: was not this strange that a foole of thirty years was borne of that Ize which would not endure the fall of a brickbat? yes it was wonderfull me thought: but every one rated him for the deed, telling him it was daungerous: he considered his fault, and knowing faults should be punished, he entreated Grumball the clowne whom he so deerely loved to whip him with rosemary, for that he thought would not smart.... (113–14)

In this passage, Grumball and the narrator seem to become one person, and many commentators – including Enid Welsford (1935) and Nora Johnson (2003), as well as *Foole Upon Foole* editors Lippincott (1979) and, earlier, Collier (1842) – suspect that Armin may have been Grumball. Jack Miller's desire to emulate Grumball, his belief that this artificial fool, Grumball/Armin, is the epitome of his class, reverses the traditional vector of influence: instead of the 'artificial' fool modelling himself on the 'natural', the 'natural' fool, recognizing his social role, looks to the theatre entertainer as his exemplar. Armin's tale suggests that, by the end of the sixteenth century, 'natural idiocy' and 'artificial folly' are engaged in a deep exchange of meaning and value. As Johnson (2003: 37) observes, 'Armin acquires cultural power by becoming more real as a fool than the fool himself is, more Grumball than Grumball'. The professionalization of folly threatens to displace the Erasmian notion of universal folly: instead of the fool representing everyman, the world is increasingly divided into natural idiots, artificial fools and the observers – those townspeople who do not want to lose their fool, and the audiences who enjoy Grumball.

But the idea of universal folly does not disappear at this point, not even from Armin, who substantially revised *Foole Upon Foole* when turning it into *A Nest of Ninnies*, primarily by adding a framing and unifying device. Whereas the first two versions of *Foole Upon Foole* present six series of sketches, which are independent of one another apart from sharing the common theme of folly, *A Nest of Ninnies* unites these tales by following each set with moral interpretations. These interpretations are provided by a new 'Philosopher' character, linked to the other six 'sottes' through his nickname 'Sotto, as one besotted, a grumbling sir' (Armin 1608: 53); the Philosopher is also termed 'Hodge' – according to Lippincott's notes to his edition, a 'generic name for an English rustic' (54) – 'the Cinnick' and 'the currish Critick', and is described as 'one that was wise enough, and fond enough, and solde all for a glasse prospective, because he would wisely see into all men but himself' (53). That the Philosopher is both wise and fond, a foolish sage who has spent all his money for a crystal ball that will give him knowledge of other men's flaws but not his own, recalls those philosophers and theologians mocked by Erasmus's Stultitia. He is joined by his student for the day, the World, who has stumbled into his cell after awakening 'wanton sick, as one surfeiting on sinne (in morning pleasures, noone banquets, after riots, night moriscoes, midnights modicoms, and abundance of trash trickt all up to turbulent revellings)' (51–52); in short, the World is exhausted and hung over from her enthusiastic indulgence in frivolities. While the World sits 'curling her locks with her fingers, and anone scratching her braine with her itching pin' (54), the Philosopher promises to reveal the offspring of her excesses:

See world in whose bosome ever hath abundance beene powred, what thy imps of impietie bee, for as they are all for the most part, as these which I will present to thee in my glasse prospective, mark them well, and see what thou breedst in thy wantonesse, sixe Children like thee, not the Father that begat them, where were they nursed, in folly? fed with the flottin milke of nicetie and wantonnesse, curdled in thy wombe of water and bloud, unseasoned, because thy mother bearing temper was ever untrue, farre from the rellish of right breede, and it is hard that the taste of one Apple should distaste the whole lumpe of this defused Chaios, but marke me and my glasse, see into some (and in them thy selfe) whom I have discride, or describde these sixe parts of folly in thee, thou shalt see them as cleare as day, how mistie thy clouds be, and what rancknesse rains from them. (Armin 1608: 54–55)

The Philosopher, then, promises to show the World six instances of folly that inhabit her, that she may cleanse herself. The text then presents the same six sets of tales it had in the previous two editions, except that after each set the 'Cinnick' draws moral lessons. These explications can strike the reader as tedious, and Lippincott hypothesizes that the Cinnick is added in order to give the text a new name and reprint it as a new work; however, we should not lose sight of the important fact that, as the tales continue, the World finds the Philosopher's lessons tedious as well. After the Philosopher's exegesis of the first set of tales (of Jack Oates), she 'humde and haide, said shee was not pleased that such lived and did promise some amendment, but desired to see further' (73–74); after the second set, the Philosopher's 'moral motion gave the world such a buffet that she skringde her face as though shee were pincht home' (91). But by the third set of tales she is laughing at the jests, although the Philosopher's moral interpretations leave her 'dimpling her chin with mere modestie as it were, throwing off variety of squeamish nicetie', and she humours the Philosopher by admitting 'sooth thou saist true, there are such tricks in mee, but I know not how to mende, I am willing but flesh is weake, preethee be more sparing, carpe but confound not, hope the best amendment may come' (105). After hearing the fourth set of tales, the World decrees them to present 'meere mirth without mischiefe and I allow of it' (117), although Sotto insists upon imposing further moral interpretations; as Armin writes, the World 'likte not this well, but bit the lip againe' (119). The tale of Will Somers opens with the observation that the World 'was in love with this merry fool, and said he was fit for the time indeede, therefore deserved to be well regarded' (120); when the Cinnick moralizes over these tales, she tries to leave, but he restrains her. Finally, after the sixth set of tales, she actively disputes the Cinnick's interpretation. Her response to the tales of John of the Hospital is the rather Morian (or Erasmian) 'surely ... this pleases well to see one so naturally silly to be simply subtill' (146), but despite this the Philosopher goes on to delineate the moral vices represented by John's adventures. The World, contesting these readings, goes on the attack, condemning those who lie in wait to 'cosin simplycitie' (147). Finally, Armin describes the World and the Philosopher in battle:

> Well the World so buffeted the Cinnicke at his owne weapon, that he playes with her as weake fencers, that carries flesh up and down for others to dresse. Such was the Cinnick, unskilful in quips and worldly flaunts, rather to play with short rods and give venies till all smart againe, not in the braines, as the world did, but in the buttocks as such doe, having their Hoses displaid, making them expert till they cry it up in the top of question.
>
> Our sullen Cinnick sets by his glasse in mallice, knits a betill brow till the roome grew darke againe, which the wanton World seeing flings out of his Cell like a girle at barly breake,[8] leaving the last couple in hell, away she gads and never lookes behind her. A whirlewinde sayes the Cinnick goe after, is this all my thanks, the old payment still, doth the world still reward mortality thus, is vertue thus bed ridden, can shee not helpe her selfe? and lookes up to heaven as hee should say some power assist. But there hee sat fretting in his owne grease, and for ought I know no body came to help him. (148–49)

A Nest of Ninnies presents a problem: how are we to understand the Philosopher? Lippincott evidently assumes that he is to be deferred to as the centre of authority in the text, and yet this interpretation hardly seems consistent with Armin's descriptions of him, isolated from humanity and exalting most in his contempt for others, especially when contrasted with the generosity and vivacity of the World. Johnson (2003: 41) suggests that the additions, in transforming the sketches into a 'series of morally beneficial tales', render the text more 'literary' than a simple jest book, thus upgrading Armin's status as an author. Certainly, the addition of the Philosopher renders the text more complex by adding an additional layer of interpretation while at the same time self-reflexively reinterpreting these interpretations. Armin's literary ambitions, though, are primarily parodic: the Philosopher denouncing the World's folly bears a close, albeit inverted, relationship to the preaching narrator of Brant's *The Ship of Fools*, much reprinted in the sixteenth century (Zeydel 1962). Even the title, *A Nest of Ninnies*, parodies *The Ship of Fools*. The distinction, of course, is that while Brant's folly-denouncing narrator is valorized as the centre of interpretative authority in *The Ship of Fools*, the Philosopher enjoys no such status in *A Nest of Ninnies*. Armin's fools may resemble Brant's degenerate and bestial beings, but they also express a worldly vitality. When the fools' jests are set against the moral certitude and restrictive authority of the Philosopher's judgement, the World sides with folly; the text asserts sympathy for the World and her fools, and even Heaven remains indifferent to the Philosopher's plight. Armin's fools are both innocent and depraved 'trickster' characters, at once the benign objects of fun, the destabilizing critics of the vanities and hypocrisies of the world's powerful, and the signs of a divine order that, while unreadable, is ultimately benevolent. But, increasingly, the power of that image relies upon the wit that composes it – that is, upon the skill of the professional clown/ author to render a convincing, compelling image of folly.

Folly and wit, the innocent and the trickster, are conjoined in Armin's carnivalesque play *The Two Maids of More-Clacke*. This play, published in 1609 but probably written as early as 1600, has drawn critical condemnation for language that is, according to John Middleton Murry, 'invariably doggerel' and 'if not fustian, thoroughly commonplace' (quoted in Liddie 1979: 41), and a plot decried by Alexander Grosart as 'involute, not to say absurd', and which, according to Harold Hillebrand, 'degenerates into episodes which defy credulity' (Liddie 1979: 53). Armin, ever self-aware, also mocks his verse 'as well blancke, as crancke' in his preface note 'To the friendly peruser', but much of the critical denigration of the play comes from an unwillingness to recognize it as a popular parodic work of contemporary comic romances; even the title echoes *The Two Gentlemen of Verona* (Liddie 1979). The play's characters are consistently 'decrowned', to borrow a term from Bakhtin, as Armin deflates both the romantic and tragic potential of his heroes and heroines, often through wild exaggeration of the traits associated with romantic and tragic plot and characterization – hence Sir William Vergir's fustian speeches, the 'involute, not to say absurd' comic subplots with the young lovers whom Vergir seeks to frustrate, and the strange nature of Vergir's own cuckolding.

The play opens after the marriage of Vergir to a widow known only as Lady Vergir, who has wed the knight partly in order to expedite the union of her son Humil to Mary, one of Vergir's daughters. However, immediately after her marriage she finds that her husband James is still alive and present in More-Clacke, despite the fact that she had received letters bearing news of his death abroad (letters that formed part of a ploy by James to test his wife's faithfulness). She manages to hold off Vergir and re-establish herself with James, although Humil comes upon them in bed and, not recognizing his own father, reports her infidelity to Sir William, thus betraying both his parents in an attempt to curry favour with his stepfather; many critics have suggested that the 'Humil' subplot parodies *Hamlet* (Felver 1961; Johnson

2003; Liddie 1979). Meanwhile, other intrigues are developing. Mary and Vergir's other daughter, Tabitha, wish to marry a pair of dashing young suitors – Sir Robert Toures and Filbon, respectively – but are forbidden by Vergir, who declares to Toures that he shall have Mary as his wife only after she has died, and to Filbon that he will have to become a woman before taking Tabitha as his bride. The young lovers are not to be stopped so easily; Toures and Mary elope, but in their flight, near an island just off England, she dies and is buried – to rise again, of course, her death being simply a temporary coma. Tabitha is incarcerated by her father, but Filbon and his servant Tutch, a witty fool formerly of Sir William's household but dismissed for being a liaison between the lovers, prepare a number of deceptions, culminating in one in which Tutch, disguised in a coat of blue motley[9] as John of the Hospital, is accompanied by Filbon disguised as John's female nurse. Vergir obligingly assigns Filbon, in nurse wear, sleeping quarters in Tabitha's chamber.

Noticeably absent from this plot summary is John, the natural fool, who appears on occasion in the play as an 'interlude' but otherwise remains apart from the main currents of the action. However, despite his apparent plot insignificance, Blue John (as he is known) forms the symbolic nucleus of the play, and his presence informs its carnivalesque valorization of folly, physicality and that particular Renaissance blending of chance and providence. John first appears as entertainment to Sir William, after the dance celebrating Vergir's marriage, where his attendant, a boy from the hospital, questions him and receives answers reflecting his particular view of the world; much of the dialogue recalls tales told in *Foole Upon Foole*. As well, much is made of John's constantly running nose. John's second appearance features him playing with the boy, who takes from him his 'point', the cord that holds up his trousers. There is more emphasis placed on John's dripping nose in this scene as well, and the scene ends with John singing a bawdy song. Both scenes emphasize bodily humour: John laughs and cries, his nose runs, his pants fall down. As such, he qualifies as a representative of what Bakhtin identifies as the grotesque body of carnivalesque literature, but he is hardly central to the plot's movement. At this point, then, we need to digress and consider the practical issues concerning the staging of the play.

The play was written by a professional clown who wished to display his own talents. As David Wiles writes, 'Armin's shape and size gave point to the recurring image of the cringing dog. His principal physical traits were ugliness and dwarfishness'; indeed, he suggests, 'Armin was obsessed with natural fools because he himself, physically though not mentally, was a natural fool' (Wiles 1987: 148). In assessing Armin's roles, he notes:

> Armin can be revealed as a fool whenever he dresses in motley, like Touchstone or Lear's fool; but he is also revealed as a fool whenever he is stripped naked, like Carlo Buffone [in Jonson's *Every Man Out of His Humour*] or Sir Morion [of *The Valiant Welshman*, thought to be written by Armin]. Armin's obsession with natural fools, and the doubt which he always projects as to whether or not he is in some sense a 'natural' himself, simultaneously derives from and exploits Armin's own stunted physique. (Wiles 1987: 150)

Charles Felver has hypothesized that Armin acted Blue John during play interludes before the actual production of this play (Felver 1961: 15), and Armin's introduction to the published version states that John was one of his roles in the original production (this would account for much of the emphasis on singing, as Armin was a notable singer).[10] In addition to playing Blue John, Armin also played the role of Tutch, the artificial fool (Felver 1961; Johnson 2003; Liddie 1979; Wiles 1987).

With Armin playing both roles, we are left with a fascinating third and final appearance by Blue John. In the final act, Tutch disguises himself as John, with Filbon disguised as the nurse, in order to facilitate Filbon's union with Tabitha. But the audience has no way of knowing that the character on stage dressed in the blue motley jacket of the hospital wards is Tutch, not John – they are not informed ahead of time, and the two roles are played by the same actor. The audience sees John on the stage just as Vergir sees John in his court, and need not be disabused of this perception until the figure stands alone on the stage during a brief interval in the action and reveals himself in a short monologue. The two characters, the 'natural' John and the 'artificial' Tutch, are fused as one, effecting the play's denouement. Thus, while John may not factor in the plot's movement, he is the play's primary symbolic figure, whose presence fills the stage when characters are openly reunited: Tabitha and Filbon; James and his wife, Lady Vergir; Humil and his parents; and, finally, Toures and the resurrected Mary. John/Tutch is the image of regeneration and reaffirmation and, as such, he provides the context – if not the catalyst – for the reunions and weddings that mark the end of the play, including Sir William Vergir's comic admission that he 'wil be generally laught at ... since our fate makes us the worlds fond idiot' (XXI, 359–66). The play concludes with an epilogue delivered by the aptly named Earl of Tumult.

Conventional authority, reason and rationality prove no match for John's folly and overt physicality, which presents a dynamic alternative to the closed, unified structures of power embodied in wealth and aristocracy; the union with the 'witty' fool Tutch incorporates and universalizes the figure of the 'natural' John, who is otherwise isolated from the plot. However, the fusion of Tutch and John does not ultimately bring John fully into the community at the end of the play. The character on centre-stage is both John and Not-John, and it is that part which is 'Not-John' whose presence is finally admitted. The image of the fool can be appropriated and used effectively, as Tutch demonstrates, but while folly can displace power, wit is needed to regenerate the community. This occurs after Tutch has revealed himself and John has all but vanished from the stage.

Armin's work bears witness to the professionalization and commodification of the fool, as he makes clear in his 'letter to the printer' that appears at the start of *A Nest of Ninnies*. 'Many now a days play the foole and want no witte, and therefore tis no wonder for me to set down fooles naturall, when wisemen before theyle be unprofitable, will seeme fooles artificiall: is it then a profit to be foolish?', writes Armin. To this last question he responds 'yea so some say, for under shew of simplicity some gaine love, while the wise with all they can doe, can scarce obtaine love' (46). Folly may be profitable, but mainly because the world loves a fool. At the end of *Foole Upon Foole* – and at the end of the final tale of *A Nest of Ninnies* – Armin eulogizes John of the Hospital, who had died shortly before 1600, and proposes an epitaph for his grave:

> Here under sleeps blew John, that gives
> Foode to feede wormes, yet he not lives:
> You that passe by, looke at his grave,
> And say your selves the like must have.
> Wise men and fooles, all one end makes,
> Gods will be done, who gives and takes.
> (146)

The witty stage fool may be a professional performing his trade, and worthy of a certain status but, in the end, natural fools like Blue John share the same fate that will befall the wise – all are subordinate before God. Armin does not directly evoke the Pauline notion of Christian folly, but his epitaph suggests that the wisdom and folly of this world ultimately count for little before God, or death.

Armin expresses a tangible affection for Blue John and his other fools; at the same time, more than any writer since Erasmus, he complicates the tension between metaphorical and mimetic images of natural folly. His fool characters refer to historical people, so that the metaphorical significance that Armin gives to folly acquires a face. Erasmian abstractions are now read directly upon the natural fools living in the towns and villages of England. And through the World confronting the 'Cinnick' in *A Nest of Ninnies*, and her clear sympathy for her foolish offspring, this image of the fool is universalized. At the same time, the professional clown develops his folly as a commodity, and defines himself in conjunction with, and opposition to, those natural fools who embody a pre-capitalist folly. This relation will later be rearticulated by psychologists, physicians and asylum superintendents, defining their professional status in conjunction with, and against, idiocy. They, however, will be working within a professional medical framework, rather than a professional theatrical one.

The image of the fool became darker and more shadowy in the Jacobean period, as representations moved from Shakespeare's wise but vulnerable innocent fool to the dangerous lunatics that abound in the works of playwrights like John Webster. The theatres were closed in 1642 under Cromwell, and when they reopened in 1660 the fool had all but disappeared. All the same, we can still sight 'folly' throughout the eighteenth century. Many of these instances are satirical, with the object of satire cast in the image of the idiot, as in Jonathan Swift's 'Dick's Variety' (1722) or Alexander Pope's *The Dunciad* (1729). Others develop the idea of the simple man whose innocence casts social hypocrisies into relief – much as in Sarah Fielding's *David Simple* (1744/53) and Henry Brooke's *The Fool of Quality* (1766/72). However, there is no sense of the natural fool in most of these representations; folly still functions as metaphor, but is detached from the character of particular, socially recognized 'fools'.

By the nineteenth century, the idea of the Christian 'idiot' has travelled far from humanist notions defined by Erasmus and More, and elaborated by popular writers like Armin. Often, the Christian 'innocent' is stripped of his 'trickster fool' qualities, and at one extreme the idiot becomes an object of pity (much like Southey's Ned) rather than a vehicle for social analysis or critique. However, other (usually secularized) examples of the innocent trickster remain, and these rearticulations of the holy or trickster fool will be explored in depth in the following chapter.

Notes

1 I have used Betty Radice's translation in Penguin Classics. Erasmus, writing in Latin, used the terms 'moriones, stultos, fatuos, ac bliteos' (25) and it is interesting to compare various translations of this passage. Chaloner goes on to note that 'if they be veraie brute Naturalles [from Erasmus's 'brutorum animantium insipientiam'], now they sinne not' (48); in John Wilson's 1688

translation, the categories have shifted slightly to 'fooles, ideots, half-wits and dolts', and those who 'come nearer even to the very ignorance of Brutes' do not sin (69); the 1941 translation by Hoyt Hopewell Hudson, which draws heavily on Wilson's version, transforms the categories to 'morons, fools, halfwits, and zanies', and to be without sin one must 'approach even more closely to the irrationality of dumb animals' (47–48). The shift from 'brute Naturalles' to 'ignorance' to 'irrationality' suggests a concomitant shift in notions of consciousness and ways of knowing: from the category 'Naturalles', with its ambivalent reference that could encompass both human and beast, to 'ignorance', implying a lack of knowledge or deficit of content, to 'irrationality', with its emphasis on processes of understanding, and Radice's 'reasoning power', with its assumption of strength and capacity.

2 Evidence for this attribution to Luther, as Goodey and Stainton (2004) point out, is profoundly circumstantial. These passages appear in *Tischreden* (published in German in 1566, and in English as *Table Talk* in 1652), a compendium of recollections of dinner conversations with Luther, taking place over several years and compiled years after Luther's death.

3 According to the *Oxford English Dictionary*, 'changeling' was used as a synonym for 'fool' by the 1640s.

4 Paul, writing in Greek, uses the words *moria* and *aphron*, both of which are translated into English as 'folly'. The citations from the first letter to the Corinthians use the former term to describe Christian folly; those from the second letter use the latter, which could refer to either a lack of understanding or a boastfulness, and has more ambiguous connotations (Maleski 1998). The original Hebrew terms translated as 'fool' and 'folly' in the King James Old Testament imply not so much an intellectual deficit as malice evidenced in the rejection of divine wisdom (MacKenzie 1965). That this wide range of terms from the original languages of the Bible could all be rendered as 'fool' in English shows just how versatile the concept of folly was at the time the King James translation was being composed, in the early 1600s.

5 See especially *The Fool: His Social and Literary History*, by Enid Welsford (1935); *A Social History of the Fool*, by Sandra Billington (1984); *Rabelais and His World*, by Mikhail Bakhtin (1984); *Reality in a Looking-Glass*, by Anton Zijderveld (1982); *Fools and Folly During the Middle Ages and Renaissance*, by Barbara Swain (1932); and *Society and Culture in Early Modern France*, by Nathalie Zemon Davis (1975).

6 This quotation is from the C-text of *Piers Ploughman* (Prologue, lines 37–38), which exists in three versions, known as A-, B- and C-texts. However, similar lines appear at the same point in the prologue of all three versions.

7 William Roper, Thomas More's son-in-law and biographer, recounts that because More's dinnertime conversation was very diverting for Henry VIII, the king insisted on More staying at his table rather than allowing him to return home to his family. Eventually, being unable to get home more than once a month, More began to suspect that he was assuming the role of jester, and in order to see his family again had to adopt a more tedious mealtime demeanor (Zijderveld 1982: 104–5).

8 R. W. Bond describes 'barly breake' (barley-brake) as 'a game ... in which two players, occupying a marked space called "Hell" in the centre of the ground, tried to catch the others as they ran through it from the two opposite ends, those caught being obliged to replace them or reinforce them in the centre'; N. W. Bawcutt adds that 'the game was usually played by pairs of men and women, who held hands and were not usually allowed to separate, and went on until each pair had taken its turn at occupying "Hell"' (both quoted in

Lomax 1987: 157–58). Lomax observes that 'In many ways, this game reflects the medieval attitude to courtship, when it was portrayed as one of the seven deadly sins and was associated with animal lust' (158).

9 As Leslie Hotson (1952) has noted, the traditional motley coat of the idiot is an inexpensively made long jacket woven of threads of different colour, with one colour dominating. Thus, John wears the blue motley coat that identifies him as a ward of the hospital; the stage fool in motley would immediately recall to mind the attire of real-life 'idiots'. As the Elizabethan writer Thomas Nashe observed, 'fooles, ye know, alwaies for the most part (especiallie if they be naturall fooles) are suited in long coates' (quoted in Hotson 1952: 53). The belief that motley was a patchwork of different colours and materials was a later misapprehension, but influenced the attire of such nineteenth-century 'idiot' characters as David Gellatley and Barnaby Rudge.

10 Records show that *The Two Maids of More-Clacke* was performed in 1607/8 by the Children of the King's Revels, a short-lived boys' company, at Whitefriars private theatre. However, Felver (1961) cites Harold Newcomb Hillebrand's article 'The Children of the King's Revels at Whitefriars' (1922) in which Hillebrand argues that plays for such speculative ventures as the Children of the King's Revels were often purchased second-hand, after having been performed successfully elsewhere, in an attempt to keep expenses down and to present a proven crowd pleaser (14, note 14). While there are no records of previous performances of this play, circumstantial evidence indicates there were some.

CHAPTER 7

History, society, economy: holy fools and idiots come home in nineteenth-century literature

The natural fool – the innocent, the trickster, the depraved – is a vibrant, complex actor in medieval and early modern society, and so it should come as no surprise that nineteenth-century writers, looking back at the store of characters and images bequeathed to them by literary and cultural history, should also light upon the fool as a means of ironic commentary and social critique. But, of course, when the social context shifts, so too do the fool's specific functions. By the nineteenth century, the 'natural' fool is an anachronism, and the individuals so designated have been replaced in the public consciousness by the more formal 'idiot'. Thus, while the associations of natural and holy folly are continuous, there are significant changes in the way authors sought to give their 'fool' characters a form that was not only accessible but also meaningful to nineteenth-century readers.

Thus, Walter Scott could use his 'fool' character David Gellatley to comment on political intrigues and developments in *Waverley* (1814), as well as to mark a certain strain of 'Scottishness'. Charles Dickens could use his fool characters, and the pervasive theme of idiocy, to present a critique of moral responsibilities, both individual and social, in *Little Dorrit* (1857). And George Eliot could use Jacob, in *Brother Jacob* (1860), as a tool for helping to carry out an analysis that blends the moral with the economic. In each case, the presence of the fool character guides how we read the fictional world they inhabit (much as with Blue John in Armin's *The Two Maids of More-Clacke* – Chapter 6) and the commentary they provide takes on a moral component. These fools are, after all, innocent – and for this quality to be relevant, it must either be shared with other characters, signifying all of their innocence (as in *Waverley*), or juxtaposed against others, thus underscoring their guilt (as in *Brother Jacob*). Of course, it can also do both (as in *Little Dorrit*). The holy innocent and trickster fool were potent images for nineteenth-century writers, and even today retain some of their power. This chapter will explore how Scott, Dickens and Eliot renovated the concept of the holy innocent or trickster fool as a more contemporary version of idiocy in order to develop social and moral critiques of the worlds they portray in their novels.

'Simply a crackbrained knave': folly, politics and Scottish identity in *Waverley*

Sir Walter Scott's 1814 novel *Waverley, or 'Tis Sixty Years Since*, tells the story of young Edward Waverley's involvement in the Jacobite rebellion of 1745, which marked the final attempt by the Stuart heirs to reclaim the British throne. It also features a simple-minded retainer, David (or Davie) Gellatley, who is used as a messenger and general servant on the Baron of Bradwardine's estate, and who exhibits a hodge-podge of mental deviance:

> It was apparently neither idiocy nor insanity that gave that wild, unsettled, irregular expression to a face which naturally was rather handsome, but something that resembled a compound of both, where the simplicity of the fool was mixed with the extravagance of a crazed imagination. (82)

Later, the Baron of Bradwardine explains to Waverley that Davie is a member of his household by virtue of having risked his own person to save the Baron's daughter, Rose, from some grave but unnamed danger, and that he is 'neither fatuous *nec naturaliter idiota*, as is expressed in the brieves of furiosity, but simply a crackbrained knave, who could execute very well any commission which jumped with his own humour, and made his folly a plea for avoiding every other' (104, Scott's italics). The novel's adherence to a certain level of realism solicits, if it does not demand, some kind of diagnosis of Davie's state, but instead Scott opts for this fruitful ambiguity, one which enables him to link Davie to literary tradition. Davie can be read as both a natural and a witty fool – a trickster fool of a sort familiar to readers and play-goers alike.

David's literary lineage is immediately established when Waverley likens him to 'one of Shakespeare's roynish clowns', observing to himself that 'wiser men have been led by fools' (83). Later, Scott illustrates Jane Gellatley's love for her son by quoting the lines 'Him whom she loved, her idiot boy' from Wordsworth's 'The Idiot Boy' (439). David is also associated, although less explicitly, with Will Somers, Henry VIII's court jester; like Somers, David sleeps with his master's hounds (441) and is linked with them throughout the story, most notably towards the conclusion, when the Baron, reflecting on the 'gratitude o' thae dumb brutes [i.e., his hounds, Ban and Buscar], and of that puir innocent', observes that he is 'obliged to Colonel Talbot for putting my hounds into such condition, and likewise for puir Davie' (484). In his final appearance, at the wedding of Edward Waverley and Rose Bradwardine, David is 'bedizened fine enough to have served Touchstone himself' (483). David is also a noted singer, 'deeply affected by that which was melancholy', whose 'prodigious memory' was 'stored with miscellaneous snatches and fragments of all tunes and songs, which he sometimes applied, with considerable address, as the vehicles of remonstrance, explanation, or satire' (104–5). Readers were not slow to pick up on the close relation of Scott's Davie to his Shakespearean precedents; as an anonymous reviewer wrote in the August 1814 *British Critic*, 'Davy appears to have been formed by the author, in some measure, upon the model of Shakespeare's fools, and we think the similarity between himself and the fool in *King Lear* is particularly striking' (quoted in Hayden 1970: 70). David is, in sum, a knavish innocent, a trickster fool, with an explicit lineage running back to Shakespeare's witty fools (characters who, incidentally, demanded the performance skills of Robert Armin to take full advantage of the theatrical potential of folly).

Davie's plot function, however, is slim. He delivers a letter from Rose to Edward Waverley when the latter is enjoying an extended visit with the Highland chieftain and Jacobite leader Fergus MacIvor. Later, when the Baron of Bradwardine is hiding in exile during the Jacobite rebellion, David appears with his elaborate grey and scarlet outfit in tatters, and supplemented by 'remnants of tapestried hangings, window-curtains, and shreds of pictures' (435) – the nineteenth century's notion of the fool's motley (Hotson 1952). Edward finds David wandering the Bradwardine estate after it has been pillaged by English troops, and follows the 'poor simpleton' (435), who, in answer to Edward's question about the fate of its inhabitants (Edward 'forgetting the incapacity of Davie to hold any connected discourse'), responds that they are all 'A' dead and gane' (436). David then leads Edward to the Baron's hideout; the Baron has gone, but is not dead after all. Yet David's deceit is not without reason, according to his mother, who asserts that 'Davie's no sae silly as folk tak him for, Mr. Wauverley. He wadna hae brought you here unless he had kend ye was a friend to his Honour' (439). David's cunning duplicity marks him clearly as a trickster as well as an innocent – the crackbrained knave whose folly cloaks his cunning.

This trickster function is even more apparent when Jane credits her son with saving the Baron, substituting himself for his master when the Baron was being pursued by English soldiers:

> Davie was in the wood, and heard the tuilzie, and he, just out o' his ain head, got up the auld grey maud that his Honour had flung off him to gang the faster, and he came out o' the very same bit o' the wood, majoring and looking about sae like his Honour, that [the soldiers] were clean beguiled, and thought they had letten aff their gun at crack-brained Sawney, as they ca'd him; and they gae me saxpence, and twa saumon fish, to say naething about it. – Na, na; Davie's no just like other folk, puir fallow; but he's no sae silly as folk tak him for. (440)

Here, Davie's cloak of folly is in fact the Baron's 'auld grey maud' (a travelling rug of grey striped plaid), but it serves to distract the soldiers and enable the Baron to elude capture.

David also foregrounds the historical and political specificity of the world of Waverley. In his first appearance, he is designated 'an innocent' by the family butler, who observes that 'there is one such in almost every town in the country' (84). Scott ends the chapter describing Waverley's arrival in Scotland by noting that 'in Scotland, a single house was called a town, and a natural fool an innocent' (85). Ina Ferris has argued that the 'distinctiveness and relativity of signifying systems' denoted by this passage marks for Waverley and the reader a specific space that is 'not simply ethical but historical and cultural' (Ferris 1991: 103). In short, David becomes a distinguishing feature of the particular world described by Scott,[1] and the innocent becomes for the protagonist, Waverley, as well as for readers of the novel, the first explicit marker of Scottish difference, both by the 'peculiarity of his dialect', as Scott says (83), and by his intellectual idiosyncrasies. The characters that speak in dialect – the Jacobite rebels and the Gellatleys – belong not just to Scotland but to a failed and discredited political enterprise, and the use of dialect renders them more foreign and primitive to a broadly British readership; that those notable Jacobite sympathizers who are successfully integrated into the pan-British culture at the end of the novel either do not speak in dialect or speak with a limited dialect further underlines this distinction (Leerssen 1991). Dialect versions of English were historically perceived as lesser or more primitive forms of the language, which parallels later notions of phylogeny and recapitulation in connection with intellectual disability: in this case, the idiot character speaks a less evolved language, while later in the century the same image will recall a less evolved race.

While Davie reappears only sporadically in the novel, he was 'a particular favorite of reviewers' (Ferris 1991: 87), a popularity due at least in part to his function as a cipher for a particular English notion of Scottishness. As the aforementioned reviewer for the August 1814 *British Critic* wrote,

> Upon the character of David Gellatley we must observe, that although this sort of personage is but little known in England, yet in Scotland it is by no means uncommon.[2] In almost every small town there is a sort of public idiot, bearing the proportion, as we conceive, of about two of knave to three of fool, who is considered so necessary an appendage to the dignity of the place, that when he grows old, there is generally a young one in training as his successor. (Quoted in Hayden 1970: 69–70)[3]

Indeed, Scott himself writes in a footnote to David's first appearance in the novel that, while he is 'ignorant how long the ancient and established custom of keeping a fool has been disused in England', Swift had composed an epitaph on Dicky Pearce, the Earl of Suffolk's fool, who died in 1728 at the age of sixty-three; however, he claims

> in Scotland the custom subsisted till late in the last century.... It is not above thirty years since such a character stood by the sideboard of a nobleman of the first rank in Scotland, and occasionally mixed in the conversation, till he carried the joke rather too far, in making proposals to one of the young ladies of the family, and publishing the banns betwixt her and himself in the public church. (85)

Clearly, Scott recognized 'the fool' as a distinct presence in Scottish culture and a marker of Scottish identity, and he was adamant that his readers also acknowledge the significance of the Scottish fool.

David straddles two literary worlds: he is a character in a historical novel, and thus is made to help populate a realistic world; and he is a figure of literary tradition – the natural fool, the innocent trickster, who, in his odd moments of inspiration, both deceives and enlightens those around him. He is also a secular version of the innocent, functioning primarily in a political context, as a participant in a hopeless rebellion. But the concept of 'innocence', however secular, necessarily invokes a Christian cosmology, and the fact that David, his master the Baron of Bradwardine, and Edward Waverley are all eventually pardoned bespeaks a political innocence analogous to the moral innocence of the 'idiots, fools, nitwits and simpletons' of Stultitia in Erasmus's *Praise of Folly* (Chapter 6). Indeed, in a letter of 28 July 1814 (exactly three weeks after the novel's publication date) to John Morritt, Scott described *Waverley*, only partly in jest, as 'a sneaking piece of imbecility' and notes that 'if he had married Flora she would have set him up upon the chimney-piece as Count Boralski's wife used to do with him' (Grierson 1932: 478) – an image which also recalls the fool at the sideboard of the Scottish nobleman described in Scott's footnote for David. Edward Waverley, like David Gellatley (and like Barnaby Rudge in Dickens's novel almost thirty years later), is an unknowing innocent, a naïf, whose intellect is weaned on chivalric romances and tales of Jacobite heroism; as Jana Davis notes, Edward Waverley suffers from what the influential Edinburgh philosopher Dugald Stewart would have diagnosed as an 'ill-regulated imagination' (Davis 1989: 445) – much akin to Davie's extravagant, crazed imagination. Waverley is motivated by his sentimental inclinations and emotional impulses, recalling Stultitia's proprietary claim to the emotions, intrinsically opposed to reason, as being part of her realm. (Notably, the young Edward is, as Scott's dedication of *Waverley* to fellow novelist Henry MacKenzie suggests, a 'man of feeling'.) But regardless of his noble sentiments and pure soul, Waverley is caught in a struggle that he does not understand and thus misinterprets; he has not the capacity to recognize the position in which he places himself, nor to judge the justice of his cause. As one who is almost as much a 'puir innocent' as Davie, Edward Waverley is spared a harsh judgement, and comes instead to a happy end by marrying Rose Bradwardine.

The novel itself rests on the boundaries of realism and romance, of history and fiction, of past and present (Dennis 1997; Duncan 1992). At the end of the eighteenth and into the nineteenth century, Scottish culture was awash in antiquarianism, partly in an effort to shape a form of Scottishness that could exist within the British union after the failed rebellion of '45. As Humphrey (1993: 25) notes, 'The dusty, rusty and musty had an irresistible lure. Antiquarianism in Scotland was a state of mind, a place of refuge, and a national and nationalist hobby', and few were as active in this realm as Sir Walter Scott, whose collection of popular ballads in *Minstrelsy of the Scottish Border* (1802/3) and his original poems in *The Lay of the Last Minstrel* (1805) helped define the nation's image. Indeed, as Scott writes in the final chapter of *Waverley*:

> There is no European nation which, within the course of half a century, or a little more, has undergone so complete a change as this kingdom of Scotland. The effects of the insurrection of 1745 – the destruction of the patriarchal power of the Highland chiefs – the abolition of the heritable jurisdictions of the Lowland nobility and barons – the total eradication of the Jacobite party, which, averse to mingle with the English, or adopt their customs, long continued to pride themselves upon maintaining ancient Scottish manners and customs – commenced this innovation. (492)

This vanished Scotland was home to the likes of David Gellatley, a character who will ultimately prove foreign to the world with which Edward Waverley must reconcile himself at the novel's end. But at the same time, Davie, and his continued maintenance within the Bradwardine household, is also emblematic of those remnants of the old Scotland that would remain acceptable – the kilts, the minstrelsy, 'the principles of loyalty ... and of old Scottish faith, hospitality, worth and honour', but not the 'absurd political prejudice' (492) of the vanished Jacobites – and which helped to carry the image of that vanished Scotland into the modern, post-Jacobite nineteenth century. Armin's Blue John was not witty enough to regenerate the community at the end of *The Two Maids of More-Clacke*, and thus disappeared; Davie Gellatley will eventually do the same, as he is simply not civilized enough for the new Britain.

Such a clever girl:
Maggy and idiocy in *Little Dorrit*

While David Gellatley's folly in *Waverley* marks him as a historical throwback, in Charles Dickens's 1857 novel *Little Dorrit*, this anachronistic 'folly' transforms directly into mid-nineteenth-century concepts of idiocy and imbecility. Early in the novel, the elderly serving woman Affery asks Arthur Clennam a pointed question: 'You're clever, Arthur, an't you?' He nods in response, 'as she seemed to expect an answer in the affirmative'. Affery then stresses that he will need to be clever if he is to confront his mother and her serving-man-turned-business-partner Flintwich: 'She's awful clever, and none but a clever one durst say a word to her. *He's* a clever one – oh, he's a clever one! – and he gives it to her when he has a mind to't, he does!' (76). In the society described in *Little Dorrit*, intelligence and 'cleverness' are the tools by which one can manipulate others and acquire dominance over them; on the other hand, a sort of worldly folly or imbecility, usually expressed as open-heartedness and generosity, becomes the means for establishing friendships and community and for achieving a qualified sort of happiness. Not surprisingly, Arthur turns out to be less clever than his antagonists, at least in worldly deliberations.

Dickens was less interested in the machinery of historical process than Scott, and his characters are rarely motivated through political conflict. Rather, Dickens builds a world in which the conflicts are moral struggles between good and evil. In *Little Dorrit*, worldly intelligence is destructive, and Dickens prioritizes the capacity for emotion, feeling and sentiment over ratiocination. In this feature the novel is not so distinct from many other Victorian works employing sentimentality and 'feeling' as vehicles for comprehending social relations. What stands out is Dickens's insistent use of idiocy imagery, which is especially interesting given that by 1857 his journal, *Household Words*, had already published two articles on the subject – the first, 'Idiots', written by Dickens himself with his editor W. H. Will, in 1853, praising the good work being done in the new National Asylum for Idiots at Earlswood.[4] Indeed, the entire novel involves a contemplation of the relative notions of idiocy, imbecility and folly in opposition to the qualities of cleverness and intelligence.

Let us match up the teams. On one side, there is the actual idiot character, Maggy, her 'little mother' Amy Dorrit, Arthur Clennam, his former flame Flora Finching, Mrs Clennam's serving woman Affery, and the various denizens of Bleeding Heart Yard, including the Plornishes, John Baptist Cavelletto and Mr Pancks. On the other side, there are the two 'clever ones', Mrs Clennam and Flintwich, the evil faux-aristocrat and murderer Blandois, the embittered Mrs Wade, the fraud Merdle and even the bureaucratic volubility of the Circumlocution Office.

Maggy is the lead fool among fools. As the grand-daughter of Little Dorrit's long-dead old nurse, Maggy is, in effect, a member of Amy's extended family. Paul Marchbanks notes that Maggy's character receives a 'fully rendered and consistent portrayal' that 'precludes her reduction to a cipher' (Marchbanks 2006b: 175), which, he suggests, is unlike some of Dickens's earlier 'idiot' characters such as Barnaby Rudge or *Nicholas Nickelby*'s Smike; he credits this change in representation to Dickens's greater awareness of idiocy, its needs and the demands placed upon those caring for idiots. This may in part be true, but Maggy's status in the novel is not guided simply by Dickens's greater concern with the apparent reality of idiocy but rather with her place at the symbolic centre of the novel's folly discourse. She is present at most significant exchanges between Arthur and Amy, initially appearing after their first discussion on the iron bridge; she is with Little Dorrit as the latter sorrows over her love for Arthur, cloaking it in the story of the princess and the shadow; she is there again when Arthur and Amy finally do express their love for one another; finally, she accompanies Amy to the Marshalsea prison to meet Arthur on the morning of their wedding.

Maggy embodies the novel's critique of both British society – especially its obsession with wealth and status – and the 'humbug' of British bureaucracy, as represented by the Circumlocution Office. While she may not quite fit the role of wise or holy fool (McKnight

1993), she remains an innocent whose self-interest and appetite have none of the manipulative features that mark those qualities in other characters; Maggy's desires – for affection, for comfort, for chicken – do not separate her from the other 'good' characters but rather serve as an expression of universal desires that are natural. As already discussed in Chapter 5, Maggy acts as the shadow figure for Amy, one who 'brings out the ambiguity, if not the deadliness, of Amy's character' and who 'betrays the appetite and the competitiveness which Amy has struggled to extinguish' (Showalter 1979: 35). Maggy provides both a foil to whom Amy can be consistently generous and an expression of that physical self that Amy so aggressively denies; she also expresses Amy's own worldly folly and innocence, both ambiguous and elusive qualities. Brian Rosenberg (1996), noting how 'Maggy tumbles into Little Dorrit as a perceptual and interpretative dilemma' (54), argues that Dickens's description of Maggy as a character is emblematic of his process of assertion, elaboration, equivocation and eventual accumulation in shaping his characters: 'Here and throughout his fiction appear contradictions, uncertainties, multiple perspectives, hints of something unexplained, together creating the picture of visual details engaged in figurative struggle' (62). One aspect of this 'figurative struggle' can be seen in how Maggy's intellectual status is defined. While Dickens establishes Maggy as a case of 'arrested development' – a twenty-eight-year-old who, because of an illness, permanently bears a ten-year-old intelligence – she is never actually called a fool or idiot or imbecile. In fact, she is one of the few sympathetic characters not to have her intelligence characterized in such a way. Instead, the single term used to describe Maggy's intelligence is applied by Amy, who stresses 'how clever' (143) Maggy is:

> 'She goes on errands as well as anyone.' Maggy laughed. 'And is as trustworthy as the Bank of England.' Maggy laughed. 'She earns her own living entirely. Entirely, sir!' said Little Dorrit, in a lower and triumphant tone. 'Really does!' (143)

Shortly after this, Little Dorrit tells Clennam how Maggy 'began to take pains to improve herself, and to be very attentive and very industrious; and by degrees was allowed to come in and out as often as she liked, and got enough to do to support herself, and does support herself' (144). Of course, we – and Clennam – realize how important a role Amy has played in Maggy's transformation. Also significant, though, is that Maggy, in her 'cleverness', confounds the folly/intelligence dichotomy. And in her capacity to support herself, meagre as this support may be, she provides a sharp contrast to Merdle's insubstantial speculations that inflate the market and, while promising riches without labour, lead thousands to ruin.

Amy Dorrit herself bears some of the markings of a holy fool, as Natalie McKnight (1993) has convincingly argued. Her diminutive size marks her as different and, traditionally, fools were often physically anomalous. Further, her casting off of the worldly values of wealth and status in favour of generosity and honesty, acts which slide somewhere between the generous and the self-effacing, prompt her frustrated sister Fanny to dismiss Amy as 'You little Fool', noting that she has 'no self-respect … no becoming pride' (289); Fanny suppresses repeating that epithet later on (549). Later, Amy's father refers to her accompanying old Nandy, the impoverished father of Mrs Plornish, as 'innocent in intention' but an act that, lowering the pride of the family, has 'cut him to the soul' (419). On the other hand, her reluctance to see Arthur Clennam because she does not want him to witness her family's humiliation is dismissed by her father as 'folly' (422) because he considers Arthur to be of appropriate social status and he appreciates the generous 'testimonials' (that is, money) that the young man gives him. Her father also labels her refusal to marry – and marry well – as 'weak and foolish, weak and foolish. You have a – ha – responsibility imposed upon you by your position' (669). She, too, acknowledges her worldly folly, writing in a letter to Clennam of 'all these foolish thoughts of mine, which I have been so hardy as to confess to you because I know you will understand me if anybody can, and will make more allowance for me than anybody else would if you cannot' (523).

Clennam, too, asserts his folly when he accepts full responsibility for the debts that have befallen his business partner, Doyce, after the bursting of the Merdle bubble. He is consequently imprisoned in Marshalsea, and consistently refuses the exhortations of his lawyer, Rugg, to 'hear reason' or to listen to 'another word of reason' (784). The slum-dwellers of Bleeding Heart Yard, on the other hand, become 'more interested in Arthur since his reverses than formerly; now regarding him as one who was true to his place and had taken up his freedom' (784) – an ambiguous assessment in which 'taking up one's freedom' becomes the act of giving up physical freedom while simultaneously asserting one's liberty from the constraints of worldly vanities. Once he is imprisoned in Marshalsea, Arthur's intellectual acumen is frequently commented upon. He is visited by Ferdinand Barnacle, of the Circumlocution Office, who comments on Clennam's insistence on trying to disturb the status quo by 'doing something', in startling opposition to the Circumlocution Office's objective of 'not doing things'. As Ferdinand says to Arthur,

'I perceived that you were inexperienced and sanguine and had – I hope
you'll not object to my saying – some simplicity.'
    'Not at all.'
    'Some simplicity....'
(805)

Not only does Ferdinand identify Arthur's actions as exhibiting 'simplicity', but Arthur willingly agrees; he has recognized himself as a
fool. In contrast, Merdle, whose fraudulent speculations create an economic bubble which, when bursting, lands Arthur in prison (and ruins
thousands of others as well), is characterized by Ferdinand as 'an
exceedingly clever fellow ... a consummate rascal, of course ... but remarkably clever! One cannot help admiring the fellow. Must have been
such a master of humbug. Knew people so well – got over them so completely – did so much with them!' (806). Shortly after his exchange with
Ferdinand Barnacle, Arthur is visited by the villain Blandois, who refers
to him mockingly as 'my friend, philosopher, man of virtue, Imbecile,
what you will' (816), and dismisses the Marshalsea as a mere 'hospital
for imbeciles' (818). By this point, Arthur's worldly idiocy has been
fully established; he is in a debtor's prison cum idiot asylum.[5]

As Arthur's example indicates, honest or generous actions are consistently dismissed as folly. The novel's resolution hinges upon a
codicil that Clennam's father had added to his will favouring Arthur's
birth mother, or, should she die, the youngest daughter or niece of
'her patron', the man who assisted her in need, but Mrs Clennam
asserts that her husband was in a state 'reduced to imbecility' when
writing the codicil, which should thus be ignored (847) – she then
evokes the same image to describe that patron himself, none other
than Little Dorrit's uncle Frederick Dorrit, when she claims that he
has been 'deservedly ruined and imbecile' (849). Even Daniel Doyce,
innovator and inventor, comes under suspicion of folly; as Doyce notes
wryly, Meagles 'extends a sort of protection to me, don't you know,
as a man not quite able to take care of himself' (234). This circumstance prompts Arthur to suspect that Meagles might harbour some
'microscopic portion' of the seed that grew into the 'great tree of the
Circumlocution Office' (238) because Meagles's sense of superiority
to Doyce is based exclusively on the suspicion that Doyce was 'an
originator and a man out of the beaten track of other men' (239); at the
same time, Clennam himself designates his partner as a man of 'great
simplicity and integrity' (782).

Among the other 'fool' figures, the serving woman Affery is 'held in
very low account by the two clever ones, as a person, never of strong
intellect, who was becoming foolish' (389); Flintwich, responding

to Blandois's question 'How is it possible to understand this good creature?', insists 'She don't know what she means. She's an idiot, a wanderer in her mind' (404). Later, Mrs Clennam refers to her as a 'foolish creature', a 'piece of distraction' (836) and a 'half-witted woman' (845); Affery in fact acknowledges herself to be 'a heap of confusion' (836), but insists that it has been Mrs Clennam and Flintwich's shared project to make her so. She is joined in the cast of fools by: Mr Plornish, who is 'foolish in the face' (179); Flora Finching, characterized by her discontinuous and absurd stream of (un)consciousness monologues; 'Mr F.'s Aunt', who exclaims, apparently in objection to Arthur, 'I hate a fool!' (200), despite, as McKnight (1993) notes, the fact that she is one; and Mr Pancks, who designates himself both a 'fool' and a 'villain' for leading Arthur to join him in following Merdle's market speculations (778).

The 'fool' characters are also associated with Bleeding Heart Yard, the slum yard owned by Christopher Casby. The name points to the importance of 'heart' in defining worth against the prevailing 'cleverness' and recalls Stultitia's observation that those who would be guided by the emotions belong to her. McKnight observes that because of their

> chaotic, creative energies, their idiocy, and their disregard for or obliviousness to Society's dictates, the Bleeding Heart Yarders achieve more freedom than any other characters in the novel.... The Bleeding Heart Yard misfits, with all their tattered clothes, their garbled idiolects, their nonsensical actions, all their decayed environs, are trash in a utilitarian world, yet Dickens upholds them ... as sources of a hidden wealth. (McKnight 1993: 124)

The Bleeding Heart Yard becomes, in effect, a fool society (or, perhaps, a fool's paradise), an alternative culture to the money-and-status society lying beyond its boundaries. The novel's one 'idiot' character who cannot escape society is 'poor Mr Sparkler', as Dickens sympathetically designates him (873): married to the clever Fanny Dorrit, the overmatched, harmless Sparkler – 'almost an idiot' in Fanny's early assessment (289), whose 'mental feebleness' later continually tries her patience (651) – is eventually appointed to a well paying position in the Circumlocution Office, further complicating the divisions between folly and intelligence.

If folly is the route to freedom, the novel also makes clear that worldly intelligence leads to distrust, avarice and despair. Society, as Mrs Merdle notes, 'will not have any patience with their making fools of themselves' (442) – she is referring to young men, but in fact the interdiction is global, and society will have no part of folly. Representing the forces of the intellect are the 'two clever ones' (as they are consistently nominated by Affery), Jeremiah Flintwich and Mrs Clennam, as well as Blandois, Mrs Wade, Merdle and Casby. In addition to their status as the 'clever ones', Mrs Clennam is a 'woman of strong head and great talent', as Flintwich bitterly notes (851). Tellingly, Flintwich's twin brother Ephraim is a 'lunatic-keeper', but one who had 'speculated unsuccessfully in lunatics, he got into trouble about over-roasting a patient to bring him to reason, and he got into debt' (852). Blandois continually asserts his status as a gentleman and, thus, a superior member of society, albeit one who is forced by circumstances to live by his wits (48); his mocking praise of Mrs Clennam's 'superior intelligence' suggests that he finds it inferior to his own (842). Mrs Wade, for her part, proclaims that she 'has the misfortune of not being a fool.... If I could have been habitually imposed upon, instead of habitually discerning the truth, I might have lived as smoothly as most fools do' (725). Merdle's 'active and vigorous intellect' (297) leads to an apparent economic marvel; he is 'the master-mind of the age' (765), until his speculations prove fraudulent and he commits suicide. Dickens even indulges in a mock phrenological praise of the patriarchal head of the slum lord Christopher Casby: 'Oh! why, with that head, is he not a benefactor to his species! Oh! why, with that head, is he not a father to the orphan and a friend to the friendless!' (187); notably, the passage's meaning could be transformed by a simple change of punctuation, from exclamation to question marks. Finally, and at a systemic level, the bureaucratic excess and evasiveness of the Circumlocution Office, with its insistence on 'How Not To Do It' and the 'genius with which it always acted' on 'not doing it' (145), represents 'the Genius of the country' (805), claims its representative, Ferdinand Barnacle. According to the arguments Dickens assigns these characters, 'openness' and 'generosity' are repeatedly reinterpreted as 'self-serving'. Thus, Miss Wade opposes 'swollen patronage and selfishness, calling themselves kindness, protection, benevolence and other fine names' (734); and when Amy and Arthur make sacrifices, Amy's father and siblings reinterpret these as attempts to humiliate the family honour (Kucich 1987). To trust another individual thus becomes no less than pure folly.

Little Dorrit ends with the marriage of Arthur and Amy, but just before they leave for the church, Maggy, who is with them, builds the fire in which Amy will ask Arthur to burn an envelop containing the codicil that would give her 1,000 guineas, that same codicil long suppressed by Mrs Clennam. Maggy's presence, and her role as the fire-builder, underscores Dickens's use of idiocy as a tool for satirizing the ills of his society. *Little Dorrit* is one of Dickens's darkest novels, in which some characters – notably those associated with Bleeding

Heart Yard – escape the real and metaphorical prisons and the oppress-ive surveillance detailed in the text, but only by living in poverty and embracing the values of folly: that is, only by being so insignificant that they do not matter. The world itself does not change, and the powers of society and the Circumlocution Office are as dominant at the end of the novel as they had been at its start. In the novel's final lines, Amy and Arthur enter into a world of 'sunshine and shade', while 'the noisy and the eager, and the arrogant and the froward and the vain, fretted and chafed, and made their usual uproar' (895); this uproar is both chaotic and restrictive, encompassing the comparatively free space of the Bleeding Heart Yard and the oppressive edifices of society. Folly and imbecility, as represented by Maggy and her double, the 'holy fool' Amy Dorrit, expose the hypocrisies of this world while at the same time offering only a very limited form of escape.

Idiocy, economics and nemesis in *Brother Jacob*

If Dickens's novel takes greed, status and the dictates of society as its satirical target, George Eliot's 1860 novella *Brother Jacob* takes aim, at least superficially, at individual greed, while offering critiques of colonialism, social identity and economic structures and processes. David Faux, 'the son of a British yeoman, who has been fed principally on salt pork and yeast dumplings' (1), is taken to a confectioner at a young age and, awed by the sugary delights he discovers, decides to follow this line of work, little knowing that 'there is satiety for the human stomach even in a paradise of glass jars full of sugared almonds and pink lozenges' (1). His trajectory is thus defined by that most blatantly childish expression of greed, the sweet tooth. David is a young man 'of much mental activity, and, above all, gifted with a spirit of contrivance' (2), who 'scorned the idea that he could accept an average. He was sure there was nothing average about him' (3). He purchases the story of 'Inkle and Yarico', in which a young Englishman looking for adventure in the West Indies has his life saved by the native American princess Yarico, whom he seduces and then sells to a slaver;[6] the story makes David 'feel very sorry for poor Mr Inkle' (3) and sets him upon the idea of stealing from his parents' savings in order to finance a voyage to the West Indies, where he imagines adventures that will lead to great wealth as well as erotic conquests. David develops a plan to steal his mother's hoard of gold guineas and hide them nearby, so that their disappearance could be blamed on an unknown thief.

However, his theft is interrupted by his younger brother Jacob, 'a very healthy and well-developed idiot, who consumed a dumpling about eight inches in diameter every day' (4) and who, as 'a large personage who went about habitually with a pitchfork in his hand', prompted in David 'considerable fear and dread' (6). David drops his bag, revealing the guineas, but he also has a box of yellow lozenges with which he distracts Jacob, tricking him into believing that if guineas are hidden in the ground, they will eventually ripen into candies; however, he discovers to his dismay that 'it's of no use to have foresight when you are dealing with an idiot: he is not to be calculated upon' (9). Jacob's interference causes David to flee immediately, thus revealing himself to be the thief and giving up his claim to a share of his father's legacy; he travels to the West Indies as 'the most propitious destination for an emigrant who, to begin with, had the broad and easily recognis-able merit of whiteness' (4), although he ends up working as a cook in a Kingstown kitchen and padding his income with some minor blackmailing. Several years later he returns to England, settles in the town of Grimworth, establishes a new confectionary business under the 'generous-sounding' name of Edward Freely (21), spins lies about his adventures in the Indies, and causes the women of the town to purchase his sweets instead of making their own, thus effecting a moral and economic alteration among the townspeople; he also suc-ceeds in becoming engaged to the daughter of one of the town's better merchant families. He resumes brief contact with his family when they advertise for him, offering a share of his inheritance if he reappears, but this act of shameless greed also reacquaints him with Jacob, who tracks his brother to his new confectionary just in time to interrupt the wedding arrangements. Jacob, speaking an English that recalls David Gellatley's primitive dialect, claims that Edward Freely is in fact his brother 'Zavy come back from z'Indies' (46), which greatly disturbs the party, who note Freely's resemblance to Jacob. Eventually the eldest brother, Jonathan, appears to fetch Jacob home, and in so doing confirms the story. The wedding is cancelled, and Edward Freely/David Faux leaves Grimworth to search for his fortune elsewhere. Concludes the narrator of her tale, 'we see in it, I think, an admirable instance of the unexpected forms in which the great Nemesis hides herself' (55).

Eliot's novella, which until recently has been largely neglected by critics, has been read as a conservative fable on the dangers of free-market capitalism (Mallen 2001; Rodstein 1991) as well as a commentary on the return of the colonial nemesis (Gregory 2002). As Mallen (2001) notes, 'before David's arrival, Grimworth possessed a pre-capitalist, status-based economy' in which all sweets were manufactured at home (50); Peter Allan Dale has also observed that David's decision to steal his mother's guineas while everyone is at church marks a capitalist's faith in 'an alternative religion in which Divinity looks after thieves and promotes the exploitation rather than love of one's fellowman' (Dale 1985: 21). For Mallen (2001), Jacob 'epitomizes greedy consumption' (50), and his very idiocy augurs a 'spontaneous economic order' that 'implicates the entire English economy' (51), while Rodstein (1991) argues that Jacob 'embodies a principle of limitless desire' (303) in fetishizing the candies David creates, and that his idiocy, which she locates primarily in his incapacity with language, means that he does not 'subordinate desire or consumption to utterance' (314). Gregory (2002), stressing Jacob's apparently 'primitive' physical attributes and pointing to Eliot's comparison of Jacob to Caliban, argues that he represents a local version of the colonial subject, the nemesis from the West Indies sugar plantations, as it were. As she argues, 'Jacob's hyper-physicalized body invokes nineteenth-century stereotypes of Africans', while his 'idiocy … definitively echoes the intellectual and moral inferiority so often assigned to colonial peoples at mid-century and beyond' (294).

Jacob's innocence is critical to his success as a nemesis; as Rodstein perceptively observes:

> Jacob, with his idiot consciousness, is capable of making the imaginative leaps and reversals that give the story its fabular quality and satirical bite. Like Wordsworth's idiot boy, for whom all kinds of magic reversals and sublime leaps are imagined possible, Jacob stands for a literal reading more accurate than David's verbal cunning. (Rodstein 1991: 313)

His desire for candy and consequent love for David, growing from the confectioner's plan to use his art to deceive his brother, transforms the fool into an unwitting trickster (unlike Scott's actively deceptive David Gellatley), so that Jacob reveals David Faux to the world in all his unsuccessful and petty machinations. While Eliot removes Jacob from an overtly Christian context in denoting him a force of the 'great Nemesis … herself', the character takes his primary significance from the tradition of the innocent trickster, while offering the threat of physical danger through his large size and pitchfork talisman – an image that might also link him to stock cartoon representations of the devil.

The related notions of the innocent and the trickster fools are venerable, versatile and tremendously resilient, informing metaphorical readings of folly from the Bible to medieval fool festivals to nineteenth-century narratives drawing on images of idiocy to explore (among other things) historical change, social hypocrisy and economic processes. In each of the works considered in this chapter, the fool/idiot character is in some way instrumental to the resolution of the novel, although often this importance is symbolic. David brings together Edward and the Baron as they hide from the English army, and their association with him underscores their political innocence; Maggy accompanies Amy as her shadow figure throughout the novel, and helps her burn the troublesome codicil; Jacob directly unveils his brother's deceits. In each instance, folly is adapted to its specific context, providing a flexible template that can be endlessly reworked to fit specific narrative or metaphorical needs; the fool thus becomes an all-purpose tool, both satirical and sentimental, appealing to the intellect as well as the emotions. The next chapter will examine in greater depth one application of the 'innocent', in focusing on Charles Dickens's *Barnaby Rudge*, with its titular idiot character.

Notes

1 Similarly, in Lady Sydney Morgan's *The O'Briens and the O'Flahertys* (1827), Robin, the porter of O'Brien manor, is described as 'one whose intellect had only been awakened to extortion, and whom indigence had almost stultified to idiotism' (vol. I, 265). He is barely communicative and is impoverished-looking, despite (or perhaps because of) his decrepit livery. Robin's mother is described as being 'scarcely more human' than her son (vol. II, 195). Like David Gellatley, Robin provides local colour for the novel, creating a particular image of 'Ireland' for Morgan's readers. Robin seems to be representative of the degenerate state of the native Irish (as well as the impoverished Irish aristocracy), and his brief appearances are limited to when the protagonist, O'Brien, returns to his ancestral home. Interestingly, at another point in the novel, the narrator describes the English in Dublin as a 'feeble race of imbecile fanatics' (vol. II, 150). According to Ferris (1991), reviewers of Morgan's work, a story of Irish subjection, generally commended her 'mimetic power' in delineating 'Irish scenery and Irish manners' (46), while decrying what they saw as 'high-strung, overwrought writing' (47) and her suspicious political sympathies. One cannot help but suspect that this criticism condones her description of the Irish servants while condemning that of the Anglo-Irish aristocracy.

2 Despite the claims of the *British Critic* reviewer, there did not seem to be a particularly large number of 'idiots' in Scotland, and provisions for their support were similar to those in England and Wales; some were boarded privately, but most who were 'at large' were cared for by their parish, living in workhouses or poorhouses (Houston 2000, 2001).

3 The concept that a 'public idiot' may have a young trainee recalls Robert Armin's position as the apprentice to Richard Tarlton (Chapter 6), further asserting the links between the Shakespearean fool and Scott's version; the 'fool-to-knave' ratio is a comic anticipation of the concept of moral imbecility that will take shape towards the end of the nineteenth century.

4 The second article, Harriet Martineau's 1854 'Idiots Again', focused on the social and familial 'burden' of idiocy and argued that this burden could be lessened by

outlawing marriages between close relations and through the proper treatment of idiocy at facilities like Earlswood.

5 Dickens's conflation of the debtor's prison with the idiot asylum reiterates Daniel Defoe's claim in his *Essay Upon Projects* (1697) to 'think no man so much made a Fool of as a *Bankrupt*' (191), discussed further in Chapter 9.

6 The story of Inkle and Yarico was popularized by Richard Steele in the *Spectator* for 13 March 1711, but comes originally from Richard Ligon's *A True and Exact History of the Island of Barbadoes* (1657). See Plasa (2005) for a detailed analysis of the importance of Inkle and Yarico to *Brother Jacob*.

CHAPTER 8

Barnaby Rudge, idiocy and paternalism: assisting the 'poor idiot'

From protests on town commons to petitions before Parliament, through the 1830s and 1840s Britain witnessed an explosion of working-class trade unionism and occasional agitation, primarily associated with the Chartist movement. 'Chartism means the bitter discontent grown fierce and mad, the wrong condition therefore or the wrong disposition, of the Working Classes of England', according to Thomas Carlyle, writing in 1839 (see Shelston 1971: 151). 'What means this bitter discontent of the Working Classes? Whence comes it, whither goes it? Above all, at what price, on what terms, will it probably consent to depart from us and die into rest? These are questions', he stressed, before offering some provisional answers (152). Chartism, he argued, grows from 'the feeling of injustice' (177) and expresses 'the claim of the Free Working-man to be raised to a level, we may say, with the Working Slave; his anger and cureless discontent till that be done' (215). These concerns occupied a great number of people, and one response considered by many – including Carlyle and the young novelist Charles Dickens – involved the development of a revamped, reinvigorated version of paternalism, one in which captains of industry assumed some of the social responsibilities formerly held (at least in theory) by the aristocracy and gentry, but which also relied on working people to develop greater moral responsibility and self-sufficiency.

Chartism was a largely working-class movement, although it involved a broad coalition of groups, that took its name from its People's Charter for social and political reform, presented to Parliament first in 1838 and again in 1842. While the events and groups associated with

Chartist ideals were generally peaceful, the 1830s and early 1840s saw a number of clashes with state authorities that prompted the pillars of British society to theorize what was amiss and how the problem could be addressed. As far as Carlyle was concerned, Chartism was the inevitable, if lamentable and appalling, outbreak of a poorly governed working class. According to his analysis, the root of the workers' complaint lay with their abusive treatment by their social superiors – industrialists as well as landowners – who should have known better. In this argument, the Chartists' call for universal male suffrage and similar legislative reforms could not be considered seriously as a political challenge but rather as the response to the moral collapse of those paternalists – the aristocracy, the landed gentry and, increasingly, captains of industry – charged with ensuring the welfare of the working people. Indeed, he implied, this moral collapse had precipitated the working classes into their own mental collapse:

> If there do exist general madness of discontent, then sanity and some measure of content must be brought about again – not by constabulary police alone. When the thoughts of a people, in the great mass of it, have grown mad, the combined issue of that people's workings will be madness, and incoherency and ruin! Sanity will have to be recovered for the general mass; coercion itself will otherwise cease to be able to coerce. (Shelston 1971: 153)

Against a frenzied population, even the threat of force is powerless. Instead, the solution for the problems posed by Chartism lay in the hands of both industrialist paternalists and their employees. The pragmatic response, Carlyle suggested, lay in both improved social structures and greater personal responsibility, in the forms of better education for the masses and of increased emigration by unemployed labourers.

Carlyle was hardly alone in advancing these arguments, and Charles Dickens was among those espousing a similar position (Christian 1947a,b; Goldberg 1972; Ackroyd 1990); indeed, Dickens, who first met Carlyle at a dinner party in 1840, later claimed that the older writer exerted a greater influence on him than any other individual (Goldberg 1972). The affinity between the two men can be seen in Dickens's 1841 novel *Barnaby Rudge*, subtitled *A Tale of the Riots of '80*, which takes its narrative from the anti-popery Gordon riots. These riots lasted from 2 to 7 June 1780, and began as a protest calling for the repeal of the Roman Catholic Relief Act of two years earlier. On 2 June some 60,000 members of the Protestant Association met to deliver a petition to Parliament; their leader, Lord George Gordon, presented the petition while the crowd waited outside. A fragment of the crowd later burned down a Catholic chapel; another church was looted and its contents burned in the street. Over the next five days, the burnings and lootings continued, while the rioters sported blue cockades and shouted 'No Popery!' (Rudé 1956). However, the novel – contracted in 1836 but, owing to a number of circumstances, delayed in both gestation and composition – also had a contemporary relevance. 'The events of 1836–41 made [*Barnaby Rudge*] almost journalistically apt', John Butt and Kathleen Tillotson observe:

> The Poor Law riots, the Chartist risings at Devizes, Birmingham, and Sheffield, the mass meetings on Kersal Moor and Kennington Common, and most pointed of all, the Newgate rising of 1839 with its attempt to release Chartist prisoners – all of these, with their aftermath of trials, convictions, and petitions against the punishment of death, gave special point in 1841 to 'a tale of the Riots of '80'. (Butt and Tillotson 1957: 82)

The Gordon riots, which quickly transformed from a Protestant protest against Catholic relief into a rebellion against wealth and authority (Rudé 1956), certainly provide a parallel to the Chartist threats of the 1830s and 1840s. Indeed, in *Barnaby Rudge*, when Hugh, the ostler at the Maypole Inn, is recruited by the rioters, he mistakenly cries 'No Property' – a radical Chartist position – instead of 'No Popery' (359).

Barnaby and the Chartists

A brief plot summary of Dickens's novel is in order. *Barnaby Rudge* mixes dramas of familial unrest with the story of the anti-Catholic riots of 1780, and is split into two main sections. The novel opens in 1775, at which point we meet many of the main characters: the idiot Barnaby, his mother and his villainous father; the benevolent patriarch Gabriel Varden and his family, including his daughter, Dolly, and his apprentice, Sim Tappertit; John Willet, the obtuse keeper of the Maypole Inn, his son Joe and the ostler Hugh; and the degenerate aristocrat John Chester and his son, Edward, whose injured body appears lying on the road in the novel's opening scenes. We discover that Barnaby's father had murdered his employer, Reuben Haredale, twenty years earlier but had managed to direct suspicion to another individual while manipulating the illusion that he had also died – and that the senior Rudge has returned from oblivion to extort funds from his noble wife, causing her to flee with her son. Joe and Edward also flee from their fathers, who are respectively too restrictive and too corrupt. The second period of the novel begins five years later, and the main action concerns the Gordon riots, led by George Gordon, manipulated behind the scenes by his secretary, Gashford, and John Chester.

The various sons are again implicated: Barnaby and Hugh – the brutish ostler is also the bastard son of John Chester – become unlikely riot leaders; Joe Willet, who had been a member of the British army, joins Gabriel Varden in trying to restrain the rioters; and Edward Chester reappears in a romantic subplot, pursuing the daughter of Geoffrey Haredale, the brother of the slain Ruben. The novel then follows the riots, their consequences and the various fates of the participants.

Some critics, notably Rice (1978, 1983) and Dransfield (1998), see *Barnaby Rudge* as a direct comment on the events of Dickens's own day; others, while wary of asserting too strong an analogy, stress that parallels certainly exist between the novel and its contemporary events, but that similarities do not necessarily breed direct allegory. Dickens's story refers most significantly to Chartism in that both the Gordon rioters and the Chartists threatened violence against the authority of the state (Brantlinger 1968, 2001; Case 1990; Magnet 1985; Stigant and Widdowson 1975; Thompson 1984); it also draws on, and responds to, the model of history and narrative developed by Scott in *Waverley* and his other fiction (Case 1990; Duncan 1992), in which events at the personal and political levels refer to one another analogically. However, while Dickens consistently opposed social injustices, he also resisted conflict and rebellion (Scheckner 1987/88), and Chartist groups such as the London Democratic Association, whose objectives involved rousing London to a state of military preparedness (Bennett 1982), would gain little of his sympathy. In 'On Strike', an 1854 article on striking factory workers in the town of Preston, published in February 1854 in *Household Words*, the journal he founded and co-edited, Dickens argues that 'political economy is a mere skeleton unless it has a little human covering and filling out, a little human bloom in it, a little human warmth in it'. He concludes, 'Masters right, or men right; masters wrong or men wrong; both right, or both wrong; there is a certain ruin to both in the continuance or frequent revival of this breach' (see Slater 1999: 210). A solution would come only when the opposing sides realized that their common interests overwhelmed their differences, which would be a result not of economic analysis but of discussion borne of respect for one another, each in his assigned role; notably, Dickens's use of the term 'masters' signals a certain affiliation with traditional notions of a paternal, organic social hierarchy.

Dickens, along with many other Victorians, read such conflicts in moral rather than economic terms – much like Carlyle's analysis of the Chartist movement. This inclination to structure social and historical conflicts in a moral framework also accords with his approach to fiction, where he stresses the need to personalize the historical struggle.[1] His concern with the proper and just exercise of authority in *Barnaby Rudge*, specifically paternal authority, clearly engages the contemporary discourse concerning the status of paternalism as a social philosophy and the role of both industry and the state in early Victorian society. Significantly, Dickens joins with this debate through the association of the 'poor idiot' Barnaby, a figure most Victorian readers would agree needs a strong paternal guide, with the violent ostler Hugh and, through them, with the disruptive and rebellious mob.

Barnaby is an odd title character, being in many ways peripheral to the main action of the novel (he disappears from Chapters 26 to 45, for instance). Still, Dickens saw fit to name the book after him instead of the locksmith Gabriel Varden, the epitome of solid middle-class citizenry, even though his working title through the novel's earlier drafts was 'Gabriel Vardon [*sic*], the Locksmith of London'. Barnaby's particular symbolic usefulness as the title character comes from his status as an idiot – the term Dickens uses to describe him both in the novel and in his discussions of the book (for example, in his letter of 28 January 1841 to illustrator George Cattermole, he writes 'Barnaby being an idiot my notion is to have him always in company with a pet raven who is immeasureably more knowing that himself' – see House and Storey 1969: vol. II, 197). Kathleen Tillotson writes in her introduction to the Oxford edition of the novel that 'Barnaby must finally be accepted less as a study of individual character than as an expression of the Dickensian compassion for the helpless and exploited' (Tillotson 1953: xii). But why does Dickens use an idiot character to express this compassion? What constitutes this idiocy, and how does it perform its symbolic work in the text?

Barnaby, fathers and authority in the novel

We first meet Barnaby as Gabriel Varden comes across him on the road to London: he is kneeling over the prostrate body of Edward Chester, the victim of a highway assault. When Varden asks 'You know me, Barnaby?', Barnaby nods 'not once or twice, but a score of times, and that with a fantastic exaggeration which would have kept his head in motion for an hour, but that the locksmith held up his finger, and fixing his eye sternly upon him caused him to desist' (73). This passage immediately establishes Barnaby's impressionable intellect and Varden's status as benevolent patriarch. Dickens then describes Barnaby's appearance:

As he stood, at that moment, half shrinking back and half bending forward, both his face and figure were full in the strong glare ... and as distinctly revealed as though it had been broad daylight. He was about three-and-twenty years old, and though rather spare, of a fair height and a strong make. His hair, of which he had a great profusion, was red, and hanging in disorder about his face and shoulders, gave to his restless looks an expression quite unearthly – enhanced by the paleness of his complexion, and the glassy lustre of his large protruding eyes. Startling as his aspect was, the features were good, and there was something even plaintive in his wan and haggard aspect. But, the absence of the soul is far more terrible in a living man than in a dead one; and in this unfortunate being its noblest powers were wanting.

His dress was of green, clumsily trimmed here and there – apparently by his own hands – with gaudy lace; brightest where the cloth was most worn and soiled, and poorest where it was at the best. A pair of tawdry ruffles dangled at his wrists, while his throat was nearly bare. He had ornamented his hat with a cluster of peacock's feathers, but they were limp and broken, and now trailed negligently down his back. Girt to his side was the steel hilt of an old sword without blade or scabbard; and some particoloured ends of ribands and poor glass toys completed the ornamental portion of his attire. The fluttered and confused disposition of all the motley scraps that formed his dress, bespoke, in a scarcely less degree than his eager and unsettled manner, the disorder of his mind, and by a grotesque contrast set off and heightened the more impressive wildness of his face. (74)

The effect of Barnaby's 'fluttered and confused disposition' is elaborated in the illustration that accompanies this passage (see also the image of Barnaby on the front cover). While Barnaby hovers ineffectively over Chester, Varden performs a quick investigation, discovers that the victim is only wounded, and transports him to safety.

Strikingly, here Dickens stresses the absence of the 'noblest powers' of the soul, those affiliated with reason and rational thought – which is a state 'far more terrible in a living man than in a dead one' and seems to come very close to the complete absence of the soul; the passage recalls John Locke's observation (see Chapter 3) that 'some Changelings, who have lived forty years together, without any appearance of Reason, are something between a Man and a Beast'.[2] At his first appearance, Barnaby clearly lacks the rationality needed to guide him through the world of deceits and conflicts described in the novel. Varden, on the other hand, is clearly capable of providing the support Barnaby needs. When Barnaby recoils from helping the wounded man because of his fear of blood, Varden, muttering 'It's in his nature, I know ... it's cruel to ask him, but I must have help', convinces 'the idiot' to assist him by appealing to his affection for the injured man (74). Immediately, then, Varden demonstrates his ability to elicit the greatest benefit from Barnaby's limited powers.

In this opening episode, Dickens places Barnaby firmly within the tradition of literary representations of the holy fool and the wild idiot, drawing on the nineteenth-century notion of the fool's motley: a hodge-podge stitching of discordant colours and fabrics (Hotson 1952). Specific literary predecessors include two characters from the oeuvre of Walter Scott, the similarly attired madwoman Madge Wildfire from *The Heart of Midlothian* (1818) and David Gellatley from *Waverley* (Chapter 7); this association was immediately apparent to some readers, being commented upon by Patrick Robinson in his 1841 review of the novel (Butt and Tillotson 1957). Iain Crawford notes that Dickens also draws on the image presented in William Wordsworth's 1798 poem 'The Idiot Boy', but alters it so that Barnaby and his world are both darker and more critically presented; thus, the idea of the 'natural', linked as it is to the murderous rioters, becomes much more ambivalent and suggests an application of the idea of 'idiocy' that is quite distinct from Wordsworth's use of the image. Indeed, Crawford says, Dickens and Wordsworth 'may be seen to be engaged in a broader shift in attitudes towards mental retardation which occurred throughout the nineteenth century' (Crawford 1991: 41) – an insightful observation, although Crawford does not elaborate.

What advantage does the novelist gain by making this character carry the symbolic weight that is placed upon him by his idiocy? To address this question, we need to consider the nature of relationships in the novel, as well as those contentious social relations identified by Carlyle.

When Dickens wrote *Barnaby Rudge*, the dominant model for the historical novel was to be found in the tremendously popular work of Sir Walter Scott. Yet while it is as commonplace to note Scott's influence on *Barnaby Rudge* as it is to note that of the Chartist movement, this influence did not inspire imitation. Instead, Dickens actively opposes Scott's view of history: rather than presenting it as driven by conflicting or opposed interests held by different groups or individuals, he casts it as a confrontation of moral positions. Dickens's response to Scott is to write not history but anti-history, to reconstruct specific struggles as timeless, ahistorical battles between good and evil (Case 1990). The moral component of Dickens's critique in *Barnaby Rudge* merges with his political critique, and is expressed as an investigation of paternal authority. Since Steven Marcus's influential reading of the novel (Marcus 1965), criticism has been divided into two streams: one focusing on the story's political subtext, and the other exploring its psychological drama (Michasiw 1989). Marcus identifies both these interests in the novel, but ultimately prioritizes the latter, and suggests the novel's engagement with history is subsumed in its concern with the Oedipal drama. The past establishes authority over the present as surely as fathers dominate their sons. And in most cases, the past's authority is expressed as meaningless and tyrannical. Interestingly, Marcus's criticism of the novel is liberally laced with references to idiocy associated with other sources of authority: the world of the novel is dominated by 'tyrannic and imbecile authority' (Marcus 1965: 178); the country justice is a 'moral imbecile' (182); and John Willet is an 'idiot father' (190). Marcus extrapolates Barnaby's idiocy to make it a general feature of abusive or irresponsible paternalist authority (both familial and social) in the novel.

Certainly, Dickens's representatives of traditional masculine authority do not fare well. The failure of the father's responsibility is most evident in the linked characters Barnaby and Hugh, both abandoned sons. Barnaby embodies his father's crime, being born an idiot because his father, bloodied from murdering his employer, Reuben Haredale, confronts his wife and charges her to say nothing of having seen him. She, pregnant, collapses in fright and gives birth to Barnaby, an idiot who has a small birthmark 'that seemed a smear of blood but half washed out' (87) and an aversion to the sight of blood. Hugh's beautiful gypsy mother is abandoned by her lover, later revealed to be the deceitful and dissolute aristocrat Sir John Chester, and is reduced to stealing to support her young child; captured and convicted, she is hanged by state executioner, Ned Dennis, who later reappears as one of the riot's leaders (Chester's abuse of his offspring transcends class stratifications, as he also exploits his legitimate son and heir, Edward). Thus, paternal authority at both the familial and societal level fails these two figures. The evils of the specific fathers, Chester and Rudge, are reconstituted in the social rebellion of the riots, led by their abandoned sons. In addition, John Willet, the proprietor of the Maypole Inn, refuses to accept his son Joe as a capable adult, a failure that drives Joe to enlist in the army; he is sent into battle, where he loses an arm.[3] Even Gabriel Varden, the locksmith who is the only successful patriarch in the novel, struggles with his apprentice, Sim Tappertit, in an economic and professional relationship modelled on that of parent and child.

The abuse or abdication of paternal authority within the family does not simply mirror the riots; it is profoundly implicated in Dickens's explanation of the mob's violence. Bad fathers (and paternalists) lead to social rebellion: incompetent fathers are mirrored by equally incompetent social authorities. George Gordon is a mentally unstable pawn, manipulated by John Chester and the secretary Gashford, and ends his days in a lunatic asylum; indeed, Dickens's description of 'the absurdity of [Gordon's] appearance' (351) at the Maypole Inn creates a visual link between the mad lord and the idiot Barnaby. Dickens also condemns the Mayor of London, who does nothing to quell the riots; after the mob's first destructive episode, he writes,

> Hot and drunken though they were, they had not yet broken all bounds and set all law and government at defiance. Something of their habitual deference to the authority erected by society for its own preservation yet remained among them, and had its majesty been vindicated in time, the secretary [Gashford] would have had to digest a bitter disappointment. (466)

The fact that this 'authority erected by society' remains silent before the wilful assertion of abusive authority – as represented by the deluded Lord Gordon, the morally degenerate Chester and the corrupt Gashford – becomes one of the novel's central issues, an expression of Dickens's concern with the use of a just and benevolent yet strong authority.

Another representative of traditional authority, the country judge who tries to buy Barnaby's raven, Grip, and later sentences Barnaby to hang, is described in conventionally flattering terms:

> this gentleman had various endearing appellations among his intimate friends. By some he was called 'a country gentleman of the true school,' by some 'a fine old country gentleman,' by some 'a thorough-bred Englishman,' by some 'a genuine John Bull;' but they all agreed in one respect, and that was, that it was a pity there were not more like him, and that because there were not, the country was going to rack and ruin every day. (435)

Yet these titles all denote a foolish, ignorant and self-important man, as Dickens goes on to demonstrate, finally concluding his description with the observation that 'Barnaby being an idiot, and Grip a creature of mere brute instinct, it would be very hard to say what this gentleman was' (435). Ned Dennis, the state hangman, also provides a vehicle for Dickens to satirize notions of justice and the corrupt authority of the state, especially in Dennis's numerous proclamations that the right to be 'worked off' by hanging is the very essence of the English constitution.

Gabriel Varden, the 'Locksmith of London' who was the novel's title character in its earlier drafts, is the only successful patriarch in the story (and his rule is only marginally successful, at that). Despite being married to a woman who never recognizes his goodness until after the riots, and being saddled with his sullen apprentice Sim Tappertit, who wishes to displace Varden and kidnap his daughter, Varden remains hearty and cheerful. In a story concerned with the failure of authority, on both the familial and societal levels, Varden clearly represents a

moral centre. Throughout, he is a model figure: he bears his ills gracefully, unlike the surviving Haredale brother, Geoffrey, who is bitter
about the death of his brother and the ongoing disenfranchisement
of Catholics. In contrast to Haredale, Varden assists those who have
wronged him, including the apprentice who would happily have seen
him dead. In the worthy locksmith, Dickens foregrounds the rights
and responsibilities of a citizen, yet Varden's occupation indicates
the ambivalent role he performs in safeguarding society. The locks he
makes both maintain safety and reinforce an authority which is not
always just. When he risks his life by refusing before the mob to break
the lock on Newgate prison, he is both affirming the sanctity of social
authority and justifying an oppressive power, an ambivalent position
of which Dickens is aware. But it would be wrong to assume that
Dickens, generally a liberal thinker, did not value or condone the ability
of the state to assert its power forcefully in a just cause; indeed, most
evidence suggests he fully endorsed the judicious application of power
(Middlebro' 1980; Scheckner 1987/88).

Interestingly, in many readings of the novel *Barnaby Rudge*, the function of the title character is glossed over. Most critics read Barnaby's
idiocy as a formal element of the literary text and within a literary tradition, rather than as an image engaged with extra-literary contexts. Juliet
McMaster, identifying Barnaby as a 'holy fool', argues that the novel
uses Barnaby to validate the 'visionary' through the eventual accuracy
of that character's dreams and perceptions; McMaster links Dickens
as imaginative novelist to Barnaby as visionary, and reads the story as
an aesthetic argument about the 'shadowy everyman's land that lies
between conscious and unconscious regions of the mind' (McMaster
1984: 15). Natalie McKnight (1993) also identifies Barnaby as a holy
fool, who, perceiving things in a manner unlicensed by authority, represents the return of society's repressed. However, she complains,
Barnaby essentially disappears towards the end of the novel (his final
speech, she notes, is before he is taken off for execution; after his
pardon, he remains silent). Barnaby becomes more 'normal' at the end
of the novel, cutting back on his wild ramblings and working harder
to assist his mother, a circumstance that leads McKnight to claim that
Dickens has 'decentered, minimalized and ultimately silenced' Barnaby
in the novel that bears his name (McKnight 1993: 91). Marchbanks
(2006b: 67–85) notes that Barnaby serves as a plot catalyst but that
his 'idiocy' is subsumed beneath these literary demands, and thus
Dickens's portrayal of Barnaby's idiocy is inconsistent. Marcus (1965)
argues that the three lead rioters, Barnaby, Hugh and Ned Dennis,
the hangman, represent a perverse Freudian trinity, with Dennis as a

superego gone berserk, Hugh as a violent and brutal id, and Barnaby as a defective ego. However, he also discusses Barnaby as a 'holy fool', but one whose innocence 'alternates with generalized emotions of anger, vindictiveness, and violence', creating behaviour 'whose consequences are indistinguishable from those which proceed from calculated wickedness' (Marcus 1965: 192). Barnaby's innocence is threatened because it can survive only 'in a society informed by the moral authority of love' (Marcus 1965: 194) and not in the world of political machinations. While Marcus interprets Barnaby primarily as being representative of the folly and madness of the crowd, Magnet (1985) argues for Barnaby and Hugh as instances of 'natural man', figures who have not experienced the civilizing although repressive father and who thus represent an undisciplined and violent unconscious.

Many of the works that consider Barnaby's idiocy tend to be of the 'diagnostic case study' genre. In 1898, George Gissing, noting that 'Barnaby himself, the so-called idiot, interests us very little', argued that

> it is a misuse of language to call him an 'idiot'. Idiocy means an imperfection of mind which degrades and possibly brutalizes; but Barnaby's weak point is a morbid development of the imagination at the expense of the reasoning powers; he is simply insane, and subject to poetic hallucinations. (Gissing 1898: 112)

In 1935 Lillian Hatfield Brush, a psychologist, reiterated Gissing's complaint: 'By the time I was a third of the way through the book I was considerably upset to find Dickens persistently terming Barnaby an *idiot*' (Hatfield Brush 1935: 24, original emphasis). She then performs a mock case study on the character in which she determines that he represents 'a clear case of a regression psychosis of the paraphrenic type' and suggests, presumably tongue in cheek, that 'so long as he remains with his mother, improvement is doubtful' (30). In 1960 the neurologist Sir Russell Brain suggested that Barnaby is a fine specimen of a mentally defective character (Brain 1960: 135), but in 1972 literary critic Leonard Manheim argued, like Hatfield Brush, that Dickens erred in calling Barnaby a 'natural' or an 'idiot' (although Manheim himself used the term 'mental defective'), and that Barnaby is in fact schizophrenic. Interestingly, while Barnaby does not count as an idiot, despite the narrator's claims that he is, John Willet, the owner of the Maypole Inn, described by Dickens as a man of 'profound obstinacy and slowness of apprehension' (45), is diagnosed by Manheim (1972: 89) as 'feeble-minded'. In 1987, Thelma Grove, with the advantage of additional work carried out in the field of clinical psychology over the years, diagnoses Barnaby as 'the first autistic hero in English literature' (Grove 1987: 147). Scott Dransfield suggests that Barnaby, 'while constructed clearly on the innocent "idiot boy" type', more significantly embodies a form of 'moral insanity' (Dransfield 1998: 80); similarly, David Oberhelman argues that 'despite the "diagnosis" of idiocy given in the novel, it is clear that Barnaby is the first victim of the paternal madness that spawns the fury of the riots and which manifests itself in Barnaby as a "wildness"' (Oberhelman 1995: 39). In their attempts to come to a psychological understanding of Barnaby, these readings ignore the symbolic function of idiocy. Barnaby is not intended to be a realistic representation of an 'idiot' any more than he is meant to be a realistic portrayal of someone with a 'regression psychosis of the paraphrenic type', schizophrenia, autism or moral insanity. Rather, Barnaby is an idiot because, for Dickens and his readers, the idea of idiocy best performs the appropriate symbolic labour in this novel.

Barnaby serves as a useful symbol both of the rioters' folly and of the undisciplined subconscious, something located within the individual. Interestingly, even those critics who acknowledge and elaborate upon the political components of the novel identify Barnaby as a creature of the subconscious, which is accurate so far as it goes. The character of Barnaby apparently lends itself especially well to readings of the psychological issues embedded in the novel. However, when critics discuss the novel's political dimensions, Barnaby is usually abandoned for other characters and events. Criticism of the character in the novel bearing his name thus constructs him as existing within a literary tradition and a psychological or philosophical discourse, but not in a social or political discourse. This is a mistake, because Barnaby, as an idiot, provides a useful metaphor for an unruly crowd deficient in proper leadership, which is much how Dickens represents the Gordon rioters. The crowd may be a social unconscious, but it is at the same time a group of people in need of government, the 'just authority' whose dormancy the novel laments.

Idiocy, politics and paternalism

The political significance of idiocy in *Barnaby Rudge* lies in its relation to the debate over the proper expression of paternalism in government and society. Even by the start of the eighteenth century, writes E. P. Thompson (1974: 385), 'economic rationalism nibbled (and had long been nibbling) at the bonds of paternalism'. By the end of that century, dramatic social and economic changes had rendered

paternalism moribund or apparently inconsequential, sparking philosophical struggles over its future. Many, notes Asa Briggs (1967: 155),
condemned the 'social disintegration consequent upon the rise of
factory industry', and the first decades of the nineteenth century saw
the publication of numerous books and novels, pamphlets and articles
espousing reinvigorated paternalist social ideas. Writers as distinct as
William Cobbett, who eulogized the 'chain of connection' that linked
the rich and poor, and Robert Southey, who similarly lamented 'the
bond of attachment' joining these groups (quoted in Briggs 1967: 155),
vigorously condemned the demise of those small industries which were
being replaced by the massive factories of the industrial revolution.

As the term suggests, 'paternalism' posits a parent–child relationship
between the classes, reiterating an ostensibly organic familial structure. In the 1830s and 1840s, the disruption of traditional paternalist
structures of relations between the social ranks prompted a search
for a sound theoretical basis for paternalism (Lawes 2000; Roberts
1979). Commentators debated whether to revive and reinvigorate the
traditional form with pure moral force (the hard Tory position) or to
transform it into some new shape that might better fit the problems of
the age. In 1825, David Robinson, writing in *Blackwood's*, a leading Tory
organ, asserted that it was

> essential for the good of the labourer, as well as for the good of the state,
> that he should be under the authority of his master in respect of general
> conduct as well as labour; that his master should instruct him in what
> constitutes a good member of society, as well as in the mysteries of his
> calling; and that his master should coerce his bad morals, as well as his
> idleness and bad workmanship. (Quoted in Lawes 2000: 33)

Similarly, William Johnstone, another *Blackwood's* contributor, wrote
in 1829:

> 'As Tories, we maintain that it is the duty of the people to pay obedience
> to those set in authority over them: but it is also the duty of those in
> authority to protect the people who are placed below them. (Quoted in
> Lawes 2000: 33–34)

Expressions of paternalism were characterized by this oft-reiterated
claim that property had its duties as well as its rights, an assertion that
became its hallmark as a social and increasingly political philosophy in
the 1840s (Roberts 1978).

Paternalism was often placed in opposition to theories of political
economics, defined by John Ramsay McCulloch, one of the latter's
leading proponents, as 'the science of the laws which regulate the production, accumulation, distribution, and consumption of those articles

or products that are necessary, useful, or agreeable to man, and which at the same time possess exchangeable value' (McCulloch 1864: 1); because man was a rational creature, continually improving himself and 'destined to be the artificer of his own fortune' (McCulloch 1864: 21), it was possible to formulate laws determined by a belief in a rational self-interest. McCulloch's *The Principles of Political Economy*, first published in 1825, was reprinted many times in the two decades following. Although both political economics and paternalism expressed largely 'organicist' notions of the state's relation to its citizens, political economy was derided by paternalists as lacking humanity; for their part, writers sympathetic to political economy dismissed the presumptions of paternalism (Gallagher 2006). In 1848, John Stuart Mill observed that, 'Considered in its moral and social aspect, the state of the labouring people has latterly been a subject of much more speculation and discussion than formerly; and the opinion that it is not now what it ought to be, has become very general'. Paternalism, he noted in his own *Principles of Political Economy*, sought to address this problem through a 'theory of dependence and protection' in which

> The relation between rich and poor … should be only partly authoritative; it should be amiable, moral, and sentimental: affectionate tutelage on the one side, respectful and grateful deference on the other. The rich should act *in loco parentis* to the poor, guiding and restraining them like children. Of spontaneous action on their part there should be no need. They should be called on for nothing but to do their day's work, and to be moral and religious. Their morality and religion should be provided for them by their superiors, who should see them properly taught it, and should do all that is necessary to ensure their being, in return for labour and attachment, properly fed, clothed, housed, spiritually edified, and innocently amused. (Mill 1848: 334)

Mill's portrayal is surprisingly mild in its sarcasm, and he acknowledges the appeal of this idealized relationship, while simultaneously stressing that, historically, it had never truly been realized.

From the perspective of the traditional paternalist, the ruling classes acted – in an ideal case – as benevolent fathers to those beneath them, to whom they had certain responsibilities, such as ensuring that their tenants and labourers were sheltered, fed and capable of meeting their needs. In return, the lower classes owed respect and deference, as well as labour, to their superiors. But at the same time, advocates of a new type of paternalism were proposing an interventionist strategy that was anathema to paternalists of the classic Tory sort (parodied by Dickens in the country judge who condemns Barnaby to death), who conceived legislation to be an interference in their realm of influence and power. Advocates for traditional paternalism – and, indeed, many non-traditionalists, such as Carlyle – argued that legislation could not address the dilemmas faced by society; instead, the problem was a question of moral soundness and firmness of purpose. According to these arguments, the country simply needed better paternalists, men who were more concerned about those beneath them in the social hierarchy. Increasingly, and especially in urban centres, the rights and duties of paternalism were broadened to apply not just to aristocracy and gentry but also to captains of industry, the leaders of the new economy. As Catherine Gallagher writes, the new paternalists believed that

> society could be regenerated by duplicating the family's benevolent hierarchy.... If employers would act like wise fathers and workers like dutiful children, antagonistic class interests would disappear, along with the extreme poverty and the class separation that accompanied early industrialism. (Gallagher 1985: 117)

Better employers – who would necessarily also be better paternalists – would raise a better society.

Dickens, who in 1841 viewed himself as something of a radical, according to his friend and first biographer John Forster, endorsed a new form of social paternalism – a union of paternalist values applied to industry leaders, focused government intervention, and local philanthropic activities – while at the same time deriding the actual representatives of traditional paternalism as self-interested bigots (Forster 1872: 277–78). He returned to this theme many times in his writing, for example opposing those good paternalists the Cheerbyle brothers to the evil Ralph Nickleby in *Nicholas Nickleby* and, perhaps most famously, contrasting Ebenezer Scrooge before and after his dream visions in 'A Christmas Carol'. In 1841 he was also anonymously composing political squibs against the Tories, and Forster (1872: 278) quotes 'The Fine Old English Gentleman, to be said or sung at all conservative dinners', as representative of the lot:

> I'll sing you a new ballad, and I'll warrant it first-rate,
> Of the days of that old gentleman who had that old estate;
> When they spent the public money at a bountiful old rate
> On ev'ry mistress, pimp, and scamp, at ev'ry noble gate,
>   In the fine old English Tory times;
>   Soon may they come again!
> The good old laws were garnished well with gibbets, whips, and chains,
> With fine old English penalties, and fine old English pains,
> With rebel heads and seas of blood once hot in rebel veins;
> For all these things were requisite to guard the rich old gains
>   Of the fine old English Tory times;
>   Soon may they come again.

And so forth. But while Dickens derided the rule of aristocratic power, he wholeheartedly endorsed the authority of the state and the need for members of a civilized society to respect this authority. Of the Rousseauian concept of the 'noble savage', he writes in *Household Words* in 1853 that:

> it is extraordinary to observe how some people will talk about him, as they talk about the good old times; how they will regret his disappearance, in the course of the world's development, from such and such lands where his absence is a blessed relief and an indispensable preparation for the sowing of the very first seeds of any influence that can exalt humanity. (See Slater 1999: 143–44)

Rather, he concludes:

> if we have anything to learn from the Noble Savage, it is what to avoid … he passes away before an immeasurably better and higher power than ever ran wild in any earthly woods, and the world will be all the better when his place knows him no more. (Slater 1999: 148)

For Dickens, natural man requires the discipline of a just civic authority.

In some areas of responsibility claimed by traditionalists, political legislation was generally considered to be an acceptable response to social need, and legislation protecting the helpless (such as the 1833 Factory Act, which placed restrictions on child labour) received support from across the spectrum of political and economic positions. As Roberts writes,

> a concrete image of the helpless, the weak, the poor, and the injured formed the rationale for government interference. Of all these images of the weak and the helpless, none was more poignant and affecting than that of the helpless child. It was the central image in all debates on factories, mines, and lace- and print-works bills just as it was on education and reformatory grants. (Roberts 1979: 190)

Helpless children had previously been incorporated as a political responsibility, as the state occasionally acted *in loco parentis* for orphans as well as lunatics, idiots and prisoners, and had long done so. 'The paternal government intervened', observes Roberts (1979: 191), 'not so much to maximize happiness or for reasons of private right or public honour, but where the weak and helpless of Her Majesty's children needed protection'. Slowly, the state was adopting new responsibilities, taking them from the less willing hands of the wealthy and powerful.

Dickens and idiots

Among those seen as deserving the protection of a paternal state were those people considered to be idiots, who were also frequently infantilized; indeed, observers constructed them as eternal children, anomalies confounding notions of age and intellect (an association also implicit in the idea of an 'innocent'), and thus gaining the attention of sympathetic Victorians. In *Barnaby Rudge*, Dickens describes Mrs Rudge reminiscing about her son's infancy, when he was 'old and elfin-like in face, but very dear to her, gazing on her with a wild and vacant eye'; later, when Barnaby becomes a man, his 'childhood' is 'complete and lasting' (250). Barnaby is forever 'a relying, loving child to [his mother] – never growing old or cold at heart, but needing … care and duty in his manly strength as in his cradle-time' (195). This confounding of age resurfaces in an 1853 *Household Words* article, 'Idiots', by Dickens and William Henry Wills, based on a visit to the Park House Asylum. Dickens refers to an 'idiot old man of eight' and an 'idiot child of thirteen … as to its bodily growth, a child of six; to its mental development, nothing' (see Stone 1968: 497).

By the mid-1830s, when Dickens began composing *Barnaby Rudge*, progressive physicians such as John Conolly were treating madness by using 'moral management', which had been pioneered by the Tukes in their Yorkshire asylum at the end of the eighteenth century. Under this system, physicians sought to train the mad to incorporate paternalist values to govern their own behaviour, if only by rote; previously, the dominant therapeutic strategy relied upon brute force (Scull 1979). The idiot asylum itself was a post-*Barnaby Rudge* phenomenon, but the ideas that led to its creation were beginning to circulate as Dickens was penning the novel. By 1840, rumours of new approaches to educating idiots, developed by Johann Jakob Guggenbühl in Abendberg, Switzerland, and Édouard Séguin in France, were making their way to England; Conolly (among many others) visited the schools of Guggenbühl and Séguin to confirm these rumours, and in 1846 Séguin published his *Traitement moral, hygiène et éducation des idiots*, sparking a pedagogical revolution. In England, these continental examples and the pragmatic philanthropism exemplified by Conolly and the Reverend Andrew Reed (see Chapter 9) – that is, a union between reformist optimism and paternalism – led to the birth of the educational asylum for idiots in the latter half of the 1840s, driven by a new belief in the possible reclamation of these most 'helpless' of individuals.

Reed and Conolly were the driving forces behind the Park House Asylum at Highgate, the first large British institution for people identified as idiots, which began accepting patients in April 1848. Two years earlier, Charlotte White in Bath had opened the Institution for Idiot Children and those of Weak Intellect, a smaller facility which housed and taught from fifteen to thirty-three students at any given time (Carpenter 2000b). These institutions mark a new understanding of the condition, an understanding also evident in Dickens's journalism. In 'Idiots', Dickens argues that, regardless of time or geography,

> the main idea of an idiot would be of a hopeless, irreclaimable, unimprovable being. And if he be further recalled as under restraint in a workhouse or lunatic asylum, he will still come upon the imagination as wallowing in the lowest depths of degradation and neglect: a miserable monster, whom nobody may put to death, but whom every one must wish dead, and be distressed to see alive. (Stone 1968: 490)

This portrayal seems greatly at odds with the character drawn in *Barnaby Rudge* and, indeed, it turns out that Dickens is setting up a straw idiot. The next paragraph refutes this bleak image:

> Until within a few years, it was generally assumed, even by those who were not given to hasty assumptions, that because an idiot was, either wholly or in part, deficient in certain senses and instincts necessary, in combination with others, to the due performance of the ordinary functions of life – and because those senses and instincts could not be supplied – therefore nothing could be done for him, and he must always remain an object of pitiable isolation. But a closer study of the subject has now demonstrated that the cultivation of such senses and instincts as the idiot is seen to possess, will, besides frequently developing others that are latent in him but obscured, so brighten those glimmering lights, as immensely to improve his condition, both with reference to himself and to society. Consequently there is no greater justification for abandoning him, in his degree, than for abandoning any other human creature. (Stone 1968: 490)

The article then describes how such individuals can be improved, and provides anecdotal evidence based partly on the works of various writers but more directly upon Dickens's visit to the asylum. He praises the institution wholeheartedly, saying it deserves 'all encouragement and support' and calling it 'truly humane' (Stone 1968: 498), and concludes his encomium to the philanthropic asylum with the wish that one may come, 'through the instrumentality of these establishments, to see the day, before long, when the pauper idiot will be similarly provided for, at the public expense' (Stone 1968: 499). Dickens's wish clearly endorses the interventionist projects for the legitimately needy that flourished in Victorian England; his desire to see them invested via legislative authority presages the development of the welfare state.

That philanthropic initiatives to assist 'idiots', 'lunatics' and other 'helpless' members of society could garner broad support from the population and the patronage of royalty testifies to the belief in neo-paternalist and interventionist solutions and to that optimism characteristic of the mid-nineteenth century. Interestingly, the internal hierarchy of Park House and other 'idiot asylums' mirrored the paternalist structures advocated by social commentators. This organizational conceit was frequently reiterated in the promotional material for Park House and later asylums. As David Wright (2001: 143) notes, the entire inmate population was 'commonly called "the family" in most Victorian asylums'; the chief medical superintendent played the role of the paterfamilias, with the inmates and junior staff fulfilling the roles of his children (Gelband 1979).

By 1850, the Park House facility was full and a sister institution, Essex Hall, Colchester, was established. A new building, which was to become the Royal Earlswood Asylum and later the National Asylum for Idiots, was under construction in Reigate by 1853, with the cornerstone laid by no less a personage than Prince Albert. These initiatives were not exercises in traditional British paternalism, but were primarily philanthropic enterprises drawing on some of the same beliefs in the responsibilities of the wealthy and powerful. Dickens argued that this sense of responsibility should be matched by state intervention in the development of institutions to support the less fortunate of society, effectively transferring the structures and responsibilities of paternalism to the state, at least in this instance. He concludes the description of his visit to the asylum and his analysis of its educational efforts with the observation that, in 'some future annotated copy of Shakespeare', one might find 'the following happy emendation':

> A tale
> Told by an idiot, full of sound instruction,
> Signifying something.

The signifying idiot

Dickens was well aware of what idiocy could signify, even when writing *Barnaby Rudge*, and had good reason for creating an 'idiot' character rather than a 'lunatic'. In 'Idiots', he presents 'the great leading distinction between Idiocy and Insanity ... that in the Insane certain faculties which once existed have become obliterated or impaired; and that, in Idiots, they either never existed or existed imperfectly' (Stone 1968: 490), thus repeating a time-worn conceptual distinction. While lunatics could be brought back to rationality and self-government through moral management, idiots were always deficient in this respect, could never be fully self-governing and would always require a strong paternal guide. Thus, the decision to make Barnaby an idiot rather than a lunatic is significant: Barnaby – and his idiocy – is associated with the rioters and, by extension, in the political context of 1841, with the working classes represented by the Chartists. This association foregrounds a belief in the inherent inability of the working classes to be fully self-governing; like Barnaby, they would always require a strong and benevolent paternalist authority to guide and rule them. Dickens's organic and hierarchical notion of society demands that each group or class assumes its share of the responsibility for the overall health of the social organism, but also that each knows its proper role and position.

At the novel's conclusion, Barnaby is incorporated into the post-riot community that grows around the new Maypole Inn. Notably, he is saved from the moral degeneration that afflicts other participants in the riots by his natural innocence, which is, of course, a feature of his idiocy. This innocence is also characteristic of Dickens's portrayal of the poorly led and manipulated working classes who reappear in works such as his 1854 novel *Hard Times* (Dickens's visit to the Preston strikers was primarily a research trip to gather material for this novel). Barnaby gains in rationality when he and his mother are incorporated into a larger community symbolically presided over by Gabriel Varden, who also is responsible for saving him from the gallows. While maternal love makes Barnaby a fundamentally decent individual, benevolent paternal authority is associated with improving his limited capacity for self-government.

The extended clan at the end of the novel does not represent radical social departure, nor an example of moral management in practice, as Dransfield (1998) and Oberhelman (1995) suggest, so much as an idealized traditional community, governed by a benevolent patriarch. Barnaby, true to traditional associations of 'idiocy' with nature, tends poultry and cattle, keeps a garden in this community and, childlike, remains devoted to his mother.

> Some time elapsed before Barnaby got the better of the shock he had sustained, or regained his old health and gaiety. But he recovered by degrees: and although he could never separate his condemnation and escape from the idea of a terrific dream, he became, in other respects, more rational. Dating from the time of his recovery, he had a better memory and greater steadiness of purpose; but a dark cloud overhung his whole previous existence, and never cleared away.

> He was not the less happy for this; for his love of freedom and interest
> in all that moved or grew, or had its being in the elements, remained to
> him unimpaired. He lived with his mother on the Maypole farm, tending
> the poultry and cattle, working on a garden of his own, and helping every-
> where. He was known to every bird and beast about the place, and had
> a name for every one. Never was there a lighter-hearted husbandman,
> a creature more popular with young and old, a blither and more happy
> soul than Barnaby; and though he was free to ramble where he would, he
> never quitted Her, but was for evermore her stay and comfort. (737)

Gabriel Varden stands alone as the novel's proper patriarch, one who
defies the rioters when they abduct him to open the locks at Newgate.
He believes in order and authority tempered with generosity and
mercy, and is responsible not only for saving Barnaby from hanging
but also for creating the benevolently governed microcosm in which
Barnaby can become a 'happy soul' (737). This soul, almost non-
existent at Barnaby's first appearance in the novel, grows healthy
under the watchful, rational eye of Varden. The locksmith guarding
the sanctity of authority is tempered by the benevolent patriarch, the
model of a good government.

Similarly, Carlyle, in his conclusion to *Chartism*, appeals to working-
class rationality – limited as it is – to confront the problems facing
society:

> These Twenty-four million labouring men, if their affairs remain un-
> regulated, chaotic, will burn ricks and mills; reduce us, themselves,
> and the world into ashes and ruin. Simply their affairs cannot remain
> unregulated, chaotic; but must be brought into some kind of order. What
> intellect were able to regulate them? The intellect of a Bacon, the energy
> of a Luther, if left to their own strength, might pause in dismay before
> such a task; a Bacon and Luther added together, to be perpetual prime
> minister over us, could not do it. What can? Only Twenty-four million
> ordinary intellects, once awakened into action; these, well presided over,
> may. (See Shelston 1971: 223)

That these intellects must be awakened is crucial; but equally important is that, once awakened, they be well presided over – that is, well
governed. The working classes, Carlyle argues, must develop intellectually under the tutelage of benevolent overseers. Dickens, for his
part, addresses the social turmoil confronting England by advocating
a type of project in which society (in place of aristocracy), through
the occasional intervention of government, behaves responsibly to
its lowest members by ensuring proper education and fair treatment,
and they repay society with their allegiance and obedience, much as
traditional paternalism was supposed to have worked in earlier eras.
The helplessness of the deserving poor, the ignorant and the 'idiot'

authorize the new approaches to paternalism championed by Dickens, and provide its fullest justification.

Barnaby himself is an obvious subject for paternal guidance – one who cannot choose for himself because he simply does not have the capacity. Presented thus as the eternal child, Barnaby becomes the perfect symbol of a people in need of good government. Barnaby is that element of the crowd that is led into folly. He is the innocent incapable of knowing the consequences of his actions, and thus requires a gentle but firm guiding hand. He is the helpless poor driven to desperation, the ignorant man exploited. He is, in his apparent 'idiocy', the perfect justification for a new political programme designed to assist and rule the helpless, subordinate everyman. And, in his untamed state, as an associate of Hugh and a leader of the rioting mobs, he also foreshadows the dangers that would come to be associated with 'idiocy', 'imbecility' and 'feeble-mindedness' in the last decades of the nineteenth century.

Notes

1 In a letter dated 5 November 1841 responding to the artist John Landseer, who had written to Dickens commenting on the central role played by the City Chamberlain John Wilkes in quelling the riots, Dickens responds, 'You are quite right in considering it very remarkable and worthy of notice, that Wilkes should have been the active magistrate in the suppression of the Gordon Riots. I determined however, after some consideration, not to notice it in Barnaby, for this reason. – It is almost indispensable in a work of fiction that the characters who bring the catastrophes about, and play important parts, should belong to the machinery of the tale' (see House and Storey 1969: vol. II, 417). The novel's machinery being driven by moral conflict, Wilkes, an individual lying outside Dickens's dramatis personae and thus being neither wheel nor cog within this machinery, could not appear in the story, despite his historical importance.

2 This passage also echoes Immanuel Kant's observation in his *Anthropology from a Pragmatic Point of View* (1798) that 'complete mental weakness which either does not suffice for even animal activities (as among the Cretins of Valais) or which is just sufficient for a mere mechanical imitation of external actions which animals can perform (such as sawing, digging and so forth) is called idiocy. This should not be called sickness of soul, but rather lack of soul instead' (108). For Kant, as for many others thinkers, rationality was an expression of the soul.

3 That the elder Willets and Chesters are both named John is significant. Dickens's own father, John Dickens, from whom he was estranged, was at the time borrowing money on his famous son's name, and occasionally simply forging his son's signature (Ackroyd 1990). Myron Magnet flirts with the claim that Barnaby is a projection of Dickens's own Oedipal fantasies, and hence is 'imbued with murderous, anticivilized Oedipal violence' (Magnet 1985: 82), although he does not pursue it with vigour, noting only that he 'cannot but note … the virtue of Freud's theory here'.

CHAPTER 9

Innocence, philanthropy and economics: the new 'asylum' idiot

When the brothers Fergus, Ronald and Archie first meet the laird, the landowner to whom they pay rent in Harriet Martineau's 1832 story 'Ella of Garveloch', from her *Illustrations of Political Economy* (1836), only Fergus and Ronald acknowledge him; Archie remains aloof. The laird naturally asks about the third brother, so Fergus answers that, different as he is, Archie 'is wiser than us about many things, and sees farther. He is always housed before a tempest, or safe in a hole in the rock, like the birds he seems to learn from' (7). 'Ella of Garveloch' provides an introduction to the workings of rental properties, using as a 'case study' Ella and her three brothers, her admirer (and eventual husband) Angus, and their improvident neighbours the Murdochs, all inhabitants of the isolated and hostile Garveloch Islands, off the west coast of Scotland. Economic activity intersects with Christian morality through the character of Archie, who is referred to as both an 'innocent', by his older sister Ella, and an 'idiot', by Callum, the self-important steward of the laird, a notably benevolent landlord. Martineau refers to 'the island superstition that the poor boy was under special invisible protection, and therefore screened from ill usage at the hand of man, as well as from natural perils' (30); the fact that Archie apparently learns from the birds, benefits from divine protection and enjoys 'a keener sight into the place of storms' (35) than the other islanders reinforces his connection to the natural world, and asserts his place in the design laid out by providence. But this story, as an 'illustration of political economy', is very much about analysing the conditions and parameters of human existence so that one may prosper in this world. Providence may provide the design, but humans are responsible for rendering this design into a social reality as wisely as possible. Archie contributes to the household economy by gathering the eggs of the birds nesting nearby and wringing the necks of the gannets too foolish not to fly away from him, tasks which Ella proudly represents 'as adding to the resources of the household, in no small degree' (37). But when Ronald suggests that Archie take a turn at handing the rent to Callum, Ella insists that 'Archie is not made to hold a money-pouch, nor to have any worldly dealings' (41) and further expresses the fear that Callum would try to have Archie sent away if he were aware of the boy's incapacity. When Ronald objects that Archie's labours 'help to fill' the familial money-pouch, Ella responds:

> And how innocently! It is his love for the things that God made that makes him follow sport. The birds are his playmates while they wheel round his head, and when he takes them on the nest, he has no thought of gain – and evil be to him that first puts the thought into him! (41)

The innocent Archie, like Barnaby Rudge, thrives in a world governed over by a benevolent authority – in this case Ella. But political economy demands self-discipline; it is, as Martineau presents it, an exercise in both morality and rationality, demanding thoughtful choices to ensure a profitable future. Martineau's tale tracks the balance needed for Ella to support her family in time of want, while at the same time making the rational economic choices that will ensure that her family survives adversity to prosper in time of plenty. However, Archie is ultimately not part of this scheme; towards the end of the story, he dies in saving his brother Fergus from a whirlpool. We are led to believe that this act involves a personal sacrifice, as throughout the story Martineau has consistently emphasized Archie's care in avoiding risk and danger, and stresses that he knows the whirlpool well.

But why is Archie's self-sacrifice necessary? More to the point, why does Archie die? In terms of moving the plot forwards, this episode is unnecessary – there is no need for Fergus to be endangered, except to have Archie perish in rescuing him. Upon his death, Ella insists that her surviving brothers tend to the daily transactions of business despite the tragedy, while she searches the beach for Archie's corpse: 'I must see that Archie is still honoured by being kept apart from that in which he had no share. The business of our days went on without him while he lived, and it shall go on now, if it were only to show that he bore no part in it', she says (141). Archie is not of the world of commerce and transactions, of political economy; he is a throwback to an older era, one in which 'naturals' could be protected by God. The bustling world of the nineteenth century, marked by industrial and population growth and an accompanying Malthusian anxiety, has no space for such quaint notions as that of the 'innocent'. This leads one to suspect that Archie appears in this story for two reasons, both related to the tale's thematic and philosophical concerns rather than narrative demands: one is to demonstrate that proper Christian morality can coexist with the pragmatic tenets of political economy, as Ella embodies both; the other is so that, once the first point is made, the 'innocent' Archie can disappear, taking with him the superstitions of a previous age.

But, of course, idiocy does not disappear because the traditional concept of 'innocence' becomes less viable (nor, indeed, do the 'innocents', although they become harder to spot). In 1846, fourteen years after the publication of Martineau's story, John Conolly, superintendent of the Middlesex Lunatic Asylum in Hanwell, was soliciting public support for the new idiot asylum to be established at Park House, Highgate, which would be the forerunner of the National Asylum for Idiots. One of his speeches included the following appeal:

> It is for the poor, poor idiot we plead – for the idiot, the lowest of all the objects of Christian sympathy, – for the idiot, the most needing charity, and for whom charity has done nothing. We ask that his soul may be disimprisoned; that he may look forth from the body with meaning and intelligence on a world full of expression; that he may, as a fellow, discourse with his fellows; that he may cease to be a burden to society, and become a blessing; that he may be better qualified to know his Maker, and look beyond our present imperfect modes of being to perfected life in a glorious and everlasting future. (Quoted in Barrett 1986: 107)

Conolly's idiot is not an 'innocent' but is emphatically a pitiable being, and the Hanwell superintendent was not alone in drawing this image of the 'poor, poor idiot': sentimental appeals to pity and charity would become commonplace as asylum advocates sought funding to establish and maintain these institutions. In a Cambridge speech around 1850 in support of the National Asylum for Idiots' second home, in Essex Hall, Colchester, Conolly calls upon his auditors to 'look with an eye of pity' on these poor idiots, and compares the parental joy at witnessing the moral and intellectual development of their children to the 'vague dread' of those less fortunate parents who eventually make the 'dreadful discovery ... full of cureless woe' that their child is an idiot (quoted in Clark 1869: 122). But the arrival of an idiot infant is not simply a blow to parental expectations, as Conolly makes clear. 'If the occurrence of an idiotic or imbecile infant is so great a disaster in ranks of life placed above mere toil and the fear of want, what is the result of such a calamity in a poor family, among the classes dependent upon daily industry for daily bread?', he asks (quoted in Clark 1869: 122–23). The idiot child is an economic burden that can never be lessened. 'Without the constant care of others it must die. But that care presses heavily always, and ruinously at last, on its poor parents', and, as other siblings grow and leave home, Conolly narrates, 'the poor imbecile alone remains, and becomes even a heavier burthen to its father and mother when years are gathering over them' (125). The images are striking, and two points stand out. One is that the idiot child sentences his parents to a life of poverty because he remains 'incapable of useful occupation' (125); the other is that it is within the power of those who can turn 'an eye of pity' upon the idiot to help relieve him, and his parents, of this fate. Conolly formulates idiocy as both a moral challenge to Christian charity and an economic disaster that imposes a penalty on the livelihood of a household, distracting its inhabitants from profitable activities while simultaneously adding greater demands on those activities by providing another mouth to feed (and often a ravenous one, as many commentators pointed out).

The period between Martineau's 'Ella of Garveloch' and Conolly's appeals for the public support of idiot asylums witnessed influential new approaches in the training and education of people identified as idiots, in addition to ongoing industrial and economic transformations. The first major British asylum, at Park House, Highgate, later the National Asylum for Idiots, opened in 1848, and those asylums established across England in the 1840s and 1850s were intended to function as residential training schools that would, among other things, instruct their residents in tasks that could then be turned to account in supporting a household economy. The less affluent parents sought to have their child 'elected' by subscription to an asylum, although the wealthier would pay; the institutions would then provide education in useful skills that could enable the child to contribute to the family coffers before the child returned home at the end of the standard five-year residency.[1] In the meantime, the financial and practical challenges of raising the 'idiot' child would also be lifted from the family. These new developments also shifted the relations between idiocy, innocence and divinity, as evident in Conolly's speeches. Previously, the idiot was credited with a closeness to God (and/or nature) that other people could not duplicate. Conolly does not explicitly refute this notion, but instead adapts it so that the 'idiot' individual becomes important not for the intrinsic qualities conferred by his privileged association with the divine but for the opportunity he affords good Christians to act charitably. These charitable acts form part of the economy of social life, and are driven by a belief in the capacity of asylums to prepare idiot children for work, thus reducing the financial and moral pressure they place on their families and guiding the 'poor idiot' into communion with his fellows.

The strategies used to generate support for such initiatives thus lay in appeals to both sentimental pity and economic rationality; the fusion of these elements is expressed in acts of charity. But when the 'innocent idiot' meets the economic prerogative encapsulated in the idea of the training asylum, the idiot's symbolic relation to society is transformed. The idiot is no longer complete unto himself, with his apparent deficiency compensated by a closeness to God; rather, he is an 'unfinished creature' who needs to be 'reclaimed', as John Conolly wrote after visiting Séguin's school at the Bicêtre asylum in Paris (Conolly 1845: 293). In effect, he becomes an exile and a burden who, through the efforts of Christian charity and professional dedication, is about to be trained for a new life as an economically productive member of society. This chapter traces the tensions inherent in attempts to model the idiot both as an object of Christian philanthropy (and occasionally even an 'innocent') and as a repository of unrealized potential, both as a moral being and as a participant in social and economic activities. But before we consider the first stirrings of the nineteenth-century idiot asylum movement, we should cast a glance further back at some instructive seventeenth-century predecessors: the relation of Mr Great-Heart to Mr Feeble-Mind in John Bunyan's *Pilgrim's Progress* (1678/84) and the fool-house proposed by Daniel Defoe in his *Essay Upon Projects* (1697).

Feeble minds and fool houses

The second part of John Bunyan's classic Christian allegory *Pilgrim's Progress* follows the party of Christiana, which, led by Mr Great-Heart, journeys past threats, trials and temptations to the gates of the Celestial City.[2] While there are no attempts to model 'idiocy' *per se* in the work, Bunyan scatters the pilgrim's route with several examples of an allegorical folly, depicted in the same pejorative manner deployed by Sebastian Brant in his *Ship of Fools* (Chapter 6). Early on their voyage, Christiana and her group come across three hanged bodies, those of Sloth, Simple and Presumption, who were 'for sloth and folly themselves' (253). Later, they come across 'one *Fool*, and one *Want-Wit*, washing of an *Ethopian* with intention to make him white, but the more they washed him, the blacker he was', which, we are told, represents the quandary of the 'vile Person' – that 'all means used to get such an one a good Name, shall in conclusion tend but to make him more abominable' (342, original emphasis, here and below). The association of folly and lack of wit with non-European people as well as moral degeneracy is striking, and underscores the set of relations that join these figures in the minds of Bunyan and his readers.

Interestingly, though, the pilgrim party also comes across one Mr Feeble-Mind, held by the giant Slay-Good; Great-Heart promptly slays the giant and rescues Mr Feeble-Mind, who describes himself as 'a man of no strength at all of Body, nor yet of Mind, but would, if I could, tho' I can but *crawl*, spend my Life in the Pilgrim's way' (317). He recounts the assistance he has received to get thus far on his journey and resolves

> to *run* when I can, to *go* when I cannot run, and to *creep* when I cannot go. As to the main, I thank him that loves me, I am fixed; my way is before me, my mind is beyond the *River* that has no Bridge, tho' I am, as you see, but of a *feeble Mind*. (317–18)

When the elderly pilgrim Mr Honest asks if he knows of another pilgrim, Mr Fearing, Mr Feeble-Mind admits to being his nephew and notes that Mr Fearing hailed from the town of Stupidity, while Mr Feeble-Mind was born in the city of Destruction. But, as Mr Great-Heart asserts,

> I have it in commission, to comfort the *feeble-minded*, and to support the weak. You must needs go with us; we will wait for you, we will lend you our help, we will deny ourselves of some things, both *Opinionative* and *Practical*, for your sake; we will not enter into Doubtful disputations before you, we will be made all things to you rather than you shall be left behind. (321)

In the narrative's allegory, Great-Heart is insisting that religious conviction be made accessible to the less intellectually sophisticated, and that all willing pilgrims be helped to complete their journey.

Feeble-Mind is joined by the physically crippled Ready-to-Halt, and the two walk along together at the end of the small group led by Great-Heart. Occasionally they are joined by the women and children in the group, when these are 'weakly' and 'forced to go as they bear' (332), and when they reach the Delectable Mountain, the good shepherds dwelling there note that Great-Heart leads 'a comfortable Company' that is welcome to join them, as they 'have for the *Feeble*, as for the *Strong*' (340). Finally, Great-Heart offers his own protection and strength to succour Feeble-Mind as they travel through the Enchanted Land, the last test before they arrive at Beulah on the edge of the river, across from the Celestial City. When Feeble-Mind is called across that river to the final end of his journey, he gathers his friends to hear his last words:

> Since I have nothing to bequeath to any, to what purpose should I make
> a Will? As for my *feeble Mind*, that I will leave behind me, for that I have
> no need of that in the place whither I go…. Wherefore when I am gone I
> desire that you … would bury it in a Dunghill. (366)

In Bunyan's dream allegory, the strong support the weak, recognizing it is their Christian duty – their commission – to do so. Feeble-Mind
and Ready-to-Halt are brought before the Celestial City in part because
they desire to complete their pilgrimage, yet do not have the capacity to
complete it alone. This image would have a potent effect on the advocates of asylums in the nineteenth century, especially those influential
reformers, including John Conolly, Samuel Gaskell and Andrew Reed,
following in Bunyan's Nonconformist footsteps. And while Mr Feeble-
Mind may not meet the diagnostic criteria of idiocy in Bunyan's day, he
is, as he stresses, 'but of a feeble Mind', a term which would resurface
in professional writings during the nineteenth century to describe an
intellectual capacity apparently greater than that of idiots or imbeciles,
but still beneath that considered normal, as well as to designate a group
of persons thought to be in critical need of guidance and supervision.
By the end of the nineteenth century, of course, this same category of
people would also seem to require surveillance and segregation.

The relation between idiocy, economics and institutions has an
interesting precedent in Daniel Defoe's 1697 proposal for a 'fool-house'
in his *Essay Upon Projects*, itself a fascinating document that proposes
numerous schemes – that is, projects – for the betterment of English
society. The *Essay* was Defoe's first major attempt at influencing policy
and public opinion, an objective which was to figure in many of his
later works (Clark 2007; Furbank and Owens 2006). Most of the *Essay*'s
proposals have to do with economic management, and even those that
more explicitly address issues of social welfare and education tend to
ultimately have an economic justification. In his introduction, Defoe
identifies a fiscal crisis being experienced by merchants as the catalyst
for the 'general Projecting Humour of the Nation' (ii), with his *Essay*
being one of many such 'projections' to appear in the 1690s. Perhaps as
significantly, in 1692, Defoe had declared bankruptcy under a staggering £17,000 debt, and some of his motivation for writing the *Essay* may
have come from his desire to reform the bankruptcy process.[3] Defoe
insists, however, that his projections are for the good of the nation, and
he posits a social fabric, a community to which all belong and which
must thrive in order for its individual members to prosper as well. This
idea is evident in his references to 'the publick Stock of the Kingdom'
(11); later, when he refers to Britain as 'a Bank to it self' (66), the
phrase, while alluding to the use of land as collateral, also evokes the

concept of the nation as a singular economic entity. As Defoe insists, humans require this sort of community – on both a personal and a social-economic scale – in order to survive.

Money is to England as blood is to the body: both must circulate efficiently to ensure health.[4] The man of trade, who ensures the circulation of wealth, is the heart of the nation. As *Essay Upon Projects* progresses, Defoe becomes more and more concerned with the element of rationality in economic exchange; first broached in projections for friendly societies for sailors and widows and for a pension office, this concern becomes even more dominant in his tirade against wagering, and not only because it is an irrational and abusive application of the probability theory that lies at the very heart of rational investing (Hacking 1990). Gambling can be easily exploited by brokers, '*those Vermin of Trade*' (173), whose 'Gaming by Rule' (177) enables them to 'command the Money out of every man's Pocket, who has no more Wit than to venture' (178). The calculated financial risks that Defoe counsels in his projections for friendly societies and assurances are parodied by the disreputable manipulation of probabilities engaged in by lottery brokers. Because wagering makes a mockery of more sincere and earnest applications of probability theory, it warrants Defoe's condemnation.

Defoe's diatribe against gambling provides the transition into his proposal for a fool house, where the link between rationality and economic security is fully realized. Here, Defoe proposes that a specific institution be established to maintain fools, and suggests that their upkeep is analogous to a divine tax on human intelligence, explicitly uniting rationality with wealth. 'We use such in England with the last contempt, which I think is a strange error, since tho' they are useless to the Commonwealth, they are only so by God's direct Providence, and no previous fault', he writes, and then follows this observation with a striking analogy:

> I think 'twould very well become this Wise Age to take care of such. And perhaps they are a particular Rent-Charge on the *Great Family of Mankind*, left by the maker of us all; like a Younger Brother, who tho' the Estate be given from him, yet the Father expected the Heir should take some care of him. (179–80)

Following this line of thought, Defoe proposes that the upkeep of fools should be provided for by

> Those who have a Portion of Understanding extraordinary: Not that I would lay a Tax upon any man's Brains, *or discourage Wit, by appointing Wise Men to maintain Fools*: But some Tribute is due to God's Goodness for bestowing extraordinary Gifts; and who can it be better paid to, than such as suffer for want of the same Bounty? (180)

Hence, Defoe suggests 'a Tax upon Learning, to be paid by the Authors of Books' (181), the proceeds from which would be applied to the maintenance of a fool house outside London. Those who have the advantages of wit – the elder sons inheriting the wealth of rationality – should share their fortune with their lessers, who are 'useless to the Commonwealth' because of their inability to participate in the activities that generate further wealth. The fool house substitutes a protective environment for the rational capacity that would enable one to thrive in a market economy. Defoe provides detailed calculations on how such a tax could work, and what funds would be needed to construct, maintain and staff a fool house. However, he acknowledges that a tax on books may prove difficult to obtain, especially as money is 'so much wanted for Wise Men' – perhaps he is here recalling his own struggles with debt – and so, noting that 'a great deal of money has been thrown about in Lotteries', he proposes an alternative: a 'charity lottery' that would 'maintain Fools out of our own Folly' (184). Thus, the irrationality of the lottery gambler – the economic fool – would support the commonwealth's natural fools.

But Defoe also fears that such a fool house could risk becoming, like Bedlam, a destination for those who wish to mock its inmates, making 'what they call Sport with the Calamity of others' (189). Folly, he stresses, 'deserves Pity, not Contempt' and, thus, he suggests that a steward assume the responsibility of keeping gawkers at bay. He also includes provision for a chaplain, noting that while critics may argue that fools 'are uncapable of reaping any benefit by Religion', it remains within the power of God to 'restore the Reasoning-Faculty to an Ideot; and 'tis our part to use the proper means of supplicating Heaven to that end, leaving the disposing-part to the Issue of unalterable Providence' (191). That fools are part of God's design is beyond doubt, and Defoe asserts that 'Ideots' are full participants in divine salvation, implying further that only by acknowledging this fact can God's design be apprehended:

> The Wisdom of Providence has not left us without Examples of some of the most stupid Natural Ideots in the world, who have been restor'd to their Reason, or as one would think, had Reason infus'd after a long life of *Ideotism*; Perhaps among other wise ends, to confute that sordid Supposition, That Ideots have no Souls. (191)

Defoe's apparently sincere concern with the souls of 'Ideots' fits with his more playful notion that these individuals are 'Rent-Charge', and also underscores his insistence on a unified, interdependent society. 'Ideots' remain members of the 'Great Family of Man' and of the British commonwealth, even if they do not contribute to it economically.

Defoe continues his association of financial mismanagement and folly by beginning his next section, 'Of Bankrupts', with a self-deprecating joke: 'This Chapter has some Right to stand next to that of Fools; for besides the common acceptation of late, which makes *every Unfortunate Man a Fool*, I think no man so much made a Fool of as a *Bankrupt*' (191). A debtor, stripped of the authority to make choices, is in effect denied the capacity for rational action which would save both himself and, argues Defoe, his creditors. A statute against a debtor

> for ever shuts up all doors to the Debtor's Recovery; as if Breaking were a Crime so Capital, that he ought to be cast out of Human Society, and expos'd to Extremities worse than Death. (194)

Loss of authority in the realm of economic exchange is comparable to expulsion from public society, as we have already seen in Chapter 4; the debtor in his despair is like the madman or the fool, removed from all communication with others. Rationality and economic activity are complementary figures, each enabling the other, neither possible without the other: to deprive a man of the capacity for acting in the marketplace is akin to stealing from him his mind and his identity.

While Defoe likens the bankrupt to the fool, the opposite comparison also works: the fool is like a bankrupt, without the capacity to act on his own behalf or to contribute to the commonwealth. The fool house can be read as a sincere proposal to address a perceived social need, and this is how it has been most often interpreted. However, it is also a satirical commentary and an anxious moment at the heart of the optimism of the *Essay Upon Projects*. The assumptions underlying Defoe's funding strategies are that the wise, while they have more than their share of intellect, do not have sufficient funds to pay a tax on their intelligence and are poor, despite their superior rationality, and that consequently the most feasible approach to funding a fool house is to tax not wisdom but folly itself, as it is in much greater supply. But as the projects proposed in the *Essay* are primarily structures that rely upon people making rational choices, such as pensions and friendly societies, the admission that the most effective way to fund a fool house is through taxing folly is, in effect, also a concession that those plans for the betterment of society that anticipate people analysing probabilities and making rational choices are profoundly optimistic and, perhaps, doomed to fail. Indeed, even Defoe, having already experienced the lessons of bankruptcy once, would do so a second time during his career (Richetti 2005), thus qualifying himself as a fool yet again. The folly that Defoe imagines is of two orders: it is a condition that afflicts some individuals from birth and, thus, necessitates the provision of a fool house, but it is also a state shared among those intermittently rational members of the commonwealth who form the great majority of mankind.

Asylum building

Through the early decades of the nineteenth century, most medical authorities accorded the idiot a dismal future. 'The moral manifestations of mind are ... deficient in a complete idiot', asserted Alexander Morison. 'He has no religious sentiment, no desires or aversions, no affections, and consequently is unconscious of the social relations; in short, he has no reason to control his will, no desires or inclinations to excite it, and no will to be controlled or excited' (Morison 1843: 218). But such despair over the capacities of idiots was slowly being eroded by reports of educational advances emanating from France and Switzerland that suggested idiots could be educated and integrated as useful, productive members of society – they need no longer be the unproductive younger brothers, the 'Rent-Charges' in the Great Family of Man, but rather participating members of the body social, perhaps even becoming capable labourers and craftsmen.

The anonymous author of the article 'Idiot Asylums', which appeared in the *Edinburgh Review* in July 1865, identifies some early advocates for the 'idiot' in Britain – notably Abercromby and Poole – but asserts that 'light ... broke in slowly and feebly' (39). The first ripples of new continental ideas appeared in 1839, according to this article, when Felix Voisin presented a series of Orthophrenic Lectures in London, apparently to present his experiences in France at the Établissement Orthophrenic, which, drawing upon ideas originated by Jean Itard in his work with the wild boy of Aveyron (Chapter 3), treated 'sufferers from mental weakness' (39). While these lectures seem to have excited little broad interest, Voisin was at the fore of a growing movement, and within a couple of years institutions for the instruction of those people identified as 'idiots' were popping up across Europe. In 1841 Johann Jacob Guggenbühl, also inspired by Itard's reports, established his school for 'cretins' on Abendberg, a mountain in the Swiss Alps; at roughly the same time in Berlin, Carl Wilhelm Saegert also opened a school for idiots. And, of course, at the Bicêtre in Paris, teacher-physicians like Voisin and Édouard Séguin, who had studied under the renowned Itard in the latter's final year, had been creating their own pedagogical revolution.

The work of Séguin has had by far the most lasting influence. Séguin was an exponent of a form of moral education; his teacher, Itard, was himself a student of Philippe Pinel, who brought the concept of moral management to France; Étienne Esquirol, who took over as Séguin's mentor after Itard's death, was also a prominent advocate of the approach. As Murray Simpson argues, Séguin developed a form of moral management that would be particularly appropriate for turning 'idiot' students into 'self-governing subjects' (Simpson 1999: 238) (Séguin's work is treated in greater detail in Chapter 10). That Conolly and Gaskell, advocates of the British version of moral management as practised initially by the Tukes, would be intrigued by Séguin's work thus comes as no surprise. His approach found audiences through a two publications in the 1840s: the first, short presentation of his work in *Hygiene et éducation des idiots*, in 1843, and the longer, more fully developed work, in 1846, *Traitement moral, hygiène et éducation des idiots*. After Séguin emigrated to the United States in 1850 and established himself there, he revised and updated this latter work in English as *Idiocy: And Its Treatment by the Physiological Method*, published in 1866.

Developing and disciplining both mind and body were key features of Séguin's approach. Idiocy was perceived as a problem of 'bodily organization', and Séguin's 'physiological method' sought to address these problems. Idiocy was 'an infirmity in the nervous system' (Séguin 1846: 107), he argued, identifying a series of physiological symptoms, ranging from mutism to physical imbalance to tactile insensitivity or excess to an unsteady gaze, and considerably fewer psychological ones. He wrote:

> We consider the idiot as a man infirm in the expressions of the trinity; and we understand the method of training idiots, or mankind, as the philosophical agency by which the unity of manhood can be reached as far as practicable in our day, through the trinitary analysis. We shall have to educate the activity, the intelligence, the will, the three functions of the unit man, not three entities antagonistic to one another. (Séguin 1866: 83)

The best vehicle for educating this trinity – that is, activity, intelligence and will – was, he argued, 'physiological education, including hygienic and moral training, [which] restores the harmony of these functions in the young, as far as practicable, separating them abstractly, to restore them practically in their unity' (Séguin 1866: 84). The objective was to take the idiot from his state of isolation and to bring him into the community of man, through a series of personalized and graduated physiological exercises that would stimulate the development of body, will and intellect. Throughout this process, moral education remains fundamental.

Reports to England

During the middle 1840s, a series of reports brought news of the accomplishments of Séguin, Johann Jacob Guggenbühl and others to English readers. In 1843 William Twining, a medical doctor and brother of social reformer Louisa Twining (Wright 2001), visited Guggenbühl's facility at Abendberg in Switzerland and wrote enthusiastically of his work in *Some Accounts of Cretinism, and the Institution for Its Cure, on the Abendberg, Near Interlachen, in Switzerland*. Twining's forty-page booklet was a focused effort in propaganda to enlist English subscribers to the Abendberg institution, which was planning to expand from Guggenbühl's cottage, where he housed eleven students, into a proposed stone hospital that would hold over fifty inmates; Twining himself distributed his work to potential supporters. The booklet also gives an overview of some of Guggenbühl's instructional methods, and helps to establish the cretin idiot as an object of sympathy to excite the generosity of English philanthropists.[5] In 1845, John Conolly, the superintendent of the Middlesex Lunatic Asylum at Hanwell, visited the educational facilities for idiots at the Bicêtre in Paris and was impressed by what he saw, writing that 'nothing more extraordinary can well be imagined' (Conolly 1845: 292); Samuel Gaskell, medical superintendent of the Lancaster Lunatics Asylum, followed Conolly to the Bicêtre a year later, and wrote in glowing terms of his visit for *Chamber's Edinburgh Journal* (Gaskell 1847a,b,c). In each instance, the visitors returned to England enthused by the prospect of educating idiots, with Conolly establishing what David Wright (2001: 27) describes as a 'pioneering but little known programme of his own at his massive Middlesex Asylum'.[6] Gaskell – like Conolly, a Noncomformist Christian – was motivated after his Parisian visit to develop his own training programme in a wing of the Lancaster Asylum and to carry out a demographic study of rates of idiocy in Lancashire (Wright 2001).

Certain themes reappear in each of the reports, most notably the contrasting 'before' and 'after' descriptions illustrating the surprising efficacy of the educational strategies, as well as an emphasis on the relation of physiological education to moral and intellectual development. Each work also included the promise – occasionally implicit, but usually explicit – that such education will render the 'idiot' students useful, productive members of society. Twining's work is the most florid, and he leads into his subject by evoking the heroic image of Alpine freedom fighters:

> There is no part of the history of Switzerland so interesting as that which records the glorious victories of the mountaineers in defence of freedom.

Still, while we may rejoice in such deeds, we should not forget that it is in the valleys, amidst these beautiful mountains, that the most pitiable of our fellow-creatures, called Cretins, are chiefly found. (Twining 1843: 5)

The cretins of the valleys are directly contrasted to the valour and glory that Twining associates with the Swiss. Fortunately, these Cretins have, in Guggenbühl, a champion to address their misery, and he is described in terms that stress the heroism of philanthropy. Guggenbühl is 'so strongly impressed with the wretchedness of the inhabitants of the valley, where Cretinism was endemic, that he determine[s] to devote all his means, time, and thoughts to ameliorating the condition' (6). Twining repeatedly stresses the 'sincere devotion' (8) and 'kind manner' (12) of that 'modest and unpretending philanthropist' (17) whose 'philanthropic labours' are 'laying down facts of high importance to the human race at large' (16) and 'who deeply feels his own responsibility which is concerned in his great work, of raising these unfortunate beings to intelligence and moral consciousness' (8). Throughout, Twining balances praise to Guggenbühl with a practical description of his plans and methodology, whose success is such that:

Cretins, whose intelligence has been thought to sink below that of brute animals, when brought under his system of education at an age sufficiently early, are capable of being trained up to social usefulness, and raised even to a sense of moral duty and religious responsibility. (17)

As for the cretins themselves, Twining adopts what would become a standard rhetorical ploy – the description (or reputation) of the cretin opposed to his later improvement. Given that the text's emphasis is on the efficacy of Guggenbühl's treatment at relieving patients of their cretinism, this approach works best if the 'before' image is especially horrific. To this end, Twining provides both his own descriptions and quotes from established authorities. For instance, he describes a three-year-old girl,

exhibiting cretinism in its highest degree.... She was wrapped in a cloth, so that her face only was visible. The lids of the eyes were constantly quivering and the eyes rolling, – the tongue large and so swollen, that the saliva was running from her mouth, and all her limbs were moving convulsively. So dreadful a sight could scarcely be imagined – a human being devoid not only of all which characterizes a rational creature, but even a healthy brute animal: and yet she is improving, so that the day will come, whether it be a year or even two years distant, when she will know the blessings of health and knowledge. (10–11)

Later, he quotes the physician Felix Platter, who wrote in 1614:

> There are some stupid creatures, who besides being born so, have other
> vices of conformation: they are chiefly seen in valleys, sitting at the doors
> of the cottages, staring upwards, playing with sticks in their hands, and
> grinning at passers-by. Their heads are misshapen, and mouths and
> tongues so thick and swollen, that many are unable to articulate sounds.
> They are indeed hideous to see. (Quoted in Twining 1843: 22–23)

In each case, the ploy is to dehumanize the subject, so that the later 're-
humanizing' is all the more striking. Interestingly, Twining suggests
that the word 'cretin' may come from 'Cretina' for 'poor creature' in
'Romance or Italian' (21), but does not mention the other oft-repeated
possibility that it comes from *Chretien*, the French word for Christian,
which refers to the cretin's presumed 'innocence'. While he concedes
that parents bestow love on their cretin offspring, believing them to
be 'blessings sent from heaven' (22), he leaves no doubt that cretinism is not a sign of divine favour but rather a plague to be eradicated.
To support this notion, he presents a breakdown of the numbers of
the afflicted (3,000 in the Canton Valais, 1,350 in Bern, and twenty-
eight villages with endemic cretinism in Argau), and suggests that
Switzerland has somewhere between 8,000 and 24,000 cretins in total.
After describing and documenting (however broadly) the problem,
Twining concludes with a plea for English subscribers to support
Guggenbühl's 'truly philanthropic and Christian plan' (32) and returns
to the imagery of his opening lines:

> Then will be the sound of chimes, re-echoed from mountain to moun-
> tain to tell the distant villages, that the dreadful malady which has long
> there raged, no longer has its victims unopposed, but that at last one has
> arisen to stop the course of that flood, which for centuries has devastated
> the valleys of Switzerland. (33)

In Twining's portrayal, Guggenbühl emerges as a philanthropic
Christian hero bringing rationality to the mentally afflicted, raising
them from a bestial state to a truly human one.[7] Far from being a
'younger brother' without the inheritance of rationality, the idiots being
described by Twining and others exist beyond the pale, until elevated
by their physician-teachers. This notion would be repeated *ad naseum* in
descriptions of the leaders of the asylum movement in Britain.

The articles by Conolly and Gaskell on the innovations at the
Bicêtre in Paris are restrained in comparison with Twining's praise of
Abendberg, but employ many of the same rhetorical strategies. In an
article that appeared in the *British and Foreign Medical Review*, Conolly
(1845: 293) wonders 'to what extent can careful and skilful instruction
make up for ... natural deficiencies; and ... reclaim for these unfinished

creatures the powers and privileges of life'. To address this 'interesting question', Conolly takes the case report of one Charles Emile, a fifteen-year-old who had been at the Bicêtre for three years. According to Conolly's interpretation of this report, the boy

> was wholly an animal. He was without attachment; overturned every-thing in his way, but without courage or intent; possessed no tact, intelligence, power of dissimulation, or sense of property; and was awkward to excess. His moral sentiments are described as null, except for the love of approbation, and a noisy instinctive gaiety, independent of the external world. (294)

With this unpromising material, the teachers of the Bicêtre have 're-deemed' the boy 'from the constant dominion of the lowest animal propensities; several of his intellectual facilities are cultivated, some have even been called into life, and his better feelings have acquired some objects and some exercise' (294). Indeed, after viewing the boy's copy-book, Conolly judged that 'his writing was steady and as good as that of most youths in his station of life' (294), an observa-tion which seems to find some common ground between class-based literacy levels and mental capacity. While the accomplishments of this particular pupil may be limited, Conolly argues that a 'great principle is established by it in favour of thousands of defective organizations' (294) and notes, in sum, that 'a wild, ungovernable animal, calculated to excite fear, aversion, or disgust, has been transformed into the likeness and manners of a man. It is difficult to avoid falling into the language of enthusiasm on beholding such an apparent miracle' (295). This miraculous metamorphosis of an animal into a man is, Conolly stresses, the consequence of hard work and adequate facilities – of the kind that he would establish in England.

Gaskell followed Conolly to the Bicêtre a year later, and published his impressions in three short articles that appeared in *Chamber's Edinburgh Journal*, a broad-ranging intellectual journal, early in 1847. He describes his visit in terms of a series of revelations – perhaps his most oft-repeated phrase involves variations of 'I was struck by...' – that begin with his experience of a choral performance by the music students, 'gone through in a manner that would have done credit to any juvenile class of singers enjoying the use of all their facul-ties' (Gaskell 1847a: 21). Gaskell, suitably impressed, notes that 'if it were to serve no other purpose than that of illuminating, by a momentary consciousness of happiness, an existence otherwise dark, blank, and joyless, it would be desirable to institute such exercises' (21–22). Similarly, he reflects that the Bicêtre idiots show 'much more spirit, and a greater capacity for playful enjoyment, than I could have supposed them capable of' (Gaskell 1847c: 105). Midway through his visit, after leaving a classroom, he reports taking time to ponder what he had already experienced:

> On passing into the open air, I became fully sensible of the crowd of novel impressions which had in so short a space of time been made upon me, and I felt tempted to pause and look back on the spot where so many ideas had been received, and with which I now associated a strong feeling of interest.
>
> In taking a rapid review of what had already been demonstrated before me, I endeavoured to systematize and fix in my own mind the principles which had been employed producing such happy results. (Gaskell 1847c: 105)

These principles included the stimulation of the senses, and it is interesting that Gaskell's description of his own state here mirrors that educational process applied to the idiot students, who were also having 'impressions' made upon their senses in order to 'awaken' them and to fix principles in their minds.

Gaskell then progresses to workrooms, where students are taught practical skills, and he enthuses over the carpentry of one individual who, upon arriving at the Bicêtre three years earlier,

> manifested all the characteristics of an inferior animal. His appetite was voracious, and he would devour the most disgusting things ... he was, moreover, passionate in the extreme, attacking and biting everyone who offered the least opposition to his inordinate and disgusting propensities.... This being, who in 1843 had been in so strange and apparently hopeless a condition, could now read, write, and calculate. (Gaskell 1847c: 105–6)

After his visit, Gaskell, clearly moved by what he has seen, observes whimsically that 'I felt in the humour to indulge my fancy by thinking of the many sources of pleasure and enjoyment in store for these, the most abject and neglected of our fellow creatures' (106). Gaskell's report is more dependent on the language of revelation than Conolly's, but certainly the two share a belief in the new pedagogical methodologies. Gaskell is the only one of the three (with Twining and Conolly) to stress the practical job skills being learned, but all three emphasize the notion of the 'reclaimed' individual, the idiot brought back into the fold of humanity – an idea that would appeal not just to those reform-minded Nonconformists at the cutting edge of the asylum movement, but to Victorian philanthropists of many different allegiances. And in each case, the narrative reduces the idiot to the status of an 'inferior animal' prior to treatment, in order to stress the success of the human reclamation project. The 'after' state is all the more striking for the depravity of the 'before' state.

The impact of these reports was almost immediate. The first British training school modelled on these examples, the Bath Institution for Idiot Children, and Those of Weak Intellect, was founded in 1846 by Charlotte White, who had, according to reports, been motivated by Twining's account of the school on Abendberg; in her own account of the creation of her school, White mentions neither Twining nor Guggenbühl, but rather writes that the 'immediate cause of the experiment being tried was the knowledge that this class of children was frequently subject to the grossest ill-usage and neglect' (quoted in Carpenter 2000a: 166). The Bath school remained small, beginning with four students and never having more than thirty, and relied on both philanthropy and boarding fees to support its operation. Like later, larger institutions, the school's pedagogical emphasis involved reading, writing and arithmetic but, as the school's annual report for 1850 notes, with 'religious knowledge and moral culture ... directly or indirectly kept in view in every pursuit' (quoted in Carpenter 2000a: 170). In addition, a number of other small schools were established around Bath (Carpenter 2000b), perhaps influenced by the example of Charlotte White, but also no doubt stimulated by the reports from abroad of the success of new pedagogical methods in training idiots.

In London, meanwhile, one Mrs Serena Plumbe, a member of the Reverend Andrew Reed's Nonconformist congregation in Whitechapel, read of these European advances in idiocy treatment and prompted her pastor, already renowned for his philanthropy in establishing orphanages, to turn his energy to creating an educational facility for idiots modelled on those existing in Paris and Abendberg. Exactly who was the prime motivator responsible for founding the National Idiot Asylum is difficult to say. Andrew Reed's sons, in their biography of their father, insist that their father was the dominant force (Wright 2001); however, Sir James Clark's biography of John Conolly claims that Serena Plumbe applied first to Conolly, then to Reed, and later to Samuel Gaskell. Then, writes Clark (1869: 111), 'Dr. Conolly and Dr. Reed set earnestly to work, and the result of their exertions in the cause of the weak-minded and helpless idiot, was the establishment of an institution which will perpetuate their names as philanthropists to future ages'. The Asylum for Idiots at Park House, Highgate, also known as the National Asylum for Idiots, was founded in 1847. And in 1848, Park House admitted one Andrew Plumbe of Whitechapel – presumably a son or other relation of Mrs Plumbe (Wright 2001).

Whither asylums?

The years following the mid-1970s have witnessed much debate over the impetus behind asylum building, although this has been focused primarily on 'lunatic' rather than 'idiot' asylums. The most recent dominant orthodoxy has been the 'social control' theory, its most notable English proponent being Andrew Scull, whose *Museums of Madness* (1979) develops in an English context the themes of confinement and moral control first explored by Michel Foucault in *Madness and Civilization* (1961). Gelband (1979) and Barrett (1986) develop Scull's hypothesis in arguing that 'idiot' asylums served primarily as a means of social control, although Wright (2001) argues that this theory does not take into account the complex reasons why people would be committed to these asylums (usually by families who could not support them) nor the fact that the institutions were originally committed to the education of individuals and insisted upon their eventual return to their family and community. Wright's conviction that Benthamite notions of social control were not the sole or even primary factor in initiating asylums provides an important corrective to what can become a reductive view of a complex situation. While social control and segregation were undeniably the most significant long-term consequences of asylums, the original motivations seem to have been a melange of factors, among which 'social control' in a very broad sense might be included, but which also involve the belief that education 'reclaimed' idiots and integrated them into the moral, social and economic life of the nation and the desire of some families to remove troublesome or expensive relatives from their care into an institution.

The role of Nonconformist Christians in the asylum movement is also striking. Nonconformist groups – that is, those Presbyterians, Baptists, Methodists, Congregationalists and others worshipping outside the Church of England – had assumed a new vigour in the nineteenth century, in part due to the repeal of many of the political and social constraints and disadvantages enacted through discriminatory legislation, and in the 1840s dissenting groups were just beginning to move 'from the fringes of religious culture' (Johnson 1999: 5) to a place of greater significance. Nonconformists argued for increased civil rights for Roman Catholics, Jews and even atheists (Larsen 1999), a logical and pragmatic extension of the principle of religious equality upon which their own existence depended. Thus, while led by Nonconformists, the idiot asylum movement was fully ecumenical, a feature Reed insisted upon in most of his philanthropic activities (Owen 1964). That Nonconformists such as Reed, Conolly, Gaskell and, later, John Langdon Down should be so active in the early asylum movement seems more than a coincidence. The idea that the idiot could achieve a higher level of humanity and share in the religious and moral as well as economic life of the state – the belief that those souls who *could* be uplifted and reclaimed, *should* be – no doubt also provided a potent source of motivation. And there were many souls to save. The Park House institution expanded to include a sister asylum at Essex in 1850, and in 1852, owing to further overcrowding, purchased the site upon which the massive Earlswood asylum was erected; the Prince Consort laid the first stone in 1853, and the institution opened in 1855.

Early Victorian philanthropy itself – whether originating among Anglicans or Nonconformists – was motivated by a number of factors: David Owen lists:

> sympathy and compassion for their fellows, the promptings of religion (and in some instances, perhaps, to compensate for a shaky faith), concern for the stability of their society, the social pressures brought to bear on them, or their own special conditions. But whatever motives, conscious or unconscious, may have actuated them, there can be no doubt that charity held a place of some importance in the Victorian world. (Owen 1964: 166–67)

Reed himself was an exemplar of philanthropic activity, leading the creation of a half-dozen charities in London, including three orphanages; in the years during which he held his pulpit in the Congregational chapel of St George's in the East, from 1811 to 1861, Reed was, writes Owen (1964: 159), 'the most important single agent in providing shelter and training for over thirteen hundred fatherless children in institutions'.

Also important in the creation of idiot asylums were the 1845 Lunacy Act, which established a permanent National Lunacy Commission and defined a tripartite division of 'lunatics, idiots, and persons of unsound mind' (quoted in Wright 2001: 16), and the County Asylums Act, passed simultaneously, which decreed that 'the Justices of every County and Borough which has no Asylum for the Pauper Lunatics shall either erect or provide an Asylum for the Pauper Lunatics of such County or Borough alone, or shall unite with some County or Borough in erecting or providing an asylum' (quoted in Arieno 1989: 31). Authorities were given three years to meet these criteria. However, like previous lunatic asylums, these new institutions rarely accepted 'idiot' inmates, doing so only if the individual was too violent or incapacitated to stay in workhouses (Melling and Forsythe 2006). But news of the pedagogical revolution to educate idiots reached England at the same time as the Lunacy Act was being drafted, prompting interest in possible approaches to treating idiocy on a large scale. Clearly, educable idiots would require a new type of institution, one developed especially to meet their specific needs.

Sentiment and idiocy

In 'Crétins and Idiots: A Short Account of the Progress of the Institutions for Their Relief and Cure' in 1853, the anonymous writer, 'RT', asserts that the establishment of idiot asylums in England was a result of the 'too long neglected branch of Christian love and charity ... gradually extending itself in the hearts and sympathies of the benevolent British public' (RT 1853: 126). But garnering public and political support for the asylums and their attempt to extend the benefits of education and rational thought – or raising the inmates 'to the level of humanity' (Anonymous 1865a: 70) – creates an important problem in representations of 'idiocy', and especially of 'innocence': if the innocent idiot is favoured by God, then why must he be 'reclaimed'? What happens to the divine favour offered to the 'idiot' if he is, in reality, no better than a brute animal? The early asylum proponents may have been prepared to offer hard answers to these questions in private, among fellow professionals, but the public image of the 'idiot' was very much implicated in the sentimental notion of 'the innocent'. As a result, asylum advocates sought to invoke a sentimental Christian pity in favour of 'the innocent' to gain the public support they needed for their projects. Indeed, the asylum proponents themselves were not immune to conflicted sensibilities: for an example we need turn no further than the co-founder of the National Asylum for Idiots, the Reverend Andrew Reed. In an 1846 entry in his journal, Reed writes of his decision to help establish an idiot asylum:

> For discipline I will do it. I have naturally a love for the beautiful, and a shrinking, almost a loathing, of infirmity and deformity. The thing I would not do, is the very thing I am resolved to do. Alas! poor Idiot! while he is the great sufferer, I am the greater sinner. (Quoted in Wright 2001: 31)

In Reed's case, the effort to establish an asylum becomes a sacrifice to Christian piety in which he overcomes his loathing for deformity in order to assist the 'poor Idiot'; his equivocations recall the ambivalence to Marie Broc exhibited by Dr Emmaneul Paul in Charlotte Brontë's *Villette* (see Chapter 5). The idiot thus functions as an object upon which one can exercise one's philanthropic Christianity, and this loose role retains some of the old 'innocent' status. But the 'poor Idiot' also becomes a loathsome subhuman who, through the intervention of heroic, dedicated Christian physicians and teachers, is transformed into a responsible moral being as well as an economically productive individual (if only marginally so).

This brand of philanthropy is closely related to the paternalist urge described in Chapter 8; the idea of the family was central to the asylum imagery and would be reiterated, with variations, for decades. The first annual report of the Highgate Asylum (in 1849) observes that 'the first gathering of the idiotic family' was

> a spectacle, unique in itself, sufficiently discouraging to the most re-solved, and not to be forgotten in time after by any. It was a period of distraction, disorder, and noise of the most unnatural character. Some had defective sight; most had no power of articulation; many were lame in limb or in muscle; and all were of weak or perverted mind. Some had been spoiled, some neglected, some ill-used. Some were clamorous without speech, and rebellious without mind; some were sullen and per-verse, and some unconscious and inert. Some were constantly making involuntary noises from nervous irritation, and others hid themselves in corners from the face of man as from the face of an enemy. Windows were smashed, wainscoting broken, boundaries defied, and the spirit of lawlessness triumphant. It seemed as though nothing less than the accommodations of a prison would meet the wants of such a family. (Earlswood archives, 392/1/2/1)

However, after a year the asylum residents formed 'not only an im-proving, but a happy family. And all this is secured without the aid of correction or coercion. The principle which rules in the house is Love – Charity – Divine Charity!' The metaphor of the Christian family and the transformative power of divine love is striking, but not uncharacteristic. The family was both a practical and an ideological model: idiocy, as Conolly's early speeches in support of institutions noted (see above), was most meaningful within the family, especially those poorer families where the idiot child was an immense economic burden. 'Family' was also an image applied to the nation itself, under the matriarch Queen Victoria; the 1865 *Edinburgh Review* article 'Idiot Asylums' repeatedly stresses the 'benevolent interest of the Queen' in the endeavours of the Highgate Asylum, and also notes visits to that institution by Prince Albert (Anonymous 1865a: 44). And as the asylum students fit into the English family, so they also form a family of their own, with the masters as paternal figures. Indeed, as the article suggests, the masters also sup-plant the mother in the world of the asylum:

> The choice of masters and teachers is by no means easy. They must be born teachers, devoted to their work, men in whom no weakness is

visible, endued with extreme patience, and able to command with calmness, force, and decision. Great medical tact and skill are also needed, and that gentle treatment of invalids which caused a youth at Earlswood to say, 'I love the doctor better than my mother'. (48)

Of course, not all praised Earlswood. In 1875, Séguin himself observed that:

> in size and number, Earlswood has no equal. It has had all the advantages that money can bring to the realization of an idea; therefore, if this all but royal institution does not stand first, it is not, as with the French schools, because the idea struggled vainly against penury and oppression...; no, it is because the idea was yet immature among the English, when their purse and will were, as usual, ready. They had determined to have the largest institution for idiots, and they have it – to build a monumental school, and here it stands. (Séguin 1875: 92–93)

While he was critical of the institution's vast size (and would eventually become an early exponent of much smaller institutions), Séguin was particularly struck by 'the TEACHING OF BUYING AND SELLING in a store-class-room, where the students are alternately buyers and sellers' (Séguin 1875: 94, original emphasis); the institution's administration did its best to deliver on promises that its charges would become participants in the economic life of the nation.

The asylum's objective of preparing inmates for economic activity was rarely achieved to the degree that its advocates had hoped, however. When one reverend wrote to the administrators of Earlswood in 1852, asking them that his 'poor boy' be allowed 'continue an inmate in the Asylum' at the end of his five-year period, he stated that 'they would be conferring upon his parents the greatest possible boon' and noted that 'the limited arrangements of home' could never have afforded the 'comforts my dear child has been permitted to enjoy in that noble institution' (Earlswood archives, 392/2/8/2). While the letter makes no explicit statement of the economic advantages to the family of having the son 'continue an inmate', this is clearly part of the 'boon' conferred upon the parents.

At the same time, well trained 'idiots' proved useful for the operation of the institutions as well. In 1861, when one inmate was about to leave the asylum after his five-year residency, Earlswood's medical superintendent, John Langdon Down, wrote to the administrators 'to urge ... as a matter of economy, without regard even to the benefit you will confer on him, to retain him in the Institution regarding his services equivalent to room and clothing'. As Down argues, the man is 'of great value in the mat shop, and is industrious and well-behaved. I have no hesitation in saying, that we could not get a man for 20 pounds per annum and his board, who would be so valuable altogether as he is' (Earlswood archives 392/2/8/3). Down's request seems motivated by two points – the economic advantages of having a reliable and capable inmate, and a concern that this individual might not prosper so well beyond the asylum. And it also demonstrates a dilemma: in no time at all, the original objectives of training people so they could be returned to their homes and integrated into the social and economic lives of their families and communities is compromised, and the asylum quickly becomes an important structure for the economic management of idiots and imbeciles – that is, it offers respite for families, as well as a form of employment for inmates. Before too long, the social and economic difficulties associated with idiocy would be transformed into threats to the health of the nation. But we are getting ahead of ourselves here – let us return to the concerns of these early asylum promoters.

Idiots and heroes

An 1868 *North British Review* article by Dora Greenwell provides an illuminating expression of some of the goals of asylum advocates. In 'On the Education of the Imbecile', Greenwell, a poet and social activist, represents the asylum movement as a heroic endeavour, and her dominant tropes are front and centre in her opening paragraph:

> In every human being, be he the mightiest or the meanest among the family of Adam, there exists a vast dimly lighted region of unknown extent and unascertained resources; a world of which we as yet know too little even to define its boundaries, and of which we can only say, in vague and general language, that it lies between mind and body, between soul and sense. It is a realm thick sown with subtle affinities, thick peopled with analogy, hint, and suggestion, some of them obscure, and some of fearful import. Far off there is a murmur as of the ocean, and we hear far inland the rush and roar of a mighty cataract; dark untracked woods are around us, and through them the river of life flows down. But who has tracked that river to its unknown source? Who through marsh and jungle, and waste of whirling burning sand, has won his way to the centre of this mysterious realm, and there ascended some height of vantage commanding it from sea to sea? (Greenwell 1868: 73)

Comparing the explorer of human nature to Cortez gazing 'Silent upon a peak of Darien', she claims that 'if we would desire, amid the complications of an incomplete and struggling existence, to be truly useful and helpful to our fellow-creatures, we must learn not to turn aside from Humanity under its more strange and conflicting aspects' (73). For Greenwell, engagement with the less fortunate idiot is critical for an understanding of humanity itself: 'it need not surely surprise us to find that we advance greatly towards the clear understanding of man's whole nature, through the contemplation of its exceptional and abnormal phases' (75). Idiocy and imbecility become, in this formulation, a realm of both intellectual and even aesthetic challenge that cannot fail to be rewarded: 'amongst the abnormal conditions of humanity, imbecility, at first sight so repulsive, so barren of all sugges- tion, will appear, when we come to look at it more closely, to be rich in analogical reference and full of tender poetry' (76). Grappling with the problem of idiocy, Greenwell suggests, stimulates creative and intellectual insights. As if to underscore the point, literary references appear throughout the article. She notes that 'The spectacle of idiocy fast bound in the iron misery of an imperfect [physical] organization, awakens in the mind the thought of a fatality more gloomy and ir- resistible than that which presides over a Greek drama' (78). The state of idiocy is also compared to 'the pit where humanity lies bound like Joseph, and forgotten of his brethren' (91); and the 'idiot' is compared to 'the lady in Comus, "locked up in alabaster"' (94).

She also cites Rousseau in her claim that 'each is created free, al- though born in chains' (74), which is especially true for the idiot, 'one who is never strong enough to cast off the swaddling-bands of infancy', an eternal child 'disinherited from his very birth' (77) of his claim to humanity. The education of the idiot is not a concern 'of mere philan- thropy', although she notes that 'it has chiefly been considered in that light'; rather, 'it is a question which connects itself most closely with almost every other social one', including psychology, education and the relation of people to one another and to God (78–79); it is, in short, an issue of broad national concern. Noting that England and Wales contain 'about 50,000 idiotic and weak-minded persons', a 'formidable battalion',[8] she asserts:

> How all-important to the life of the family, to the well-being of the nation, becomes the question of their susceptibility to improvement! How worthy of the attention of the Government of every Christian State! For the idiot, as it has been truly remarked, does not sink alone. (79)

The task of educating the idiot becomes one of critical domestic and national importance (a noteworthy conflation) and must fall to the best men and women that the nation can produce, people of 'zeal and devotion' (91) who call forth

> the powers of genius itself.... Not to breathe life into a statue or to bid the canvas speak; not to command a listening senate or to win the smile of beauty and love; not to gain the coveted laurel or to obtain a name

among our fellow-men; but to awaken a ray of intelligence in some poor sickly and repulsive child, whose nature is perhaps too torpid to respond to kindness, and whose faculties are certainly too dull to guess at the great sum of time and thought and care that is spent over his improvement. (98)

Greenwell's representation of the heroic task of educating people identified as idiots or imbeciles is directed here at an intellectual and reformist readership, and her Christian hero exploring the poetic and uncharted dark continent of the human intellect clearly draws upon the language of British imperialism; the 'idiot' thus becomes another unmapped territory to be colonized. But the imperialist imagery of Greenwell's argument works effectively because it is linked with another stream of discourse, that of the Victorian family.

As 'children' (and they were, before the law, considered to be like children), 'idiots' were part of a larger social family, one which represented by Victorian society as a whole. As Greenwell makes clear, the education of idiots was crucial to the happy functioning of the national family and, indeed, the family of humanity. While she presents the 'idiot' as an infant 'who may perish with cold and hunger, although he is the Father's son' (78), Greenwell wishes to ensure that this fate is avoided:

> It is time that England, who for her 50,000 imbeciles has as yet provided asylums for just *one thousand*, to ask whether we are to continue to allow the weakest, the least fortunate among us, to drift hither and thither as chance and fate direct, the very *flotsam* and *jetsam* of humanity, or to decide whether as a nation we will seek to emulate the wise and loving economy of our Divine Founder, and strive to heal that which is sick, to bind up that which is broken, to bring back that which is driven away, to gather up of these fragments and leavings of human existence, 'so that nothing may be lost'. (80–81)

God provides the paternal model as well as the divine economy of selfless love compensated by heavenly rewards, an economy within which the idiot will function productively. The human family under God the Father is implicitly paralleled by the paternalist organization of the asylum, whose Christian organization is a significant feature; indeed, John Langdon Down's religious convictions were quite likely instrumental in his selection as Earlswood's medical superintendent in 1859 (Zihni 1990). The family, as the model for the Victorian brand of paternalism that shaped understandings of society and the economy, becomes for Greenwell a dominant paradigm for understanding idiocy and imbecility. The colonial imagery which also illuminates Greenwell's argument must be seen in this context: Greenwell's explorers are missionary-adventurers bringing new lands into the Christian fold. As the following chapters will make clear, by 1868 the notion that people identified as 'idiots' are also potential partners in society is by no means uncontested; Greenwell is writing in an environment which is increasingly perceiving such people to be examples of degeneration, on the levels of both individual families and the British race.

The innocent in the asylum

Asylum advocates rarely endorsed the notion of innocence, at least not in conversation among their own, and no less an authority than Séguin (1846) claimed that the belief that idiots were innocents favoured by God was one of the obstacles standing in the way of initiatives for their education. However, the notion of the 'innocent' was not fully abandoned by asylum advocates, but was modified, and the parameters within which the 'idiot' could also be read as 'innocent' were made more narrow. Writing in 1873, Bucknill claimed that the idiot

> is always that which our fine old English synonym represents him to be – an Innocent. Not always, indeed, an innocent in one sense of the term, innoxious and harmless, but certainly innocent of his own lamentable condition, Innocent also of any sin or crime to which that condition may lead, as well as that of the Shrieves Fool, mentioned by Parolles, in 'All's Well that ends Well', *'He was whipped for getting the Shrieves-fool with child, a dumb Innocent who could not say him nay.'* (Bucknill 1873: 171, original italics)[9]

But Bucknill was addressing a largely lay audience, the governors of a new idiot asylum. Among works for a general audience, the prohibition on 'innocence' imagery was less consistently observed than it was in professional discussions, but even then many writers strove to elicit sympathy and pity by drawing on notions connected to traditional 'innocence' without explicitly using the term 'innocent'. In 1856, Elizabeth Grove released a collection entitled *Narrative Poems; and a Beam for Mental Darkness for the Benefit of the Idiot and His Institution*, meant to raise both money and awareness for the work being done at the Earlswood asylum. In her poem 'The Idiot', a piece explicitly meant as propaganda for the institution, parents who gaze happily upon 'the intellectual brow' of 'the fair child' are asked to 'Pity the Mother, who has wept / Over her dear first-born, / Watching and waiting long to see / The light of reason dawn.' Such light is, of course, denied, and worse is in store. Soon, we are told that 'A mental blindness seals his eye' and he is immune to the beauties of the world. But, stresses the narrator, there is hope:

> Yet not upon him may we gaze
> With cold despairing eye,
> Tis not decreed the Idiot born
> Must a poor Idiot die
>
> And 'tis a blessed charity,
> The fetters to unbind,
> That hold the dull imprisoned soul,
> The dark and hidden mind.
>
> And God will surely give to those
> His blessing and his love,
> Who rightly use their better gifts
> Affliction to remove.

Grove's poem follows the rhetorical trajectory defined in the writings in the previous decade by Twining, Conolly and Gaskell, contrasting the unassisted, unenlightened idiot to that new individual promised by new pedagogies, and bestowing praise upon those responsible for the transformation. Her accompanying essay stresses that

> There are, amongst the male inmates, some very credible tailors, shoe-makers, carpenters, glaziers, matmakers, plaiters, basketmakers and gardeners; while others are trained for porters, or to assist the in-door servants in the duties of the establishment. Many of the girls are really expert at plain needlework, knitting, crochet, patchwork, beadwork, &c. &c. (73)

Similar observations were made by others. J. C. Parkinson's 'A Day at Earlswood', originally appearing in the *Daily News* and reprinted as a pamphlet in 1869 to help raise funds for the Royal Albert Idiot Asylum in Lancaster, writes that 'a plain record of our experience [i.e., his visit to Earlswood] may possibly help to remove some erroneous theories respecting idiots' (5). He then describes what he finds there:

> a happy united family, proud of its occupations, attached to its instructors and friends, harmonious in its relations, and quiet and peaceful in its life. You have constantly to ask which are inmates and which attendants as you progress through the house and grounds. On inspecting the substantial block of workshops which have been built and opened within the last few years, and in which various industrial occupations are in full progress, you are amazed at the intelligence and skill displayed. (Parkinson 1869: 5)

In such writings, the promise is clear: the idiot, after long exile, is being welcomed into the social and economic activities of the family and the nation.

The idea of the innocent idiot remained viable, and is still evident, albeit through a mist, in Parkinson's article:

> The idiots … are in certain respects better citizens than some stupid people we have heard of. They do their work bravely, find no pleasure in inflicting pain, or in annoying one another, and are not without a sense of humour. Some of them babble incoherently, but all are harmless, and all full of enjoyment in their simple way. (6–7)

That traditional character also figures heavily in an 1869 booklet edited by Dora Greenwell to solicit support for the Royal Albert Asylum. This collection included previously published works that reflected the place of idiots in the family of God, asserting their innocence and providing a model for what Greenwell considered proper and desirable attitudes towards people identified as 'idiots'. Notable among them are Caroline Bowles Southey's 'Harmless Johnny', an excerpt from 'Chapters on Churchyards', first published in 1824 in *Blackwood's Magazine*, and George MacDonald's 'The Wow o' Rivven', first published in 1864 in *Good Words for 1864*.

Caroline Bowles Southey's 'Chapter in Churchyards' begins (not surprisingly) as a meditation on mortality; after the narrator ponders several other graves, she comes to the humble site, already 'quite level with the even sod', where lies 'the poor outcast of reason … the workhouse idiot' (Southey 1824: 319). He is described as 'one for whom no heart was tenderly interested' (319), his parents being long dead; Johnny was an orphan, although at seventy years of age, and the absence of family provides much of the pathos of the story. However, at the same time he is represented as a figure whose status in the community is secure (albeit marginal). The fact that the story is over forty years old when Greenwell republishes it underscores its nostalgic appeal for a time when the community seemed, at least in retrospect, to mirror more accurately the family; the world of Southey's tale is already passing when she writes of it in 1824 (a story about graveyards can hardly help but be elegiac). The text emphasizes Harmless Johnny's role in the community performing odd tasks, his pleasure in dressing in military clothing and playing at soldiers with the village children, and his inevitable tearful response to music (except in church, where he very decorously, but with great effort, controls himself). But he is now dead to all music, notes that narrator as she brings the readers back to the present. Harmless Johnny shall sleep undisturbed

> till the call of the last trumpet shall awaken him, and the mystery of his earthly existence shall be unfolded, and the soul, emerging from its long eclipse, shall shine out in the light of immortality – At that day of solemn

reckoning, how many, whose brilliant talents, and luminous intellect, have blazed out with meteoric splendour, not to enlighten, but to dazzle and mislead, and bewilder the minds of their fellow-mortals, in the mazes of inextricable error – How many of those who have so miserably abused the great trust reposed in them, shall be fain to exchange places with that unoffending innocent.... (320)

As a part of Greenwell's fund-raising collection, the story reminds readers of the innocence of the idiot (as well as of the vanished pre-industrial England), although at the same time these readers are expected to make the link between Johnny's salvation and those spiritual benefits which will also accrue to them through the support of an asylum – that is, those who do not abuse 'the great trust reposed in them'.

In George MacDonald's 'The Wow o' Rivven', the Colonel, so named for his wardrobe of tattered military clothes,[10] wears on his sleeve, where the military stripes would normally be, a piece of fabric in the shape of a bell. The bell is more than decoration, as the narrator assures us: 'It was, indeed, the baptism of the fool, the outward and visible sign of his relation to the infinite and unseen' (MacDonald 1864: 131–32). The Colonel had been found as an infant almost seventy years earlier by a traveller from the village, crying in the moss, 'hardly wrapt in rags, and untended, as if the earth herself had just given him birth'; rescued and taken into the village, he grew to be 'what he was now – almost an idiot' (134). The Colonel's relation to the divine is mediated through his relation to the natural world, the earth being presented as his mother.

Occasionally mocked by children and villagers, but generally accepted and tolerated, the Colonel befriends the story's heroine, Elsie, who lives a life of self-deprivation. Elsie, like the Colonel, is an outcast; she has grown up without parents, although 'she had faint memories of warm soft times on her mother's bosom, and of refuge in her mother's arms' (135). Instead, she is raised by an unsympathetic brother, and while 'Tenderness was the divine comforting she needed ... it was altogether absent from her brother's character' (137). A bond grows between Elsie and her fellow sufferer, the Colonel, and eventually she discovers that his call 'Come hame, come hame, the Wow o' Rivven', refers to a church bell and graveyard in the nearby ancient parish of Ruthven. Elsie, through the narrator, ponders the revelation:

It was no wonder that the fool, cast out of the earth on a far more desolate spot than this, should seek to return within her bosom at this place of open doors, and call it *home*. For surely the surface of the earth had no home for him. (152)

The church becomes an entry into the bosom of the maternal earth, a portal through which the Colonel could return to his true home. And, indeed, his notion of home becomes elevated symbolically:

> It is possible that in the mind of the idiot there may have been some feeling about this churchyard and bell, which, in the mind of another, would have become a grand poetic thought; a feeling as if the ghostly old bell hung at the church-door of the invisible world, and ever and anon rung out joyous notes (though they sounded sad in the ears of the living), calling to the children of the unseen to *come home, come home.* (153)

The Colonel's 'iambic cry' (159) is related to creative activity in this significant passage; the call to return to the home, to the lost phantasmic family, is an articulation of the divine (Manlove 1990). When the Colonel dies, he is buried in the Ruthven churchyard; when Elsie soon after also sickens and dies, she is buried next to the Colonel.

The Colonel, designated both a 'prophet-fool' (154) and a 'defenceless idiot' (156) by the narrator, acts as a guide for the more intelligent and perceptive Elsie. His disability allows a passage to both eternal and domestic bliss.

> Side by side rest the aged fool and the young maiden; for the bell called them, and they obeyed; and surely they found the fire burning bright, and heard friendly voices, and felt sweet lips on theirs, in the home to which they went. Surely both love and intellect were waiting them there. (165)

Heaven in this passage becomes a domestic Victorian hearth, an idealized home and family. Not only is the Colonel called to the heavenly fireside, but through association with him and her willingness to care for and sympathize with him, Elsie, too, finds a home. In treating kindly the least of her earthly brethren, she assures herself a place in the celestial family, where the benevolent patriarch is God himself. Interestingly, MacDonald's images of divine bliss are domestic and maternal, and this particular version of the Victorian God assumes shape in the warmth of the family parlour.[11]

The asylum anticipates this divine home by providing an earthly abode for idiots; it also provides a means by which good Christians can help both poor idiots and their own souls, simultaneously.[12] At the same time, the 'idiots' in these two works bear the traditional qualities of the 'innocent' – and if Wordsworth's critics from 1800 could have witnessed the drawing power of the 'innocent' as a means of engaging sympathy, they might well have been astonished. The idea of the 'natural innocent' formed such a powerful tool that Greenwell uses the stories despite the fact that the ideology of the asylum is clearly opposed to this interpretation of idiocy.

Significantly, though, not all representations of the Christian innocent within the family could be mobilized in the service of the asylum
movements. The works of Charlotte Mary Yonge, a high-church
Anglican novelist very popular in the latter half of the nineteenth
century, occasionally include 'idiot' children as part of a family environment, but these characters are not institutionalized, even though
asylums may be briefly presented as options. In the high Anglican
world of Yonge's *Hopes and Fears* (1860) and *The Pillars of the House*
(1873), the 'innocents', Maria and Theodore respectively, become the
responsibilities of their families, especially of one particularly devoted
sibling. As late as the 1880s most families of all classes opted to care
for their own if possible, seeing the asylum as a last resort (Saunders
1988), so Yonge's families are thus reasonably accurate portrayals of
mid-Victorian social realities. However, her representation of idiocy
is also meaningful in the context of her own political agenda and
the strongly evangelical impetus behind the asylum movement. An
adherent of the Oxford movement in its earlier incarnations, she was
a vigorous apologist for a conservative version of social responsibility
in which the upper classes, in alliance with the Church of England,
exercised the responsibility for the poor and helpless.[13] If one could
personally care for the unfortunate, then one did. Both authority and
responsibility in Yonge's novels are located within the family, with
the 'authority of the human parent [being] intimately equated with
the divine authority of the Anglican Church' (Storr 1965: 110). The
surrogate family of the institution was a lesser family, an impersonal
mimicry of the natural, true family, which is, in itself, the earthly expression of the divine family.

In Yonge's 1860 novel *Hopes and Fears*, Phoebe commits herself
to looking after her sister Maria, a 'poor innocent' (321). Maria's
intellectual disability comes to light only when the governess, Miss
Fennimore, points it out to Phoebe, her affectionate sister having perceived only that Maria 'was not clever' (241). Phoebe consoles herself
with the knowledge that 'such people cannot do wrong in the same
way as we can', although her rationalist governess notes only that
Maria 'cannot be treated as otherwise than deficient' (242). Yonge explicitly contrasts Fennimore's interpretation with Phoebe's Christian
response, and valorizes the latter. The revelation of Maria's handicap
in fact stimulates Christian sympathy in the sister:

> There was a fresh element in Phoebe's life. The native respect for 'the
> innocent' had sprung up within her, and her spirit seemed to expand
> into protecting wings with which to hover over her sister as a charge
> particularly her own. (243)

Phoebe's urge to become her sister's guardian angel is significantly seen as a 'native' respect for 'the innocent', the natural response but also one sadly atrophied in those who have suppressed their Christian inheritance. Later in the novel, after their mother has died and Phoebe has committed herself to caring for Maria, her sister Julianna announces that she has 'found a capital place … for Maria – a Dr. Graham, who boards and lodges such unfortunates. Sir Bevil had an idiot cousin there who died' (356–57);[14] another sister, Augusta, insists that Phoebe cannot stay with Maria because she 'could not receive [Maria]; she can never be made presentable' (357). Phoebe's integrity is revealed through her struggles to resist the pressures of her family and, indeed, her heritage. Her father had made his fortune from a gin distillery; Phoebe and her brother Robert, a priest working the very slums created by his father's industry, owe their spiritual education to Honora Charlecote, a neighbouring landowner and high Anglican, rather than to their own family. Eventually Honora's nephew, Humfrey Charlecote, newly returned from Canada, provides Phoebe with a happy ending, pursuing her to be his wife and gallantly accepting Maria as part of a holy trust. Thus, the family, and the responsibility entailed within, prevail: Maria remains both as a maiden sister and an innocent child.

A similar position is occupied by Theodore Underwood in Yonge's 1873 novel *Pillars of the House*. Theodore and his twin sister, Stella, are born just before their father, a minister, succumbs to consumption (he has time to name and baptize the twins, and then he departs from the novel). Theodore is more clearly disabled than Maria of *Hopes and Fears*, and the family (excepting the mother, who dies three years after the father) acknowledges his disability from his childhood.[15] Still, he grows up with the family, tended to primarily by Felix, the oldest child, who is sixteen at the start of the novel, and later also by Stella. While a constant presence in the family, Theodore is rarely more than alluded to in passing (usually to say that he is in the background humming and playing on his concertina, a favourite occupation as he gets older). His status in the family is never contested in the same manner as Maria Fulmont's is in *Hopes and Fears*, although at one point, in a state of pique, his sister Alda mutters of asylums (vol. I, 338); however, when her good humour is restored, the asylum threat disappears from the novel.

Theodore's central moment in the novel is his last – at seventeen, he is in a river-boating accident with his family and drowns (the river on the estate is reputed to claim one Underwood every generation – Theodore, obviously, in this case). Felix, in pulling the failing Theodore to shore, arouses his consumptive tendencies and within the year he, too, has died, at thirty-four, and the novel, *sans* protagonist, ends. But Yonge's goal (or one of them, at any rate) is to demonstrate true Christian charity and responsibility through Felix, who lives a life of labour and self-denial, coming into his heritage – the Underwood estate that was taken from his father through a trick of inheritance – only at the end of the novel. There is little else for Felix to do after he has assumed the estate; he has raised his siblings, seen them married and settled (he dies days after Stella's wedding) and lost the only one who would depend upon him in the future. Without Theodore, Felix's work is done, and he can go on to his heavenly reward; indeed, the earthly Underwood estate, the family heritage, is merely foreshadowing Felix's final inheritance. The novel's subtitle, *Under Wode, Under Rode*, alludes to the cross ('the rode') the Underwoods (especially Felix, it would seem) must bear to achieve their destiny. As with MacDonald's 'The Wow o' Rivven', the story ends in a graveyard: the plots of Theodore and Felix next to one another, with the family estate and the natural world surrounding them. Theodore becomes representative of Felix's means to salvation; he does not provide the catalyst for Felix's goodness, but through his helplessness he provides a symbolic expression of this quality. The union of graveyard, family estate and nature reinforces the connection between the significant components of Yonge's universe: the eternal and Christian, the familial and the natural worlds. Just as Archie had no part of the world of commerce and exchange in Garveloch, Theodore has no place in the mundane world of the Underwoods, although a place still exists for him, as an innocent, in heaven.

Innocence in conflict

In the mid-Victorian years, asylums, created by philanthropists as educational institutions, promised that debased humanity would be redeemed by love and discipline, ingenious innovation and zealous devotion. They sought to take that which was bad, and make it good. However, this objective created a representational dilemma. The figure of the 'idiot' as the 'poor innocent' favoured by God was a useful tool for gaining popular support, yet the 'idiot' also had to be reconstructed as needing the redemption the asylum offered. At the same time, even when appearing in works by writers like Charlotte Yonge, the innocent was stripped of his more disruptive 'trickster' qualities, those very characteristics that denoted the innocent's divine protection: the ability to speak truths, to mock the comfortable, to resist the categories of rational and worldly life. The growing authority of the asylum movement was slowly casting a shadow over the 'innocent idiot', although not obscuring it entirely. The figure of the innocent drew its power from its mystery, and asylums sought to solve this mystery, to make it known and mundane. In effect, they sought to remove that which connected the innocent to the divine, the very essence of the image itself. However, reconstructing the figure of the 'innocent' as someone needing redemption implied a question left untreated in the literature of early asylum apologists: that of the irreclaimable idiot. What if 'innocence' cannot be redeemed? What does it then become?

The first enthusiasm for building asylums to educate the idiot grew from educational innovations supported by both philanthropic and economic arguments. The image of the childlike Christian innocent was joined by that of the poor idiot waiting to be reclaimed into the social and economic community; the choice of which representational approach was to appear in a particular document seems to have depended on the intended audience, with, as a broad rule, the 'innocent' appearing most often in general fund-raising efforts written by those outside the professions directly related to asylum management – that is, pedagogues and medical men. On the other hand, the reclaimable, semi-bestial idiot is a stock character in early descriptions of continental institutions, as well as in professional writings and focused fund-raising attempts in Britain.

But these images do not exhaust the representational repertoire of the time. Let us return to the writer with whom we opened, Harriet Martineau, who in 1854 – more than twenty years after her *Illustrations of Political Economy* – wrote 'Idiots Again' for Charles Dickens's *Household Words*. In this article she observes that 'it used to be thought a very religious and beautiful thing (it certainly was the easiest thing) to say that it pleased God to send idiots, and other diseased or defective children, to try and discipline their parents by affliction, and so on' (Martineau 1854: 197). She then cites arguments published by the American Samuel Gridley Howe that present idiocy as most often the consequence of the morally degenerate behaviour of the parents, enhanced by the immoral proclivities of the afflicted offspring themselves; and she recalls Robert Southey's macabre narrative from his poem 'The Idiot' (discussed in Chapter 2). Throughout, Martineau assails the idea of the 'innocent', decrying it as a strategy for eluding responsibility, first for the very presence of people so identified, and then for their care and education; instead, she writes, the responsibility for idiots belongs with individuals, society and the state:

> Our business is, in the first place, to reduce the number of idiots to the utmost of our power, by attending to the conditions of sound life and

health; and especially by discountenancing, as a crime, the marriage of blood-relations; and, in the next place, to try to make the most and the best of such faculties as these imperfect beings possess. It is not enough to repeat the celebrated epitaph on an idiot, and to hope that his privations here will be made up to him hereafter. We must lessen those privations to the utmost, by the careful application of science in understanding his case; and of skill, and inexhaustible patience and love, in treating it. (Martineau 1854: 200)

As Martineau's example indicates, the advocates of asylum-based care and education shared fundamental notions with a parallel discourse just beginning to take form: that linking 'idiocy' to ideas of degeneracy. Initially, this degeneracy is an individual attribute, a flaw in the bodily organisation of the idiot, demanding the cultivation of a sort of corporeal sensitivity, a development of the senses, in order to stimulate the intellect. Eventually, though, people will come to think of this degeneracy as an attribute threatening the health of the race and the stability of the state. The remaining chapters will explore these notions of degeneracy, from the corporeal to the cultural, more thoroughly.

Notes

1 According to William Ireland, the election process placed restrictions on the social class of children entering institutions, while also providing benefactors with a laudable substitute for gambling at the racetrack: 'To the parents of imbecile children the system of voting had some unpleasing features. Instead of a timely relief, the hope of gaining a sufficient number of votes was dangled before the eyes of the competitors, whose private circumstances were published in a printed roll sent to each voter. In general, the candidates whose parents were poorest and most helpless had the least chance of being elected. Their only chance often was that a well-meaning lady with redundant leisure, or a male philanthropist at a loss for something to do, should take the case in hand, and run a candidate against the rest. Combining the excitement of the polling booth with that of the betting ring, this system had a charm for those to whom, from the holiness of their lives, the pleasures and excitements of the turf were forbidden' (Ireland 1886: 183–84).
2 Christiana's travels make up Book Two, published in 1684, on the heels of the 1678 publication of the protagonist Christian's pilgrimage in Book One. Christiana is the wife of Christian.
3 According to biographer John Richetti, Defoe lost huge sums of money insuring ships and cargo that were then captured by French privateers. 'Defoe clearly played for high stakes and lost, but he also seems to have dealt at times from the bottom of the deck', writes Richetti. 'In other more serious cases, Defoe was accused of fraud, and in the most grimly amusing of his financial entanglements he was involved in a botched project to farm civet cats in Stoke Newington for their secretions, used in making perfume. Sued by the person from whom he had borrowed the money to buy the cats, he sold them to his widowed mother-in-law, Mary Tuffley, who in turn sued him when it turned out that Defoe did not really have title to the cats, having used the money he

had borrowed initially to pay a creditor' (Richetti 2005: 16). Richettti estimates Defoe's £17,000 debt in 1692 as being roughly equivalent to £2 million in 2005.

4 The Bank of England was formed in 1694, three years before Defoe's *Essay*, to manage the government's debt (accumulated through military activities in Ireland and France) by selling it in shares and trading it on the open market, where prices rose and fell dramatically; to add to the instability, individual banks were also circulating unguaranteed paper money (Bigelow 2003). In Defoe's terms, the Bank is fit primarily to encourage exchange, to have a 'proper regard to the Ease of Trade in General, and the Improvement of the Stock in Particular' (41), but the new Bank of England is 'nothing but so many Goldsmith's shops' (40); while he endorses the concept, he is critical of its execution.

5 'Cretinism' is today known as 'hypothyroidism' and may be congenital or acquired; it is essentially a condition in which the thyroid gland is underdeveloped and thus secretes insufficient levels of hormones, which results in both physical and intellectual impairment. While its causes remain uncertain, the condition is also associated with iodine deficiency, a condition not uncommon in landlocked areas such as the Swiss Alps.

6 Conolly himself writes of this project in 'On the Management of Hanwell Lunatic Asylum' (1849).

7 Guggenbühl's reputation did not outlast his fame. In 1858, sparked by complaints of neglect and disorder at Abendberg, an official investigation yielded extremely negative results. Guggenbühl's claims to have effectively cured and educated cretins were found to have been heavily exaggerated; indeed, only one-third of the institution's residents were, in fact, 'cretins', and his successful pupils, those presented as exemplars of his work, were not 'cretins' at all but simply regular children (Scheerenberger 1983). By the time Guggenbühl died in 1863, his work had become synonymous with fraudulence in the world of idiot education. Dr W. Carmichael McIntosh suggested, with some restraint, that 'it is very doubtful if this institution answered the purposes for which it was erected, either on physiological or psychological grounds' (McIntosh 1864: 17) and an anonymous review in the *Journal of Mental Science* dismissed Guggenbühl by noting that 'his undertaking was a miserable failure, not to say imposture' (Anonymous 1866c: 608). But by 1887, John Langdon Down could look back on Guggenbühl as one 'who entered on his work with true enthusiasm – an enthusiasm which one regrets was quenched by the flattery of English drawing-rooms' (Down 1887: 2). Down seems to attribute Guggenbühl's fall at least in part to the success of the public relations efforts begun by Twining and other early visitors. As Down writes: 'I shall never forget the feelings of disappointment and chagrin when, on reaching the summit of the Abendberg, which I had mounted as a pilgrim to a shrine, I found the pupils in a state of physical and mental neglect while the patron saint was being enervated by the Capua-like influence of the West End of London. Fortunately for the pupils the Commune stepped in and closed what had become a parody on philanthropic effort' (Down 1887: 2).

8 This number is debatable. The unsigned article 'Idiot Asylums', which appeared in the 1865 *Edinburgh Review*, notes that there were 18,611 pauper idiots according to an 1862/63 report of the Poor Law Board and also alludes to the unverified number of '50,000 idiots or imbeciles, as has been asserted' (Anonymous 1865a: 38, 69). Michael Donnelly refers to an 1830s estimate that put the number of idiots and lunatics in England, Scotland and Wales at 20,000

(Donnelly 1983: 88); Michael Barrett quotes an 1877 survey identifying 10,599 'idiots and imbeciles under 20', 17,749 adult idiots and imbeciles, and 7,615 'harmless lunatics', for a total of 35,963 in England and Wales (Barrett 1986: 144).

9 The innocence of the 'Shrieves-fool' would not survive the coming decades, as the supposed sexual availability and promiscuity of 'feeble-minded' women would be blamed for the apparent proliferation of people with low intelligence at the end of the nineteenth century and the start of the twentieth, leading to the 1913 Mental Deficiency Act, treated in Chapter 13.

10 Both Harmless Johnny and the Colonel wear tattered military clothing, suggesting that idiocy in these instances parodies traditional martial notions of masculinity; in both cases, the characters are marked by their capacity to sympathize with, rather than rule, others.

11 MacDonald's conception of divinity was somewhat outside the mainstream. A Congregationalist minister, MacDonald proved too non-conforming even for his chapel, and was eventually removed by his constituents following his heterodox hypothesis that animals might well have souls (Prickett 2005).

12 The 'innocent' providing a means for redemption remained an important figure for Victorian writers, and these writings, while used as asylum propaganda, were not necessarily written with that objective in mind. Elizabeth Gaskell's 1850 short story 'The Well at Pen-Morfa' is a case in point. The story features Nest Gwynn, beautiful and beloved of all the villagers, who injures herself in a fall on icy stone while fetching water from the well, and loses not only her strength and beauty, but also her betrothed. Nest is nursed by her mother, whom she reproaches for not letting her die; eventually, the mother, finding that she 'had no power to console the poor wounded heart' and weakened by these 'sorrowful, hurrying events', herself dies (Gaskell 1850: 136), and Nest is bereft and repentant. 'Nobody loves me now', she observes (137), but is gently reprimanded by an elderly itinerant Methodist preacher, who tells her that while no human may love her, God does, and she must now learn to cast aside youthful love for a version more profound – she must learn to love 'like Christ himself' (138). She does this by taking in Mary Williams, who is described as 'half-witted', a 'poor crazy creature' and a 'regular savage' (139), rescuing her from a home where her discipline had been enforced by beatings rather than solicited by Christian love and patience. Nest lives with Mary for thirty years, with Nest repeating to her neighbours stories of Mary's 'docility, and her affection, and her innocent little sayings' but suppressing mention of those times when Mary is 'overpowered by the glooms and fancies of her poor disordered brain' (141). Finally, Nest decides she would like to see the well at Pen-Morfa once again, for the first time since her near-fatal accident; when she arrives there, she sits to rest against a stone, and there she dies peacefully. Mary is removed to a workhouse, where she is generally 'good and tractable' but occasionally has 'paroxysms' that are calmed only by the mention of Nest's name. The story ends with Mary's plaintive words: 'Mary has tried to be good. Will God let her go to Nest now?' (143). The 'half-wit' Mary clearly serves as the catalyst for Nest's redemption, but is also a double for Nest, betrayed by circumstance and by her husband-to-be. Mary becomes the means by which Nest exercises her essential goodness and can thus be taken to heaven, as well as the expression of Nest's despair and solitude.

13 Yonge's affiliation with the Oxford movement has been explored most thoroughly by Barbara Dennis (1992) in her *Charlotte Yonge (1823–1901): Novelist of the Oxford Movement.* See also Raymond Chapman's *Faith and Revolt*

(1970). The Oxford movement (also known as the Tractarian movement) was founded in the early 1830s by Oxford-based theologians and philosophers, including John Keble, John Henry Newman, Henry Edward Manning and Richard Hurrell Froude, who were influenced by (among other things) the liturgy and ceremony of the medieval church. Their 'High Anglican' or Anglo-Catholic advocacy has been influential in the subsequent development of the Church of England, although the movement itself suffered when some of its leaders, notably Newman and Manning, converted to Roman Catholicism. For more information, see Brad Faught's *The Oxford Movement* (2003) and Newman's own *Apologia pro vita sua* (1864).

14 Not all asylum reports were laudatory, as Yonge's readers no doubt were aware. On 5 August 1858, the *Daily Telegraph* identified 'filth, obscenity, discomfort, semi-starvation, and, worse than penitential monotony' as characteristics of idiot asylums, and noted that, at the Earlswood asylum, 'everything appears to exist that could render a human abode a den of misery and degradation: bad water, insufficient diet, no stated rations, irregular and often tainted supplies of meat, a dilapidated building; and regulations which have not yet received the sanction of the Secretary of State'. The asylum board contested this report and invited the editor of the newspaper to visit the asylum, and, after this visit, the *Telegraph* largely retracted its claims. However, these newspaper reports were not wholly without substance. On 15 September 1858, the Earlswood administration paid one woman £250 after her daughter, in care at the institution, suffered 'chilbains' and did not receive proper treatment; her toe subsequently 'mortified' and fell off. The daughter had entered Earlswood in December 1857, and was removed by her mother in August 1858. After the payment, the case was closed and never made public (Earlswood archives 3247/2/2).

15 Mrs Underwood suffers a fall days before giving birth to the twins, and in the novel this is the explanation for Theodore's disability. Interestingly, Annis Gillie suggests that 'Theo Underwood was the child of parents exhausted by procreation. His appearance was not that of a mongol, though his musical capacity was characteristic of that group. All subnormal children were grouped together [at the time of the novel's publication], and Charlotte Yonge generalized below her usual standard of observation' (Gillie 1965: 104–5). Theo was the youngest of the thirteen Underwood children.

CHAPTER 10

Sensational idiocy

In May 1862, Margaret Oliphant's review article 'Sensation Novels' situated the popular new literary genre as an offspring of its era:

> Ten years ago the world in general had come to a single crisis in its existence. The age was lost in self-admiration. We had done so many things that nobody could have expected a century before – we were on the way to do so many more, if common report was to be trusted. (Oliphant 1862: 564)

But all that had changed. 'What a wonderful difference ten years makes!', Oliphant writes. The 'distant roar' of war abroad – that is, the American Civil War – she explains

> has come to form a thrilling accompaniment to the safe life we live at home and we ... begin to feel the need of a supply of new shocks and wonders ... it is only natural that art and literature should, in an age that has turned to be one of events, attempt a kindred depth of effect and shock of incident. (564–65)

Domestic fiction is no longer sufficiently exciting to hold the attention of readers, she suggests, and on this flat literary landscape Wilkie Collins's 1859 novel *Woman in White* emerges as a phenomenal success, effectively establishing a new genre: sensation fiction. Notably, this literary triumph comes by the novel employing 'not so much as a single occult agency', but rather producing its sensation 'by common human acts' (566) – that is, by acting on the human emotions to stimulate the senses, it renders the apparently mundane thrilling. Oliphant's contemporary H. L. Mansel describes sensation writers as 'preaching to the nerves', and suggests that the 'rule' of this school of fiction might be 'les nerfs, voilà tout l'homme' (quoted in Daly 1999: 466).

Oliphant's analysis of her times may err on the side of the disingenuous, as sensational reportage on everything from murder to sexual deviance to aristocratic abuses of station had been a staple of the newspaper reader's diet throughout the 1850s (Boyle 1989). More recently, critics of the 'sensation fiction' genre, which flourished throughout the 1860s and beyond, have added their own rationales for its popular success. Elaine Showalter writes that the form's popularity 'came from its exploitation of repressed sexual fantasy and covert protest against the restrictions of domestic respectability', with an 'emphasis on secrecy as the condition of middle-class life' (Showalter 1976: 2); Jonathan Loesberg (1986) has identified the genre as being characterized by an anxiety over establishing and maintaining identity, often understood in terms of legal and class status; Nicholas Daly, following the arguments of Walter Benjamin, suggests not only that sensation fiction is 'concerned with the subject's response to modernity', but also that the 'hyperstimulation of the nerves is itself a component of historical *modernization*' and that 'heightened consciousness – low level anxiety, that is – is the subject's *defense mechanism* against shock' (Daly 1999: 465, original emphasis). Similarly, Deborah Wynne argues that sensation fictions

> constituted an important response to the issues of the day, particularly anxieties surrounding shifting class identities, financial insecurity, the precarious social position of single women, sexuality, failed and illegal marriages, insanity and mental debilitation, fears of criminality, and perceptions that modernity itself was undermining domestic life. (Wynne 2001: 2–3)

Many of the items in Wynne's list could fit under the more general rubric of an anxiety around degeneration, a notion that resurfaces repeatedly in the genre.[1] Sensation fiction played with notions of physical and mental deviance, and idiotic and imbecilic characters (along with insane and crippled ones) were staples of the genre. But often the 'idiot' is only vaguely defined; even in terms of intellectual capacity, status is blurred, uncertain and provisional. In addition, the idiot is also a figure specifically played against the notion of sensation: the individual for whom sensations come slowly, ineffectively and often mistakenly, and for whom the thrill of sensation, as understood in the genre, was inevitably misdirected – if it was felt at all.

When Oliphant's article appeared in *Blackwood's Magazine* in 1862, it ran alongside the serialized version of her own stab at sensational fiction, *Salem Chapel*; at the same time, Wilkie Collins's *No Name* was

appearing in *All the Year Round,* one of Charles Dickens's publishing endeavours, and Mary Elizabeth Braddon's *Aurora Floyd* in *Temple Bar.* All
three appeared as books the following year (with Collins's novel being
published on 31 December 1862), and each contained characters identified as 'idiots', 'imbeciles' and 'softies'. This burst of idiocy imagery
repeats some of the issues engaging the burgeoning asylum movement: the educability of idiots and the curability of idiocy; the need for
kindness in instruction; the danger posed by 'unreclaimed' idiots; and,
perhaps most significantly given the genre, the need to develop the
bodily organization of idiots by educating their fundamental sensory
capacities. So let us consider these case histories.

Collins's regeneration of the moral degenerate

Early in Wilkie Collins's *No Name,* the narrator poses a timely question: 'If we dare to look closely enough, may we not observe, that
the moral force of character and the high intellectual capacities in
parents seem often to wear out mysteriously in the course of transmission to children?' (11). The spectre of degeneracy is thus invoked
right away: Magdalen Vanstone, Collins's problematic heroine, is
scheming and ambitious; Norah, her morally upright older sister, is
without vitality or initiative. Norah and Magdalen are young women
displaced because of a secret – they are illegitimate children – that is
revealed only when their parents, newly married after the death of Mr
Vanstone's first wife in North America releases him from a youthful
error, both meet sudden and unexpected ends; then, owing to a trick
of the law, the sisters are disinherited and cast into a world where they
have no money, no status and no legal claim to their father's surname.
Magdalen leaves her sister and their elderly guardian, Mrs Garth, to
make her living as an actress, a morally questionable profession that
muddies the frontier between the real and the assumed, and in so doing
meets her distant cousin Captain Wragge. As Collins writes, Magdalen
'had hitherto seen nothing but the successful human product from the
great manufactory of Civilization. Here was one of its failures – and,
with all her quickness, she was puzzled how to deal with it' (197). If
Magdalen is a slightly debased version of her parents, she is capable of
much further decline, as Wragge's example indicates.

Magdalen has much less difficulty in learning how to deal with the
Captain's wife, Mrs Matilda Wragge, whom he had married for her small
inheritance. Collins develops Mrs Wragge's character around several

blurred categories. For instance, her enormous size – she is over six feet tall and, in her husband's words, is constantly 'uneven' in some way or another – runs counter to conventional notions of femininity and wife-liness (David 1990). Her intellectual status is also ambivalent at best: Collins describes her as having 'a large, smooth, white round face – like a moon – encircled by a cap and green ribbons; and dimly irradiated by eyes of mild and faded blue, which looked straightforward into vacancy' (202). The Captain suggests she is 'only a little slow. Constitutionally torpid'; on the other hand, he notes, 'externally speaking … [she is] the crookedest woman I ever met with' (203), an observation that under-scores Mrs Wragge's anomalous bodily organization. Soon, Magdalen and the Captain become partners in deception, with Wragge managing her stage career and later assisting her plot to disguise herself and marry the sickly, selfish miser Noel Vanstone, inheritor of her father's wealth and her cousin, and thus to claim back the family fortune. The web of familial relations is significant to the novel's 'degeneracy' subtext: both Noel Vanstone and Captain Wragge are cousins of Norah and Magdalen, on the paternal and maternal side respectively. This degeneration appears more strongly as a moral trait than as a physio-logical one, despite Noel's sickliness, thus leaving the possibility of redemption. Notably, Collins never presents Mrs Wragge herself as degenerate, despite giving plenty of instances of her mental weakness. Wragge fears that his wife is 'too great a fool' to participate in their intrigues (254), and that her 'imbecility may … lead to consequences which we none of us foresee. She is nothing more or less than a grown-up child' (255). Magdalen has more sympathy for the beleaguered Mrs Wragge, though. When the Captain suggests that, were it not for the possibility of her gaining a further inheritance, he would 'probably have long since transferred [his] wife to the care of society at large', and that for the duration of their scheme he could 'see no objection to having her comfortably boarded or lodged out of our way', Magdalen insists that 'The poor creature's life is hard enough already … and I won't allow her to be shut up among strangers while I can help it' (352–53). And when the Captain later questions Magdalen's decision to share rooms with Mrs Wragge, she 'burst[s] out vehemently' that Mrs Wragge 'is the only innocent creature in this guilty house' (391). Throughout, Collins uses Magdalen's sympathy for Mrs Wragge and appreciation of her innocence to establish his protagonist's essential goodness. And this essential goodness – a moral quality – also spares Mrs Wragge the taint of degeneracy that marks the other main characters.

   One point of suspense in the novel concerns whether or not Mrs Wragge will be able to remember her lessons – that is, remember their assumed characters if queried. When she is finally confronted by Mrs Lecount, Noel Vanstone's cunning housekeeper, she immediately forgets the subterfuge and gives away the plot, thus forcing the Captain and Magdalen to accelerate their plans to lead the sickly Noel to the altar. Unlike Dickens with *Little Dorrit*, Collins does not use intellectual incapacity to offer a critique of society; however, he raises the emotional stakes by having the honest Mrs Wragge intuitively recognize the dangers facing Magdalen as she plots her seduction of and marriage to Noel. Mrs Wragge is also expressing those responses that the novel hopes to elicit from its readers – concern for the protagonist and fear for her future – and, as such, she becomes not merely a sympathetic figure but an exemplar of Collins's audience, part of the authorial strategy for maintaining sympathy for his heroine. Matilda Wragge's insightful anxiety for Magdalen, her 'expression of … artless gratitude' and her 'cry of … guileless love' on the wedding day shakes Magdalen 'as nothing else had shaken her during that day' (512), Collins tells us. At that point where Magdalen is her most insensate, suppressing all emotional responses like an automaton, Mrs Wragge expresses the fearful truth that Magdalen so vigorously denies: her prescient exclamation 'I am frightened for you!' gives words to the fear that Magdalen suppresses – her fear subordinated to her desire to reclaim the family name and fortune by marrying the sickly, selfish miser Noel, and her 'guileless love' lost when her previous fiancé, Frank Clare, proved shallow and unworthy. This juxtaposition of the insensate heroine against her emotionally expressive 'imbecile' companion is significant in terms of theories of the defective nervous system of those people identified as idiots and imbeciles. But I will build upon this point later; for now, let us stick to the novel.

Mrs Wragge is both a comic figure and a parodic double to Magdalen; as Deirdre David observes, each is 'a woman deprived of her identity as inheriting daughter and disciplined by laws that legislate legitimacy and correct irregularity' (David 1990: 193). However, the sexuality often associated with idiot girls is here carried exclusively by Magdalen instead. Interestingly, the notion of degeneracy alluded to at the start of the novel experiences some slippage at the end: Magdalen marries Captain Kirke, a steadfast seafarer whose father had been a friend of Magdalen's father and who had admired her upon first sight; Captain Wragge becomes the successful vendor of an allegedly revitalizing medicine, using Mrs Wragge's image as the 'revitalized woman' on the bottle's label; Mrs Wragge's honesty and love are eventually rewarded when she is invited to join Magdalen's household; and the passive, virtuous Norah marries George Bartram, who inherits the Vanstone fortune from Noel after his death (which follows his discovery that the woman he has married is in fact Magdalen Vanstone, plotting to get his money), thus bringing the legacy to its rightful recipient. While at the start of the novel Collins presents a theory of degeneracy vaguely connected to the idea that vital energies and virtues dissipate over generations, by the denouement this decline is understood primarily in moral terms, and even the flawed heroine can atone for her sins and recover her moral worth. As Magdalen observes at the novel's end, 'poor narrow people who have never felt and never suffered' would 'fasten on my sin, and pass all the suffering by' (740) – but she is, in the symbolism of Collins's nomenclature, the fallen woman, like the Biblical Magdalen, redeemed by Kirke, who, through his affinity with the ocean, seems here a natural or secular version of the 'church' alluded to by his name.

Much of *No Name* involves exposing social hypocrisies. Magdalen sets out to deceive and marry Noel Vanstone in order to reacquire her father's legacy; later, when she is preparing to exchange roles with her maid as part of a further subterfuge, she advises her servant how to impersonate a lady: 'Shall I tell you what a lady is?... A lady is a woman who wears a silk gown, and has a sense of her own importance' (613). These concerns find a parallel in Collins's portrayal of Matilda Wragge. Mrs Lecount cannot determine whether or not Mrs Wragge – using the alias Mrs Bygrave – is a lady kept in seclusion because of 'some remote nervous illness' so that she is 'forbid all excitement' (368), as Captain Wragge claims, or rather has a 'defective capacity for keeping her husband's secrets' (379), which both underscores the ambiguity of Matilda's status and destabilizes the definition of the 'lady'. Later, Lecount determines that Mrs Wragge 'was little better than an idiot' and that the best way to unravel Magdalen's plot 'lay through deluding the imbecile lady and not through bribing the ignorant servant' (443). When finally meeting Mrs Wragge, Mrs Lecount takes note of everything, even her 'imbecile foot ... searching blindly in the neighbourhood of her chair for a lost shoe' (458), and introduces herself with an 'artless truthfulness of manner which the Father of Lies himself might have envied' (459). Lecount 'probe[s] her way tenderly into Mrs. Wragge's feeble mind' (463), and Mrs Wragge, thus probed, gives away the game almost immediately. Mrs Wragge's imbecility is exposed through her incapacity with the secrecy and deceit demanded by social interactions; she is innocently honest, and her general resistance to the sensations that the novel seeks to elicit underscores this incapacity: as she is honest, she suspects no one and she feels no nameless anxiety.[2]

Oliphant's innocent degenerate girl

Margaret Oliphant's contribution to the 'sensation' genre, *Salem Chapel*, shares some features with Collins's work – especially in the concern with degeneracy and sexual exploitation (or, alternatively, the exploitation of sexuality). *Salem Chapel* and other novels in the Carlingford series were written with an eye to high sales, and took as exemplars the successful forms of the day, including the sensation novel (Colby and Colby 1966); as Oliphant herself noted, the series – and especially *Salem Chapel* – '*almost* made me one of the popularities of literature' (see Coghill 1974: 70), and it did so (at least in part) by building tension between different notions of innocence – including moral, legal, intellectual and something we might call 'worldly' innocence – and moral, sensual degeneration.

In this novel, Arthur Vincent, the new minister trying to establish himself as the pastor of the dissenting congregation of Salem Chapel, becomes intrigued by one of its less regular members, Mrs Hilyard, an eccentric needlewoman (and, it turns out, a fallen gentlewoman) who has had an apparently imbecilic daughter with her sensual and deceitful husband, Colonel Mildmay. They have separated, she living under an assumed name and sending her daughter, Alice, away with an attendant, as she fears what her husband would do with his beautiful but simple girl. The 'sensational' version of the story is told by Adelaide Tufton, the invalid daughter of the retired pastor, who amuses herself by observing the locals from her wheelchair and analysing their motives; in the history she recounts to Arthur, Mrs Hilyard and her husband

> had one baby, and then she left him – one baby, a girl, that has grown up an idiot; and here this lady lives – a poor needlewoman – to keep her girl safe, somehow, out of her father's hand. Why he should want to have her I can't exactly tell. I suspect, because she's pretty, to make a decoy of her, and sell her somehow, either to be married, or worse. (253)

Adelaide's version of the story, with its clear sexual threat, becomes, by virtue of the lack of alternative narratives, the dominant explication of the sensation subplot. This plot impinges on Arthur's life when his mother and sister, living in the town of Lonsdale some miles away, take in a boarder who gives his name as Fordham but who is in reality none other than Colonel Mildmay searching for his daughter, whom he knows is being kept in a town called Lonsdale; while there, in what seems to be an act of casual amorous adventurism, he becomes engaged to Arthur's sister, Susan. Once he finds that his daughter is not there, he departs for one of the other many 'Lonsdales' in

England, and his wife, learning that her husband has left this particular
Lonsdale and believing her daughter would be safe with the family
of the upright, honest minister (but ignorant of Mildmay's assumed
name), sends Alice to live with Arthur's sister and mother. However,
Mildmay, through a stroke of fortune, intercepts both Susan and Alice
while Arthur's mother is visiting him in Carlingford. He absconds with
the two young women, and the remainder of the subplot concerns the
minister's attempt to recover his sister, with attendant concerns over
the status of her sexual innocence. When Susan reappears, nearly
senseless, after Mildmay has been shot in the head (not fatally), her
legal innocence also comes into question – as does whether or not
she will survive the coma into which she falls. Eventually, the sound
of the voice of the 'idiot' girl, Alice Mildmay, who has been driven to
the patient's bedside by an unconquerable desire to see her protector
again, helps recall Susan to consciousness. Mrs Vincent interprets the
recovery as a 'wonderful victory of innocence over wickedness' (421).

The novel exploits tensions between differing notions of innocence
and degeneracy, and Alice embodies this conflict: while her fundamental innocence is repeatedly asserted, she is also the offspring of
overly sensual, impassioned and perhaps criminal parents; Mrs Hilyard
describes her husband as 'not a man, but a fine organisation capable
of pleasures and cruelties', and, in a variant of the 'maternal impressions' theory of the causes of idiocy, claims that her discovery of her
husband's deceits caused her daughter '[to come] into the world with
a haze on her sweet soul'. Mrs Hilyard justifies some of Adelaide's
more sensational hypotheses in her own assessment of the threats
Mildmay poses to his daughter: 'how could I tell what he might have
done? – killed her – but that would have been dangerous; poisoned
what little mind she has left – made her like her mother' (394). This
mother's moral status is also uncertain, especially as she is guilty of
having shot her husband, the crime for which the comatose Susan is
originally thought responsible; throughout the novel Oliphant opposes
the sensual Mrs Hilyard to the innocent and worthy Mrs Vincent,
mother to Arthur and Susan. In direct contrast to the corrupt bloodline of Alice's parents, the humble Vincents have something much
preferable: Dr Rider, one of the centres of moral authority in the novel,
compliments the Vincent family for bearing 'such pure blood in [their]
veins; not robust ... but far better – such sweet, perfect health as one
rarely meets with nowadays' (330).

Despite their differing blood (and intellectual status), Alice's condition mirrors Susan's: both are threatened sexually by Colonel Mildmay
and both are (as the novel repeatedly asserts) innocent. The term is

loaded and refers to Alice's moral innocence associated with her intellectual incapacity, Susan's legal innocence of the attempted murder of her abductor and, in both their cases, their sexual innocence and general lack of worldliness. In fact, Susan's mother is also repeatedly designated 'innocent', as is her household before it was defiled by Fordham/Mildmay. In the world described by Oliphant, this innocence has a regenerative quality. The novel ends three years after its main action has been completed; Susan remains Alice's guardian, and Arthur sees the two of them as emissaries from an 'enchanted country' (459): 'two beautiful young women, unexpected apparitions, who transformed life itself and everything in it. Was one his real sister, strange as it seemed? And the other – ?' (460). Alice's final status is ambiguous, and the text hints that she has been cured of her imbecility by the pure love offered by Susan – while at the same time lending Susan some of her strangeness, and making her an other-worldly (but not 'worldly') 'innocent' by association.[3] However, this reading demands an extrapolation – it would be more accurate to say that we are left uncertain what degree of intellectual recovery, if any, Alice has made by the end of the novel. She remains both innocent and alluring, though, and, in the novel's final lines, we are told that 'Seeing [Susan and Alice] as they went about the house, hearing their voices as they talked in perpetual sweet accord, with sweeter jars of difference, surprised [Arthur's] life out of all its shadows; – one of them, his sister – the other –. After all his troubles, the loves and hopes came back with the swallows to build under his eaves and stir his heart' (461). Alice resurrects the promise of love for Arthur, regenerating his own damaged spirit, but she herself is unnameable, undecipherable and innocent. In the end, the beautiful Alice, like the rumour of her cure, remains a mystery, her insensibility supplanted by authorial obscurity.

Braddon's dangerous softy

Mary Elizabeth Braddon was, with Wilkie Collins, one of the most popular of the 'sensation' novelists, and when her *Aurora Floyd* was published in January 1863, at roughly the same time as Collins's *No Name* and Oliphant's *Salem Chapel*, the sensation novel was at the height of its popularity. As with the previous two examples, concerns with degeneracy lurk throughout Braddon's novel. The pure blood running in the veins of Talbot Balustrade is compared to that hybrid blood fuelling the impassioned Aurora Floyd, who is the daughter of the wealthy banker Archibald Floyd and Eliza Prodder, an actress whom

Floyd had first seen on-stage performing in a second-rate Liverpool theatre. The only daughter of a seafarer, Eliza dies shortly after giving birth to Aurora, although her seafaring brother will appear late in the novel to assist in solving the murder mystery that threatens his niece. Throughout the novel Braddon mocks Balustrade's obsession with selecting a wife worthy of perpetuating his aristocratic lineage: he and Aurora become engaged to marry, but when she refuses to divulge the secret of what happened during several unaccounted-for months of her youth, Talbot, fearing to pollute his illustrious bloodline, retreats from her and she frees him from his engagement. Talbot then marries Aurora's kind, passive and thoroughly insipid cousin Lucy, and Aurora, in turn, marries John Mellish, a wealthy Yorkshire landowner, who has accepted that his wife will be the keeper of her secret.

Aurora's secret is that, as an eighteen-year-old attending a boarding school in France, she had run off to marry James Conyers, the groom to her father's horses, who had followed her to the continent. Before long she realizes that Conyers' 'outward beauty' was matched by an 'inward ugliness' (180–81); 'Nature', Braddon writes, 'had created a splendid image, and had chosen a soul at random, ignorantly enshrining it in her most perfectly-fashioned clay' (298). Once Aurora realizes that Conyers is interested in her hefty inheritance (also, presumably, in her virginal beauty, although the text is less explicit on this point), she abandons him, and returns to her father with the story that she had married the groom but that he had died. Then, while being courted by Balustrade, she comes across a news article reporting Conyers' death in a riding accident, freeing her to accept his marriage proposal. But she chooses to keep her secret, thus precipitating her break with Balustrade and marriage to Mellish.

All begins well for the newlyweds, but when Aurora and Mellish arrive at his estate, they meet the 'one person who did not join in the general voice when Mrs Mellish was spoken of', Stephen Hargraves, 'a man of about forty, who had been born at Mellish Park, and had pottered about the stables from his babyhood, doing odd jobs for grooms, and being reckoned, although a little "fond" on common matters, a very acute judge of horseflesh' (134). His first appearance is inauspicious:

> He was a squat, broad-shouldered fellow, with a big head, a pale haggard face, – a face whose ghastly pallor seemed almost unnatural, – reddish brown eyes, and bushy, sandy eyebrows, which formed a penthouse over those sinister-looking eyes. He was the sort of man who is generally called *repulsive*, – a man from whom you recoil with a feeling of instinctive dislike, which is, no doubt, both wicked and unjust; for we have no right to take objection to a man because he has an ugly glitter in

his eyes, and shaggy tufts of red hair meeting on the bridge of his nose, and big splay feet, which seem to crush and destroy whatever comes in their way. (134)

Aurora experiences this revulsion and, like the narrator, tries to suppress it as an unworthy response: 'she was angry with herself for the involuntary shudder with which she drew back from the sight of this man', who, she quickly learns from the trainer, is also known as the 'Softy', being a bit 'touched in the upper story – a bit "fond", as we call it here' (135). The Softy had lost his mental capacities in a horse-riding accident over twenty years earlier, but even if his 'fondness' may not be congenital,[4] Hargraves' degeneracy is innate.[5] Aurora's instinctive feeling of dislike is the correct response to the softy, and although the text describes Aurora 'reproaching herself … for that repugnance which she could not overcome' and which was 'a repugnance closely allied to terror', this is quickly followed by a direct address: 'Reader, when any creature inspires you with this instinctive unreasoning abhorrence, avoid that creature. He is dangerous.… Nature cannot lie; and it is nature which has planted that shuddering terror in your breast' (136).[6] When Aurora finds Hargraves kicking the dog she has owned since childhood, she horsewhips him; her husband then expels him from the estate where he has lived all his life. Unlike Matilda Wragge and Alice Mildmay, Hargraves is denied status as an 'innocent': his incapacity is, after all, apparently derived from a misadventure, and he behaves brutally. Instead, his mental weakness becomes an explicit marker, along with his repulsive appearance, of his fundamental degeneracy; at one point the narrator even describes his 'slow, side-long gait' as 'having some faint resemblance to that of the lower reptiles, but very little in common with the motions of his fellow-men' (248).

Stephen Hargraves is solemn and unemotional; his 'higher sensations' have been replaced by a simple longing for revenge and with an intelligence that expresses itself only as a debased, devious cunning. His face is described as 'expressionless almost always', conveying nothing but 'stolid indifference; the stupid indifference of a half-witted ignoramus' with an 'impenetrable intellect' (387). After his expulsion from the Mellish estate, he hangs about the town 'in a lounging, uncomfortable manner, sitting in some public-house taproom half the day and night, drinking his meagre liquor in a sullen and unsocial style peculiar to himself, and consorting with no-one' (424). When John Mellish hires the new groom to look after his stable of horses, this groom decides, upon arrival, that he needs a 'humble drudge' for his servant, and so takes on the 'ignorant and brutish' Hargraves (188). The new groom is none other than James Conyers, not dead after all, but hiring his wife's enemy in order to provoke her, and at this point the reader (if not Mellish) learns of Aurora's secret. Conyers blackmails Aurora and she agrees to pay him but insists he leave for Australia – but minutes after she hands him the promised £2,000, a gunshot takes his life and the money disappears. Soon the secret of Aurora's first (and only legal) marriage is out, and the remainder of the story involves John Mellish and Talbot Balustrade setting out to find the murderer.

While the first suspicion falls on Aurora herself, the murderer, of course, is Hargraves, mocked too many times by Conyers to harbour any affection for him (even if that were in his nature), too fond of money and entirely without moral scruples; he also hopes to frame Aurora for the crime in revenge for his expulsion. Upon the discovery of his crimes, and his capture, the story moves quickly to his execution and its conclusion. As presented by Braddon, Hargraves is very much a type – 'Them softies is allus vicious', proclaims one character, generalizing broadly (285). But Hargraves is also a *new* type: the degenerate, 'softy' criminal, unrestrained, manipulated by the more intelligent Conyers, whom he then turns upon. He goes to his death having never 'been either help nor comfort to any one of his fellow-creatures'.

> [While] there was an attempt made to set up a plea of irresponsibility upon the part of the 'Softy', and the *sobriquet* which had been given him was urged in his defence ... a set of matter-of-fact jurymen ... saw nothing in [the murder] but a cold-blooded assassination, perpetrated by a wretch whose sole motive was gain. (547–48)[7]

Hargraves is physically, morally and intellectually degenerate – a set of distinctions that probably did not exist for Braddon, whose portrayal belies a belief that they are all expressions of the same fundamental depravity. This belief would become more widespread over the coming decades.

The ambivalent, insensible imbecile

Matilda Wragge, Alice Mildmay and Stephen Hargraves are ambivalent figures, and because none appears immediately to be idiotic, other characters cannot decide how to respond to them, although the issue is raised repeatedly. In *No Name* and *Salem Chapel*, the 'imbecile' women carry little threat, but rather are vulnerable to those in a position to exploit them. For Matilda Wragge, the oppressor is her husband (and to a lesser degree Mrs Lecount) and the threat rarely seems particularly ominous; as readers, our concerns are reserved primarily for her 'double', Magdalen. In Oliphant's novel, though, the threat of sexual exploitation hangs over Alice and Susan both. In addition, both novels raise questions of degeneracy of the physical, genealogical sort as well as the moral variety. Mrs Wragge herself is never represented as specifically degenerate, despite her intellectual failings; however, both Captain Wragge and Magdalen can be read in this way. Alice, with her ethereal appearance and redemptive powers, is drawn within the 'innocent' tradition, but, as the child of overly sensual parents, she is clearly linked to both moral and physical degeneracy, which are implicitly opposed to the 'pure blood' of the virtuous Vincents. Hargraves, however, remains thoroughly unreclaimed and threatening, from his first appearance to his execution: he is consistently depraved and dangerous – 'one of the most notorious murderers in Victorian fiction', according to Robert Lee Wolff (1979: 150). But despite their differences, all three of these characters existed on the border at which normality (itself a new concept in the 1860s) slipped into deviance, the mundane into the sensational.

This liminal status is not the only feature shared by these characters. According to D. A. Miller, sensation fiction provides

> one of the first instances in modern literature to address itself primarily to the sympathetic nervous system, where it grounds its characteristic adrenaline effects: accelerated heart rate and respiration, increased blood pressure, the pallor resulting from vasoconstriction, and so on. (Miller 1988: 146)

These physiological responses mark characters in sensation novels as well as readers of the genre. But while readers of sensation fiction may be stimulated and impressed, their sensations thrilled by the narrative, and while the characters in the novel are often in states of high agitation – Magdalen Vanstone, Arthur Vincent and Aurora Floyd pass most of their respective narratives in extreme emotional states – the idiot characters are generally passive, stoic, insensate and otherwise unreceptive to normal impressions and sensations: Mrs Wragge is uneven and moon-faced, and experiences a buzzing in her ears that keeps her from understanding the world outside; Alice Mildmay is semi-comatose, impervious to the external world; and Stephen Hargraves is capable of only the grossest and basest of feelings, and plods sullenly through his attempts to frame Aurora for the murder of James Conyers.

Given this consistency in the representation of idiocy in sensation novels, we might ponder just what the significance of this idiot insensibility may be to the reader. That is, what functions do these 'idiot' characters perform in sensation fiction? One, clearly, is to serve as a point of contrast for the reader, whose understanding of the novel's social conflicts and tensions stands in opposition to the apparent ignorance of the idiot characters: that is, the ability of readers to experience sensations is directly contrasted to the incapacity of the idiot characters to receive these same sensations, thus providing an aesthetic strategy for intensifying the story's suspense and emotional impact. But the idiot characters, in their insensate ignorance, are also vulnerable. They live in constant danger: Mrs Wragge loses her meagre inheritance to the Captain, whose insistent commands leave a constant and confusing 'buzzing' in her ears, and she must be hidden to avoid being manipulated into revealing the truth of the marriage plot; Alice Mildmay is, in her idiocy, morally and sexually vulnerable to her depraved father; even the repellent Stephen Hargraves is exiled from the only home he has known because of a newcomer, and is later exploited by Conyers. Hargraves' condition does not share the quality of 'innocence' associated with Matilda Wragge and Alice Mildmay, but rather is the vulnerability of the wounded, dangerous and unpredictable animal – indeed, as Braddon describes him in his last battle to escape capture, he 'glared ... with something of the savage terror of some ugly animal at bay – except that in his brutalized manhood he was more awkward, and perhaps more repulsive, than the ugliest of the lower animals' (453). In each of these novels, the conclusion demands that the vulnerability of these characters somehow be resolved: Magdalen offers Matilda Wragge a safe home; Alice Mildmay remains with her guardian Susan; and Stephen Hargraves is hanged for the murder of James Conyer.

Training the insensible idiot

The insensate idiot is not simply a phenomenom of sensation fiction. In 1861 P. Martin Duncan and colleagues argued that 'idiocy was quite as much a disease of the nervous centres and their expansions, as a deficiency of mental attributes' (Duncan *et al.* 1861: 238) and the anonymous author of 'Idiot Asylums' wrote in 1865 that

> the body is but the instrument, the mind of the unseen musician, and the strings must be in tune or no harmony can be produced by the most skillful hand. Thus the corporeal state of the idiot being disordered, discord results from the agency of the mind upon it. All that can be said of what the idiot really is terminates in this – that an idiot is one wanting in power, greater or less, to develop and manifest the normal human faculties by reason of organic defects ... the nerves of motion and sensation are without due action. (Anonymous 1865a: 46)

Both these passages draw on the authority of Édouard Séguin, whose major writings reiterated the argument that the bodily organization of the idiot was deficient and that consequently such individuals needed careful stimulation and discipline to learn how to properly receive and act upon sensations. His methods of physiological and moral education, a prominent pedagogical technique in the early asylum movement, are meant to address this apparent incapacity. Séguin's 'trinitarian hypothesis' proposes that 'man ... is artificially analyzed ... into his three prominent vital expressions, activity, intelligence, and will' (see Chapter 9). According to this schema, the idiot is 'a man infirm in the expressions of his trinity', and so, writes Séguin, 'we consider the method of training idiots, or mankind, as the philosophical agency by which the unity of manhood can be reached as far as practicable, though the trinitary analysis'. This analysis, applicable to idiots as well as the rest of mankind, demands that one 'educate the activity, the intelligence, the will ... not with a serial object in view ... but with a sense of their unity in one being' (Séguin 1866: 83). This objective can be achieved only by a blend of physical and intellectual exercises under the careful eye of the enlightened pedagogue. In Séguin's system:

> all the senses are considered as modifications of the tactile property, receivers of touch in various ways. In Audition, the sonorous waves *strike* the acoustic nerves; in Vision, the retina is *touched* by the image carried by the luminous waves assembled at the focus; the Taste and Smell are yet more proximate modifications. (Séguin 1866: 133)

This emphasis on the tactile is significant, as the concept of 'sensation' is itself most closely aligned to the sense of touch, in how one *feels*. Séguin then stresses the importance of determining 'the point or points where lies the deficiency of a nervous function', especially as, he writes

> the senses may be in themselves normal, yet left in the same state of impotence to perceive sensations, in which we have seen the motor organs incapable of moving, as if paralyzed, by mere deficiency of the will and of the intellectual synergy. This last incapacity may be more or less aggravated by sensorial ones. (Séguin 1866: 135)

The treatment was intended to be, in a sense, holistic: the corporeal idiot is treated in conjunction with the intellectual and moral being. But, as Murray Simpson shows, Séguin's pedagogy demands that all activity be 'moralised': that, for instance, a moral function be applied to basic activities such as eating meals, in which 'control over the appetite must be learned through the intimacy of family-sized eating areas and the judicious timing of serving' (Simpson 1999: 234), and in labour, which must be 'linked to production, immediately visible and tangible to the idiot' (Simpson 1999: 235). As Séguin writes,

> Moral treatment involves employing every means available to develop and regulate the activities, intelligence and passions of the idiot. From the first day to the last, from the most simple exercise to the most complicated and abstract, from the simplest acts of hygiene observed to the most demanding or difficult instructions given, at every moment, every one of the master's actions, his every word, gesture, every manifestation of his being and his moral will must help logic prevail over the instinctive and negative inclinations of the subject. Without moral treatment, hygiene is an extravagance; withdraw moral treatment and education is reduced to nonsense, and any progress halts immediately. According to my method, moral treatment is at the heart of all things, it is the beginning and the end; it is the entire method, because everything dwells within it. (Séguin 1846: 642)

The 'moral education' of the idiot also frames Séguin's basic physiological training. For example, he writes, the influence of the eye:

> as an instrument of moral training, [the eye] cannot be overrated, whether we consider it from the master's or from the pupil's side. For if the look of the former is alternately inquiring, pressing, exacting, encouraging, caressing, etc., the look of the latter is avoiding, opposed, submitted, irate or grateful, borrowing its expressions from feelings incited by the former. To obtain this result, the master's look must have taken possession of the other, have steadily searched, penetrated, fixed, led it; and here the constant use of the look, already described in the physiological training, is found corroborated by its use in moral training, and *vice versa*. (Séguin 1866: 222–23)

Séguin develops 'activity' in the case of the eye by taking 'possession' of the idiot's eye to instruct the student in the 'use of the look'. Even the basic senses, when being physically trained, were also being 'morally' educated as Séguin sought to strengthen the deficient will of the idiot.

Séguin's approach was tremendously influential, and his impact was reflected in a publishing boom in books, articles and pamphlets on the education of idiots. The review article 'Idiot Asylums', appearing in the July 1865 issue of the *Edinburgh Review*, covers fourteen works published between 1846 (Séguin's *Traitement*) and 1864, with half coming after 1860. In their *Manual for the Classification, Training and Education of the Feeble-Minded, Imbecile and Idiotic*, published in 1866, Duncan and Millard present what was rapidly becoming the new orthodoxy: 'The defects of the mind in idiots have a very close relation to those of their bodies, and it may be stated as a general rule, that the greater the bodily defect the greater the idiocy' (6). However, these defects are not consistent. As they note:

The sense of feeling may be universally dull, and both hot and cold may produce very slight effects, or the defective sensibility may be restricted to one or more patches of skin. Sometimes it is universally great, or only small patches upon the skin are exquisitely sensitive. (7)

While 'the special senses may be defective or perverted' (7), there is no consistency across these defects. In addition, they note,

the whole or part of the muscles of the limbs, hands and feet have greater or less want of coordinating power, hence a general clumsiness, a shuffling, hobbling gait, waddling, inelegant running, with odd and eccentric movements generally ... [indeed, there may be] a general inertness of the body. (9)

Overall, they conclude 'that there is a great scope of bodily and mental deficiency, amongst idiots, imbeciles, and the feeble-minded, but that only a few defects are really characteristic of the states' (11). Duncan and Millard go on to provide specific diets, sleeping and bathing regimens, gymnastic exercises and speaking lessons to aid in the development of these deficient nervous and muscular systems.[8]

The development of sensorial awareness is seen as critical for establishing a moral identity – a position with roots in the work of John Locke and his followers, such as Étienne Bonnot, Abbé de Condillac, who stressed the importance of sense impressions in the growth of the consciousness. If one was of a particularly sensitive constitution, these sense impressions would be more deeply experienced. By 1733, the physician George Cheyne noted that people with 'weak Nerves' were especially likely to be quick-witted and imaginative, owing to their nervous system's higher level of receptivity:

the common division of Mankind, into Quick Thinkers, Slow Thinkers, and No Thinkers, is not without Foundation in Nature and true Philosophy. Persons of slender and weak Nerves are generally of the first Class: the Activity, Mobility, and Delicacy of their intellectual Organs make them so, and thereby weakens and relaxes the Material Organs of the intellectual Faculties. (Cheyne 1733: 189)

'No Thinkers', at the other end of this spectrum, would have nervous systems with very poor levels of receptivity. This weakening must then be addressed by moderate regimens of diet and exercise, many of the latter similar to those later encouraged by Séguin and his followers. The point was to bring the body back into harmony, and Cheyne used a familiar analogy to illustrate this state: 'the best Similitude I can form ... is that of a skilful Musician playing upon a well-tun'd Instrument. So long as the Instrument is in due Order, so long is the Musick perfect and compleat in its Kind' (Cheyne 1733: 69).[9] The development of sensory awareness and, eventually, moral identity became a central concern in the education of 'idiots'. In 1865, the anonymous writer of 'The Psychology of Idiocy', in the *Journal of Mental Science*, asserted that:

> the first suggestion and impulse in the philosophical analysis, and in the education and cure of the imbecile mind, originated with the Philosophers, or with medical men acting as Philosophers, and not with Physicians. They desired to solve a problem rather than relieve humanity; to decide a controversy, not to eradicate an evil. (Anonymous 1865b: 14)

This philosophical impulse led Jean Itard to apply the axiom 'the senses are the soul' to his development of exercises for the wild boy of Aveyron, and although 'no such magnificent results as were hoped followed ... the attempt was not altogether fruitless' (Anonymous 1865b: 15). The writer cites the case of the blind, deaf and dumb prodigy Laura Bridgeman to suggest that 'if the sense of personal identity can be, or can arise as, an element of one class of perceptions, taste, for example, it may be inferred that such sense will gain extension and clearness in proportion as such perceptions are multiplied' (Anonymous 1865b: 8). Idiots, though, seem especially deficient in their capacity to develop independent personal identities:

> The rarity of the use of the personal pronoun by idiots is remarkable. They pronounce their name, they avoid substitution, or speak impersonally, perhaps from the feeble sense of personal identity which they possess, and from their still feebler volition. Egoism is undoubtedly involved in many of the brief expressions used; but I is a revelation. They are, in fact, parasites. They are part of their parents or guardians, they depend upon their personality, responsibility, thoughts and acts. Even after their powers have been developed and trained, and they have become self-reliant, so far as the sense of the capacity to perform certain acts within a given circle of contingencies is concerned; they still require an impulse from without, they wait for the governance and guidance of another, in order to be moved. (Anonymous 1865b: 16)

While the goal of education was to help create this identity, idiots remained 'parasites', dependent upon a 'host' – a parent, a guardian, a teacher – to assign them an identity.[10] This analogy is worth pursuing a bit further, as it illuminates certain symbolic labours performed by the idea of idiocy. First, though, let us consider the relationship of identity to the imagination. The writer notes that

> so far as the sense of the beautiful, the inventive faculty, or that speculation which carries us into the true but the unrealized, are concerned, the aspirations of this class are feeble and puerile; but so far as the idealisation of ordinary life, the addition of qualities to visible objects so as to confer like, animation or elevation, so as to form pictures and romances,

which are event pictures, can be regarded as the suggestions of imagination, many of weak mind share the gift with their fellow mortals. But as in those who dwell and revel in the supersensuous, and as in the insane, many of these creations are dreams and phantasmata, over the origin of which they have little control, and from which, as in the same classes, they cannot withhold their assent and belief. (Anonymous 1865b: 22)

Intriguingly, then, while idiots are deficient in productive imagination, they are similar to the 'supersensuous' in their capacity for experiencing and succumbing to phantasms over which they have no power. Their imagination is delusional rather than creative, and they become, in effect, parasitically dependent upon these phantasms for motivation, as they do upon their guardians.

The tendency of 'idiots' to give themselves over as 'parasites' to a dangerous host, or to yield unresistingly to dangerous phantasms, made them particularly vulnerable individuals. As Duncan and Millard (1866: 156–57) noted, 'the feebleminded are easily affected and influenced by the conduct and example of their superiors in intelligence, and they therefore generally reflect the moral condition of those around them'. As such, they are particularly susceptible to abuse, and Duncan and Millard repeatedly stress the importance of 'great good temper, kindliness of disposition, cheerfulness, and a decidedly firm and persevering manner' in the care of 'idiots, imbeciles and the feeble-minded'; a 'good nurse and teacher produce good pupils, just as a scolding nurse and an unamiable instructor soon add to the disobedience, inertia and misery of the children' (81). One idea for reducing this vulnerability involved stimulating the will, and Séguin's treatment explicitly strives to create a moral being by imposing the will of the teacher on that of the idiot student:

the moral treatment is the systematic action of a will upon another, in view of its improvement; in view for an idiot, of his socialization. It takes possession of him from his entrance in to his exit from the institution; from his opening to his shutting his eyes; from his acts of animal life to the exercise of his intellectual faculties. It gives a social meaning, a moral bearing to everything around him. The influences destined to give moral impulse to the very life of the idiot come upon him from prearranged circumstances, from prepared association with his fellows, and, above all, directly from the superior will which plans and directs the whole treatment. (Séguin 1866: 214)

This result is achieved through the 'moral treatment [being] blended with the physiological training' (Séguin 1866: 214). The idiot becomes a moral being by experiencing subordination to the teacher, and through this process being dragged from the solitude of idiocy into the social and moral life of humanity. But, as the anonymous author of 'Idiot Asylums' writes, 'the first care ... must be to put the *instrument* as far as may be in tune' (Anonymous 1865a: 48, original emphasis).

Collins's post-sensation idiot

' The dormant intelligence of my curious cousin is like the dormant sound in a musical instrument. I play upon it – and it answers to my touch. She likes being played upon', says Miserrimus Dexter of his cousin Ariel in Wilkie Collins's 1875 novel *The Law and the Lady* (212–13). Dexter is vividly conscious of his cousin's deficiencies and describes their relation in terms consistent with notions of idiocy in the 1870s. In making Ariel into a musical instrument, Collins is re-peating a common refrain: the same image was used by George Cheyne in 1733, as well as Samuel Gridley Howe in 1848 and the writer of 'Idiot Asylums' in 1865 (see above), and would soon be used again by Henry Maudsley, in 1879. Dexter, in his arrogance, believes that he plays elegantly on this flawed instrument.[11]

The Law and the Lady is the first-person narrative of Valeria, who dis-covers that Eustace Woodville, the man she has married, is not what he had claimed: instead, he is Eustace Macallan, recently found 'not proven' of poisoning Sara Macallan, his previous wife – an instance of the 'Scotch verdict' that provides a third alternative to 'guilty' or 'not guilty' in Scottish law, and one which does not remove the taint of guilt, but merely concedes that there is insufficient evidence for a clear conviction. Eustace abandons his wife when she discovers his secret, fearing she will eventually grow suspicious and afraid of him, so Valeria sets out to prove her husband's innocence, and quickly decides that Miserrimus Dexter, one of the key witnesses in the case – and apparently an ally of her husband – may be able to provide some assist-ance in her quest.

When she first meets him, Dexter – brilliant, mercurial and born without legs – flies about his room in his wheelchair, a 'fantastic and frightful apparition, man and machinery blended in one – the new Centaur, half man, half chair' (206); as Valeria had noted earlier, 'Never had Nature committed a more careless or a more cruel mistake in the making of this man' (173).[12] In the mystery at the core of the novel, Dexter eventually proves to be the villain, and he precipitates Sara's suicide by informing her that Eustace does not love her (in this, Dexter is correct – Eustace did not love his first wife); his objective is to gain Sara's love, or at least gain admission to her bed. Dexter's mental eccentricity (and eventual insanity), his physical disability and his lust all mark him as degenerate. While Collins plays Dexter's physical disability against stereotype at first, and has Valeria marvelling at his vitality and energy, Dexter soon becomes what Daly calls 'one of the most memorable figures of Victorian technological nightmare ... animated by an almost superhuman energy, and possessed of considerable creative powers[;] but he also represents for Collins a falling off from the human' and 'seems to demonstrate that the human/machine hybrid is unstable, and like other hybrids, sterile' (Daly 1999: 477). Dexter is described later in the novel (328) as 'a monkey', a more assertive representation of his degeneracy.

This degeneracy is also signalled through Dexter's association with his cousin Ariel, with her 'round, fleshy, inexpressive face, her rayless and colourless eyes, her coarse nose and heavy chin' (210). To Valeria, Ariel is both formless and unfeminine, a 'creature half alive; an imperfectly developed animal in shapeless form, clad in a man's pilot-jacket, and treading in a man's heavy laced boots: with nothing but an old red flannel petticoat, and a broken comb in her frowsy flaxen hair, to tell us that she was a woman' (210). Dexter, who has named her Ariel in a fit of irony, describes her as 'a mere vegetable. A cabbage in the garden has as much life and expression in it as that girl exhibits at the present moment.' However, he boasts, there is more to his charge than meets the eye, and he asks Valeria, 'Would you believe there was latent intelligence, affection, pride, fidelity, in such a half-developed being as this?' (211). When Dexter, in a perverse parody of an 'idiot doctor', boasts that he holds the key to Ariel's dormant intelligence and asks her if she would like to comb his hair and 'anoint [his] beard', she responds 'Yes! yes! yes!' eagerly, supplementing this enthusiasm with the jealous assertion that 'Nobody, as long as I live, will touch you but me'. When Dexter suggests that Valeria might like to perform these ministrations, Ariel threatens Valeria with a 'burst of sudden rage', exclaiming 'Let her touch you if she dares!' (212).

The relation between the cousins Dexter and Ariel is covertly incestuous, with Valeria posed between the two. Ariel also substitutes her own body for Dexter's; when he offends Valeria and she refuses to see him, Ariel delivers his penitent letter to her home, and also offers her body for the beating she believes Valeria would like to give to her cousin and 'Master', as she repeatedly calls him. Collins plays with the notion that if one can earn the affection of the innocent idiot, one must carry some germ of goodness – a characterization strategy that he had used in *No Name*, where the friendship between Mrs Wragge and Magdalen signals to the reader that Magdalen truly is good-hearted.

At one point, Valeria asks herself, 'Could a man who was hopelessly and entirely wicked, have inspired such devoted attachment to him as Dexter had inspired in [Ariel]', although she also recognizes that 'the greatest scoundrel living always has a friend – in a woman, or a dog' (303). Later, Valeria, accompanied by Benjamin, a friend of her father, visits Dexter and comes upon a strange scene:

> The unfortunate Ariel was standing before a table, with a dish of little cakes placed in front of her. Round each of her wrists was tied a string, the free end of which (at a distance of a few yards) was held in Miserrimus Dexter's hands. 'Try again, my beauty!' I heard him say, as I stopped on the threshold of the door. 'Take a cake.' At the word of command, Ariel submissively stretched out one arm toward the dish. As soon as she touched a cake with the tips of her fingers, her hand was jerked away by a pull at the string, so savagely cruel in the nimble and devilish violence of it, that I felt inclined to snatch Benjamin's cane out of his hand, and break it over Miserrimus Dexter's back. (326)

The performance is a grotesque parody of the instructional techniques described in training manuals; Duncan and Millard (1866), for instance, suggest a series of exercises involving poles, wands and pulleys, for the improvement of motor skills, and it is not difficult to see in Dexter's manipulation of Ariel a perverse reinterpretation of such practices. Whether Collins intends this episode as a critique of practices used in 'idiot' education is an open question but, at any rate, Dexter insists, in response to Valeria's outrage, that 'Ariel has no nerves – I don't hurt her', and his cousin reiterates his claim, saying of herself, 'Ariel has no nerves.... He doesn't hurt me' (326). Yet if Ariel is at times a puppet, at others a musical instrument to be played upon by her cousin, she also assumes a number of other standard images of idiocy. She communicates with Valeria 'by imitation, as a savage might have' (302); she then assumes an attitude 'more like a dog than a human being' (302) and finally bursts out of Valeria's home 'like a wild animal escaping from its cage' (303). All of these images point to her less than human (or less than European) status, which would also have made her, according to the ideas of the day, someone whose sensory capacities were, like those of the wild boy of Aveyron, woefully unrefined.

Ultimately, although Ariel is Dexter's puppet, she also manipulates him, the two eventually becoming indivisible. Ariel precipitates Dexter's final mental decline by insisting he finish the story he is telling her and Valeria, in which, his wandering mind brought back to the path by Ariel's insistence, he unwittingly reveals his role in the death of Sara Macallan. From this point, Dexter grows irrevocably mad and is sent to the asylum; a subscription is taken up to enable Ariel to attend him there as well. After he dies, Ariel escapes the asylum, seeks out the cemetery and is 'found towards sunrise, dead of cold and exposure, on Miserrimus Dexter's grave', recounts Valeria. 'Faithful to the last, Ariel had followed the Master! Faithful to the last, Ariel had died on the Master's grave!' (408). The death of Ariel recalls that of Robert Southey's 'Idiot' Ned (Chapter 2), wringing pathos from its audience, but with a significant difference: Southey's idiot follows his mother to the grave, but Ariel follows her morally and physically degenerate cousin whom she thinks of as her 'Master'. Filial love is displaced by incestuous desire, and the means through which Dexter earns the affection and fidelity of the idiot Ariel are based upon nothing less than self-interested manipulation and exploitation – far from Southey's 'Old Sarah', who 'lov'd her helpless child' (line 5). Collins's portrayal of Ariel suggests a new anxiety around idiocy in 1875: not simply as degenerate in itself, but also as an extension of the will of others. The coming years would see a growing fear that people of lower intelligence could fall under the sway of unscrupulous manipulators, who would exploit them to perform any number of depraved and criminal acts. Ariel does no such thing – she simply provides necessary aid to her own degenerate master. But she is a harbinger of these new degenerate 'idiots' and 'imbeciles' who would soon populate the public imagination.

The insensate, 'parasite' idiot taking identity from another being leads to two broad possibilities in these sensation novels. One is that the vulnerable idiot is linked to a benevolent but also vulnerable protector, who is, like the idiot character, in danger of losing identity or status, although both idiot and protector achieve a level of relief at the novel's conclusion. This is the case with Magdalen Vanstone and Matilda Wragge, and again with Susan Vincent and Alice Mildmay. Alternatively, the idiot 'parasite' could attach to a being whose moral integrity is flawed, corrupt, or non-extant, as is the case with Stephen Hargraves and James Conyers, and with Miserrimus Dexter and Ariel. And in these instances as well, the 'parasite' shares the fate of the host. The term 'parasite' functions surprisingly well in these representations, but, to pursue the zoological analogy further, these relations can also be symbiotic. Both Magdalen and Susan benefit from their relations: Mrs Wragge presents a fount of goodness and innocence for Magdalen, while Susan is recalled to life by Alice. On the other hand, both Conyers and Dexter are destroyed by their 'parasites': Hargraves literally murders his master, while Ariel insists on Dexter telling the story that finally breaks his fragile mental stability and plunges him into the madness and fits that take his life. After the hosts die, so do their parasites. The drama of the parasite and the host is being played out in broader social relations as well. The asylum movement benevolently offers to aid society both morally and economically by at the same time assisting the idiot, but the closed space of the asylum, with its emphasis on the moral government of its inmates, also embodies the lurking fear that the relationship will not prove symbiotic after all, that perhaps the threat of the degenerate idiot could prove more powerful than ever previously imagined.

Intellectual incapacity in the sensation novel remains an individual concern. While it can be caused by morally corrupt progenitors, the 'idiot' character carries no particular consequence for broader society. The idiot was innocent even if the idiocy itself is the consequence of parental degeneracy and so long as that degeneracy remained within the individual, all was (relatively) well. But even as Collins, Oliphant and Braddon are writing their novels, the idea of degeneracy is moving beyond the individual to infect the social bloodstream. Idiocy is becoming symptomatic of a broader decline, just as folly had been a metaphoric expression of a vast range of vices for Sebastian Brant at the end of the fifteenth century (Chapter 6). In the latter decades of the nineteenth century, the infrastructure supporting the concept of the degenerate idiot is built with evolutionary theories, both the new theory of natural selection and the Lamarckian concept of acquired characteristics. But even those notions of degeneracy based on the theory of natural selection are attached to older ideas of moral decrepitude that had long been instrumental in defining a particular stream of discourse around idiocy. The following chapters will explore these fears of degeneracy – both moral and 'racial' – in greater detail.

Notes

1 As Deborah Wynne observes, the serial publication of Wilkie Collins's *No Name* in *All the Year Round* was accompanied on 26 April 1862 by the short story 'Out of the House of Bondage', featuring as its heroine Clara, a white, middle-class daughter of a wealthy American slave-owner, who, despite her efforts to be morally and politically advanced, looks down upon the slaves as 'lower animals'. To her shock, she discovers that her mother was also a slave, and her father, with his 'fantasy that she is a white daughter' destroyed by her knowledge of her mother, also 'views her as a slave'; eventually she leaves for England and freedom. In addition to reiterating the themes of identity, displacement and degeneration that pervade Collins's novel, the short piece also illustrates Oliphant's link of distant war and sensation fiction (Wynne 2001: 104–5). For more on degeneracy in the sensation novel, see, for instance, Andrew Maunder's '"Stepchildren of Nature": *East Lynne* and

the Spectre of Female Degeneracy, 1860–1861' (Maunder 2004), and Mary Rosner's 'Deviance in *The Law and the Lady*: The Uneasy Positionings of Mr. Dexter' (Rosner 2004).

2 Mrs Wragge does experience fear of a more old-fashioned, gothic nature, however, as she takes a disguised Magdalen to be a ghost. The gothic dread, a staple of popular fiction of the early nineteenth century, is here placed against the more modern 'sensational' anxiety stimulated by the novel.

3 Some critics, such as Shirley Jones (1999), interpret Alice as having been cured of her idiocy at the novel's end.

4 According to some contemporary definitions, non-congenital imbecility could be caused in those 'born with perfect intelligence' by 'disease of the brain, by epileptic convulsions, by water on the brain, or by injury to the head'; this sort of imbecility forms class 5 of Duncan and Millard's eight classes of feeble-mindedness, imbecility and idiocy (Duncan and Millard 1866: 13).

5 Hargraves is kept on at the Mellish estate because, as John Mellish explains, 'He was a favourite groom of my father's twenty years ago; but he got a fall in the hunting-field, which did him some injury about the head, and he's never been quite right since. Of course this, with my poor father's regard for him, gives him a claim upon us' (135). It is tempting to see this explanation as a description of outdated tolerance for 'fond softies', as his ongoing employment is associated with the deceased Mellish senior. When Mellish turns to his groom, saying 'we put up with [Hargraves'] queer ways, don't we, Langley?', the trainer responds 'Well, we do sir, … though upon my honour, I'm sometimes half afraid of him, and begin to think he'll get up in the middle of the night and murder some of us'. Mellish jokingly responds that this will not happen until one of them has 'won a hatful of money…. Steve's a little too fond of the brass to murder any of you for nothing' (135).

6 Braddon is inconsistent on this point, as her description of James Conyers shows: 'Mr James Conyers, puffing lazy clouds of transparent blue smoke from his lips, and pondering thus looked as sentimental as if he had been ruminating upon the last three pages of the "Bride of Abydos". He had that romantic style of beauty peculiar to dark-blue eyes and long black lashes; and he could not wonder what he should have for dinner without a dreamy pensiveness in the purple shadows of those deep-blue orbs. He had found the sentimentality of his beauty almost of greater use to him than the great beauty itself. It was this sentimentality which always put him at an advantage with his employers. He looked like an exiled prince doing menial service in bitterness of spirit and a turned-down collar. He looked like Lara returned to his own domain to train the horses of a usurper. He looked, in short, like anything but what he was, – a selfish, good-for-nothing, lazy scoundrel, who was well up in the useful art of doing the minimum of work, and getting the maximum of wages' (190). In this instance, nature *does* lie.

7 Braddon makes mocking reference to a current theatrical conceit of innocent parties delivered from the gallows through the last-minute 'evidence of an idiot, or a magpie, or a ghost, or some other witness common and popular in dramatic criminal courts' (396); she refers explicitly to the play *Susan Hopley; or The Vicissitudes of a Servant Girl*, an 1841 a popular domestic tragedy by George Dibdin Pitt. However, this narrative turn might not work so well if the accused is understood to be something of an 'idiot' himself.

8 Séguin had prescribed similar exercises, and noted that 'Our Gymnasium differs from the ordinary one in its general object, being intended to create an equilibrium of the functions, not by the towering of the muscular above the

other systems, but, on the contrary, by paying more attention to the nervous, as being the most shattered in idiocy' (1866: 99).

9 Cheyne's theories had a direct impact on English literature through his close relation, as both friend and physician, to Samuel Richardson, author of such profoundly influential sentimental novels as *Pamela* and *Clarissa*; their correspondence is marked by an ongoing exchange of advice on matters both literary and medical, with Cheyne diagnosing his friend as being 'born originally of weak Nerves', which became apparent only in middle age, by which point, Cheyne tells Richardson, 'the Nerves have been wasted and relaxed by your sedentary Life and thinking attentively' (see Mullett 1943: 104).

10 Other writers expressed the relation between 'idiots' and other people in less pejorative terms and commented upon the educative advantages of the idiot's apparent propensity for identifying closely with others. John Langdon Down, in a review of Seguin's 1866 work *Idiocy: And Its Treatment by the Physiological Method*, noted that 'the idiot is to some extent a hero-worshipper, and he loves to bask in the sunshine of his hero's approval. That person will not be a successful moral trainer of idiots who fails to exercise by the threat of his displeasure one of the most potent punishments that he can inflict. He can only do this, however, by being consistent, truthful, and loving, with a tender appreciation of all the traits of his patients, and by holding the supreme place in their affectionate regard' (Down 1867: 195). Furthermore, education was critical if idiots were to be kept from becoming dangerous parasites or, at least, drains on the energy of their healthy carers. As Down wrote in the same review, 'An idiot left uneducated is not only shut out from the enjoyments of this life, and incapable of taking his part in the world's work, but he uses up the energy of a sane life, and nullifies, to some extent, the existence of a more perfect creation' (192).

11 Ironically, when Dexter does play music, it is described as cacophonous.

12 Teresa Mangum notes that 'Collins perceived his own body as deformed', especially his 'delicate feet and hands ... his small body and large head, and his misshapen forehead. His left temple was partially collapsed and his right temple bulged outward, which probably resulted from the use of forceps during a difficult birth' (Mangum 1998: 289). At the same time, she proposes that photographs and drawings of Collins suggest that he perceived these deformities to have been worse than they actually were. In addition, in the 1860s and 1870s, Collins was afflicted with 'what he called "gout" of the eyes', during which time, according to some who knew him, his eyes 'were literally *enormous bags of blood*' (quoted in Mangum 1998: 289). Collins used laudanum to treat this condition, which has led one biographer, Catherine Peters, after noting that Dexter embodies the 'dangers of the imaginative and creative inner life', to suggest that the 'extraordinary portraits of Dexter and his willing slave Ariel ... may come as much from opium visions as from an imaginative extension of reality' (Peters 1991: 374). However, the opium was probably unnecessary to create these characters: the growing discourse of degeneracy would probably have been sufficient nourishment for these images.

CHAPTER 11

'The sins of the fathers': idiocy, evolution and degeneration

' Everybody knows the consequences of prolonged intermarriages between any sort of people who are few enough to be almost all blood relations', wrote Harriet Martineau in her 1854 *Household Words* article 'Idiots Again'.

> The world was shocked and grieved, some years since, at the oldest baronage in England 'going out at the ace of diamonds' – expiring in the disgrace of cheating at cards. The world ought to be quite as much shocked and grieved at seeing – what has been seen, and may be seen again – the honours of the same ancient birth being extinguished in a lunatic asylum. (Martineau 1854: 197)

The country's oldest families were being led to lunacy and idiocy thanks to consanguineous marriages, she argues. Martineau then draws on Dr Samuel Gridley Howe's *On the Causes of Idiocy* (published in 1848 in the United States but not printed in Britain until a full decade later[1]), quoting his assertion 'in his Report on Idiocy in Massachusetts, that "the law against the marriage of relatives is made out as clearly as though it were written on tables of stone"' (197). And then she cites his evidence: Howe's study of seventeen families with parents who were blood relations. Across these households, she notes, there were ninety-five children. 'What were these children like?', Martineau asks.

> Imagine a school of ninety-five children, of all ages, or the children of a hamlet at play, and think what the little crowd would look like; and then read this! Of these ninety-five children, one was a dwarf. Well, that might easily be. One was deaf. Well, no great wonder in that. Twelve were scrofulus. Well, that is sadly common, and especially in unhealthy situations. Well, but FORTY-FOUR were IDIOTS! (197, original emphasis)[2]

The lesson was clear: marriage among relations was reducing the health of family blood-lines, which were consequently degenerating into intellectual squalor.

In the latter half of the nineteenth century, ideas of degeneracy stimulated concern over the possible decline of what was thought of as the 'British race', an anxiety that found expression in novels, journal articles, medical and sociological works, and social initiatives. The concern with intermarriage and idiocy – so prominent in Martineau's piece – is an early instance of degeneration anxiety, and would before long represent only one limited aspect of it. This degeneration anxiety arose from a number of converging factors: a national population that had doubled between 1800 and 1850, with attendant shifts in economic and social structures (Wrigley and Schofield 1981); increased immigration, especially Irish; the growing urbanization of London and industrial centres such as Manchester; and the growing acceptance of evolutionary theories such as Darwin's, as set out in *The Origin of Species* (1859), and their application to social structures (for example, natural selection and a laissez-faire economic structure merge in Herbert Spencer's rephrasing of evolutionary theory as the 'survival of the fittest', a doctrine that seemed both to explain the growth of the British Empire and to justify the inequalities of class structure). This chapter tracks the evolution of the idea of degeneration in relation to idiocy, which, in its earlier manifestations, is confined to specific individuals, but eventually becomes – in worst-case scenarios – a feature of society: a loss not simply of individual vitality, or the vitality of a particular familial line, but of the vitality of the entire Anglo-Saxon race. The first intimations of this change appear in the 1850s, but even those notions of degeneracy that draw on the theory of natural selection are attached to older ideas of moral decrepitude that had long been instrumental in defining a particular discourse around idiocy. In the years immediately before Darwin's book appeared, the moral discourse had been revitalized by writers such as the American reformer, teacher and asylum builder Samuel Gridley Howe, whose ideas were quickly reproduced in Britain.

Samuel Gridley Howe's theory of moral degeneration

As head of the Massachusetts Asylum for the Blind, in Boston, Howe had already achieved fame by educating the deaf and blind prodigy Laura Bridgeman, for which he was lauded by Charles Dickens in his *American Notes* (1842); Howe had also successfully trained blind students who had been mistakenly diagnosed as idiots. In 1846, inspired by reports of Édouard Séguin's work in Paris and John Conolly's moral training of the insane in England, he began to advocate similar facilities in Massachusetts and was appointed to chair a commission on idiocy, leading to a report in 1848 to the Massachusetts legislature (Trent 1994). This report was accompanied by the supplement *On the Causes of Idiocy*, written by Howe, which, with the report itself, made his a particularly strong voice in the transformation of dominant notions of idiocy in both the United States and Britain – as Harriet Martineau's use of his work indicates.

In his report to the governor of Massachusetts, excerpted in the British (1858) edition, Howe proclaimed that:

> We regarded idiocy as a disease of society; as an outward sign of an inward malady. It was hard to believe it to be in the order of Providence that the earth should always be cumbered with so many creatures in the human shape, but without the light of human reason. It seemed impious to attribute to the Creator any such glaring imperfection in his handywork. It appeared to us certain that the existence of so many idiots in every generation *must* be the consequence of some violation of the *natural laws*; – that where there was so much suffering there must have been sin. We resolved, therefore, to seek for the sources of the evil, as well as to gauge the depth and extent of the misery. (vi)

Once they began to look, Howe and his committee had no difficulty in finding evil practices abounding, and these discoveries form the basis of *On the Causes of Idiocy*. Howe, following Conolly and Séguin, insisted that idiocy was a manifestation of physiological disorder. The physical, material basis of idiocy and insanity was a claim reiterated with increasing force throughout the latter half of the century, especially as 'materialists' and 'alienists' (who used psychological moral treatment to cure insanity) struggled both for priority in the profession and for control of the prestigious and lucrative asylum industry (Jacyna 1982). Locating idiocy in physiology provided a means to link the physical state of the idiot child with that of the degenerate parent, and identified practices that could, in weakening the parent, lead to idiocy in offspring. It also helped to consolidate the notion of the idiot as a degenerate, if not depraved, being. While conceding that specific causes remained shrouded in secrecy, Howe argued that:

> The whole subject of idiocy is new. Science has not yet thrown her certain light upon its remote, or even its proximate causes. There is little doubt, however, that they are to be found in the CONDITION OF THE BODILY ORGANIZATION.... If any bodily peculiarities, however minute, always accompany peculiar mental conditions, they become

important; they are the finger-marks of the creator, by which we read his work. (ix, original emphasis)

The relation of the body to the soul Howe likened to that of a musical instrument and its musician, except that 'the idiot's body is a wretched thing, and its few strings are so sadly awry, that even in a seraph's hand it could give nothing but jarring and discordant sounds' (12). The task of the educator was to tune these strings as close to proper pitch as was possible.

Howe identified three categories of idiot, which he called 'pure idiots', 'fools' and 'simpletons' (noting that this latter group were known as 'imbeciles' in Britain), and gave case descriptions for all three. Seeking the causes of idiocy in family history, he landed upon five primary factors: poor physical organization, intemperance, masturbation, marriage between close relations, and failed attempts at abortion. With the first (and most all-encompassing) of these categories, Howe anticipates the later criticisms of the enfeebling qualities of urban environments and does so with a particularly vivid moralizing rhetoric:

> It is said by physiologists, that among certain classes of miserably paid and poorly fed workmen, the physical system degenerates so rapidly, that the children are feeble and puny, and but few live to maturity; that the grandchildren are still more puny; until, in the third or fourth generation, the individuals are no longer able to perpetuate their species....
>
> It would seem that startled nature, having given warning by the degenerated condition of three or four generations, at last refuses to continue a race so monstrous upon the earth.
>
> We see here another of those checks and balances which the exhaustless wisdom of God pre-established in the very nature of man, to prevent his utter degradation ... a race of men, abusing the power of procreation, may rush on in the path of deterioration until, arrived at a certain point ... the procreating power is exhausted. (25)

Howe's conflation of moral and physiological degeneracy is striking, as is the tone of judgement from the pulpit that characterizes this passage (a tone that would become familiar enough in Britain in the 1860s and beyond). While the afflicted progenitors may be 'miserably paid and poorly fed workmen', they assume responsibility for degeneration by 'abusing the power of procreation' until nature, and God, denies their monstrous race the possibility of life. Scrofula, with its broad range of symptoms, is a constant in his case histories: Howe admits that it is 'difficult to describe exactly the marks which characterize this low organization', but stresses that 'the eye of a physiologist detects it at once' (25). However, he also hedges his bets with scrofula, noting that he is using the term 'in its popular sense, without any pretension to pathological accuracy. Indeed', he writes, 'it is difficult to give a correct idea of scrofula, because its symptoms are so manifold and so various': these include poor posture ('they seem ... to be trying to hold their head and shoulders up by their muscles than to rest firmly and gracefully poised upon the spinal column and lower extremities'); 'red and sore eyelids, turgid lips, spongy gums, swelling in the glands, liability to eruptions and diseases of the skin', which is itself 'generally fair'; muscles that are 'flabby'; and hair that is 'light –, seldom hard, crispy and strong' (26). The catalogue of symptoms is broad enough for it to be hard for any one individual to avoid all of them, and a physiologist determined to examine each patient for evidence of scrofula – one of the 'finger-marks of the creator' that identifies degeneration – would probably not have to try very hard. Howe paints a physical image of a type of human inclined to produce idiocy, but these descriptions remain, for all their apparent detail, profoundly inconclusive.

Idiocy is even more closely linked to immoral behaviour in his second cause, intemperance. Howe reports a study of 359 'idiots' in which 99 were the children of confirmed drunkards – and, he notes, the parents of many of the others may well have also warranted the label. 'Thus', he concludes, 'directly and indirectly, alcohol is productive of a great proportion of the idiocy which now burdens the commonwealth' (28). Furthermore, he notes, alcohol is probably involved in the process that creates the low physical organization of many scrofular parents. His third cause of idiocy, masturbation, Howe does not support with statistics; instead, he rages against the practice, 'a monster so hideous in mien, so disgusting in feature, altogether so beastly and loathsome, that, in very shame and cowardice, it hides its ugly head by day, and, vampyre-like, sucks the very life-blood from its victims by night' (29). While conceding that his language 'may be extravagant' (30), he justifies it with the assertion that

> there are among those enumerated in this report some who not long ago were considered young gentlemen and ladies, but who are now moping idiots, – idiots of the lowest kind; lost to all reason, to all moral sense, to all shame, – idiots who have but one thought, one wish, one passion, – and that is, the further indulgence in the habit which has loosed the silver cord even in their early youth, which has already wasted, and, as it were, dissolved, the fibrous part of their bodies, and utterly extinguished their minds. (30)

Howe's concerns here express what G. J. Barker-Benfield calls the 'pervasive and obsessive masturbation phobia that took hold of America during the early nineteenth-century' (Barker-Benfield 1976: 167), linked to the belief in the 'spermatic economy', whereby loss of sperm weakened both the body and the mind, which dictated that semen must be rationed for appropriate usage (181).[3] The concern to discipline deviant sexual practices also frames Howe's final two categories, marriage between close relations and failed abortion: he identifies 17 of 359 people designated idiots as having parents 'nearly related by blood', and extrapolates this to suggest that 'idiocy is only one form in which nature manifests that she has been offended by such intermarriages' (34); and he notes that idiocy caused by attempts to procure abortions is 'one of the forms in which the fruit of sin reappears to punish the sinner and forewarn all beholders' (36).

Howe's insistence that idiocy is the consequence of moral crimes was not a cry from the fringe. As Leo Kanner notes in his *History of the Care and Study of the Mentally Retarded*, Howe warrants the credit for establishing 'institutional care for retarded children' in the United States (Kanner 1964: 42), and Scheerenberger (1983) in *A History of Mental Retardation* also stresses Howe's influence in establishing an education asylum in the States; both Kanner and Scheerenberger quote the same passage from the Preface of the 1848 report to illustrate Howe's significance:

> The benefits to be derived from the establishment of a school for this class of persons, upon humane and scientific principles would be very great. Not only would all the idiots who should be received into it be improved in their bodily and mental condition, but all the others in the State and the country would be indirectly benefited. The school, if conducted by persons of skill and ability, would be a model for others. Valuable information would be disseminated through the country; it would be demonstrated that no idiot need be confined or restrained by force; that the young can be trained for industry, order, and self-respect; that they can be redeemed from odious and filthy habits, and there is not one of any age who may not be made more of a man and less of a brute by patience and kindness directed by energy and skill. (xiv)

In this passage, Howe's tone is little different from that of Conolly or Gaskell (see Chapter 9), promising to raise the brute idiot to the status of man, and to see him included in the social and economic life of the state. Like his peers in Britain, Howe stressed the economic benefits of the asylum system:

> There are at least a thousand persons of this class who not only contribute nothing to the common stock, but who are ravenous consumers; who are idle and often mischievous, and who are dead weights upon the material prosperity of the State.... Many a town is now paying an extra price for the support of a drivelling idiot, who, if he had been properly trained, would be earning his own livelihood, under the care of discreet persons who would gladly board and clothe him for the sake of the work he could do. (Quoted in Trent 1994: 24–25)

However, Howe's insistence that idiocy was evidence of moral degener-acy is a revision of the symbolic function of idiocy, making it a repository of anxieties regarding class (witness the emphasis on scrofular progeni-tors, drunkenness and consanguinity, all thought more common among members of lower social strata in the United States) and sexuality (in his passages on consanguinity, masturbation and abortion).

Howe's influence in Britain was, given cultural differences, not as great as in the United States, and British asylum doctors often tried to distance themselves from Howe's work. 'It would appear that the statistics of one nation will not apply to the idiots of another, unless the social and climatic conditions are the same; and this is clearly seen from the results of the Massachusetts report (1848)', Duncan *et al.* observed in 1861, after noting a dearth of reliable statistics on idiocy.

> This report, which would form a good model, for one which ought to be set on foot by our own government, applies to an energetic, rude, hard-working race, fighting earnestly, against external circumstances, and whose vices are very positive. But many of its conclusions become doubtful, when they are examined and tested by our experience amongst our own countrymen, whose social condition is different, whose difficul-ties, as a rule, are not nature's, and whose vices are more secret and less prominent. In America there is hardly a case whose history does not bear upon its cause; here it is quite the opposite. (Duncan *et al.* 1861: 237)

But despite cultural (and climatic) differences, Duncan's peers did not succeed in freeing themselves from Howe's statistics, although they often struggled to resist them. Often they were uncertain how to inter-pret the American results. While in 1864 Henry Maudsley noted – albeit without explicit reference to Howe – that 'It has already been shown that the drunkenness of parents may become the idiocy of children' (Maudsley 1864: 519–20), three years later he dismissed the 'oft-quoted statement that out of 300 idiots in the State of Massachusetts 145 were the result of parental drunkenness' as 'not the sober con-clusion of science but the intemperate conclusion of an intemperate zeal for temperance', objecting that 'were it an accurate and adequate assessment of causation, the wonder would be that so many habitual drunkards fail to beget idiots'. Rather, he suggests 'the most favourable conditions for the production of idiocy to be these – to be begotten by a drunken father off a half-witted mother' (1867/79: 343) – a for-mulation that recalls the common association of female sexuality and idiocy. On the other hand, in 1873 John Charles Bucknill asserted that 'The most trustworthy authority we possess on the causes of idiocy is contained in the report of Dr. S. G. Howe', and, echoing Howe's pen-chant for the Biblical, notes that 'Emphatically the stern text is true of idiots that "The fathers have eaten of sour grapes, and the teeth of the children are set on edge"' (Bucknill 1873: 170–71).

In 1877, in a presentation entitled 'Intemperance as a Cause of Idiocy' at the forty-fifth annual meeting of the British Medical Association, George Shuttleworth, medical superintendent of the Royal Albert Asylum, opposes Howe's analysis of the role of intemperance among the causes of idiocy; Shuttleworth notes that during his visits to the 'principal idiot asylums' in the United States, he found that 'parental drunkenness occupied, in the estimation of the physicians in charge of those institutions, by no means a conspicuous place in the causation of idiocy'. Of 800 cases in Earlswood, he suggests, 'six only were probably occasioned by drunkenness; in two of these, other hereditary influences being also noted' (Shuttleworth 1877: 308). But despite these findings, he was reluctant to dispense with the notion that alcohol abuse was somehow implicated in the production of idiocy. He notes in summary:

> Congenital idiocy was not, as a rule, the *immediate* legacy of the drunkard to his offspring, but physical and mental degeneracy were doubtless the heritage, and scrofulous disease, nervous instability, and even moral obliquity, might ofttimes be amongst the direct bequests. It needed, however, but one step more, the conditions remaining unfavourable, to reach actual idiocy; and thus, in very truth, was visited 'the iniquity of the fathers upon the children unto the third and fourth generation'. (Shuttleworth 1877: 309, original emphasis)[4]

And John Langdon Down, as late as 1887, noted that in his attempts to define the causes of idiocy he has 'endeavoured ... to keep [himself] free from the bias of former statistics, especially those of the late Dr. Howe, of Massachusetts' (Down 1887: 32).

These commendations and qualifications among British writers demonstrate how wide Howe's influence spread, and for how long his work remained a force; the British medical establishment, while often at pains to distinguish itself from his positions, still had no alternative but to acknowledge his influence. At the same time, his work carried a certain authority in educated lay writing, as Martineau's citation of his report suggests (presented at the start of this chapter). Even while his statistics failed to convince many, his association of idiocy with moral crimes, his conjunction of sin and physical and intellectual degeneracy, found increasingly sympathetic audiences among British physicians as well as lay people. Howe's theories were also timely, their circulation no doubt bolstered by a number of other works transforming how people thought about heredity and morality. In 1857, the year before Howe's work was published in Britain, Bénédict Morel had published his influential *Traité des dégénéresences physiques, intellectuelles et morales de l'espèce humaine* in Paris. And a year after Howe's British publication, in 1859, Charles Darwin would present the world with a scientific structure that would soon alter how degeneration was understood.

Degeneration after Darwin

According to Howe's formulation, the degeneracy evident in idiots was of a vaguely Lamarckian sort – that is, it was the consequence of depraved parental will, the striving towards evil rather than good, which was embodied in the unfortunate offspring. The social ills embodied in the idiot were those of an excess of corruption among his progenitors, the legacy of diseased inclinations – the will of parents was misdirected, and a sort of moral righteousness needed to be re-established in order to remove the blight of idiocy.[5] The Lamarckian theory of acquired characteristics informed most of these notions, but when Charles Darwin published *On the Origin of Species by Means of Natural Selection* in 1859 – with its faintly ominous subtitle *The Preservation of Favoured Races in the Struggle for Life* – the concept of degeneracy acquired a new framework, in which it could pose a threat to the health of an entire society, rather than the individual blood-lines of depraved progenitors. And that threat came not only through moral degeneration, but also, according to many of Darwin's followers, as a result of profound flaws in social organization that demanded active reparation.

Notions of class and race were instrumental in the development of evolutionary theory. Both Charles Darwin and Alfred Russel Wallace, who developed the theory of natural selection independently from and co-terminously with Darwin, found not just inspiration but also (in Darwin's case) a theoretical framework in the writings of Thomas Malthus on population (Ospovat 1995; Young 1969). As Darwin wrote in his autobiography:

> In October 1838, that is, fifteen months after I had begun my systematic inquiry, I happened to read for amusement Malthus on *Population*, and being well prepared to appreciate the struggle for existence which everywhere goes on from long-continued observation of the habits of animals and plants, it at once struck me that under these circumstances favourable variations would tend to be preserved, and unfavourable ones to be destroyed. The result of this would be the formation of a new species. Here, then, I had at last got a theory by which to work; but I was so anxious to avoid prejudice, that I determined not for some time to write even the briefest sketch of it. (Quoted in Young 1969: 126)

Even before the publication of Darwin's epoch-changing work, though, social philosophers such as Herbert Spencer were redefining the relations of humans to society. Spencer's *Social Statistics*, first published in 1850 and much reprinted (and, eventually, much revised), observed that 'All evil results from the non-adaptation of constitutions to environments', and, if this assertion were not emphatic enough, stressed that 'This is true of everything that lives' (Spencer 1850: 54). Indeed,

> Every suffering incident to the human body, from a headache up to a fatal illness – from a burn or a sprain to accidental loss of life – is similarly traceable to having placed that body in a situation for which its powers did not fit it. Nor is the expression confined in its application to physical evil; it comprehends moral evil too. (54–55)

Thus, the body strives to adapt to environments, to minimize evil, as seen with 'the drunkard who needs an increasing quantity of spirits to intoxicate him, and ... the opium eater who has to keep taking a larger dose to produce the usual effect' (56). Furthermore, this adaptation is evident not just in individuals but also in entire cultures:

> The multitudinous differences of capacity and disposition that have in course of time grown up among the Indian, African, Mongolian and Caucasian races and among the various subdivisions of them must all be ascribed to the acquirement in each case of fitness for surrounding circumstances. (56)[6]

This is not precisely Darwinian natural selection that Spencer is describing, but it is a set of observations particularly amenable to Darwin's theory, anticipating the role Spencer, along with Thomas Huxley, played in modifying natural selection to describe social structures and to naturalize the idea of progress as applied to human societies. In his *Principles of Biology*, first published in 1866, Spencer famously describes Darwinian natural selection as 'the survival of the fittest' (444) and while he is writing at this point about organisms in general, throughout the work he has used social and economic analogies to explicate organic, biological processes. For instance, his extended description of the economics of shipbuilding in periods of great and lesser demand to illustrate the modifications that an organism might undergo in changing environments (197–98) would resonate powerfully, as the shipbuilding industry had experienced a boom in the early 1860s but would collapse between 1865 and 1871 (Stedman Jones 1971: 24); biological and socio-economic processes follow similar patterns in Spencer's work, and these processes were not necessarily progressive. The analogy of society to an organism is nothing new at this point – the king had long been the head of the 'body politic', after all – but soon society would come to be seen not *like* an organism, but rather *as* an actual organism, subject to the same laws and the same threats. Like any other organism, it could become infected, ill and degenerate. And, increasingly, idiocy was understood to be an incontrovertible symptom of this infection, illness and degeneracy.

Not surprisingly, the belief, exemplified by Howe, that idiocy was the consequence of moral degeneration and, thus, a sign of moral decay entered a broader discourse concerning evolution and degeneration. In 1868, William Rathbone Greg, in 'On the Failure of "Natural Selection" in the Case of Man', published in *Fraser's Magazine*, drew on Darwin's work to argue that the human proclivity to compassion and sympathy weakens societies:

> We have kept alive those who, in a more natural and less advanced state, would have died ... thousands with tainted constitutions, with frames weakened by malady or waste, with brains bearing subtle and hereditary mischief in their recesses, are suffered to transmit their terrible inheritance of evil to other generations, and to spread it through a whole community. (Greg 1868: 359)

The danger is to be found at the two ends of the class hierarchy, with the aristocracy and the poor, according to Greg:

> The *physique* and the *morale* of both the extreme classes are imperfect and impaired. The physique of the rich is injured by indulgence and excess – that of the poor by privation and want. The morale of the former has never been duly called forth by the necessity for exertion and self-denial; that of the latter has never been cultivated by training or instruction. (360)

Unfortunately, though, both classes marry young and breed with impunity, with the consequence that

> the imprudent, the desperate – those whose standard is low, those who have no hope, no ambition, no self-denial, – on the one side, and the pampered favourites of fortune on the other, take precedence in the race of fatherhood, to the disadvantage or the exclusion of the prudent, the resolute, the striving and the self-restrained. The very men whom a philosophic statesman, or a guide of some superior race would select as most qualified and deserving to continue the race, are precisely those who do so in the scantiest measure. Those who have no need for exertion, and those who have no opportunities for culture, those whose frames are damaged by indulgence, and those whose frames are weakened by privation, breed *ad libitum*; while those whose minds have been hardened, strengthened and purified by temperance and toil, are elbowed quietly aside in the unequal press. (360–61)

The problem is not with natural selection *per se*, but with the aberrant social structures that enable the weak, the lazy and the inferior to survive and procreate. The answer, Greg suggests, could lie in selected breeding for the amelioration of the race, although he concedes that there is little popular or political support for such a programme. Greg's proposal is philosophically dependent upon the notion of evolution as 'progressive', as the term would be understood from the perspective of Victorian socio-economics, and now seems unintentionally ironic: he advocates selected breeding to restore the notion of natural selection, presuming, clearly, that there could be little dispute over which class deserves to be perpetuated. His social analysis of the theories of natural selection and degeneration was widely circulated and received a good deal of approval from his contemporaries, not least from Darwin himself, who refers to the issue of natural selection in humans as 'ably discussed' by Greg in his 1871 work *The Descent of Man* (130), and then reiterates Greg's points in his own discussion.

One aspect of evolutionary theory was that, for many mid-Victorian writers, non-Anglo-Saxons, as well as Anglo-Saxons of lower social classes, occupied a lower rung on the evolutionary ladder.[7] Evolution – and devolution – quickly became part of Victorian discourse, to the extent that Charles Kingsley was able to incorporate an instance of degeneration into his 1862/63 children's tale *The Water-Babies*, when he describes the Doasyoulikes, who abandon their home country of Hardwork to frolic in the land of Readymade. They degenerate into 'no better than savages', living on 'poor vegetables instead of roast beef and plum pudding', so that 'their jaws grow large, and their lips grow coarse, like the poor Paddies who eat potatoes' (128) (Kingsley's description here is another notable moment of anxiety over the immigration of those degenerate Irish); eventually, they devolve further into speechless, ape-like creatures, 'grown so stupid, that they can hardly think' (129). The lesson is made clear by Mrs Bedonebyasyoudid, who tells Tom, the story's protagonist, and his companion Ellie that the Doasyoulikes could have been saved:

> if only they would have behaved like men, and set to work to do what they did not like. But the longer they waited, and behaved like dumb beasts, who only do what they like, the stupider and clumsier they grew; till at last they were past all cure, for they had thrown their own wits away. (130)

Tom, she points out, saves himself from a similar fate by deciding to 'see the world, like an Englishman' (131). Kingsley's audience would also have understood the lesson: Englishmen sat atop the evolutionary ladder by virtue of their ability to perform difficult work, which also allowed them to reap the rewards of good health, roast beef and plum pudding.

What was good for the nursery was good for the university. Gillian Beer observes that Victorian anthropological journals present

> a conversation among gentlemanly peers, a conversation that frequently fails in irony, does not sufficiently observe itself, and makes possible that strange and characterizing locution of the time: 'mankind' as meaning white, implicitly middle- and upper-class, Europeans, distinguished from all other ethnic groups. (Beer 1996: 80)

With evolutionary theory came discussions of the relation of ontogeny and phylogeny – the idea that the stages through which an individual passes *en route* to mature adulthood are reflected in the advancement of different races as they achieve maturity. As C. S. Wake argued in 'The Psychological Unity of Mankind', one of the *Memoirs Read Before the Anthropological Society of London* (1867–69),

> It is a familiar idea, and one which appears now to be accepted as a truth, that 'mankind' (a term which, in this relation, has probably been used as synonymous with the Caucasian, or Indo-European, race) resembles in its totality an individual man, having, like him, an infancy, a childhood, youth, and manhood. In the early ages of the world man was in his infancy: and from that stage he has progressed, by gradual steps, until now he may be said to have attained – at least in peoples of the European stock – to a vigorous manhood.... The fact, which appears to have hitherto escaped attention, is the present existence of various families, exhibiting every stage of the supposed development. (Quoted in Beer 1996: 80–81)

The theory expressed by Wake was characterized by the German zoologist Ernst Haeckel's 1866 claim that 'ontogeny is the short and rapid recapitulation of phylogeny,' so that 'During its own development … an individual repeats the most important changes in form evolved by its ancestors during their long and slow paleontological development' (quoted in Gould 1977: 76–77). Even in 1862, Henry Maudsley had shared the 'interesting reflection that, in the formation of the individual, the same gradual changes that have preceded the appearance of the race on earth, are more or less passed through' (Maudsley 1862: 464). Recapitulation theory, the belief that the growth of an individual follows 'a series of stages representing adult ancestral forms in their correct order, … ranks among the most influential ideas of late nineteenth-century science', writes Stephen Jay Gould; according to this theory, 'the gill slits of an early human embryo represented an adult ancestral fish; at a later stage, the temporary tail revealed a reptilian or mammalian ancestor' (Gould 1981: 114).[8] The same could be said for the organization of human hierarchies: in this schema, 'the *adults* of *inferior* groups must be like *children* of *superior* groups, for the child represents the primitive adult ancestor' (Gould 1981: 115, original emphasis). Recapitulation theory thus served as a scientific justification of British imperialism, as it constructed colonized peoples as 'children' in relation to their 'adult' overlords.[9] In addition, it provided a framework for an understanding of the apparent decline of the British race.

John Langdon Down and the recapitulating idiot

When he became the medical superintendent at the Earlswood asylum in 1858, John Langdon Down was a young, ambitious man who, despite not yet having completed his medical education, had already won the support of John Conolly (Wright 2001). Today, he is one of the leading figures in the histories of intellectual disability, from the traditional whiggish medical narratives of Kanner (1964) and Scheerenberger (1983) to Wright's (2001) social history. Down played a central role in advancing the medical study of idiocy, frequently publishing papers in the *Lancet* and the *Journal of Mental Science*. In 1867, Down met with George Shuttleworth (who had begun his career as Down's assistant at Earlswood), Fletcher Beach and William Ireland – the four leading medical figures concerned with idiocy in Britain, and all early in their careers – in the first medical conference on idiocy (Wright 2001). The year before, in 1866 – the same year that Haeckel's *Generelle Morphologie der Organismen* appeared – Down had published the article for which he remains most well known, 'Observations on an Ethnic Classification of Idiots', in the *London Hospital Reports*.[10] After studying his institution's residents, Down reached a startling conclusion: 'I have been able to find among the large number of idiots and imbeciles which come under my observation ... that a considerable portion can be fairly referred to one of the great divisions of the human family other than the class from which they have sprung' (Down 1866: 121–22). He hypothesized that many forms of idiocy were in fact genetic throwbacks, avatars of earlier, less evolved races: while he observes that 'of course there are numerous representatives of the great Caucasian family', he describes the others – the Ethiopian, the Malay, the native American and the Mongolian – in more detail, identifying each 'race' according to stereotypical physical features. Thus, the Ethiopian variety is marked by 'the characteristic malar bones, the puffy lips, and retreating chin', as well as 'the woolly hair ... although [it is] not always black, nor has the skin acquired pigmentary deposit'. Down concludes that these individuals are 'specimens of white negroes, although of European descent' (122). The Malay variety are identifiable by their 'soft, black, curly hair, their prominent upper jaws and capacious mouths', and the American by 'shortened foreheads, prominent cheeks, deep-set eyes, and slightly apish nose' (122). The most common of Down's varieties, though, and that which he focuses on for the second half of his paper, is the Mongolian. Indeed, he writes, 'a very large number of congenital idiots are typical Mongols. So marked is this that, when placed side by side, it is difficult to believe that the specimens compared are not children of the same parents' (122). He concludes from the evidence before him that 'there is no doubt that these ethnic features are the result of degeneration' (122). This point has, he suggests, 'considerable philosophical interest', in that these 'examples of retrogression, or, at all events, of departure from one type and the assumption of characteristics of another' help to 'furnish some arguments in favour of the unity of the human species' (123).

Lilian Zihni (1990) credits John Conolly with bringing recapitulation theory to Down's attention and, noting that the American Civil War was being fought at this period, suggests that this 'discovery' of racial regression was motivated in part by his abolitionist sentiment. By providing evidence for the monogenic argument that all races were part of a single linear human development, Down could oppose polygenists, whose belief that other races had sprung from a different evolutionary lineage from Europeans was used to justify their enslavement.[11] David Wright (2001) suggests that Down's ethnic divisions also result from an attempt to unite phrenological theories involving the analysis of the skull (again, an interest that may have been stimulated by Conolly) with Darwinian natural selection. Gould, on the other hand, has argued that Down's classifications 'embody an interesting tale in the history of scientific racism' (Gould 1982: 162), and suggests that Down's identification of mimicry among 'Mongoloid' children has its roots in the European strategy of dismissing the complexities of Oriental culture as due to a 'facility for imitative copying, rather than to innovative genius' (166).

Whatever his original motivation (or motivations), Down's use of recapitulation theory was its first elaborate application to idiocy, and no other scientist or physician pursued his line of thought quite so vigorously. The 'European negroes' and others discerned in his article thus remained in the realm of undeveloped theory (despite being supported by F. G. Crookshank almost sixty years later) rather than acquiring the aura of scientific truth achieved by 'Mongolism', which was the only one of Down's categories to be widely adopted; it even received a challenge for precedence from Sir Arthur Mitchell's identification in 1876 of very similar 'Kalmuc' idiots, who were also, suggested Mitchell, the results of recapitulation (Fraser and Mitchell 1876).[12] Not everyone was convinced, of course, with the American physician Hervey Wilbur in 1877 accepting the category as useful but finding 'little constant resemblance to the Mongolian race in these degenerate human beings' (quoted in Wright 2001: 172). Ultimately, 'Mongolism' became the dominant appellation, remaining in popular use well into the 1970s; now, of course, the condition it designated is known as 'Down's syndrome', and the characteristic physical features of people with it are traced not to a primitive Mongolian emerging from the depths of evolutionary history but to an extra twenty-first chromosome, a condition known more formally as trisomy 21.[13] Down's recapitulating idiots may never have been fully accepted by the scientific community, but they remain all the same an important illustration of a discourse that had significant consequences for the people who were gathered into the 'ethnic categories'.

Perhaps most important is that Down's recapitulation theory quickly merges with the more pervasive belief that much so-called degeneracy was the consequence of moral weakness. Although Down does not address causes of idiocy in his paper on ethnic classifications, in another document, published in 1867 in *The Lancet*, 'On Idiocy and Its Relation to Tuberculosis', he claims that:

> No-one who has had an opportunity of investigating the influences which are at work in the production of congenital mental diseases can fail to be struck with the fact that they are, for the most part, to be traced to some inherent vice of constitution in the progenitors. He will discover in the parents elements of degeneracy which must have had their share in producing the catastrophe. He will notice how by degrees the stock has deteriorated. He will be able to estimate how intemperance or sensuality leads slowly but surely to idiocy – how physical weakness of the parents culminates in the mental blight of the child. (See Down 1887: 132)

Down would develop this position further over the course of his career. In his 1887 work *Mental Affectations of Childhood and Youth*, he argues that 'one of the great causes [of idiocy] is heredity', and supports his claim with that observation that, of those cases (numbering over 1,200) in which he could trace the family history,

> only in 16 per cent. did I fail in obtaining a grave history of physical or psychical decadence from one or another of the progenitors. But even where there was no evidence of gross departure from the normal

standard, one could not fail to notice frequently cranial and other signs of racial degeneration, such as narrow palates, rabbit mouths, bad foreheads and facial exaggerations. (Down 1887: 32)

Indeed, he argued, even those of a gentle constitution and modest demeanour risked generating idiot children. Drawing on data from his own studies of 'four hundred cases with fair social antecedents', he claims that 'no less than 18 per cent. are the children of members of the clerical profession', while only 4 per cent are the children of fathers from the medical profession and a mere 3 per cent are children of lawyers (Down 1887: 40). For further evidence, Down unleashes statistics drawn from Francis Galton's *Hereditary Genius*, which show that 'while lawyers give origin to nearly three times as many scientific men as do the clergy, the clergy, on the other hand, beget six times as many feeble-minded children as do lawyers' (Down 1887: 40–41). These discrepancies are no accident, he asserts, but rather arise from the differences in the vitality of body and spirit required for each profession:

> The life of a lawyer is such as to aggregate to that profession men of strong resolve, of mental and physical vigour, men who must be conscious that it is an avocation in which they must bring to their aid an imperturbable will and a good digestion. In the medical profession there is a larger average of moderate success. The race is not so urgent and the claims not so imperious; an aggregation of feeble element is likely to ensue. But in the clerical profession a moderate success is still more ensured, and there is less claim among the rank and file for great mental and physical exertion.... It is a profession which, by its very gentleness, is likely to draw to its enclosure less the powerful will, the vigorous thought, and the ratiocinative brain, than those with bodies weak and emotions strong; men who may be classed as gently good than as grandly great. (Down 1887: 41)

The grandly great class of men – lawyers, doctors and scientists – were, thus, less likely to have intellectually disabled offspring due to their 'mental and physical vigour'. Down's argument here recalls that moment in Oliphant's *Salem Chapel* when Dr Rider compliments the 'pure' but not 'robust' blood of the Vincents (see Chapter 10), and one wonders if the relatively unsophisticated notion of pure blood ascribed to the clergyman's family by Oliphant some twenty-five years earlier is simply being dressed up with an apparently more scientific rationale.

Ultimately, Down argues, these statistics

> point to the importance of training our sons to be temperate and our daughters to be self-possessed. They indicate that we should seek alliances for our daughters with men from a healthy stock, that our sons should avoid women whose emotions are developed at the sacrifice

of their judgment and self-control. They show that idiocy is often the natural outcome of a gradual process, in which the strain becomes more and more degenerate, requiring only an insignificant factor to produce the direst results. (Down 1887: 53)

This passage marks Down's endorsement of the eugenic programme that Galton had proposed in his *Inquiry into Human Faculty and Development* a few years earlier (in 1883) – but we are now getting ahead of ourselves. Still, throughout Down's explanations of the form and causes of idiocy, one supposition remains clear: the condition is an expression of degeneration, perhaps not specifically (or at least not always) the moral degeneration insisted upon by Howe, but all the same a decline in vitality that is passed from one generation to the next.

Degeneration anxiety

Down's observations on idiocy and degeneracy were part of a much larger discussion about the apparent association between the two, carried out in professional and popular arenas alike. The causes of idiocy were ascribed not only to intemperance and sensuality, however, and much of the discussion involved trying to identify and treat the physiological and social as well as the moral roots of degeneration. As early as 1861, W. A. F. Browne had written of endemic idiocy as follows:

the occurrence of diseases which are confined to a particular community or locality, or are attributable to the habits and modes of life of a particular race or district ... is intimately connected with the consideration of those causes which determine the progress or deterioration of the human race, and with an estimate of the amount of control which may be exercised, through external circumstances, upon the development of the highest intelligence and the highest qualities of our nature. (Browne 1861: 66)

Research into the causes of idiocy was essential, he insisted, for addressing the question of human progress and degeneration, and he argued that 'extend[ing] the inquiry to the etiology of mental disease, generally, may involve the whole problem of the destinies of the human race' (66–67). Browne's article stands as an early assertion of the importance of conceiving idiocy as a subject of both medical treatment and research.

To some observers, racial deterioration was clearly linked to the new urban environments. In 1866, John Morgan, physician to Salford Hospital and honorary secretary of the Manchester and Salford Sanitary Association, argued in *The Danger of Deterioration of Race from the Too Rapid Increase of Great Cities* that not only were populous cities a risk even to healthy citizens, but also the immigrants who came to them from the countryside were generally the most hardy of the native stock, whose emigration to the city caused them to decline and also left the countryside populated with an inferior rural stock. Once healthy country folk come to the city, Morgan argues, they are subject to three primary evils: 'vitiated air, constitutional syphilis, and the abuse of alcohol' (Morgan 1866: 25). The 'noxious gases' forming a 'murky mass' that 'hangs like a shroud over the city' (29) charge a serious toll on the health of the urban dweller; as for syphilis and alcohol abuse, these, while 'originating in the vicious courses of individuals, are not confined in their consequences to the guilty sufferers, but are passed on to the offspring, and thus become, year by year, more generally diffused among the great mass of the people' (26). Yet, despite his dire warnings, the 'deterioration of race' described by Morgan did not necessarily involve the British race degenerating, or travelling backwards on the path of imagined evolutionary progress. Indeed, while he refers to 'that lowered standard of the public health ... under the ominous title of "deterioration of race"' (35), he suggests that the answer to the problem is to be found in better public hygiene, increased emigration from crowded urban areas to the colonies, and the creation of suburban communities along train lines, enabling urban workers to live in relative proximity to nature, with its attendant health benefits. In Morgan's view, the English race may be less healthy, but it is not, as a consequence, less English. It is degenerating, but not devolving. His warning received wide recognition and, although its immediate impact is difficult to discern, *The Lancet* of 23 June 1866 commented in an article entitled 'Deterioration of Race':

> If the consequences, then, of this social agglomeration be, on the one hand, increase of political power, of wealth, of commercial and social prosperity, and successful competition with other nations, they are, on the other, an overtaxing of the physical and mental energies at our disposal, and a premature consumption of national life-blood. (691)

Earlier that year, on 17 February 1866, a *Lancet* article entitled 'Race Degeneration' had lumped Morgan with Bénédict Morel, whose theories of racial degeneration were gaining currency in France; *The Lancet* credits the supposed French degeneration to changes in modes of living brought about by the rise of manufacturing industries and to the subdivision of agricultural land.

Morgan's thesis suggested that degeneration resulted from the combination of both sociological and individual factors: the explosion of urban centres in the early nineteenth century had created unhealthy environments, and at the same time presented even more opportunity for vice. As already noted, much degeneration theory of this period involved a blend of Lamarckian notions of acquired characteristics and Darwinian natural selection. Henry Maudsley, the editor of the *Journal of Mental Science* from 1863 to 1878, was one of the most audible and controversial medical voices of his day and a powerful influence on ideas of intelligence and idiocy, as well as degeneration, from the 1860s into the 1890s (Turner 1988; Pick 1989). In an 1879 *Fortnightly Review* article, 'Materialism and Its Lessons', Maudsley makes explicit the links between idiocy and racial degeneracy while also opposing materialist theories to 'spiritualist' notions (i.e., those founded in religious thought) of moral and intellectual development, arguing that moral depravity is a physiological concern. Employing a Biblical image also used to effect by Howe and Shuttleworth, he writes:

> It was not a meaningless menace that the sins of the fathers shall be visited upon the children unto the third and fourth generation; it was an actual insight into the natural law by which degeneracy increases through generations – by which one generation reaps the wrongs that its fathers have sown, as its children in turn will reap the wrong which it has sown. (Maudsley 1879: 255)[14]

From the threat of degeneration, Maudsley develops the idea of ontogeny recapitulating phylogeny expressed a few years earlier by Down. European brains, he argues, stand in relation to bushmen's brains as they do to microcephalic idiots, a comparison he returns to several times. For good measure, he also claims that 'it is a well-known fact that many savages cannot count beyond five, and that they have no words in their vocabulary for the higher qualities of human nature' (254), features which recall earlier criteria for the diagnosis of idiocy. Furthermore, he claims, 'the small brain-weight of the Bushman is indeed equalled among civilized nations by that of a small-headed or so-called microcephalic idiot' (252), which suggests that

> If we were to have a person born in this country with a brain of no higher development than that of the low savage – destitute, that is, of the higher nervous substrata of thought and feeling – if, in fact, our far remote pre-historic ancestor were to come to life among us now – we should have more or less of an imbecile, who could not compete on equal terms with other persons, but must perish, unless charitably cared for, just as the native Australian perishes when he comes into contact and competition with the white man. (254)[15]

Indeed, recapitulation could see the human regress even to the 'lower' vertebrates. Writing in his 1873 work *Body and Mind*, Maudsley noted that 'in the conformation and habits' of some 'idiots' he had observed, 'the most casual observer could not help seeing the ape'; he supports this claim by citing Sir Arthur Mitchell, who had reported an 'idiot' who was not only 'ape-faced', but 'grins, chatters, and screams like a monkey' and 'puts himself in the most ape-like attitude in his hunts after lice' (Maudsley 1873: 48). Pinel, too, had 'recorded the case of an idiot who was something like a sheep in respect of her tastes, her mode of life, and the form of her head', Maudsley writes. He then refers to the example of 'a deformed idiot girl' in the West Riding Asylum, 'who, in general appearance and habits, has ... striking features of resemblance to a goose' (so much so that the nurses who had received her described her as just like 'a plucked goose') and who, when angry, 'flaps her arms against her sides, and beats her feet on the floor'; we are also told that the girl is 'very fond of her bath, cackling when she is put into it, and screeching when she is taken out of it' (48–49). These animal traits seemed like murmurings from the phylogenetic past to observers like Maudsley, thus making the comparisons – to apes, sheep and geese – more than simply descriptive, but investing them with a certain level of scientific reality. 'No doubt such animal traits are marks of extreme human degeneracy', Maudsley insisted, and, he asserted:

> degenerations come by laws, and are as natural as natural law can make them. Instead of passing them by as abnormal, or, worse still, stigmatizing them as unnatural, it behooves us to seek for the scientific interpretation they must certainly have.... When we reflect that every human brain does, in the course of its development, pass through the same stages as the brains of other vertebrate animals, and that its transitional states resemble the permanent forms of their brains, and when we reflect further, that the shapes of its development in the womb may be considered the abstract and brief chronicle of a series of develop-ments that have gone on through countless ages in nature, it does not seem so wonderful as at the first blush it might do, that it should, when in a condition of arrested development, sometimes display animal instincts. (51)

Maudsley concludes by noting that:

> there is truly a brute brain within the Man's; and when the latter stops short of its characteristic development as *human* – when it remains arrested at below the level of an orang's brain – it may be presumed that it will manifest its most primitive functions, and no higher functions. (52)[16]

The idiot brain thus can slip below the human to the brute brain, according to this hypothesis, although whether this degeneration is so precise as to lead to the goose or sheep level of development, or simply that of some undifferentiated lower animal, Maudsley leaves

unresolved. However, we may suspect that the belief in this sort of recapitulation, that human brains could have their development arrested
at less-than-human stages, might easily have nourished the desire
to see certain not uncommon behaviours (like waving or 'flapping'
one's arms when agitated) and physiognomies as more than simply
'goose-like', 'sheep-like', or 'ape-like', but indicative of the individual's
atavistic goose, mutton or monkey coming to the surface.

In his *Fortnightly Review* article, Maudsley also takes up the 'musical
instrument' analogy previously used by Howe (and, as we have seen in
Chapter 10, by Wilkie Collins) to describe the brains of lesser humans:
the savage brain, like the idiot brain, is a poor instrument, rendering
to the most sensitive touch at best 'a few feeble intellectual notes and
a very rude and primitive sort of moral feeling' (Maudsley 1879: 253).
Finally, he reasserts the association of insanity with evolutionary degeneration leading to idiocy:

> What we call insanity or mental derangement is truly, in most cases, a
> form of human degeneracy, a phase in the working out of it; and if we
> were to suffer this degeneracy to take its course unchecked through
> generations, the natural termination would be sterile idiocy and extinc-
> tion of the family. (255)

Such evolutionary regressive births must arise, he argues, from
'hereditary antecedents': 'in fact', he claims, 'a person may succeed in
manufacturing insanity in his progeny by a persistent disuse of moral
feeling' (256). Maudsley uses this argument to claim that the medical
theory of materialism reinforces moral behaviour, perhaps more so
than more conventionally religious moral approaches do, as it poses
the threat of racial degeneration in this world, along with loss of one's
soul in the next.

Maudsley's theories of degeneracy informed medical researchers
who searched for evidence of degeneration along family lines. In
1885, Fletcher Beach published a short patho-genealogy in which he
traces, through four generations, the case of 'G. B., aged 15', who had
been admitted to the Clapton Asylum as an 'imbecile' in 1875: his
great-grandfather was 'not bright', his grandfather 'very reserved', his
grandmother 'excitable and queer', and his father 'irritable, excitable,
bad-tempered, and formerly intemperate'; in addition, the eldest children of his paternal uncles are 'affected in their intellects in the
same way as the patient', and 'the eldest daughter of the father's
sister is queer and excitable' (Beach 1885: 198). Beach proposes that
the great-grandfather's apparent 'weak-mindedness' leads to the
'very reserved' son – a 'disposition [which] cannot be considered a
normal one, and much resembles a man of insane temperament' (199).

Anticipating possible objections to identifying 'irritability, queerness and excitability' as signs of 'the insane temperament', he refers to the authority of Maudsley (200); at the same time, it is difficult now (as it presumably was then, given Beach's apparent defensiveness) to ignore how indefinite the terms are – 'not bright', 'queer', 'excitable' and 'irritable' – by which insanity and imbecility are designated in support of the 'degeneration' argument.

While Beach does not identify a root cause for the degeneration of this particular family line, other writers were developing theories to explain such phenomena, and some of the ideas articulated by John Morgan in 1866 (see above) were looking increasingly prescient. In 1889, another physician commentator on urban life, J. Milner Fothergill, discerned not just degeneration but also recapitulation among city-dwellers, observing that 'While the rustic remains an Anglo-Dane, his cousin in London is smaller and darker, showing a return to the Celtic-Iberian race' (Fothergill 1889: 113). The reversion, writes Fothergill, can go back even further:

> The cockney reared under unfavourable circumstances, manifests a decided reversion to an earlier and lowlier ethnic form. In appearance, the East-Ender, to the mind of the writer, bears a strong resemblance as to figure and feature, to the small and ugly Erse who are raised in the poorer districts of Ireland. (114)

He concludes that

> this tendency in town dwellers to degenerate on the lines of reversion to older racial types, has an interest of its own for the anthropologist. While the deterioration, both physical and mental, of town bred organisms, is a matter not meant for the philanthropist, but for the social economist. (114)[17]

For these writers, idiocy was an image presaging the end of the race, the inevitable consequence of the infernal blend of immoral acts and noxious environments.

Happily, the 'social economists' already had by this point a champion to provide a framework for racial amelioration. Francis Galton's *Hereditary Genius*, published in 1869, had introduced the idea of measuring mental capacity by deviations from a norm, with genius at one extreme and idiocy at the other, and argued for the hereditary nature of both. In his 1883 work *Inquiries into Human Faculty and Its Development*, Galton investigated human heredity

> to learn how far history may have shown the practicality of supplanting inefficient human stock by better strains, and to consider whether it might not be our duty to do so by such efforts as may be reasonable,

thus exerting ourselves to further the ends of evolution more rapidly and
with less distress than if events were left to their own course. (Galton
1883: 1)

He proposed to deal with 'the cultivation of race, or, as we might call
it, with "eugenic" questions', which he defines in a footnote, and adds
that 'We greatly want a brief word to express the science of improving
stock' (17). Immediately after this definition, he establishes certain
parameters:

> Energy is the capacity for labour. It is consistent with all the robust
> virtues, and makes a large practice of them possible. It is the measure of
> the fullness of life; the more energy the more abundance of it; no energy
> at all is death; idiots are feeble and listless. (17)

Further, he notes, 'Energy is an attribute of the higher races, being
favoured by all other qualities of natural selection' (18). In Galton's
formulation, idiocy is linked to those allegedly lower races, with both
idiots and these racial others exhibiting diminished energy. Idiocy is
also, apparently, in its feeble listlessness, very close to death – in fact,
a form of living death.

In Galton's writings we find ourselves a long way away from the
notion of idiocy and innocence, still alive and relatively vibrant a mere
two decades earlier (and, truth be told, still lingering on in the 1880s,
but with considerably less energy). The reservations on selective breeding for racial improvement expressed by Greg in his 1868 article (see
above) proved no barrier to Galton fifteen years later. So far as Galton's
audience was concerned, almost twenty years of public discussion of the
degenerating British race had convinced them that they were nearing a
crisis – if they were not already in its midst.[18] As Galton's eugenic
proposal suggested, if certain lines were on an inevitable decline, might
it not be best to stop them before they reached the point of 'sterile
idiocy'? Would it not be best to arrest the degeneration as quickly as
possible, as soon as it becomes apparent? Such questions would lead
to the increased use of a third informal division of idiocy, that of the
feeble-minded, to supplement the common bipartite division of idiocy
and imbecility. The feeble-minded idiot was at the upper end of imbecility, the very lower end of normal, on Galton's scale. By embracing the
notion of the quasi-idiotic feeble mind, the anxious quest to identify
degenerate beings had enacted a self-fulfilling prophecy. The addition
of the broad category of the 'feeble-minded' under the even broader
umbrella of idiocy meant there were many more people who could con-
ceivably be idiots than there had ever been before. Clearly, according to
Galton and like thinkers, something had to be done.

Degenerate aristocracy, regenerate labour

Even though it would have been difficult to avoid coming across the idea of degeneration, given its prevalence, not everyone was sold on the notion. Margaret Oliphant is a case in point, a writer who seems to have absorbed some of the discourse of degeneration into her work, but leavens it with a heavy dose of scepticism. Her 1892 novel *The Cuckoo in the Nest* is a tale of 'these degenerate days' (1), as she writes (with at least partial irony) in her opening paragraph: Gervase Piercey, the only son of the aged and enfeebled Sir Giles and the querulous Lady Piercey, is heir to Greyshott, the family estate, but he is also a 'Softy', as 'all the county called him' (20), with 'a fluid brain in which everything gets disintegrated, and floats about in confusion', so that he can 'never … lay hold upon a subject distinctly either by head or tail' (37). The intemperate Gervase likes his beer, and he also likes Patty Hewitt, the barmaid, whose family, like his, also boasts a long descent, having run the Seven Thornes Inn and alehouse for generations (Oliphant's riposte at the prizing of lineage). Patty sets out to marry the Softy. After his mother dies, Patty moves into the great house with her new husband, and the novel carries out its exploration of class and social identity. Gervase, to Patty's dismay, soon bores of domestic life and returns to his old alehouse haunts, passing out one cold evening on the moor in a drunken stupor; he is returned to Greyshott by Roger Pearson, Patty's previous lover, and then falls into a fever and dies. Patty nurses Sir Giles, Gervase's ailing father, and when he dies she receives the estate. However, she is snubbed mercilessly by the local gentry and eventually realizes she will never be accepted into the social world that comes with Greyshott. Her cast-aside lover Roger, now one of the top cricket players in England and a respectable and wealthy man, returns to marry her, and they move into a modern new house – 'her own 'Andsome 'Ouse', as Oliphant writes (450), the dropped 'h' signifying the low origins of the *nouveau riche*. In a final gracious act, prompted by Roger, Patty returns Greyshott to the 'natural heir', Gerald Piercey, who marries his widowed cousin Meg – a *distant* cousin, Oliphant asserts, perhaps concerned about the theories linking consanguinity and idiocy – and they, with her son Osy, the sole offspring of her first marriage, are left to regenerate the family line. Thus, the old order is affirmed only on the sufferance of the new. Gervase and his family are gone, yet the obsolete world they represent remains as the softy brother in the national family, supported in its place by hardworking relatives and benevolent social underlings.

Oliphant's narrator seems to voice opinions very close to those of Oliphant herself and claims to 'be no great believer in heredity' (39), but her story of degenerating gentry bested by a vital lower-middle-class barmaid, who becomes a cuckoo in the nest of the blue-bloods, cannot help but draw upon some of her culture's prevailing notions. Of most interest, perhaps, is Gervase's intermediary status as a 'Softy'. He is emphatically not an idiot, as the novel asserts repeatedly, but, even though he is twenty-eight, his father still optimistically awaits his coming 'fully to man's estate' (112). His cousin Meg, who is in many ways the moral centre of the novel, counsels Gervase's mother that her son is 'very innocent' (113), and explains to her cousin Gerald that Gervase is 'not a madman, nor even an imbecile, yet not like other people. He might be imposed upon – he might be carried away' (154). Later, responding to Gerald's exclamation that Gervase is 'next to an idiot', she insists that 'Gervase is not an idiot. He has gleams of understanding, quite – almost, as clear as anyone.' And, she notes, there is little chance of Gerald claiming the estate by arguing Gervase's incompetence: 'Aunt Piercey examined into all that. They could not make him out to be incapable of managing his own affairs. To be sure, he has not had any affairs to manage up to this time' (232), she says, but Gervase's potential difficulty managing his responsibilities may be mitigated by his marriage, she suggests, noting that 'Poor Gervase is not an idiot, but he is not like other people…. It is the best thing that could have happened for him to marry Patty' (232–33).

Gervase's 'softness' also has physical markers: his 'silly laugh in the wrong place' or an 'equally foolish question' that would interrupt speakers (10), his 'wavering gait and stooping shoulders', his 'uncertain step' (20); when he walks in the moonlight, he even casts 'a villainous blotch behind him on the clear white line of way' (21). We are told more than once of his 'moist hanging under-lip' (305) and later, as he lies in the fever that will kill him, Patty ponders his constitution:

> He was a little loose in the limbs, not very firmly knit perhaps, with not so much colour as the rustics around – but he was young, and healthy, and strong enough…. As for being a little soft, perhaps, in the mind, that was because people didn't know him; and even if they did, the mind had nothing to do with the body. (326)

But, of course, theories of idiocy and intelligence had been linking mind and body for most of the nineteenth century, and Patty blinds herself to her Softy's signs of degeneracy. Gervase may not be an idiot or an imbecile, but he is something rapidly becoming equally, if not more threatening: he is almost normal, but not quite.

The cultural meaning of idiocy was transformed by the degeneration theories that began to flourish in Britain (as well as Europe and America) in the second half of the nineteenth century, and by the tension these theories created with the concurrent discourse on the reclaimable idiot discussed in Chapter 9. Both these ways of understanding idiocy assume the initial bestial nature of the idiot, but the increasingly potent degeneration theory did not include the promise that the idiot could be reclaimed and integrated into the moral, social and economic life of the nation. Instead, the idiot became the marker of an irreversible decline. In the later decades of the century, degeneration, as Jenny Bourne Taylor has observed, was 'no longer one explanatory model interwoven with others. It became the dominant paradigm' (Taylor 1988: 212) – so much so that some of the concept's original advocates were growing wary of its vulgarization. In an article in the *British Medical Journal* of 28 September 1895, Henry Maudsley complained:

> Has not the theory of degeneracy been abused of late? As used by Morel the term has scientific meaning and value, but much has been done to rob it of definite meaning by stretching it out to cover all sorts and degrees of deviations from an ideal standard of thinking and feeling, deviations that range actually from wrong habits of thought and feeling to the worst idiocy, and some of which are no more serious marks of morbid degeneracy than long legs or short legs, long noses or short noses. Moreover, as often happens with big-sounding words that have no definite meaning, but are used habitually as if they had meaning, the meaningless name has been converted into a quasi-metaphysical something, so that many persons think, when the word degeneracy has been spoken, that all has been said that need be said, though nothing actually has been said. (771)

But Maudsley's complaint (and it seems a bit disingenuous, coming from one who had used this 'big-sounding word' to great effect for the previous thirty years) fell on deaf ears; his voice had no longer the power it once commanded, and degeneration moved from a theory with 'scientific meaning and value', dealing primarily with notions of evolution, race and physiology, to a much broader concept, embracing a diverse range of social and cultural phenomena. From mid-century on, anxieties about urban paupers and racial decline and reversion had been growing, and people identified as idiots or imbeciles – and, increasingly, as feeble-minded – were more and more often being perceived as signs not simply of racial decline, but also of social and moral degeneration, the corporeal evidence of vice. The image of the idiot is rapidly becoming a cipher for those characteristics and behaviours, including sexual promiscuity, economic ineptitude and criminal inclinations, that fell under the banner of this new, expansive notion of degeneracy.

Notes

1 The British edition, published in Edinburgh, was financed by the estate of William Ramsay Henderson, who had left his trustees to distribute his wealth in 'whatever manner they might judge best for the advancement and diffusion of the science of Phrenology, and the practical application thereof in particular' (xvi).

2 Martineau's article was reprinted in the United States as 'A Chapter on Idiocy' in the June 1854 *Harper's Magazine*, 9: 101–4.

3 English writers were more circumspect about the link between masturbation and idiocy, although 'class VIII' in Duncan and Millard's classification of idiocy contains individuals who 'had more or less perfect mental and bodily gifts up to a certain period', but whose indulgence in 'the solitary vice has gradually undermined the constitution, the mind and the passions' (Duncan and Millard 1866: 56). As a cure, they recommend 'abundant exercise, the use of aperients, less stimulating diet, total abstinence from all spiritous liquors, less sitting still, change of scene and companions, and a careful selection of the books to be read', supplemented by 'careful cat-like watching'; they also observe that 'horsehair gloves are very useful' with some patients (79–80). Finally, they suggest that 'there is nothing like hard work … by way of a cure,' and propose 'send[ing] the cases to sea with a kind and determined commander' (80). John Langdon Down refers to masturbation, especially in puberty, as 'liable to lead to disastrous results', but elaborates no further in his *On Some of the Mental Affections of Childhood and Youth* (Down 1887: 13). In his 1866 'Account of a Second Case in Which the Corpus Callosum Was Defective', he presents the case of a patient whose friends 'were very desirous of asserting the non-congenital nature of the mental condition, and attributed it to masturbation', but 'the diagnosis formed, however, was that it was congenital, and that masturbation was an accidental circumstance. The diagnosis was strengthened by reference to the other members of the family, who, although occupying good positions in the world, were manifestly not of average intellectual power. The habit of masturbation became entirely broken, and he gave himself up to simple employments, such as wheeling invalids in a Bath chair' (reprinted in Down 1887: 110). Robert MacDonald has noted that nineteenth-century British physicians were reluctant to discuss masturbation at all, although it was referred to in medical texts as 'leading to degeneration' (MacDonald 1967: 428–29). Meanwhile, Peter T. Cominos links prudence in economic matters with 'thrift' in the expenditure of semen in nineteenth-century British writings: 'Continence in sex and industry in work were correlative and complimentary virtues. The Respectable Economic man must not be the sensual man who had failed to conquer himself, but the Respectable sublimated sensual man' (Cominos 1963: 37).

4 According to the report on the annual meeting in the *British Medical Journal*, responses to Shuttleworth's paper included those from a veritable 'who's who' of the era's 'idiocy' experts. J. C. Bucknill, despite respect for Howe – and in opposition to his approval of Howe's statistics only four years earlier – expresses doubts over his methodology; Séguin confirms Shuttleworth's US report and applauds his new work; Down generally approves and notes 'he

knew the immense practical difficulty in arriving at the truth with regard to the existence of vicious habits on the part of parents of idiots admitted to public institutions'. Of special note is Daniel Hack Tuke's belief 'that the American statistics, if not entirely accurate, might nevertheless have served a useful purpose, and on that ground were entitled to respect' (*British Medical Journal*, 1 September 1877: 309). The *British Medical Journal* does not report what this 'useful purpose' might be; we are left to our own hypotheses. One that comes to mind is that Howe's statistics may have frightened people into behaving 'morally'; another is that they may have raised the profile of idiocy as a subject of medical and scientific concern and enhanced the professional reputations of the individuals working in this field.

5 This concern with the moral weakness of the parents being embodied in the children is also evident, on a grander social level, in Carlyle's explanation of Chartism as the consequence of the moral failure of political, social and industrial leaders, as discussed in Chapter 8.

6 Interestingly, early in *Social Statistics*, Spencer identifies the different forms of happiness which appeal to different peoples: 'To the wandering gypsy a home is tiresome, while a Swiss is miserable without one. Progress is necessary to the well-being of the Anglo-Saxons; on the other hand, the Eskimos are content in their squalid poverty, have no latent wants, and are still what they were in the days of Tacitus. An Irishman delights in a row, a Chinese in pageantry and ceremonies, and the usually apathetic Javanese gets vociferously enthusiastic over a cockfight' (5). This analysis of different cultural pleasures plays upon the theme of Anglo-Saxon superiority, and the Anglo-Saxon desire for progress, with all its evolutionary implications, which will be reflected in later writings on evolution and degeneration.

7 For instance, Greg's critique seems closely connected to anxiety around the flood of Irish immigrants who had appeared in Britain since the 1850s, as he decries the fact that 'the careless, squalid, unaspiring Irishman, fed on potatoes, living in a pig-stye, doting on a superstition, multiplies like rabbits or ephemera: – the frugal, foreseeing, self-respecting, ambitious Scot, stern in his morality, spiritual in his faith, sagacious and disciplined in his intelligence, passes his best years in struggle and in celibacy, marries late, and leaves few behind him'. But quality will win out, Greg insists. 'Given a land originally peopled by a thousand Saxons and a thousand Celts, – and in a dozen generations, five sixths of the population would be Celts, but five sixths of the property, of the power, of the intellect, would belong to the one sixth of the Saxons that remained' (361).

8 Gould writes that 'the law of recapitulation was "discovered" many times in the decade following 1859', including in Fritz Müller's *Für Darwin* (1864), the neo-Lamarckists E. D. Cope's and A. Hyatt's independent publications of 1866, and Haeckel's *Generelle Morphologie der Organismen* (1866), the last being praised by Thomas Huxley as 'one of the greatest scientific works ever published' (quoted in Gould 1977: 76).

9 Recapitulation theory is the biological equivalent of 'stadial' theories of society popular in the eighteenth century and articulated by de Gérando, Jean Itard's ally in his early studies of the wild boy of Aveyron (see Chapter 3). According to John Locke's formulation, in stadial theory, 'each specific society has experienced a similar history in terms of its internal constitution, and each passes through numerous organization stages with varying degrees of success until the highest stage is attained, namely, that of [Locke's] contemporary Europe' (Jacques 1997: 203).

10 The article reached a broader audience when it reappeared the following year
    in the *Journal of Mental Science* (it was reprinted yet again, along with a number
    of other shorter pieces, in 1887, as part of his last major publication, *On Some of
    the Mental Affections of Childhood and Youth*).

11 The debate concerning the evolutionary roots of humanity preceded Down,
    and would linger for years after. In 1844, Robert Chambers, the publisher of
    Chambers' Edinburgh Journal, wrote his *Vestiges of the Natural History of Creation*
    (published anonymously for its first twelve editions), an early evolutionary
    work which raised the hackles of many a theologian and conservative scientist
    (Bowler 1989). The idea of progress that informs Chambers' theory of evolution
    would not only popularize the idea of evolution prior to Darwin; as Peter Bowler
    suggests, it 'offered a progressionist and largely non-Darwinian approach to
    evolutionism that almost certainly preconditioned the way in which the *Origin
    of Species* would be understood' (Bowler 1989: 89–90). In his landmark work,
    Chambers wrote of 'a curious physiological speculation' that 'some of the
    broader features of the great families of mankind are expressly connected with
    the principle of development' (Chambers 1853: 261). According to this line
    of thought, 'the brain of one of the most favoured specimens of humanity,
    after completing the series of animal transformations, passes through the
    characters in which it appears in the Negro, the American, and the nations of
    Northern and Eastern Asia (sometimes comprehensively called Mongolian),
    and finally assumes that perfect character which it bears in the superior
    nations comprehensively called Caucasian by Cuvier. The face partakes of these
    alterations' (261). Chambers' progressive monogenic theory, which provides
    a theoretical structure for Down's ethnic divisions, was opposed by Carl Vogt,
    who, in his *Lectures on Man*, published in English in 1864, argued that 'However
    much we may indulge in theological speculations on the origins and differences
    of mankind, however weighty proofs may be adduced for the original unity of
    the human species, this much is certain, that no historical, nor ... geological
    data can establish this dream of unity. However far back our eye reaches, we find
    different species of man spread over different parts of the globe' (Vogt 1864:
    424). These different species Vogt credited to three different types of anthropoid
    ape: the orang-utan, the gorilla and the chimpanzee. 'None of these stands
    next to man in all points, – the three forms approach man from different sides
    without reaching him', writes Vogt, observing that the chimpanzee approaches
    man 'by the cranial and dental structure; the orang, by its cerebral structure;
    and the gorilla, by the structure of the extremities' (464). Other anthropoid
    apes – gibbons, macaques, baboons and New World apes – are capable of
    entering into the mix, too, he suggests, and notes that if 'in different regions of
    the world anthropoid apes may issue from different stocks, we cannot see why
    these different stocks should be denied the further development into the human
    type, and that only one stock should possess the privilege' (466). Ultimately, he
    concludes, after describing the 'species of mankind and their history', 'all these
    facts do not lead us to one common fundamental stock, to one intermediate
    form between man and ape, but to many parallel series, which, more or less
    locally confined, might have been developed from the various parallel series
    of the apes' (467). In Vogt's version of human history, 'Our savage ancestors
    stand opposed to each other – stock against stock, race against race, species
    against species. By the constant working of his brain man gradually emerges
    from his primitive barbarism; he begins to recognise his relation to other
    stocks, races, and species, with whom he finally intermixes and interbreeds.
    The innumerable mongrel races gradually fill up the spaces between originally

so distinct types, and, notwithstanding the constancy of characters, in spite of the tenacity with which the primitive races resist alteration, they are by fusion slowly led towards unity' (468). Vogt's schema was influential. Eugene Talbot, in his 1898 work *Degeneracy: Its Causes, Signs and Results* – an introduction to the topic published as part of a wide-ranging Contemporary Science Series edited by Havelock Ellis – endorses Vogt's polygenic division into 'descendents of the anthropoid apes' (95). And as late as 1924, F. G. Crookshank's *The Mongol in Our Midst* (part of E. P. Dutton's 'To-Day and To-morrow Series' of popular science and philosophy, also featuring works by J. B. S. Haldane and Bertrand Russell) refers back to Down in arguing that the ethnic divisions of idiocy were, in fact, atavistic, but denies Down's monogenic conclusion. Rather, argues Crookshank, in a variant of Vogt's theory, there are at origin three human 'races', the negro, the Asian (or Mongol) and the semitic, which had intermixed heavily over the centuries; following Vogt, he traces these races to the gorilla, the orang-utan and the chimpanzee, respectively. According to Crookshank, all humans are either a pure version of one of these races or a blend. Writing of Down's theory of Mongolian idiocy, Crookshank insists that 'it is the "Mongolian" rather than the idiocy that it is important to stress. For the "Mongolian" that is so evidently displayed by a proportion of our indigenous population is far from being a mark of idiocy or imbecility, but is a kind of physical and psychical make-up that is coarsely and brutally displayed in certain idiots and imbeciles' (6); further, he argues that he had 'never seen a Mongolian imbecile of whom one or both parents were not clearly Mongoloid and that, when both parents show signs of Mongolism, the Mongolian children are more than usually resemblant to racial Mongols' (81). Among literary characters, Crookshank proposes that Micawber, from David Copperfield, while not a Mongoloid idiot, was in fact a relatively low-grade adult Mongoloid, a sub-genre of the form, which, he suggests, 'Dickens' description with Phiz' etchings serve well to illustrate' (12); so, he notes, is Job Trotter of *The Pickwick Papers* (55). In Virginia Woolf's 1925 novel *Mrs Dalloway*, Clarissa Dalloway's daughter, Elizabeth, is described as having Mongolian characteristics; Donald Childs suggests that Woolf may be drawing upon the theories of 'racial hybridization' propagated by writers like Crookshank (Childs 2001: 48).

12 David Wright (2001) notes that both 'Mongolian' and 'Kalmuc' idiots began to appear in American medical literature in the late 1870s, probably due to the influence of Shuttleworth and Fletcher Beach, who had attended the first meeting of the Association of Medical Officers of American Institutions for Idiotic and Feeble-Minded Persons in 1877; Wright suggests that Down's inclusion of a reprint of this article and others in his 1887 work was in part an attempt to reassert his claim for precedence in identifying this condition.

13 In 1976, art-punk band Devo – short for 'devolution' – released the satirical song 'Mongoloid', in which the 'Mongoloid' in question is a bourgeois everyman whose extra chromosome is hidden to all, but 'determines what he could see'.

14 This common proverb – the sins of the fathers visited upon the children – involves some interesting gender associations regarding the causes of idiocy, and recalls Maudsley's earlier comment that one of 'the most favourable conditions for the production of idiocy' is 'to be begotten by a drunk father off a half-witted mother' (Maudsley 1867/79: 343). It is the depraved father who sows the seeds of degeneracy, although the feeble- or weak-minded woman was eventually to become the dominant image associated with racial decline (Saunders 1988; Gladstone 1996). According to this model, degeneracy is carried within men, but perpetuated through women.

15 The analogy between savage and idiot brains had been gaining medical
    legitimacy for some time; in 1867, John Marshall had published 'On the Brain
    of a Bushwoman; And on the Brains of Two Idiots of European Descent', in
    which he noted signs of the 'structural inferiority' (102) of the bushwoman
    brain in comparison with the European brain, even though 'no suspicion either
    of idiocy or other defect exists as concerns the Bushwoman' (103). Of the
    idiot brains, he writes that both seem to have reached a level of development
    somewhere between that normally achieved by the fetus between six and seven
    and a half months; the deficient condition of the cerebra, he writes, 'consists
    essentially in an imperfect evolution of the cerebral hemispheres or their parts,
    dependent on an arrest of development ... occurring at one stage or other of
    their metamorphosis from a simpler to a higher form' (107). The important
    point here is the notion of simpler to higher forms; while Marshall does not
    directly compare idiot and bushwoman brains, the first section of the article
    clearly establishes the bushwoman brain as a less developed form. The analysis
    of both bushwoman and idiot brains is assumed to be a study of inferior forms
    of intelligence, with the aim of throwing light on the later development of
    complexity in the brains of Europeans.

16 Thanks to Tim Stainton for bringing the foregoing passages from Maudsley
    (1873) to my attention.

17 In a telling move, Fothergill dedicates his book 'To the shades of the Norse
    rovers'; later in his text, he begins a paragraph 'Assuming the Norse to be the
    highest type of mankind...' (112). His idealization of Norse culture is not
    entirely anomalous for the age; however, Fothergill's is a particularly clear
    instance of early Aryanism, anticipating the racial ideologies (most notably
    those of the Nazis) of the early to mid-twentieth century.

18 Many proponents of eugenic beliefs were members of what N. G. Annan
    (1955) described as Britain's 'intellectual aristocracy' and wielded a great
    deal of authority in intellectual and academic circles. Annan identifies a group
    of families bearing the illustrious names Galton, Darwin, Huxley, Stephens,
    Haldane, Keynes, Macauly, Arnold, Trevelyan and Booth, among others, who
    had intermarried and sustained their status as intellectual elites over two or
    more generations, their example thus demonstrating (according to Galton's
    theory) the possibility of successful racial amelioration. Interestingly, Galton's
    marriage, despite the best attempts of he and his wife, remained childless.

CHAPTER 12

Danger and degeneracy: the threat of the urban idiot

The crowd of parents, awaiting their appearance before a school board 'B' committee, mills outside the room on the second floor of the school building. The year is 1883, and they have been summoned to the meeting to explain before a group of school board officers why their children have been missing school, which had been made compulsory with the 1870 Education Act. When Mrs Jones, 'a decent-looking woman', takes her turn to explain why her daughter has been missing classes, she is accompanied by her nursing baby and 'a small boy, with staring eyes that seem fixed upon nothing in particular – a strange, uncanny, big-headed child, who attracts attention directly'. As reported by George R. Sims, a popular journalist and playwright attending the meeting as part of his research for a series of articles under the general rubric 'How the Poor Live' for *The Pictorial World*, a London tabloid, Mrs Jones then claimed:

> it's that boy as is the trouble. Ye see, sir, he can't be lef' not a minnit without somebody as can get after him quick. He's allers settin' hisself afire. He gets the matches wherever we 'ides 'em, and he lights anything he sees – the bed, the baby, hisself. Bless you, gen'lemen, it's orful; he can't be off settin' somethin' alight not five minnits together. He ain't right in 'is 'ed, sir.

Sims then picks up the narrative:

> The idiot incendiary paid not the slightest attention; his wild, strange eyes were wandering about the room, probably for a box of matches with which to set us alight, and make one big blaze of the 'B' meeting, chairman, officers, himself, and all.

The woman's wish that her daughter be allowed off school half time is granted, and she departs, 'dragging the young gentleman with a tendency to commit hourly arson after her' (Sims 1889: 39–40).

The anecdote is short but illustrative. Sims's incendiary idiot is visibly anomalous, with his large head and unfixed, staring eyes; he is an economic challenge to his working-class family, demanding his sister's supervision while disrupting her schooling; and he is an embryonic, comic version of what was thought to be a growing threat: those urban 'idiots' who seemed to be stealing, burning, drinking and procreating along their inauspicious road through life.[1] Sims's travels in London's 'Povertyopolis' (19) were republished as a book in 1889 (along with another set of articles, 'Horrible London', originally appearing in the *Daily News*), when they joined the deluge of travelogue-type accounts exploring the shadowy depths of London for the benefit of middle-class audiences. Some writers, like Sims, professed to be interested in bringing aid to the downtrodden; as he noted, perhaps disingenuously, in his Preface, 'If an occasional lightness of treatment seems ... out of harmony with so grave a subject, I pray that [the reader] will remember the work was undertaken to enlist the sympathies of a class not generally given to the study of "low life"' – that is, the regular readers of *The Pictorial World*. But many instances of the genre were frankly exploitative, titillating their more comfortable readers by recounting the sins of the disreputable, who were clearly to blame for their poverty.

Eleven years after that 'B' meeting, another incendiary attempted to blow up the Greenwich Observatory but succeeded only in killing himself, and while London's mainstream press credited the mysterious plan to anarchists and left it at that, the rumour among those with links to the anarchist community was that the bomber was an 'unfortunate idiot ... talked by *agents provocateurs* into taking a bomb to Greenwich Park, where the bomb exploded in his pocket and blew him into many small fragments' – at least, so claimed Ford Madox Ford in his memoirs (Ford 1911: 122). The bomber was named Martial Bourdin; his brother-in-law, H. B. Samuels, edited an anarchist newspaper but was also a police informant, according to accusations levelled in the anarchist press of the time, and may have intended that Bourdin be arrested for carrying explosives (Sherry 1967). Ford's inside information was no doubt channelled through his cousins Olivia, Arthur and Helen Rossetti, the children of William Michael Rossetti, who as adolescents in 1891 began to publish an anarchist journal, *The Torch*, in the basement of their parents' house, and knew many of the main actors in what the press was soon calling the 'Greenwich bomb outrage'. There is no direct evidence that Bourdin was an 'idiot', as Ford claimed; nor did he blow himself into small fragments (he survived the bombing long enough to die in hospital) (Sherry 1967). However, contemporary insider accounts portray him as having been easily impressionable. The anarchist pamphleteer David Nicolls recalls 'little Bourdin' at Christmas 1893, 'sitting at the feet of Samuels, and looking up into his eyes with loving trust. To the little man he was evidently a hero to be loved and revered' (quoted in Mulry 2000: 54); in *A Girl Among the Anarchists*, a fictionalized memoir published in 1903 by Helen and Olivia Rossetti under the name Isabel Meredith, the bomber, Augustin Myers, is manipulated by his older sibling, Jacob, 'who had appeared to exercise undue influence and power over his brother' (Meredith 1903: 49). Most famously, the Greenwich bombing forms the basis of Joseph Conrad's 1907 novel of intrigue and urban degeneration, *The Secret Agent*, in which an idiot, Stevie, accidentally blows himself to fragments while carrying his brother-in-law's bomb to the Greenwich Observatory (this novel is discussed in detail in the following chapter). Thus, the innocent idiot boy of Wordsworth's 1798 poem becomes, a century later, the malleable tool of criminals and murderers.

From the 1860s people increasingly read both idiocy and pauperism as signs of degeneration. The previous chapter explored the scientific framework of theories connecting idiocy and degeneration, and also considered the representations of idiocy that took shape in that framework. But scientific and social understandings of idiocy grew together, and idiots, if examples of racial decline, were also increasingly an urban phenomenon, thieves or prostitutes in the making, or at the very least an economic burden on their more successful brothers and sisters. As Dora Greenwell, writing in 1868, noted:

> scientific researches bring into clear light a fact which has been long familiar to the chaplains of jails and others practically interested in our criminal population, that a large proportion of it is made up of weak and mentally deficient people, whose infirmities have made them the easy victims and the ready tools of the vicious and designing. (Greenwell 1868: 79)

Her assertion was supported by the findings of James Bruce Thomson, the physician at Perth General Prison, Scotland, who reported in 1866 that 11 per cent of prisoners exhibited 'mental weakness' (345); by 1869 he had raised the estimate to 12 per cent, but both numbers were significantly disproportionate to the ratio in the mainstream population, figured by Charles Goring (whose work is considered below) at less than 0.5 per cent. In concluding her argument for a more comprehensive, expanded system of idiot asylums, Greenwell pleaded,

Let no one think of the idiot, as persons wholly uninformed on the subject are apt to do, as a happy and harmless if limited being, shielded by his very infirmity from the awful burden of responsibility, and freer than are wise people from care and pain…. The experience of few grown-up people is so limited as not to have shown them something of the evil which a poor being so fearfully left to his own guidance may suffer and cause, a risk of course greater in the humble order of life, where continual care and watching of a weak-minded person is impossible, and where, unless the tone of the family life is unusually good, such persons too often become the centre of wide-spread moral debasement, – for the idiot, be it ever remembered, *does not sink alone*. (Greenwell 1868: 98, original emphasis)

Greenwell's idiot is a gullible patsy for criminals and threatens to bring down those around him, debasing his family, friends and community. While she presents this aspect of her argument only in her final pages, it provides a potent rationale for the expanded support of idiot asylums that she advocates.

Idiocy found its conceptual home in the impoverished slums and rookeries of London and other major cities, places often represented as lairs of depravity from which only degraded humans issued forth. Fears of degeneration, as well as of crime and pauperism, led to the enlarging of the concept of idiocy at its marginal category, the 'feeble-minded', as this term was increasingly being used to designate those apparently inferior beings whose capacity to pass as 'normal' excited the anxiety of many commentators (Jackson 2000). The term itself was not new: Duncan and Millard (1866) had used it in the title of the first book-length English manual for the education of the 'feeble-minded, imbecile and idiotic' in 1866, and of course John Bunyan's Mr Feeble-Mind makes his literary appearance in 1684. The borderline between the 'idiot' and the 'imbecile' and again between the 'imbecile' and the 'feeble-minded' was vague, and while many of the people identified as 'feeble-minded' in the early 1900s may well have escaped the designation in previous decades, others may have been formally identified as 'idiotic' or 'imbecile'. Indeed, the end of the century saw increasing concern over this grey zone, as Mark Jackson (2000) has shown, with the *British Medical Journal* noting in a December 1894 editorial that 'those inhabiting the borderland of imbecility' – that is, the 'feeble-minded' – were 'more to be pitied, and certainly … a greater danger to the State, than the absolutely idiotic' (quoted in Jackson 2000: 1). But, as we will see, 'feeble-mindedness' soon comes to play a significant role in defining idiocy itself; indeed, Havelock Ellis, writing in 1912, suggested that the term 'feeble-minded' 'may be used generally to cover all degrees of mental weakness', although he conceded that full precision would demand the recognition of imbecility and idiocy as the two other degrees of 'congenital mental weakness' (Ellis 1912: 32).

The rise of the term 'feeble-minded' points to a growing anxiety about the burgeoning numbers of unemployed poor and casual labourers, as well as fears of increased criminal activity; and 'feeble-mindedness', in its late-nineteenth-century manifestation, is born of degeneration theory and the pathologization of poverty. Scientific, social and cultural discourses fuse to shape a new image of a dangerous urban idiocy, the degenerate threatening not just racial decline but also social order: an economic burden, a small-time law-breaker, an innocent tool for the more ambitious and unscrupulous criminal, and, perhaps worst of all, a fecund progenitor of more of the same, promising ever-accelerating social decline. The category of the 'feeble-minded' expanded the (dis)franchise of 'idiocy', effectively exporting the condition's apparent degeneracy to a broader population and licensing the development of repressive action to control what seemed, at least to some observers, a growing menace. Early in the twentieth century, the formal use of 'idiocy' as a blanket term was also coming to an end, and in 1913 'idiocy' was just one condition, along with imbecility, feeble-mindedness and moral imbecility, covered by the Mental Deficiency Act. The increase in the formal, legal use of terms such as 'feeble-minded' and 'defective' also made possible a reconfiguring of the idea of idiocy into something broader and, not coincidentally, more ominous: the innocent idiot becomes the dangerous defective.

Degenerate paupers:
the urban face of degeneration theory

From the 1840s, interested and concerned citizens struggled to comprehend the poverty of the teeming metropolis. In 1842, Edwin Chadwick's *Report on the Sanitary Condition of the Labouring Population of Great Britain* raised the alarm about the decline of health in urban centres; the primary cause of increased disease and mortality rates, he argued, was 'atmospheric impurity' (79), but his report also documented many accounts of vice and criminality among the labouring classes. Henry Mayhew's *London Labour and the London Poor*, written from 1849 to 1851, explored income and expenditures in the city's different regions, while at the same time characterizing groups such as costermongers, fruit vendors and street poets. In describing the 'nomadic races of England' (ranging from the 'purely vagabond' to 'those who follow some itinerant occupation in and round about the large towns'), Mayhew offers a hypothesis concerning their general physical and intellectual characteristics:

> Whether it be that in the mere act of wandering, there is a greater determination of blood to the surface of the body, and consequently a less quantity sent to the brain, I leave to physiologists to say. But certainly be the physical cause what it may, we must all allow that … there is a greater development of the animal than of the intellectual or moral nature of man, and that they are all more or less distinguished for the high cheekbones and protruding jaws – for their use of a slang language – for their lax ideas of property – for their general improvidence – their repugnance to continuous labour – their disregard of female honour – their love of cruelty – their pugnacity – and their utter want of religion. (2–3)[2]

The following years saw countless articles and books dedicated to outlining this unsettling urban underworld, ranging from carefully detailed reports to exploitative reportage. When in 1889 Charles Booth began publishing the first volumes of his massively researched, minutely detailed and highly influential *Life and Labour of the People in London*, a comprehensive social and statistical analysis of London's labouring classes, he was following decades of publications, ranging from the sociological to the sensational, concentrating on the urban poor. Booth, like Mayhew, was very much in the former camp, painstakingly compiling record books of statistics on the city's workers, but he was certainly aware of the potential for dramatic narrative. As he explained in his Introduction:

> The materials for sensational stories lie plentifully in every book of our notes; but, even if I had the skill to make use of my material in this way – that gift of the imagination which is called 'realistic' – I should not wish to use it here. There is struggling poverty, there is destitution, there is hunger, drunkenness, brutality, and crime: no one doubts it is so. My object has been to attempt to show the numerical relation which poverty, misery and depravity bear to regular earnings and comparative comfort, and to describe the general conditions under which each class lives. (Booth 1889: 6)

George Longstaff's *Studies in Statistics* (1891) and Seebohm Rowntree's *Poverty: A Study of Town Life* (1901), focusing on York, also tried to assess urban poverty and disease numerically. As Longstaff explained in his conclusion, 'My hope throughout has been that increased knowledge of facts, alike in matters political and matters medical, may tend to make legislative and administrative efforts more reasonable…' (442), and the same objectives seem evident in Rowntree's work. Notably, while explicit references to degeneracy rarely surface in these works, the scenes described and numbers produced by Booth, Longstaff, Rowntree and others provided further sustenance for worried degeneration theorists:

for example, consider the possible interpretations of Rowntree's discovery that, compared across three neighbourhoods, 'the proportion of defective children to the total population' is by far the highest in the poorest area (255). The impressionistic, fearful reports of earlier writers acquire a retroactive authority with this new statistical buttressing.

As early as the 1850s and 1860s, before the fears of degeneration infiltrated thinking on so many different issues, there was a palpable unrest over the numbers of poor, expanding and cramped neighbourhoods in London, and much of this unrest expressed itself as concern over immorality, disease and crime. Early works like Thomas Beames's *The Rookeries of London*, published in 1850, held out hope for some form of reconciliation. Beames, citing Mayhew as his exemplar, is concerned with the social and economic factors circumscribing life in the 'rookeries'. While he labels them 'fraternities' (164) that are 'a means of demoralizing the present generation' and which serve as 'beds of pestilence' and 'rendezvous of vice' – indeed, 'not only the lurking places, but the *nurseries* of felons' (149) – he tempers his condemnation by identifying the social forces making them thus, and ultimately labels the sober British middle classes as a whole the 'degenerate offspring' (212–13) of their ancestors for failing to address the health and economic problems constraining the poor in the 'rookeries'. In Beames's formulation, these social problems are interpreted in terms of a bad (or dysfunctional) family; at issue is a moral decline, not just among the poor but also among those others whose inaction and indifference have allowed social conditions to deteriorate to the point where people are living in 'rookeries' – a position not so different from the paternalist stance adopted by Carlyle just over a decade earlier in his critique of Chartism (Chapter 8).

But by the 1860s and 1870s, few writers proposed bettering the lot of paupers, and more constructed travelogues rather than treatises, for the mixed pleasure and disgust of their readers (Stedman Jones 1971). In 1861, John Hollingshead wrote in his *Ragged London*:

> We are evidently surrounded by a dense population, half-buried in black kitchens and sewer-like courts and alleys, who are not raised by any real or fancied advance in wages; whose way of life is steeped in ignorance, dirt, and crime; and who are always ready to sink, even to death, at their usual period of want. How many they really number, what they really profess to be, and in what proportions they may be found in different parts of the metropolis, are secrets that no census has ever fully exposed.
> (Hollingshead 1861: 6)

Hollingshead opposes the civilized, middle-class 'we' to the shadowy, unmeasured threat of 'ragged London', but perhaps even more disconcerting to his readers was his claim that pauper children of London were surprisingly, even perversely, healthy:

> Where are the emaciated children who have often been dangled before our eyes? Certainly not in the black-holes inhabited by the poor. What is it that gives fulness [sic] to the cheeks, agility to the limbs, and even bone and sinew to the form? It cannot be food. A block of coarse bread, taken at uncertain intervals, is far from forming the supposed necessary three meals a day, and yet those children who get nothing but this plain and scanty fare astonish those who know them best by their healthy vigour. These children live in the streets, and draw their nourishment from wind and mud. They are not stunted, far from it, and with few exceptions are stronger than the children of the middle class. (9)

The image of the impoverished child, which earlier in the century was so often used to elicit middle-class sympathy, is displaced by a healthy specimen from ragged London who poses a threat to the less rugged middle class.[3] Recalling those members of Mayhew's 'nomadic tribes', these ragged Londoners are hardy beasts, seemingly immune to cold and filth (like Victor of Aveyron – Chapter 3) and with a brutal strength inversely proportionate to their degraded state.

This strange and unlikely union of pauperism with a perverse vitality nourished by wind and mud resurfaces in other writings on degeneration in Victorian cities.[4] In George Gissing's 1884 novel *The Unclassed*, Slimy, as fine an example of an urban degenerate that one can find anywhere in late-Victorian fiction, first appears when the novel's protagonist, Waymark, is beginning his new job as a rent collector: awakened in surprise, and with one good eye, Slimy looks 'much like a wild beast which doubts whether to spring or shrink back'; he lives among 'heaps of rags and dirty paper, bottles, boots, bones', and claims to be involved in 'trade in general' – presumably as a rag-and-bone vendor (101); the narrator later explains that in Slimy there are 'depths beyond Caliban, and, at the same time, curious points of contact with average humanity.... He was not ungrateful for the collector's frequent forebearance, and, when able to speak coherently, tried at times to show this' (229). While Gissing never identifies Slimy as an 'idiot', the character is explicitly presented as a degraded moral and intellectual being, more beast than human. As Slimy grows ill in his hovel, his sickness 'exhibit[s] itself as it would in some repulsive animal, which suffers in captivity, and tries to find a remote corner when pains come on' (229). Eventually, ill as he is, Slimy compels Waymark to submit to being bound carefully to the floor and then steals the rent money Waymark has collected, in order, as he explains, to 'drink myself dead!' (233); after his capture, he requires three police officers to control him in his cell before he dies of alcohol poisoning. The perverse strength and occasional cunning (evident especially in the way he carefully binds Waymark to constrain him without actually hurting him seriously) become emblems of the degraded urban pauper: a degenerate being, occasionally but only sporadically capable of human discourse, marginally sympathetic but with the dangerous ability to overwhelm his more civilized social and biological superiors.

Perhaps the most prominent literary manifestation of this inversion can be seen in the relation between the Morlocks and Eloi in H. G. Wells's *The Time Machine* (1895). When Wells's Time Traveller arrives in the year 802,701 AD, he is shocked to find the Eloi, who had first struck him as being like 'the more beautiful kind of consumptive', with a certain 'child-like ease' (45), 'to be on the intellectual level of one of our five-year-old children' (46): they have declined both physically and intellectually, and even gender distinctions have been muted, if not erased entirely. Before long, he discovers that humanity had evolved into both the Eloi and the Morlocks, those 'ape-like' (60) 'lemurs' and 'vermin' (64) who raised and fed upon the 'Upperworld' Eloi as upon 'mere fatted cattle' (71), and that the division between these creatures grew from that between 'the Capitalist and the Labourer' (63). The 'too-perfect security of the Upperworlders had led them to a slow movement of degeneration, to a general dwindling in size, strength, and intelligence' (63); while the Eloi may once have been 'the favoured aristocracy, and the Morlocks their mechanical servants', they were 'sliding *downwards* toward, or had already arrived at, an altogether new relationship' (68, emphasis added). Ultimately, concludes the Traveller, the 'human intellect had enjoyed a brief dream', but 'had committed suicide' (81). Wells's characters embody his critique of the relations between property and labour, but simultaneously exploit contemporary fears about the growing power of the under-classes: long before receiving reports of the future from Wells's fictional Time Traveller, British readers were imagining the carnivorous hordes in the dark allies of urban rookeries and ghettos.

That this degeneration is embodied in both the physically strong and the intellectually weak suggests more about social anxieties concerning the ever-increasing urban poor than anything else. If the individuals were not, in truth, particularly healthy, they were still strong in numbers and social impact, and this strength translated into unsettling figures such as Gissing's Slimy and Wells's Morlocks, the literary offspring of Hollingshead's ragged Londoners. By the 1880s, most likely exacerbated by such social phenomena as the London housing crisis (Stedman Jones 1971), theories of degeneration informed discussions across a broad range of topics, including urbanity, poverty and idiocy. In

his 1885 tract *Degeneration Amongst Londoners,* James Cantlie argued that
healthy Londoners were inevitably no more than second-generation
town-dwellers; it was impossible to find a fifth-generation cockney,
he claimed, simply because a family dwelling in the city for that long
suffered from 'urbomorbus', or 'city disease' (24–25), in which 'the
close confinement and the foul air of our cities are shortening the life
of the individual, and raising up a puny and ill-developed race' (33).
Constitutional vitality is mitigated further with each generation, until
'Nature steps in and denies the continuance of such; and weakness of
brain-power gives such a being but little chance in this struggling world'
(23). But before becoming extinct, these cockney families produce a
generation or two of physically and mentally weak offspring, marked in
Cantlie's descriptions by a expressionless 'solemnity' (21, 22, 23) that
telegraphs a lack of mental vigour.[5] Cantlie's weak-minded degenerates
have precedents in social reportage. For instance, in Thomas Archer's
1865 exploration of the London underworld, *The Pauper, the Thief, and the
Convict; Sketches of Some of Their Homes, Haunts, and Habits,* the narrator
visits a workhouse, only to find that

> in the warmest corner of the yard … a whole row of female idiots, of
> various ages, sit blinking and lounging, as it seems to me, with a vague
> consciousness of superiority in the fact of nothing at the moment being
> expected of them. The same stout, beef-faced young woman who is the
> peculiar representative, I fancy, of all pauper idiocy, offers her hand
> as we pass, and asks after our health in the same thick utterance as
> though she spoke during sleep, and while suffering from greatly en-
> larged tonsils. (75–76)

Archer's workhouse idiots,[6] the sensational-reportage literary antecedents of Cantlie's sterile generation, occupy the most desirable plot
of real estate in the workhouse, despite doing nothing to warrant this
boon. They also represent one of many moments where the pauper
merges with the idiot, and especially the female idiot, a fusion making
more and more sense to British readers in the latter years of the nineteenth century. As the arch-degenerationist Arnold White argued in
The Problems of a Great City, 'tainted constitutions, brains charged with
subtle mischief, and languishing or extinct morality, transmit a terrible
inheritance of evil to the next generation, there to taint once more a
whole community' (White 1886: 8). The degenerate are not simply a
set of individual problems; rather, their tainted constitutions have vast
societal consequences.[7]

These fears of the waning generation are reiterated in Margaret
Harkness's 1889 novel of social analysis *Captain Lobe* (published under
the pseudonym John Law and republished as *In Darkest London* in

1891[8]), when the narrator observes that 'The thing that strikes one most about East End life is its soddenness; one is inclined to think that hunger and drink will in time produce a race of sensationless idiots' (17); later, one character, a physician, observes that 'if the poor were not so wonderfully generous to one another, the result would be a generation of idiots' (75). An ironic variant of degeneration theory informs Harkness's novel, in which, as Gillian Beer (1996: 142) writes, 'the voice of the missing link is itself heard, perhaps for the first time in fiction' – the voice also of 'the present-day poor and the handicapped, those ignored by a factitious "civilization"'. Harkness's novel, while documenting the trials of the poor, also debates different approaches to the problem, placing the faith-driven efforts of the Salvation Army's diminutive Captain Lobe against the political solutions of socialists, communists and anarchists, as well as the aggressive moralizing of groups like the Charity Organisation Society (discussed below). Harkness does not offer any solutions, and at the novel's open-ended conclusion her protagonist emigrates to Canada.

Idiot, criminals and measures of the feeble mind

The growing concerns about the poor were increasingly (but not exclusively) expressed through a moral condemnation that imagined them as responsible for choosing their condition. In Charlotte Yonge's 1864 novel *The Trial*, the patriarchal physician-protagonist, Dr Henry May, identifies an outbreak of scarlet fever as emanating from 'those wretched Martins, in Lower Pond Buildings … living in voluntary filth' (6).[9] The condition of the poor becomes an issue of moral deterioration for Yonge, whereas fourteen years earlier Beames had seen it as the consequence of unfair social structures. As Stedman Jones (1971: 286) writes, especially of the 1860s and 1870s, 'pauperism, poverty's visible form, was [perceived as] largely an act of will. It had been freely chosen and was therefore sinful.' This problem was not necessarily irreversible, but rather simply demanded increased moral strength. Many works urged the self-improvement of the working and middle classes and, thus, the nation. The most notable among these was the much-republished ouevre of Samuel Smiles, including *Self-Help* (1859), which opens with the assertion that 'the spirit of self-help is the root of all genuine growth in the individual; and, exhibited in the lives of many, it constitutes the true source of national vigour and strength' (35). 'Self-help' was an oft-invoked formula for personal success, and examples of the poor who strive to improve their station were commonly presented as exemplars in the works of Smiles and others.

One way to improve the lot of the poor was through mandatory education. The Education Act 1870 established a national system of elementary schools, meaning that for the first time many poor and working-class children appeared in formal classrooms; however, many did not prosper as well as hoped in this environment (Simmons 1978; Thomson 1998). The journalist George Sims, while endorsing compulsory education, also noted the hardships imposed by the 1870 Act, observing that 'many a lad whose thick skull keeps him from passing the standard which would leave him free to go to work, has a deft hand, strong arms and a broad back – three things which would fetch a fair price in the labour market' (Sims 1889: 29). But the slightly thick-headed manual labourer was only part of the problem. The sheer numbers of struggling and unsuccessful students hinted that the apparently deficient were more plentiful than previously suspected and, perhaps even more worryingly, many of these people seemed to be travelling through life unnoticed, passing their tainted constitutions along to their offspring.[10]

At the same time, if many children were not succeeding at school, they did seem to be showing up later on in prisons. In the mid-1860s, Dr George Wilson's research into cranial measurements had demonstrated an apparent link between habitual criminality and imbecility, with 40 per cent of the convicts in his study allegedly being 'weak-minded' (see Davie 2005: 76); not long after, the Scottish prison physician James Bruce Thomson argued that 'All who have seen much of criminals agree that they have a singular family likeness or caste.... Their physique is coarse and repulsive; their complexion dingy, almost atrabilious; their face, figure, and mien, disagreeable. The women are brutally ugly; and the men look stolid, and many of them brutal, indicating physical and moral deterioration' (Thomson 1866: 341). Furthermore, we have already noted, Thomson estimated that 'a large proportion' of prisoners – 11 per cent, in his 1866 article – were 'weak-minded congenitally' (341). Thomson's like-minded American contemporary Samuel Royce (perhaps with unwonted enthusiasm) summarized Thomson's research as showing that one-third of juvenile criminals were imbeciles, and that 'professional criminals are hopeless imbeciles and hardly amenable to moral treatment' (Royce 1878: 31). That champion of British degeneration theory, Henry Maudsley, also referred to Thomson's research in his 1874 work *Responsibility in Mental Disease* when observing that there is a 'distinct criminal class of beings, who herd together in our large cities in a thieves' quarter' and that 'this criminal class constitutes a degenerate or morbid variety of mankind, marked by peculiar low physical and mental characteristics' (quoted in Davie 2005: 81). In the United States, family-history studies like Richard Dugdale's 1877 work *The Jukes* also claimed to demonstrate the hereditary nature of criminality, immorality and mental deficiency.

Meanwhile, Italian criminologist Cesare Lombroso was developing his theories by which hereditary physiognomy could reveal innate degenerate and criminal personalities. According to Lombroso's theories, law-breakers carried a hereditary taint and were, in effect, 'born criminals'. This taint suggested an atavistic recapitulation: Lombroso argued in *Criminal Man* (1876) that cranial abnormalities in criminals 'recall the black American and Mongol races and, above all, prehistoric man much more than the white races' (49), a point he reiterates in a section entitled 'Atavism and Punishment', where he notes that 'those who have read this far should now be persuaded that criminals resemble savages and the coloured races' (91).[11] Lombroso's findings, while always controversial, caught the degeneration-saturated imagination of many Europeans. As Mary Gibson and Nicole Hahn Rafter note in the introduction to their translation of *Criminal Man*, 'Lombroso's image of the atavistic offender – with his small skull, low forehead, protruding jaw, and jutting ears – fired the imagination of not only jurists and doctors but also writers, journalists, and artists throughout Europe' (Gibson and Hahn Rafter 2006: 28–29).

But compelling as Lombroso's theories were, they consistently drew fire from other criminologists. In his 1913 statistical study of English convicts, Charles Goring 'claimed to have destroyed the theory of the born criminal by proving that physical anomalies were no more widespread in criminals than in the general population', write Gibson and Hahn Rafter, who note, however, that Goring's interpretation of his findings tended towards the opposite conclusion. Indeed, Lombroso's daughter, Gina Lombroso-Ferraro, 'perceptively realized that "Goring was more Lombrosian than Lombroso" because his conclusion … echoed her father's ideas' (Gibson and Hahn Rafter 2006: 29): Goring's analyses showed the very Lombrosian result that between 10 and 20 per cent of prisoners were 'mentally defective', as opposed to 0.45 per cent for the general population (Goring 1913: 255). Goring writes:

> On the average, the criminal of English prisons is markedly differentiated by defective physique – as measured by stature and body weight; by defective mental capacity – as measured by general intelligence; and by an increased possession of wilful anti-social proclivities – as measured, apart from intelligence, by length of sentence to imprisonment. (370)

Thus, he concluded, the 'high and enormously augmented association of feeble-mindedness with conviction for crime' indicated that this

condition, along with related 'heritable qualities', was 'chiefly responsible for the social phenomenon of crime' (372).

Measuring the 'defective physique' was a regular strategy in the
process of trying to define criminal types: Lombroso, Goring and others
had all collected physical, cranial and physiognomic data, although
they were at odds as to precisely which specific features conveyed
what information. Meanwhile, Francis Galton had since 1878 worked
on developing a rudimentary form of composite portraiture which
could be used to define facial characteristics of different classes of
people, including criminals. Physiognomic studies became all the more
frequent with the development of photography. This sort of portraiture
eventually made its way into studies of idiocy. In 1861, Duncan *et al.*
had identified what they felt to be the most important 'physiological
anomalies of idiots', which were primarily non-visual, and certainly non-
physiognomic: these included insensitivity to heat and cold, deficient
fine senses (i.e., taste and smell), and difficulties in vocal expression
and physical coordination. But with photography, the characteristics of
idiocy were increasingly visually identifiable, physiognomic features. As
early as 1858, the American Isaac Kerlin included photographs in his
work *The Mind Unveiled, or, a Brief History of Twenty-Two Imbecile Children*;
the anonymous reviewer in the *Edinburgh Review* suggested that the
work was 'embellished by photographs' in order 'to make it as attractive
as possible' (Anonymous 1865a: 62) and not particularly to point
out the physiognomic characteristics of the twenty-two individuals so
illustrated. But by 1904 the American physician Martin Barr included
numerous photographs in his work *Mental Defectives: Their History,
Treatment and Training*, using them to illuminate conditions from 'low-
grade imbeciles' and 'idiots – superficial excitable' to, oddly, 'echolalia'
(the repetition of words or phrases). In 1908 Alfred Tredgold used
photographs extensively to illustrate variations of mental deficiency in
his *Mental Deficiency*, which was to become the standard textbook in the
field for most of the twentieth century; and in 1911 C. Paget Lapage
used careful measurements and photography to help delineate the
physical stigmata of degeneracy and feeble-mindedness, focusing, like
Lombroso, on cranial contours, ear shapes and the 'protruding jaw' (55)
noted so often by others. These approaches, following earlier attempts
at the description of physical anomalies and stigmata by Down, Duncan,
Shuttleworth and others (Chapter 11), insisted that it was possible to
recognize and assess idiocy visually. The degenerate idiot bore the
stigmata of his condition (Halliwell 2004; Jackson 2000).

The claim that criminality is associated with mental deficiency was,
as we have seen, not new with Goring; nor is the attempt to define the

physical and physiognomic markers of the condition. But the notion of a measurable 'general intelligence' is still novel. When in 1883 Galton proposed the term 'eugenics', he also suggested the use of 'psychometric experiments' to track the thought processes, as well as (with echoes of George Cheyne – Chapter 10) the measurement of 'sensitivity' by employing such approaches as sound and weight discrimination tests. William Brown, writing in 1911, claimed that 'the history of the use of the theory of correlation in Psychology can hardly be said to have begun earlier than the commencement of the present century', and he identified Clark Wissler's attempts in 1901 as 'the first investigation showing any mathematical precision' (Brown 1911: 81). Soon, a number of other strategies were developed for the assessment of levels of intelligence, and within a few brief years intelligence measuring had become an important area of research. Ultimately, the work of French psychologists Alfred Binet and Theodore Simon, first published in 1905, proved the most influential; they had developed their measure with the pragmatic intent of identifying children whose intellectual abilities meant they would not thrive in standard classroom environments. However, they cautioned that 'intelligence cannot be estimated as can the height', and stressed that their measurement was based on the adoption of a convention, which, 'be it the best possible, will always give to the proceeding an artificial character'; indeed, 'the estimate of the amount of retardation or precocity depends partially on the conventional proceeding which we have adopted' (Binet and Simon 1905: 67–68). All the same, their tool was broadly seen as the most effective available, and in 1911 the British Board of Education recommended the use of the Binet–Simon tests to assess mental capacity (Jackson 2000); in 1912 Havelock Ellis could claim confidently that 'the method of Binet and Simon renders possible a fairly exact measurement of feeble-mindedness' (Ellis 1912: 32). With intelligence testing, the feeble mind was appearing to assume a more tangible (because measurable) reality. But we have moved ahead of the story here. Feeble-mindedness, as a significant category of mental deviance, takes shape well before Goring and his early-twentieth-century peers.

The Charity Organisation Society and the proliferation of the feeble mind

One of the major forces redefining idiocy, and especially 'feeble-mindedness', was the Charity Organisation Society (COS), founded in 1869 to organize and assign charitable assistance throughout London.

The COS, while revolutionizing the profession of social work, also became something of a 'new urban gentry', extremely unpopular among working people for its moral interpretation of the causes of poverty (Stedman Jones 1971: 269); Fraser (2003: 142) describes the 'essential duality of the C.O.S.: it was professionally pioneering but ideologically reactionary'. The COS, prompted by the increased number of students struggling in school since the 1870 Education Act, commissioned a report that was produced in 1893 under the title *The Feeble-Minded Child and Adult*. This report argued that the children struggling to learn in the new compulsory classrooms were 'all probable social failures – now at the child-stage' (quoted in Simmons 1978: 389) who needed immediate attention in order to avoid costing society dearly in later years. In her retrospective of the COS's development, Helen Bosanquet[12] singles out this group as being particularly significant:

> Another class of afflicted persons for whom the Society has worked strenuously down to the present day consisted of those known forty years ago as 'Improvable Idiots'; and with respect to these [the COS] has been the pioneer of a great movement which followed almost exactly on the lines laid down by it. The problem of the Feeble-minded is one which has only slowly differentiated itself from those of the lunatic and the idiot.... (Bosanquet 1914: 195)

Notably, Bosanquet here equates the feeble-minded with the educable (improvable) idiots – or imbeciles – of previous years. At least in its early COS usage, the 'feeble mind' was not so different from previous concepts of idiocy: as a category, it is not so much new as reconceived. Equating feeble-mindedness with educable idiocy provides the notion with a formally recognized antecedent, and, of course, the term 'feeble-mindedness' itself had long been used with varying degrees of formality. At the same time, the emphasis placed on this relatively new terminology opens the conceptual space for a refiguring of the image of the idiot in order to affix a synonym for 'idiocy' onto people to whom traditional labels might not have adhered sufficiently. Although the term 'feeble-minded' had been used on many instances previously, Bosanquet claimed that it was coined by Sir Charles Trevelyan in an 1876 motion at a COS meeting, in which he proposed that 'feeble-minded' children should not be allowed to associate with adult 'idiots'. The motion was withdrawn after discussion, with opponents arguing that 'under certain circumstances, mutual aid might with advantage be interchanged among those diversely afflicted, and the elder might act as nurses and helpers to the younger' (Anonymous 1876: 504); Bosanquet retrospectively calls this objection 'unconvincing' (Bosanquet 1914: 196). It is not entirely clear that Trevelyan is not simply using 'feeble-minded' as a synonym for 'imbecile' – or 'educable idiot' – in this motion, as he clearly opposes the feeble-minded to 'idiots' only. In any case, that Bosanquet credits the COS with first describing the 'feeble-minded' underscores how important the notion of feeble-mindedness was to the organization, which, more than any other group, attempted to assert ownership of the concept, to determine what kinds of individuals might be so designated, and to shape the popular image of the feeble-minded person. When Duncan and Millard had defined 'feeble-mindedness', they noted that:

> the cases to be included in this class may have been born idiotic, and may have belonged to either of the former classes [i.e., idiocy and imbecility] during early childhood, and the decided advance in mental gifts and especially in bodily power, is either due to the ordinary growth, to an applied education, or both. (Duncan and Millard 1866: 41)

Alternatively, while some children improve from 'idiocy' to the level of the 'feeble-minded', in others, who had originally seemed more or less 'normal', the condition appears later – although they are 'readily distinguished, as years progress, by their general inaptitude to everything useful, their imprudence, improvident conduct, and general feebleness of purpose' (Duncan and Millard 1866: 42). This definition is based on the ability to perform mental and physical tasks. However, when the COS articulates its concept of feeble-mindedness, the condition is characterized not only by these features but also, and more importantly, by a dangerous absence of moral sense.

The COS's engagement with the education of 'feeble-minded' and other 'defective' children translated into participation in a number of commissions, which led to new legislation. In 1889, the Royal Commission on the Blind, the Deaf and Dumb released its report proposing that compulsory education be provided for blind, deaf and dumb children, and that special educational provisions also be made by school authorities for imbecilic and feeble-minded children; the Elementary Education (Blind and Deaf Children) Act 1893 and the Elementary Education (Defective and Epileptic Children) Act 1899 made these recommendations into law. However, despite these Acts, education was often haphazard. As Rowntree wrote in his 1901 analysis of poverty in York,

> [while] there are ... in some of the York schools special classes for teaching backwards children ... in one school in 1899 there was a class of thirty children, between eight and nine years old, who had hitherto succeeded in evading the vigilance of the School Board officers, and who could neither read nor write. (Rowntree 1901: 401)

Such reports would undoubtedly raise the hackles of COS activists, whose solution to the problem of the feeble-minded reached well beyond the limits of the 1899 Act. By the turn of the century, the COS and others were calling for the permanent support – that is, the segregation – of the feeble-minded, both for their own good and for that of society; to this end, the National Association for Promoting the Welfare of the Feeble-Minded was formed in 1895, working in close collaboration with the COS, with Sandlebridge schools founder Mary Dendy and with allies in the eugenics movement (Wright 2001; Jackson 2000). As Wright observes, while the Association's original goals 'stressed the care, self-sufficiency and protection of the feeble-minded', there was an inherent tension: it also 'sought to protect society from future social problems', such as crime and pauperism, by isolating this population (Wright 2001: 186–87). Segregation was necessary both to maintain social order, as desired by the COS, and to ensure the biological health of the race, as the eugenicists wished. Mary Dendy, the sister of Helen Bosanquet, put this programme into action at her Sandlebridge boarding schools, which opened in 1902 (Jackson 2000), but the facilities needed for initiatives such as these at the national level could not be supported solely by philanthropy: government assistance would be necessary. 'It was a long pull before the State could be brought to consider a program even approaching that urged by the Society, but the C.O.S. continued to pound away with reports, resolutions and deputations', writes David Owen (1964: 236), noting that initially there was little political interest in the issue. But in 1904, after much energetic lobbying by the COS and its allies, the government appointed a Royal Commission on the Care and Control of the Feeble-Minded. Feeble-mindedness had achieved official state recognition as a problem that needed to be solved. The next chapter examines in more detail this apparent problem, as well as proposed solutions.

Notes

1 Interestingly, in his 1913 work *The English Convict*, Charles Goring claims that 'stack-firing', a form of arson, was by far the crime most intimately associated with idiocy, with 52.9 per cent of criminals apprehended for this act being 'mental defectives' (Goring 1913: 258).
2 Most of Mayhew's work consisted of economic analysis intended to '[make] intelligible the economic behavior of the London poor', according to Gareth Stedman Jones (1971: 263), and, as E. P. Thompson notes, Mayhew's writings 'commenced as an effort at social reconciliation' after the cholera plagues of 1849 and the decline of Chartism (Thompson 1967/68: 45), but formed 'a reconciliation so searching that it was profoundly disturbing' (47). By the time

Mayhew's *London Labour and the London Poor* was republished in 1861, it was already being 'typed as quaint', according to Thompson (43).

3 The editor of the Everyman edition of Hollingshead's *Ragged London*, Anthony Wohl, flags this passage and notes that 'This is certainly questionable, for the infant death rate among urban working-class children was certainly higher than that for middle-class children' (Wohl 1986: 196).

4 For a comprehensive investigation of images of degeneracy in nineteenth- and twentieth-century literature, see William Greenslade's *Degeneration, Culture and the Novel 1880–1940*; see also Daniel Pick's *Faces of Degeneration* (Greenslade 1994; Pick 1989).

5 In an interesting variant on inter-generational politics, Cantlie claims that it is the young of London who are prematurely old, shaping manners for their elders and telling them how to behave, whereas 'it is the old, not the young people who are enthusiastic' (49); he concludes his lament on the 'good behaviour … fine manners … apathy [and] perfect morals' of the young generation (opposed to the 'ambition, energy, enthusiasm and love of enterprise' of their elders) by observing that 'it is beyond prophecy to guess even what the rising degeneration will grow into, what the Empire will become after they have got charge of it' (52).

6 The workhouse idiot was not simply a figure of sensational reportage. Also in 1865, Francis Edmund Anstie, a London physician, undertook a census of insane and idiotic inmates of workhouses. At Clerkenwell, he noted, there were 'eighty-three insane and imbecile patients', with 'the more harmless imbeciles mix[ing] with the ordinary inmates' (Anstie 1865: 331). St Pancras had twenty male and thirty-four female 'imbeciles', among many other inmates falling broadly under the category of 'insanity', a circumstance he uses to argue that the workhouse was 'becoming assimilated to a great public asylum' (332). In his summing up, Anstie argues that, of all those 'insane' and 'idiotic' inmates, 'none but the class of harmless imbeciles who are devoid of dirty habits ought to be retained in workhouses'; 'the idiotic', he stresses, 'require special *education*, and do *not* get it in workhouses' (335, original emphasis). He also notes the telling difference between town and country workhouses, 'the former containing a very much larger number of cases of imbecility from age, and of congenital weakness of mind, while the metropolitan districts furnish a larger number of actively troublesome cases' (335). While he does not further define 'actively troublesome', we can infer that this phrase refers to those who exhibit those moral and social vices increasingly associated with mental degeneracy.

7 According to White (1886: 60–61), this state of affairs rendered it 'desirable, therefore … to sterilize the unfit' by raising the age of matrimony, preventing 'reckless marriages', and permanently segregating habitual criminals. White was a particularly enthusiastic proponent of both degeneration theory and eugenics.

8 Harkness's new title alludes to Henry Stanley's *In Darkest Africa* as well as to William Booth's *In Darkest England and the Way Out*, both of which appeared in 1890. 'General' Booth, who founded the Salvation Army in 1878 (which grew out of his 'Christian Mission', based in east London since 1865), was the most prominent of a group of poverty activists whom Stedman Jones (1971: 311) identifies as 'social imperialists'. According to Booth's *In Darkest England*, the poor should be moved out of the city, to farming colonies, where they could receive both moral and agricultural training, 'continuing the process of regeneration'. From there, they would emigrate 'to the virgin soils that await their coming in other lands keeping hold of them with a strong government,

and yet making them free men and women; and so laying the foundation, per chance, of another Empire to swell to vast proportions in later times' (quoted in Stedman Jones 1971: 311). The 'In Darkest...' formulation became something of a cliché, with Ford Madox Ford also using 'In Darkest London' as the title for the chapter recounting the exploits of his cousins the Rossettis and their anarchist activities of the 1890s in his 1932 memoirs *Return to Yesterday*.

9 Interestingly, martins (a type of swallow) also live in large colonies like rookeries; thanks to Robert Martin for this observation.

10 These concerns helped give new impetus to the Idiots Act 1886, in which institutions formalized a ranking of 'idiots' and 'imbeciles', the latter exhibiting a higher cognitive capacity and thus showing greater promise for educational efforts. While the 'idiot' and 'imbecile' division had appeared in medical, social and popular parlance for some time, under the legislative authority of the Lunacy Act 1845 only the term 'idiocy' had any legal status. The primary push for the 1886 Act, though, came from those physicians managing 'idiot asylums', who argued that 'idiocy' should be recognized as something distinct from 'lunacy' and thus demanded its own legal status. The Idiots Act was supplanted by the Lunacy Act 1890, although this Act retained the crucial 'idiot' and 'imbecile' distinctions; asylums especially targeted the latter as those most likely to benefit from educational opportunities.

11 'Genius' was also, Lombroso argued in *The Man of Genius* (1889), a degenerate condition, observing that 'nothing so much resembles a person attacked by madness as a man of genius when meditating and moulding his conceptions' (22); indeed, ignorant parents and teachers can mistake 'the distraction or amnesia of genius' for 'mental obtusity, or even idiocy' (17).

12 Helen (Dendy) Bosanquet was the COS's honorary secretary from 1895, and author of a number of works on social welfare and individual morality and responsibility. She was the sister of Mary Dendy, founder of Sandlebridge schools for the feeble-minded, and the wife of philosopher Bernard Bosanquet. In the words of Charles Mowat, she was 'the C.O.S.'s most redoubtable champion of individualism' (Mowat 1961: 125) – that is, the belief that individuals were responsible for creating their own well-being.

CHAPTER 13

The problem of the feeble-minded: the Royal Commission, eugenics and eternal chaos

In his 'author's note' to his 1907 novel *The Secret Agent*, Joseph Conrad recalls a conversation with an unnamed friend about the 1894 Greenwich Observatory bombing, which Conrad called a 'blood-stained inanity of so fatuous a kind that it was impossible to fathom its origin by any reasonable or even unreasonable process of thought'. It was an 'outrage [that] could not be laid hold of mentally in any sort of way, so that one remained faced by the fact of a man blown to bits for nothing even most remotely resembling an idea, anarchist or other' (39). Conrad recounts that his friend – in fact Ford Madox Ford – replied 'in his characteristically casual and omniscient manner: "Oh, that fellow [i.e., the bomber] was half an idiot; his sister committed suicide afterwards"' (39).[1] By the time the Royal Commission on the Care and Control of the Feeble-Minded was struck in 1904, the Charity Organisation Society (COS) and others had fixed with some success the reputation of the idiot as dangerous to himself and others, and thus needing both care and control. By 1907, the broad belief in the dangerous degenerate would have made it especially easy to believe that the man with the bomb was 'half an idiot'. It should come as no surprise, then, that Conrad's novel presents an 'idiot' character as the gullible bomber. The unfortunate idiot anarchist Stevie is more than simply a character in a novel, though: he also informs Conrad's commentary on the 'degeneration anxiety' of his day, and provides a useful gloss on the 'idiot' imagined by the Royal Commission report, issued in 1908. But there were even larger issues: not only were the feeble-minded, those who were 'half an idiot', potentially dangerous, but they were also growing in number. To many observers, the predictions of writers like William Rathbone Greg (Chapter 11) were coming true: the towns and cities – especially the cities – of Britain were being overrun by rapidly reproducing hordes of 'marginals', who threatened to overwhelm the nation's healthy eugenic stock as well, creating a nation populated by imbeciles.

The 'imbecile world' of *The Secret Agent*

In *The Secret Agent*, the middle-aged Adolphe Verloc, proprietor of a 'stationery' shop that deals in pornographic materials and the odd anarchist journal, lives with his young wife Winnie, her aged mother and Winnie's brother – 'a terrible encumbrance, that poor Stevie' (48). Stevie, we are told, is 'delicate and, in a frail way, good-looking, too, except for the vacant droop of his lower lip' (49), and Winnie has nurtured a 'quasi-maternal affection' for him, from the time when their father would attempt to beat his son and Stevie would 'run for protection behind the short skirts of his sister' (49). Later, Winnie recalls the nature of her protection: intercepting blows meant for her brother, ineffectively trying to hold a door shut against her drunken father and, once, throwing a poker at him, with the consequence that the father complains of being 'accursed since one of his kids was a "slobbering idjut and the other a wicked she-devil"' (220). After the father's death, Winnie and her mother had run a boarding house, where Stevie was 'the unconscious presiding genius of all their toil' (220); Winnie gives up a lover who will not include her brother as part of the marital bargain and instead marries Verloc when it becomes clear that she can bring her brother and mother with her. The novel opens in the seventh year of their marriage, with Stevie in his abundant spare time occupied by 'drawing circles with compass and pencil on a piece of paper' (50).

Verloc's shop doubles as the meeting place for a group of anarchists, but he himself is a police informer and a secret agent in the employ of the embassy of a major foreign power, one which is growing impatient with the freedom offered by Britain to anarchists who have fled their own nations. Verloc is directed by Vladimir, the embassy's new first secretary, to play the *agent provocateur*: that is, to organize an assault on the Greenwich Observatory that will spawn terror and, thus, bring the law down upon London's anarchist community. Verloc's anarchist associates include the robust womanizer Ossipon, the ticket-of-leave apostle Michaelis, the poisonous, bitter Yundt and, slightly apart from this circle, the Professor, who searches for the perfect detonator and is renowned for carrying with him a bomb with which to kill himself and anyone nearby should the law try to apprehend him. Unfortunately, these anarchists are of little use in such activities as bomb-throwing (although the Professor provides the explosives), preferring malediction, the composition of inflammatory articles or benign idealism. In searching for some way to carry out the attack without exposing himself to any undue danger, Verloc realizes Stevie's particular malleability and decides to have his brother-in-law place the bomb at the Observatory. But Stevie trips on a tree root, falls and, instead of damaging the Observatory, blows himself into fragments. Winnie, eventually realizing what has happened to her beloved brother, kills Verloc and then seeks aid from Ossipon, who, fearing her as another degenerate, 'a degenerate of the murdering type' (Conrad 1907: 254), betrays her. She finally throws herself from a ship while fleeing to France.

But the novel contains much more than what is described in this simple plot summary. It is, as Avrom Fleishman argues, a 'world pervaded by dominant symbols' (Fleishman 1967: 189), dense with repeating, overdetermined images. Degeneration imagery and allusions play an important role in the novel's symbolic exchanges: the London of *The Secret Agent* is characterized by idiocy, imbecility and weakness. Yet while characters refer constantly to the degeneracy or idiocy of others, the power to ascribe these traits is never granted to any one group: police, anarchists and government bureaucrats all struggle to wrest authoritative control of the concept to pathologize their opponents, but the struggle is never resolved. Stevie, however, is one character whom audiences would infallibly recognize as degenerate. He is, after all, an idiot and, thus, according to the logic of degeneration narratives, the inevitable issue of a declining lineage. Stevie is also a literary figure whose symbolic function is shaped in part by his place in the tradition of idiot imagery: Irving Howe calls him 'a literary cousin of Dostoevsky's Myshkin' (Howe 1973: 145), and Thomas Mann more emphatically (and mistakenly) asserts that 'without Dostoevsky's *Idiot* Stevie is unthinkable' (Mann 1973: 110), while other critics have located him in the tradition of truth-telling court fools or Dickensian eccentrics. But while these observations have something to recommend them, as Stevie does indeed function in the traditional role of 'fool as social critic', he is also very much an offspring of late-nineteenth, early-twentieth-century degenerate London.

Stevie first appears in the action of the novel when Verloc and the anarchists open a door to let some air into their congested room:

> and thus disclosed the innocent Stevie, seated very good and quiet at a deal table, drawing circles, circles; innumerable circles, concentric,

eccentric; a coruscating whirl of circles that by their tangled multitude of repeated curves, uniformity of form, and confusion of intersecting lines suggested a rendering of cosmic chaos, the symbolism of a mad art attempting the inconceivable. The artist never turned his head; and in all his soul's application to the task his back quivered, his thin neck, sunk into a deep hollow at the base of the skull, seemed ready to snap. (76)

Stevie is the artist as idiot: his intellectual limitations are no barrier when it comes to trying to represent a rationally incomprehensible, metaphysical reality, the chaotic eternal. Stevie's allusive circles re-appear later, as Winnie, after learning of her brother's death, sits 'where poor Stevie usually established himself of an evening with paper and pencil for the pastime of drawing those coruscations of in-numerable circles suggesting chaos and eternity' (216).

Stevie is an ambiguous being, interpreted variously by the novel's characters. For Winnie, he is 'amiable, attractive, affectionate and only a little, a very little peculiar' (170). Verloc 'extends as much recognition to Stevie as a man not particularly fond of animals may give to his wife's beloved cat' (72); when meeting his brother-in-law unexpectedly, he realizes 'with some surprise that he did not know really what to say to Stevie' (83). The anarchist Ossipon presents a contemporary scientific interpretation: Stevie is not only a 'degenerate' but a 'very good type, too, altogether, of that sort of degenerate. It's good enough to glance at the lobes of his ears', he notes, then referring to the dubious authority of Lombroso (77); and, shortly after, the nar-rative describes Ossipon's 'thick lips' that accentuate 'the Negro type of his face' (80), an ironic observation that marks him as another of Lombroso's degenerate beings.[2]

Despite his apparent degeneracy, Stevie is also, in some sense, the moral centre of the novel. When he learns from an evening cabman the realities of the night cabby's trade, pushing himself and his 'infirm and lonely steed' (168) to earn money for his wife and four children, Stevie repeats to himself 'Poor brute, poor people!', until he stops with the 'angry splutter "Shame!"' Finally, 'as though he had been trying to fit all the words he could remember to his sentiments in order to get some sort of corresponding idea', he successfully formulates a conclu-sion: 'Bad world for poor people' (168).[3] Whatever difficulties Stevie has in formulating his thoughts, he is quick to develop a response: 'The tenderness of his universal charity had two phases as indissolubly joined and connected as the reverse and obverse sides of a medal. The anguish of immoderate passion was succeeded by the pain of an inno-cent but pitiless rage' (166); as a result, 'being no sceptic, but a moral creature, he was in a manner at the mercy of his righteous passions'

(169). Interestingly, Stevie's 'morality' here runs counter to prevailing discourses that constructed the 'idiot' as fundamentally lacking moral capacity. Stevie, told by his sister that no one could help the world being a bad place for the poor, and that this was not something that would concern the police – his conception of the organizing authorities of the world – is baffled and irritated. Unlike his sister, whom we are told 'put her trust in face values', he 'wished to go to the bottom of the matter' (169), but as his understanding of 'the bottom of the matter' is limited, Verloc can easily nourish in Stevie an inarticulate hatred of a system that oppresses night cabbies and their horses. Under Verloc's political tutelage, Stevie abandons his favourite pastime, so that 'when discovered in solitude would be scowling at the wall, with the sheet of paper and the pencil given him for drawing circles lying blank and idle on the kitchen table' (179). Eventually Stevie becomes the circle, entering that world of chaos and eternity his drawings had so often intimated, in the explosion at the Greenwich Observatory – as summarized in the early news reports, an 'enormous hole in ground.... All round fragments of a man's body blown to bits' (95). Stevie is transformed out of space and time, at the point of the first meridian.

Writing to Henri Davray, his French translator, on 8 November 1906, Conrad describes his new novel as containing 'half a dozen anarchists, two women, and an idiot. They're all imbeciles, what's more, including an Embassy Secretary, a Minister of State, and an Inspector of Police' (see Karl and Davies 1983: 372–73). The novel, as Conrad accurately observes, is permeated by imbecility, idiocy, weakness – all terms used by authorities, both official and anarchist, to describe others. Idiocy and degeneration exist in the eyes of the beholders and are, almost inevitably, what they perceive outside themselves but never within. Verloc, the narrator tells us, is 'not devoid of intelligence', although it is of a sort that prefers not to sweat in exertion (52). At the embassy of the unnamed great power, the first secretary, Vladimir, suggests that the embassy's previous staff was 'soft-headed' (59) – the previous ambassador, we are told, had 'enjoyed in his lifetime a fame for an owlish, pessimistic gullibility', and was said to have exclaimed on his deathbed 'Unhappy Europe! Thou shalt perish by the moral insanity of thy children!' (63). Asserting that he will set things straight, Vladimir assesses his predecessor's secret agent, the man designated by his predecessor only by the symbol Δ (in contrast to Stevie's circles), as 'impudently unintelligent' (63); Verloc, in opposition, dismisses those fluent in Latin (including, by implication, Vladimir) as 'only a few hundred imbeciles who aren't fit to take care of themselves' (60). Vladimir then proposes that the only anarchist plot capable of waking the 'imbecile bourgeoisie' of Britain (64) out of their stupor is an assault on 'the sacrosanct fetish of today' (66), science, which 'any imbecile that has got an income believes in' (67). Such an attack, 'an alarming display of ferocious imbecility' (68), would squeeze a few howls from the 'intellectual idiots' (67) gathered at an upcoming international conference in Milan to deliberate upon means to suppress political crime, thus prompting a restriction of liberties in England; Verloc eventually comes to see this plan as Vladimir's 'truculent folly' (224), but only after the fact, as he laments the endeavour in which Stevie had 'stupidly destroyed himself' (227).

But there is more: the Assistant Commissioner of the police notes that there was 'a peculiar stupidity and feebleness' evident in the planning and execution of the Greenwich attack (146). Chief Inspector Heat, 'by a sudden illumination', recognizes newspapers to be 'invariably written by fools for the reading of imbeciles' (197). Sir Ethelred's secretary, Toodles, refers to the minister's 'massive intellect' (149) but this seems an ironic description, given the source and the minister's refusal to hear details, as well as the minister's complaint that his police force is making him 'look a fool' (142) by having previously assured him that there was no chance of an anarchist attack. Among the anarchists, Karl Yundt dismisses Lombroso's theories of physiognomy by exclaiming 'Did you ever see such an idiot?' and then denouncing Lombroso as an 'imbecile who has made his way in this world of gorged fools by looking at the ears and teeth of a lot of poor, luckless devils' (77–78). The Professor combines the 'extreme, almost ascetic purity of his thought' with 'an astounding ignorance of worldly conditions' (102), while Michaelis is set apart by 'the innocence of his heart and the simplicity of his mind', a point reiterated when the narrator explains that 'a certain simplicity of thought is common to serene souls at both ends of the social scale' (121). In the Professor's dismissive account at the end of the novel, Michaelis is 'elaborating ... the idea of a world planned out like an immense and nice hospital, with gardens and flowers, in which the strong are to devote themselves to the nursing of the weak' (263); further, the Professor complains, Michaelis's 'poverty of reasoning is astonishing. He has no logic. He can't think consecutively' (263). The Professor, for his part, dismisses 'that multitude, too stupid to feel either pity or fear' (264), but at the same time laments that he suffers from 'the oppression of the weak' and that 'the fools, the weak and the silly ... rule the roost' (268); 'the weak, the flabby, the silly, the cowardly, the faint of heart, and the slavish of mind' are, he insists, 'our sinister masters', who must be exterminated (263).

And there is even more: Winnie thinks, watching Verloc and Stevie walk away together in coats and hats, that they 'might be father and son' (179), a vision that fuses the intelligence agent with the degenerate idiot, and one which she bitterly recalls after Stevie's death (221). Verloc, we are told, 'lacked profundity' (213), while Winnie, for her part, is guided by an intellectual policy in which things 'did not stand looking into very much', so that she should not go about 'troubling her head'; she is a woman of 'singularly few words, either for public or private use', and whose thought processes are primarily visual (219); Stevie's death, however, 'stimulate[s] … her intelligence' (226), giving her the mental focus to plot and perform the murder of her husband. Ossipon first lusts after Winnie and then, once he realizes she has killed Verloc, fears her as 'the sister of the degenerate – a degenerate herself of a murdering type … or else of the lying type' (254). When she reveals how Verloc had led Stevie to his death, Ossipon exclaims 'The degenerate – by heavens!', surprised because he had believed Verloc, not Stevie, to have died in the explosion, but Winnie interprets this as a denunciation of Verloc, who is, in her mind, the 'degenerate'. Ossipon, 'nicknamed the Doctor … late lecturer on the social aspects of hygiene to working men's clubs' – that is, on eugenics – observes to Winnie that 'It's almost incredible the resemblance there was between you [and Stevie]' (259–60), as he trembles with fear that he struggles to hide.

Conrad's reader has already seen this resemblance between Winnie and Stevie, just before she murders her husband. When Verloc says 'I wish to goodness … I had never seen Greenwich Park or anything belonging to it', Conrad describes the sound waves filling the room: 'The waves of air of the proper length, propagated in accordance with correct mathematical formulas, flowed around all the inanimate things in the room, lapped against Mrs Verloc's head as if it had been a head of stone'. The waves of sound emanating from the voice of Verloc recall Stevie's inscribed circles, stimulating her imaginative reconstruction of his death:

> smashed branches, torn leaves, gravel, bits of brotherly flesh and bone, all spouting up together in the manner of a firework…. Mrs Verloc closed her eyes desperately, throwing upon that vision the night of her eyelids, where after a rainlike fall of mangled limbs the decapitated head of Stevie lingered suspended alone, and fading out like the last star of a pyrotechnic display. (232–33)

She imagines Stevie as a circle of fire, and when Verloc calls her to the couch, and she noiselessly grasps the knife from the table, she is transformed: 'as if the homeless soul of Stevie had flown for shelter straight to the breast of his sister, guardian and protector, the resemblance of her face with that of her brother grew at every step, even to the droop of the lower lip, even to the slight divergence of the eyes'. She stabs her husband, putting into the thrust 'all the inheritance of her immemorial and obscure descent, the simple ferocity of the age of caverns, and the unbalanced nervous fury of the age of barrooms' (234). The murder completed, 'her extraordinary resemblance to her late brother' fades. This passage draws upon dominant theories of hereditary as well as urban degeneration: the Winnie of the caverns, an instance of biological recapitulation of the sort Ernst Haeckel had described (Chapter 11), is complemented by the Winnie of the bar-rooms, a creature exemplifying the moral degeneration attacked by groups like the COS. Prehistory and urbanity combine to create the regressive human brute.

Conrad had previously contemplated a world populated by degenerate beings in his early short story 'The Idiots', published in 1898 as part of his *Tales of Unrest*. 'The Idiots' is a dismal, blunt tale of degeneration in which a woman bears four idiot children, is beaten and abused by her husband for failing to produce a proper heir, kills him and then, in a fit of insanity, takes her own life (albeit accidentally). The idiot offspring live with their grandmother, and the narrator comes across them while driving through the countryside. 'They lived on that road, drifting along its length here and there, according to the inexplicable impulses of their monstrous darkness', Conrad writes. 'They were an offence to the sunshine, a reproach to empty heaven, a blight on the concentrated and purposeful vigour of the wild landscape' (58). In his author's note to a later edition of that collection, Conrad (1923: ix) describes the story as 'an obviously derivative piece of work' suggested by 'actual idiots', and his wife Jessie Conrad recalls how, when honeymooning in France, they 'came across the idiots, who became the subject of one of the short stories written on the spot'. However, she writes:

> In his story ... he has not given quite the full number of unfortunates. I pointed out to him that there were two more at least and was quite startled by his unexpected violence: 'Good God, my dear, I've put enough horror into that story in all conscience. Two more! More than enough without them, to my mind'. (Jessie Conrad 1935: 37)

Conrad's 'unexpected violence' may have been stimulated by his artistic conscience, but, as Martin Bock (2002) has pointed out, may also have sprung from his fears based on his long history of illness and depression, and perhaps especially strong as he had just wed, about sexuality and what he suspected to be his own inherent degeneracy. Daphna Erdinast-Vulcan argues convincingly that the story – which she calls 'one of Conrad's most pointless' – is 'interesting mainly for its symptomatic significance, but the anxiety it articulates, in the most inarticulate manner, is not merely the private mental torments of a troubled individual trying to adjust to the marital state, but a much wider cultural malaise' (Erdinast-Vulcan 1996: 186). This anxiety she discerns in the story's very pointlessness, its refusal to end properly and the telling failure of the father to produce offspring to work his land and perpetuate his line: in her reading, at the heart of 'The Idiots' lies the 'anxiety of Modernism' (193), a phrase which here functions as a broad concept to designate the impact of a *mélange* of social and cultural forces expressed through the very specific fears of degeneration.

But if the idiots of 1898 are almost artlessly rendered as mere instances of degeneration, Stevie's symbolic function in *The Secret Agent* is much more complex – and just as he is the moral centre of the novel, he is also, as Martin Halliwell points out, the 'true secret agent' at the novel's 'symbolic centre' (Halliwell 2004: 108). Idiocy, imbecility, weakness and degeneracy characterize the novel's world, which in this sense resembles that of Dickens's *Little Dorrit* (Chapter 5), although there are also profound differences. In *Little Dorrit*, it matters that one embraces folly; such is the means of surviving, and even finding pleasure, in a world of deceit and self-pride. In *The Secret Agent*, embracing idiocy is not desirable, but rather unavoidable. Terry Eagleton suggests that:

> [Stevie's] human tenderness is at once a function of his muddled, mentally regressive naivety, and a 'mystical' intimation of values critical to bourgeois society – values which are in him, however, literally inarticulable, mere broken murmurs of dissent. The silence of Stevie is ideologically determinate: the text is unable to endorse the callous inhumanity of the social world, but unable to articulate any alternative value because *value itself* is 'metaphysically' trivial. (Eagleton 1986: 26, original emphasis)

The novel leads to a 'stalemate' of competing perspectives (Eagleton 1986: 29), each cancelling out the others, so that the 'message of the book's metaphysical materialism' becomes 'nothing can really be changed' (Eagleton 1986: 30). There are also contradictions in characterization, so that Stevie 'is a type both of the anarchists themselves and of their innocent victims' (Eagleton 1986: 31), a product of conflicting ideologies drawing on the same imagery. The silence of Stevie, his language replaced by mystical circles of chaos and eternity, becomes the inarticulate centre of the text's ideological contradictions: it becomes the inevitable idiocy of urban humanity.

This collapse of urban humanity into idiocy is rooted in the same sort of ideological contradiction that Eagleton describes. The social values of liberal bourgeois democracy meet the profound and implacable opposition of anarchist ideals in Eagleton's reading, and while the novel satirizes and undercuts the authority of the bourgeois, it also despises the anarchists. This conflict between the dominant ideological 'choices' offered by *The Secret Agent* creates a void, expressed in Stevie's death, and a deferral of authority to the metaphysical in place of the social and political: Conrad's answer to the novel's conflicting ideological positions lies in the eternal chaos of Stevie's circles. Similarly, according to the argument proposed by degeneration theorists and social hygienists, as humanity reaches the point where it does not only struggle but prospers – when it becomes *civilized* – then human society not only enables the survival of the fittest, but also of the enfeebled: social structures provide aid to the weakly, thus enabling them to breed and perpetuate their deficiencies. Under this model of humane and philanthropic civilization, humanity, especially in its urban form, must inevitably decline.

While novelists can reach for metaphysical resolutions, social activists and politicians (if not theologians) require more quotidian, pragmatic responses to perceived problems. As Conrad's novel was appearing before the reading public, the Royal Commission on the Care and Control of the Feeble-Minded was deliberating about what to do with people like Stevie. And, just as Conrad's character disintegrated under the contradictory symbolic burdens he carried, so, too, were the 'feeble-minded' muted and their individuality erased before the interpretative regard of those who made up the Commission, for whom 'feeble-mindedness' was connected to many of the ills afflicting Britain and was embodied in a class of people in apparent need of both 'care' and 'control' – notions that find their sources in the respective educational and punitive discourses of the school and the prison.

'The feeble-minded in our midst'

'No doubt there are some who would regret the disappearance of the feeble-minded in our midst', suggested Havelock Ellis in 1912. 'The philosophies of the Bergsonian type, which today prevail so widely, place intuition above reason, and the "poor fool" has sometimes been enshrined and idolized'. Then, as if to assuage the fears of those deluded Bergsonians who would miss the presence of the 'poor fools', Ellis notes that 'Eugenics can never prevent absolutely the occurrence of feeble-minded persons, even in the extreme degree of the imbecile and the idiot. They come within the range of variation, by the same right as genius so comes' (Ellis 1912: 32). This Bergsonian fool may be no more than a figment of Ellis's imagination, but it provides him an opportunity to take a swipe at a rival philosopher, one whose theories of intelligence differed substantially from his own. In his 1907 work *Creative Evolution*, Henri Bergson proposes theories of intelligence and instinct in which the two complement one another and emerge in a higher form, as intuition. So, while Bergson describes the intellect as 'characterized by a natural inability to comprehend life', instinct 'is moulded on the very form of life. While intelligence treats everything mechanically, instinct proceeds, so to speak, organically' (Bergson 1907: 182). Later, he argues that 'instinct is sympathy', which, if it could 'extend its object and also reflect upon itself ... would give us the key to vital operations – just as intelligence, developed and disciplined, guides us into matter'. Thus, while intelligence is turned towards 'inert matter', instinct is directed 'toward life' – and that intuition decried by Ellis is defined by Bergson as 'instinct that has become disinterested, self-conscious, capable of reflecting upon its object and enlarging it indefinitely' (Bergson 1907: 194). This intuition then becomes, for Bergson, the source of artistic insight and the creative mind; whether these arguments led Bergsonian philosophers to idolize 'pure fools' is another question, but it is worth noting the similarity between the intuitive morality of Stevie, in Conrad's *Secret Agent*, and Bergsonian notions of intuitive apprehension. Similarly, Stevie's circles of eternity and chaos, and his explosion at the Greenwich Observatory, the first meridian of human divisions of time, recall Bergson's notions of time as fluid, both compressive and extensive.[4] If a Bergsonian version of a 'pure fool' exists, he might look very much like Stevie.

By the time Ellis opposed Bergsonian fools, plans to have the feeble-minded disappear from British society were already well underway. In 1908, after four years of inquiry and meetings with 248 individuals (Thomson 1998), the Royal Commission on the Care and Control of the Feeble-Minded reported its findings:

> Of the gravity of the present state of things, there is no doubt. The mass of facts that we have collected, the statements of our witnesses, and our own personal visits and investigations compel the conclusion that there are numbers of mentally defective persons whose training is neglected, over whom no sufficient control is exercised, and whose wayward and ir-responsible lives are productive of crime and misery, of much injury and mischief to themselves and to others, and of much continuous expendi-ture wasteful to the community and to individual families. (Quoted in Davey 1914: 2)

The most significant recommendation was the creation of a system of institutions for the permanent segregation of the feeble-minded. An abstract of the multi-volume report was published in 1909 under the title *The Problem of the Feeble-Minded*, accompanied by appendices penned by Francis Galton, the Reverend W. R. Inge, A. C. Pigou and Mary Dendy. This abstract, which made the report's research and recommendations available to a much broader population than the report itself ever could have reached, particularly stressed the threat of immoral behaviour, including promiscuity, drunkenness and criminal activities:

> a large proportion of the evidence points unmistakably to the fact that mentally defective children often have immoral tendencies; that they are greatly lacking in self-control; and moreover are peculiarly open to suggestion, so that they are at the mercy of bad companions. (Royal Commission on the Care and Control of the Feeble-Minded 1909: 6–7)

(One might wonder whether children who were not 'mentally defective' often had 'immoral tendencies' as well.) The Commission gathered an impressive range of voices to support its findings. For instance, Dr Kerr, Medical Officer (Education) to the London County Council, told the committee that feeble-minded children constituted 'a very serious social danger, developing in many cases into dangerous criminals who only come into the care of the law after they have committed crimes, such as assault, theft or arson' (7), and he suggested that if these children were to be fingerprinted 'it would probably be found that in the succeeding ten years very many would be found under different names in the hands of the police or in maternity hospitals' (7). The 'maternity hospitals' were particularly significant, as 'feeble-minded' women were imagined to be sexually promiscuous threats to the eugenic health of the state, bringing forth a flood of mentally deficient offspring who would overwhelm the nation's healthy sons and daughters.

Thomson argues that the motivation for and findings of the report itself are not primarily eugenic, and that the 1913 Mental Deficiency Act that adopted the report's recommendations (discussed below) should not be seen primarily as a eugenic measure but rather 'fitted into a broader vision of the reorganization of mental health care which had little to do with eugenics' (Thomson 1998: 32). However, the appendices published with *The Problem of the Feeble-Minded* explicitly highlight the advantages of the report's eugenic proposals. Galton, the father of eugenics, who was in 1908 named President of the Eugenics Education Society, created the year earlier, argues that 'the feeble-minded, as distinguished from the idiots, are an exceptionally fecund class, mostly of illegitimate children, and a terrible proportion of their offspring are born mentally deficient' (82). While the Reverend Inge, a Cambridge theologian, expresses some reservations about eugenics, he repeats Galton's position, noting that 'the rate of illegitimate births would be appreciably reduced if the seduction of the half-witted were made impossible and if males equally deficient in moral sense were placed under restraint' (91). He then conflates intellectual and moral deficiency, in observing:

> it is by no means uncommon for a high-minded man or woman to abstain from marriage on account of some hereditary taint, and such conduct is universally commended. Can there be anything morally objectionable in prescribing the same abstention for those who are too deficient morally to choose it for themselves? (91)

The economist A. C. Pigou argues that:

> by means of a little money spent now in segregating the mentally defective, it is possible to cut off at the source what would otherwise become a permanent stream of imbecile and idiotic persons, almost certain to fall into pauperism or crime, and to constitute a continuous and increasing charge on the community. (100)

Finally, Mary Dendy, founder of the Sandlebridge boarding schools, the prototype for later segregated institutions, provides a requisite humanitarian touch in suggesting that 'if persons who are not criminals are detained partly in the interests of society, it is the duty of society to see that they are made happy' (105) – after all, the Commission was concerned with not just the control but also the care of the mentally defective. She adds:

> Fortunately, the feeble-minded are much more easily made happy than sane persons ... though no normal man or woman could live a happy life in the restricted conditions which ought to be provided for the weak in intellect, it is perfectly easy to make the great majority of the weak-minded happy without ever letting them see anything of the outside world. It is indeed essential to their happiness that they should be so secluded; there is probably no more miserable being on earth than the weak-minded person who is at large. (105–6)

Dendy's claim lightens what might easily be interpreted as a proposal for a set of measures more restrictive than anything previously imposed by the British state upon people who had committed no crime. The other writers, however, overtly express the anxiety that the feeble-minded, and especially feeble-minded women, posed a national danger that must somehow be neutralized.

The Commission recommended that the state undertake permanent custodial guardianship of feeble-minded individuals, unless 'the parents are able and willing to provide proper care and training' (66). Such an enterprise would demand the construction and maintenance of many more facilities than were available at the time but, as Pigou argued:

the money that the Commissioners require for improving the treatment of the feeble-minded would not be merely *a gift to them*. It would also be an *investment*, calculated to yield a return to the community just as real and tangible as is yielded by investment in buildings and machinery. (99, original emphasis)

Segregation of the feebleminded thus becomes, like buildings and machinery, part of the critical infrastructure of the modern state, and social engineering takes its place alongside civil and mechanical engineering.

While the control and care sections of these appendices are divided upon gender lines – Galton, Inge and Pigou citing the biological, moral and economic advantages that would accrue to the greater society by the proposed restraints on the feeble-minded, with Dendy providing the palliative 'care' passages – all are part of the same project: constructing the 'feeble-minded' as both dangerous and childlike. As Dendy writes three years later in her appendix to *Feeblemindedness in Children of School Age* (1911), by the Manchester physician and social hygiene lecturer C. Paget Lapage, 'there is no hard and fast line which can be drawn dividing the childhood of the feebleminded from their manhood; – their school-life from their industrial life' (Dendy 1911: 291). Even as adults, the feeble-minded are 'grown-up children' (296), a point reinforced by photographs in Lapage's book. The frontispiece photograph is captioned 'Group of Boys Working at Sandlebridge', but the five 'boys' pictured all appear to be physically mature adults; in another instance, an image of two young men working in a field shares the caption 'Feebleminded Children of the Ordinary Type' with another photograph of three young girls peeling apples in a kitchen (Lapage 1911: 48). These images demonstrate the therapeutic labour carried out at Sandlebridge while simultaneously working to reinforce the 'childishness' of the individuals portrayed, lest anyone mistakenly assume that these labourers could also perform their work in an non-segregated community, without trained, professional supervision.

Care and control do not always fit easily together, but blending 'feeble-mindedness' with 'childhood' helped make the union palatable. Pigou's observation that society has the power, 'with but little severity to any living person', to remove the threat of 'race deterioration' (Royal Commission on the Care and Control of the Feeble-Minded 1909: 101) makes the mildly uncomfortable admission that some degree of severity is involved. Inge, like Dendy, conflates the 'feeble-minded' with children, arguing that 'persons who are mentally defective are not in a natural state (though in vulgar parlance they are sometimes called "naturals")'; as a result of this unnaturalness, he concludes, 'we have a right to treat them like children, supplying by gentle compulsion the lack of moral and rational will-power which constitutes their infirmity' (92). The 'gentle compulsion', like the 'little severity', is that point where care and control collide, demanding a clear strategy for licensing the proposed restrictions. Figuring the feeble-minded as children needing guidance provides the necessary rationale – even if the 'children' have certain adult interests and desires. Rendering the 'feeble-minded' childlike also effaces their sexual maturity, a very real characteristic given their oft-noted fecundity. Of course, the association with children is not new: the 'childishness' of Barnaby Rudge is critical to the symbolic exchanges at play in that novel (Chapter 8), and in the fifteenth-century Court of Chancery, finding a person an 'idiot' meant that his 'age of majority' was permanently deferred or, in effect, revoked (Chapter 4). What is new, though, is that an even broader group of people have become 'like children' and must be managed on a large scale. Further, this management is especially critical because, as sexually mature beings capable of procreating, they pose a threat to the nation's eugenic health. This new type of idiot, the 'feeble-minded', must be constructed as 'childlike' precisely because they can (and did) have children, and needed to be restrained from indulging in this adult behaviour – a far cry from the Court of Chancery, where the ability to procreate was taken as proof that one was *not* an idiot (Bell 1953). The transformation that began in the 1840s, with the sub-human idiot who needed reclamation in order to become a social participant, has come to this point: the mentally deficient individual is fundamentally bereft of moral and rational will-power, and thus cannot possibly engage in larger society. A caring control, a permanent paternalism, is required: the mid-nineteenth-century ambitions of welcoming the idiot into the social and economic life of the nation are culminating instead in the mental defective's permanent exclusion.

Eugenics, the evil of amentia and the 1913 Mental Deficiency Act

The publication of the Commission's report coincided with the burgeoning eugenics movement, and while eugenics was not the sole impulse behind the report (or perhaps, as Thomson argues, even the dominant impulse), eugenicists consistently wrote in its support in an effort to see its findings translated into law – and often these eugenicists

were the same people who, through their positions with the COS and
Royal Commission, had played significant roles in dictating the national
agenda on the problem of the feeble-minded. The first issue of *Eugenics
Review*, published in 1909, included articles by Miss A. H. P. Kirby, secretary to the COS-affiliated National Association for the Feeble-Minded,
and A. F. Tredgold, medical expert to the Royal Commission, in addition
to Francis Galton, Arnold White and Havelock Ellis. Kirby lays out
the problem, arguing for the hereditary nature of the major problems
traditionally associated with the feeble-minded: their propensity for
procreation; their criminality – referring to a study in which thirty-seven
'defective' convicts, averaging thirty-five years old, 'began their known
criminal life at the average age of 14½ years' and had since committed
515 serious crimes between them (Kirby 1909: 89); and their drunkenness – noting that 'the feeble in mind can only drink half or quarter
the amount of alcohol taken by other men, before reaching the stage of
complete inebriety' (90).[5] She concludes by observing that, thanks to
the misguided support given to 'the worst type of our wastrels ... we
are looking on at a process of selective degeneration, carried out on a
somewhat extensive scale, by State and private philanthropy' (94).

In his contribution to the issue, White suggests that the danger of
the feeble-minded lies with their threat to 'national efficiency', which
he defines as 'the sum of spiritual, mental and material conditions,
each of them affecting, whilst none alone determines, national identity' (White 1909: 104). Britain, endowed by nature and good fortune,
has grown lethargic and indifferent, White laments: 'While boasting
of the finest horses, sweet-peas, delphiniums, bull-dogs, and grass-fed
beef in the world, we have hitherto left to chance the future of our own
race' (107). This danger can be addressed by 'the Sterilisation of the
Unfit', but the solution is not without its own complexities: who, after
all, are the 'Unfit'? As White points out:

> That each one of us is in a measure *among the Unfit* is known to every
> human soul honest with itself. The question of unfitness, therefore, is
> one of degree, and the medical tyranny that would extirpate breeding-
> beds of mental degeneracy at the wholesale sacrifice of personal liberty is
> out of court, not because it is stupid, but because it is impractical. (108,
> original emphasis)

Ultimately, he argues:

> the answer to the question, therefore, what is the unfitness that justifies
> sterilisation is that the unfitness shall be of a kind that is as dangerous
> to the community as murder or forgery, and the sanction for interference
> shall rest, as all sound laws rest, on the solid foundation of public policy.
> (109).

Those to be sterilized are those beings whose very existence poses a threat to 'national efficiency' comparable to the social threat posed by murderers and forgers, whose crimes rob the nation of manpower and money.

Perhaps the most powerful and influential arguments were those presented by Alfred Tredgold, who, in his explicitly named 'The Feeble-Minded: A Social Danger', stressed the threat posed by the problem of 'National Degeneracy', and noted that 'more nations have sunk to a position of utter insignificance or have been entirely blotted out of existence, as the result of the moral, intellectual, and physical degeneracy of their citizens, than of wars, famines, or any other conditions'; the 'feeble-minded and their relations form a considerable proportion, if not the whole, of the social failures – the degenerates of the nation' (Tredgold 1909: 100). Thus, the future of the nation rests upon the ability of the state to confront this problem. In 'modern civilisation', the 'struggle for existence' no longer weeds out the feeble, as this natural process is 'thwarted by sentiment, which ignores the race in its concern for the individual', he writes.

> The result is that in the present day many delicate and diseased individuals, who in former times would have undoubtedly have perished, are enabled to reach maturity through the intervention of the physician. I am not saying that this is wrong, for I believe it to be the duty of my profession to fight disease in every shape and form; but I do say this, that if social science does not keep pace with medical science in this matter the end will be national disaster. In other words, I would lay it down as a general principle that as soon as a nation reaches that stage of civilisation in which medical knowledge and humanitarian sentiment operate to prolong the existence of the unfit, then it becomes imperative upon that nation to devise such social laws as will ensure that these unfit do not propagate their kind. (101)

So far, he makes clear, the social laws that would ensure the national health have been sorely neglected, a sign of lamentable sluggishness on behalf of the state. 'But delay is dangerous', Tredgold prophesized, and he stressed that 'each of us, as intelligent citizens of a great Empire, [must] bestir ourselves to see that this great social evil is removed and that this tide of degeneracy is stemmed' (104). Tredgold's arguments would become profoundly influential, as his 1908 *Mental Deficiency (Amentia)* would live through a dozen editions as the field's standard textbook for most of the twentieth century, being used to instruct social workers, teachers, therapists and physicians for over sixty years.[6] But his work also had a more immediate impact: in 1911 Winston Churchill, then Home Secretary, circulated Tredgold's paper among his government colleagues, noting that it provided 'a concise, and I am informed, not exaggerated statement of the serious problem to be faced' (quoted in Davie 2005: 208). Eugenics may not have been the driving force behind the Commission, but eugenicists were energetic supporters of the push to turn its recommendations into law. And many wanted laws that extended far past segregation, to include sterilization as well.

The rhetoric would soon grow even more insistent. 'Feeble-mindedness is an absolute dead-weight on the race. It is an evil that is unmitigated', Havelock Ellis asserted dramatically in 1912, in laying out his programme for social hygiene.

> The task of Social Hygiene which lies before us cannot be attempted by this feeble folk. Not only can they not share it, but they impede it; their clumsy hands are for ever becoming entangled in the delicate mechanism of our modern civilization. Their very existence is itself an impediment. (Ellis 1912: 43)

The feeble-minded clearly were not to be participants in the ideal society. But bringing this society to fruition was proving frustrating. The government moved slowly to propose legislation, so in 1912 two private members introduced bills drafted by the Eugenics Education Society (the Feeble-Minded Control Bill) and the National Association for the Care of the Feeble-Minded (the Mental Defect Bill); these, however, did not get very far (Jones 1972). The government then proposed its own Mental Defect Bill in May 1912, but withdrew it in the face of opposition. However, concerted lobbying, most prominently by Mary Dendy, the founder of Sandlebridge, and Ellen Pinsent, a prominent member of the National Association for the Care of the Feeble-Minded and of the Royal Commission, won over local governments, commissions and school boards and kept the issue on the agenda (Jackson 2000); as a result of their advocacy, local authorities began to send to the government resolutions demanding legislative action, and by the end of 1912 the Home Office had received 'no less than 800 resolutions from public bodies, including resolutions from 14 county councils, 44 borough councils, 110 education committees, and 280 boards guardians' (Jones 1972: 199). On 19 July 1913, the Mental Deficiency Act passed Parliament by a vote of 180 to 3, and took effect on 1 April 1914.[7] Josiah Wedgwood, one of the leading opponents of the Bill within the House of Commons (along with Sir Frederick Banbury and Handel Booth), claimed retrospectively that the Bill, 'whereby prostitutes could be sent to feeble-minded houses to save mankind from infections', was a 'clear case of expediency over justice' (quoted in

Jones 1972: 201).[8] Wedgwood's reference to prostitutes points to one of the major issues in the debate over the Act: the control of the sexual behaviour of those apparently 'feeble-minded' women who, according to the dominant theories, were responsible for the growing population of the mentally deficient.[9] While the opposition mounted by Wedgwood and his allies could not keep the bill from passing, they were able to add over 200 amendments, including one ensuring the parents' right to refuse to send a child to a residential school, between the government's initial 1912 effort and the final version (Thomson 1998).

'Mental defective' officially replaced 'idiot' as a general designation. The Act defined four levels of 'mental defectives' – idiots, imbeciles, the feeble-minded and moral imbeciles (this fourth category being at the recommendation of the Royal Commission)[10] – thus both refining and broadening the concept of idiocy. The terms 'feeble-minded' and 'moral imbecile' would have encompassed people who may well have escaped the ignominy of such notice sixty years earlier.[11] Mental defectives at all levels could, under appropriate circumstances, be committed to segregated homes or asylums.

Why was the government able to pass the Mental Deficiency Act, legislating for the segregation of one apparently risky population when similar proposals for other populations – the hopeless drunkards, promiscuous women and habitual thieves – gathered no momentum whatsoever? According to the jurist A. V. Dicey, 'the Mental Deficiency Act is the first stage along a path [towards responsibility to the social collective] on which no man can decline to enter, but which if too far pursued, will bring statesmen across difficulties hard to meet without considerable interference with individual liberty' (quoted in Thomson 1998: 46). Thomson (1998) observes that 'because of the very nature of their defect, mental defectives were the one group who were widely accepted as lacking will or the potential for self-improvement' (34); instead, they 'were marked out as lying outside the boundaries of responsible citizenship: … with the right to be given humane care, but too irresponsible to exert their own civil right or to have the right to liberty' (55). The parliamentary support for the 1913 Act reflected broad public opinion, certainly as expressed by local governments, boards and commissions, as well as the media; ultimately, Thomson notes, the Act 'seemed to provide a rational administrative solution to a series of social problems' (39). Of course, the Act also provided a covert means to segregate habitually inebriate and criminal individuals and, most importantly for the eugenicists, promiscuous women, thanks to the relatively new concept of moral imbecility, here making its formal debut as a subcategory of mental deficiency.

The 1913 Act and the eugenic proclamations regarding feeble-mindedness had a profound impact on the way idiocy – or mental deficiency – was understood. In her diary entry for 9 January 1915, Virginia Woolf tells of how, while out on a walk:

> on the towpath, we met & had to pass a long line of imbeciles. The first was a very tall young man, just queer enough to look at twice, but no more; the second shuffled, & looked aside; and then one realised that every one in that long line was a miserable ineffective shuffling idiotic creature, with no forehead, or no chin, & an imbecile grin, or a wild suspicious stare. It was perfectly horrible. They should certainly be killed. (See Bell 1977: 13)

While the first 'very tall young man' warranted only a glance, the 'long line' is repellent to Woolf, and one wonders how much the clustering of the apparently feeble-minded made the concept more disquieting by presenting the threat en masse. According to Childs (2001), this passage indicates the degree to which Woolf had absorbed extreme eugenicist arguments, and while I suspect that diary entries cannot be accorded the same weight as published writings, her passage recalls Arnold White's commentary on 'national efficiency' and the desirability of sterilization in his 1909 *Eugenics Review* article.[12]

The concept of mental deficiency serves a similar function to that which informed John Locke's 'changeling', as Chris Goodey has shown (1994, 1996): Locke's idiot, like the mentally deficient individual of 1913, forms the contrast group which, by being denied political rights, enables an argument for the extension of rights to others. In 1918, a mere five years after the passage of the legislation segregating those identified as mentally deficient, the Representation of the People Act tripled the number of eligible voters in Britain, but did not include the mentally deficient; as Thomson (1998) suggests, the paucity of parliamentary debate on the position of 'mental defectives' under the Representation of the People Act may indicate that MPs 'assumed that mental defectives were already automatically excluded from the franchise because of their permanent mental incompetence' (53), although prior to 1913 many of the 'feeble-minded' would have been undifferentiated members of those groups of people made eligible to vote in 1918. If democracy was to be extended to include all, then the mentally deficient, by their incapacities, forced the failure of that ideal; but their segregation is the pragmatic compromise that enables its partial realization. Indeed, the Mental Deficiency Act can be seen as the logical political outcome of Locke's isolation of the 'changeling' at the fringes of humanity over 200 years earlier (see Chapter 3). By the early twentieth century, the eugenic dream that mental deficiency could be bred out of the population expresses a desire to make the 'mentally deficient' literally disappear rather than to move them into segregated communities, thus pushing the reality of human diversity to conform to the social, political and philosophical theories that demanded these contrast groups in the first place.

For a moment let us consider the Mental Deficiency Act not as a pragmatic compromise but as a collision, a space where the ideals of the culture cannot cohere. The Act is the political equivalent of the explosion of Stevie in *The Secret Agent*, with Conrad's metaphysical faith in the eternal circles replaced by the promise of a hygienic society bequeathed to future generations. It may be the pragmatic solution to the question of how to share the responsibilities of a functioning society among a rational populace demanding more rights, while at the same time ensuring control over the health and well-being of the British nation and the British (or at least English) race. But, just as Conrad's metaphysical solution follows upon the death of Stevie, this political solution is not possible without the overt and enforced exclusion of a section of the population: those whose intellect is apparently deficient, whose morality is apparently suspect, whose hereditary legacy is apparently degenerate, and whose claims to an equal share of humanity is, thus, forfeit.

Notes

1 According to one of Ford's later accounts of the conversation, 'what the writer really did say to Conrad was: "Oh that fellow was half an idiot! His sister murdered her husband afterwards and was allowed to escape by the police. I remember the funeral..." The suicide was invented by Conrad. And the writer knew – and Conrad knew that the writer knew – a great many anarchists of the Goodge Street group, as well as a great many of the police who watched them. The writer had provided Conrad with Anarchist literature, with memoirs, with introductions to at least one Anarchist young lady who figures in the *Secret Agent*.... Indeed the writer's first poems were set up by that very young lady on an Anarchist printing press' (Ford 1924: 231). Ford had published his first poem in *The Torch*, a journal edited by Helen, Arthur and Olivia Rossetti, the teenage children of William Michael Rossetti (Sherry 1967), and which appears in the opening paragraphs of Conrad's novel as one of the journals sold at Verloc's shop. While Conrad may have invented the suicide of the bomber's sister, Ford invented her murder of her husband (Sherry 1967). Both Conrad and Ford are recalling the conversation fifteen to twenty years after it had taken place, a length of time which allows the memory plenty of opportunity to revise details.

2 The novel's many instances of Lombroso's theory and other physiognomic observations have been explored thoroughly by Allan Hunter (1983), who notes how Conrad uses Lombrosian ideas while taking issue with them. After the passage quoted here, Yundt dismisses Lombroso's science – and Ossipon's – as bourgeois folly.

3 Lori Kelly describes how this passage with the cab-horse in *The Secret Agent* was used by Charles Dana (1909) in his short article 'The Zoophil-Psychosis' in the *Medical Record* as an 'illustrative case study ... identifying a new kind of mental disorder – zoophil-psychosis' (Kelly 2003: 99), in which individuals showed an 'inordinate sympathy for animal suffering'. She argues that pathologizing sympathy for animal suffering enabled the medical establishment to equate anti-vivisectionists with 'mentally deficient individuals' (102). Of course, such pathologizing also creates an even more restrictive range of *non*-pathological behaviour, a tightening of the concept of normalcy.

4 Some literary critics have already identified certain Bergsonian influences in *The Secret Agent*, primarily in the relation of Conrad's use of comedy to theories Bergson develops in his 1900 work *Laughter*: see James F. English's 'Scientist, Moralist, Humorist: A Bergsonian Reading of *The Secret Agent*' (1987) and M. A. Gillies' 'Conrad's *The Secret Agent* and *Under Western Eyes* as Bergsonian Comedies' (1988). See also R. W. Stallman's 'Time and *The Secret Agent*' (1975).

5 Like many other writers on mental deficiency, Kirby also acknowledges that it appears in the best of intellectual families, but provides an intriguing mathematical rationale: 'we have the undoubted appearance, in families of an average ability high above the normal, of individuals much below the normal; denoting possibly the effort of nature to return to the mean' (p. 93). The suggestion that 'nature' exerts a mathematical will-power, rather than operating by simple random variation, belies a faith in statistics not as a measuring tool but as a prescriptive rule.

6 Tredgold's use of the Latin term 'amentia', denoting 'senselessness' or 'without mind' as a synonym for 'mental deficiency' (and in opposition to 'dementia') and his reference to 'aments' throughout his writing, is particularly striking; the use of the term was rare if not unprecedented in the field, and Tredgold's adoption of it marks an effort to solidify the scientific status of the field by employing a term remote from popular usage, as well as to stamp the field with his own peculiar nomenclature. The twelfth and final edition of his work, re-titled *Tredgold's Mental Retardation* and edited by Michael Craft, was published in 1979.

7 The Act applied specifically to England and Wales, and remained in force until it was supplanted by the Mental Health Act 1959; there was a separate Mental Deficiency (Scotland) Act in 1913.

8 In 1912, Josiah Wedgwood had joined G. K. Chesterton, H. G. Wells and Hilaire Belloc to form a short-lived Freedom Defence League (Wedgwood 1951); Belloc and Chesterton also used their journal *New Witness* as a vehicle for opposing the Act (Jackson 2000).

9 A number of writers have demonstrated how the 1913 Act sought to control the sexuality of women: see, for example, Walmsley (2000); Gladstone (1996); Saunders (1988); and Stainton (2000).

10 The term 'moral imbecile' was replaced by 'moral defective' in the 1927 amendment to the Act; according to Thomson (1998), this change 'reflected the view that a person should only be certified as a mental defective if he or she had a mental (intellectual) defect in the first place; the moral defect was to be only a secondary factor' (55). Some of the other amendments, though, made the law more restrictive: the condition that one should be proved 'mentally defective' from an early age was 'liberally reinterpreted to include those who had not been detected until 18; education authorities were given greater power to notify school leavers directly to the mental deficiency authorities; it was made easier to obtain care for defectives who came from homes where the care

was already adequate; and local authorities were compelled to provide training facilities in day centres for those defectives who remained in the community', writes Thomson (56).

11 The Act defined these terms as follows: idiots were 'persons so deeply defective in mind from birth or from an early age as to be unable to guard themselves against common physical dangers'; imbeciles were 'persons in whose case there exists from birth or from an early age mental defectiveness not amounting to idiocy, yet so pronounced that they are incapable of managing themselves or their affairs, or, in the case of children, of being taught to do so'; the feeble-minded were 'persons in whose case there exists from birth or from an early age mental defectiveness not amounting to imbecility, yet so pronounced that they require care, supervision, and control for their own protection or for the protection of others, or, in the case of children, that they by reason of such defectiveness appear to be permanently incapable of receiving proper benefit from the instruction of ordinary schools'; finally, moral imbeciles were 'persons who from an early age display some permanent mental defect coupled with strong vicious or criminal propensities on which punishment has little or no deterrent effect' (quoted in Davey 1914: 31–34).

12 Interestingly, on 17 January, just over a week later, Woolf's diary recounts a conversation with Marjorie Strachey in which Strachey confesses that she is in love with 'a married man! Jos Wedgwood!' 'We both gasped', writes Woolf (Bell 1977: 21); Wedgwood was, of course, the most vocal opponent of the 1913 Act. On Tuesday 19 January – ten days after meeting the 'long line of imbeciles' – Woolf announces that she is reading Dostoevsky's *The Idiot*. While there is not nearly enough evidence to demonstrate that Woolf's meeting with the imbeciles and the chance of her friend's love affair with Wedgwood would have led her to explore the artistic and philosophical potential of the idea of idiocy in *The Idiot*, it remains an interesting possibility. Shortly after these entries, in February 1915, Woolf's diary is disrupted for two years, in large part because she suffered a mental breakdown; it is not difficult to read her response to miserable imbeciles as a projection of her own anxieties about her mental coherence and efficiency.

Epilogue

Despite efforts to nail down its true being, to define its causes, its significance and its parameters, 'idiocy' has remained elusive. John Charles Bucknill admitted in 1873 that, notwithstanding his confidence that he did 'know what an idiot is', a definition might be difficult to render all the same. Forty years later, with the Mental Deficiency Act 1913, idiocy was subordinated under the newer banner of 'mental deficiency', and while the concepts designated by this new term may have seen their formal legal and medical status solidified thanks to both the Act itself and the enthusiasm of its supporters, in reality these notions remained as slippery, as contentious and as challenging to define as the 'idiocy' described by Bucknill. Consequently, these newer notions of mental deficiency did not pass unchallenged. 'A man is not an imbecile if only a Eugenist thinks so', G. K. Chesterton argued in his 1922 critique *Eugenics and Other Evils*:

> That which can condemn the abnormally foolish is not the abnormally clever, which is obviously a matter in dispute. That which can condemn the abnormally foolish is the normally foolish. It is when he begins to say and do things that even stupid people do not say or do, that we have a right to treat him as an exception and not the rule. It is only because we none of us profess to be anything more than man that we have authority to treat him as something less. (Chesterton 1922: 37–38)

In his criticism of the eugenic impulse given authority by the 1913 Act, Chesterton emphatically resists 'professional' notions (medical or otherwise) of mental deficiency, and especially the borderline categories of 'feeble-mindedness' and 'moral imbecility', in favour of socially based definitions, dependent upon public perception and consensus. 'It is as plain as the nose on Punch's face that no scientific man must be allowed to meddle with the public definition of madness', he insists. 'We call him in to tell us where it is or when it is. We could not do so, if we had not ourselves settled what it is' (42). And given the tendency of even the 'ablest and sanest' of doctors to have 'some little ... half-discovery of their own, as that oranges are bad for children, or that trees are dangerous in gardens', when these medical men set out to identify idiots, 'each man would have his favourite kind of idiot. Each doctor would be mad on his own madman' (53). Just such a motivation lies behind the eugenic impulse, he insists, albeit in a more sinister form:

> Feeblemindedness ... conveys nothing fixed and outside opinion. There is such a thing as mania, which has always been segregated; there is such a thing as idiotcy, which has always been segregated; but feeble-mindedness is a new phrase under which you might segregate anybody. (61)

In effect, he argued, the 1913 Act offered physicians (and others) the chance to isolate and segregate their own 'favourite kind of idiot' under the new and expansive formal category of mental deficiency, especially as 'feeble-minded' or 'mental imbeciles', categories given new status by the Act.

Chesterton's populist approach to defining mental deficiency hearkens back to the broadly social (and occasionally legal) criteria pre-dating the asylum movement and the professionalization of idiocy 'care and treatment'. All the same, the public 'we', that community which defines idiocy, imbecility and feeble-mindedness in Chesterton's ideal schema, remains a circumscribed 'we' for all its unprofessionalism: it is still a largely Anglo-Saxon, largely middle- and upper-class, largely masculine 'we' capable of singling out idiocy in which ideas of intelligence and its lack are filtered through notions of class, race or gender (among other markers of difference), and it remains the position from which, over history, a wide range of qualities have been denigrated as folly or idiocy.

Eugenic philosophies may or may not have been the driving engine behind the Mental Deficiency Act 1913, but the Act was enthusiastically received as a mechanism of social engineering, a means of bettering the national genetic stock, by many of its supporters. 'Feeble-mindedness' was, as Chesterton pointed out, a new category under which the state might isolate individuals, and the growth of this category, as a feasible way of perceiving and classifying certain people, was linked closely to social demographic movements such as the rise of urban immigration and urban poverty (themselves linked to shifting

economic environments), scientific theories of natural selection and degeneration, and the political lobbying of eugenicists, whose philosophy
prospered in the wake of these other factors. But, despite Chesterton's
claims to the contrary, at one time idiocy had also been a new category,
and had not always been segregated; even by Chesterton's own terms,
idiocy, as we have seen, would not have existed in a state fixed outside
opinion. The borders of idiocy have always been moveable, and the
condition has been defined by vastly different criteria from one place
and time to the next. And as with idiocy's borderlands, so also with
its heartland. While in each time and place we will find some people
who indeed require more assistance than others owing to the difficulties they experience in navigating the complexities of their world, the
fundamental meaning of idiocy, its primary being within a culture,
has shifted dramatically over the years, along with the qualities used
to define it. The fourteenth-century individual who is a 'private' man,
deprived of civil power, may or may not be the same as that individual
who becomes the legal and moral 'innocent'. And this person may
again be different from those 'degenerate' beings of the late nineteenth
and early twentieth century.

With the 1913 Act, idiocy was both reconfigured and expanded to
include new groups of people – but so had it been in the 1850s and
the following decades, with its growth as a subject of medical and
scientific interest, its comprehensive pathologization, and its reconceptualization as a threatening degeneracy; so had it been in the first
half of the nineteenth century, with the transformation of local econo-
mies brought about by the industrial revolution, and the subsequent
demand for new kinds of labourers; so had it been in the sixteenth
century, when the nascent merchant classes began to have family
members legally declared 'idiots', just as the gentry had done since the
thirteenth century, and when 'folly' had designated everything from a
vaguely recognizable 'witlessness' to atheism to dwarfism to a particular thespian demeanour.

Idiocy's symbolic meaning also proves to be a moving target. For
Wordsworth, looking at a disappearing rural England, Johnny Foy fits
snugly within, and acts as one representative of, the inclusive community that is being threatened by the spinning gears of industrial
change. In the early 1840s, the push to educate 'idiots' and bring
them into the social, moral and economic life of the nation follows
from a number of factors, including this shifting economic landscape,
with its emphasis on industrial production, an environment within
which 'idiocy' would become a more explicit and dramatic problem
than it had been previously. The traditional countryside might be

characterized by a pervasive 'idiocy of rural life', in Karl Marx's memor-
ably dismissive phrase (1848: 84), but in the new and primarily urban
economy there were machines to operate, schedules to follow, jobs
to compete for. Those who did not succeed in this new world would
become more visible than they ever were in an agrarian community,
and more 'disabled' in competition. The effort to minimize this dis-
advantage by educating the idiot and making him a productive member
of society – an effort fed by both Christian and economic impulses – led
to the creation of institutions through which the people so designated
could be transformed and welcomed to undertake their full responsibilities in the commonwealth. But the prosperity of the latter half of
the nineteenth century became concentrated into fewer hands, leaving
vast numbers of people struggling to stay alive in rapidly expanding urban centres, and in this context idiocy becomes emblematic of
failure. Increasingly, it is also seen as the cause: the idiot becomes the
face of poverty, the promise of degeneration, the wellspring of criminality. And each of these shifts in the symbolic function of idiocy is
accompanied by shifts in the criteria for identifying people as idiots, or,
later, mentally defective. The idea of idiocy is changeable – its borders
move and its meanings shift very much according to where and when
one is standing while observing the phenomenon.

As I have argued, these changes are often most evident in the cultural representations of idiocy, which do not presume objectivity or
spin a narrative of medical progress, but instead use the idea of idiocy
as a tool to perform certain acts, to convey certain kinds of information. When writers insert an 'idiot' character into their narratives,
that character has a job: to portray certain aspects of humanity; to
evoke abstract notions – such as love, or compassion, or fear – that are
more easily intuited than rationally understood; to symbolize certain
abstractions related to God, the devil, the innocent or the degenerate;
to express possibilities of relations between individuals or (as in the
late nineteenth century) between different social classes, 'races' and
even species. This list is not exhaustive, but rather indicative of the
versatility of the image of idiocy across time and space. At any given
time, in any given context, the symbolic possibilities of idiocy are
shaped by their environment. These symbolic possibilities also lurk in
the subtext of professional discourses, where they appear much more
covertly than in cultural texts. The medical concept of idiocy, while
identifying certain individuals who need extra assistance or support
in their lives, is also a tool, used by physicians and others to convey
information and suppositions about the viability and significance of
certain people in different contexts: these professional formulations of

idiocy also portray certain aspects of humanity, evoke abstract notions, express relations between individuals, groups and divinities. The professional, social and cultural understandings of idiocy are not separate things: they share common sources and perform common functions.

I believe that historical study has an important role to play in current attempts to reimagine the idea of 'intellectual disability' and its various conceptual siblings. Recent years have seen a growing number of opportunities for people identified as having intellectual or learning disabilities to participate in the processes and discourses that help shape their lives, in areas including social policy development and management of resources (Stainton and Boyce 2004), academic research (Walmsley 2001) and social and cultural self-representation (Atkinson and Walmsley 1999; Atkinson and Williams 1990; Dybwad and Bersani 1996; Hevey 1992). This change has grown with the move, beginning in the 1970s, from institutional to community-based living arrangements and support services. And, as in the nineteenth century, this shift is intimately linked to a number of other factors: a growing discourse of civil and human rights seeking to create a space for people identified as having intellectual or learning disabilities, initially led by parents and other support providers (Bérubé 1998, 2003; Stainton 1994); a new sense of pedagogical and social possibilities offered by models such as 'normalization' (Wolfensberger 1972); a rearticulation of philosophical notions of identity focusing on models of interdependence and assessments of vulnerability (Greenspan 2006); a displacement of control from physical efforts at segregation to scientific efforts at genetic screening, which moves the eugenic moment from post-natal control to pre-natal (Duster 2003); and economic and demographic shifts that have altered the feasibility of large institutions.

The last factor is often overlooked, but is significant all the same: most large institutions were built in the nineteenth century, on land that was relatively close to urban centres, but still distant enough to have space for subsistence farming and gardening (Conolly 1847; Park and Radford 1999). But with the expansion of cities and the growth of public transport, these institutions now rest upon prime real estate. The Earlswood asylum – eventually known as the Royal Earlswood Hospital – closed its doors in 1992. A few short years later, the facilities were sold to developers, and today Royal Earlswood Park offers luxury housing at a reasonable price a mere forty minutes from downtown London. It is still an institution, with rules defining good behaviour posted at various points on its grounds, but now it is inhabited by young professionals climbing onto the property ladder. Nothing about Royal Earlswood Park today acknowledges its role as a model institution, the first and the largest of its genre in Britain, meant to transform the place of the 'poor idiot' in society.

'Idiocy' has a history, but for too long has been accepted as a stable and non-problematic medical and social category, unworthy of analysis or criticism. My main objective with this book has been to demonstrate that the idea of idiocy is neither timeless nor a purely objective quality of those people defined as idiots – who, thus, might be the earthly incarnations of ideal, transcendent idiots – but rather a notion constituted by a number of discourses, some quite remote from the individuals who end up being designated as 'idiots', and one which performs important symbolic, ideological labour in professional, social and cultural narratives. To demonstrate this argument, I have tracked how idiocy changes and moves, primarily by focusing on nineteenth-century Britain, though with a few brief forays into other times and other places. Within these constraints, I have tried to isolate at least some of the factors involved in the representational and ideological transformation of the idiot: the growing importance of sentiment and sympathy as tools for imagining and structuring human relations; the development of new pedagogical strategies and policies; the changes in the economic and demographic structures of English society, such as the growth of cities, the increase in the poor and working classes, the influx of (primarily Irish) immigrants, and concern about criminal tendencies being nurtured in the rookeries of London and other urban centres; the growth of the medical profession and its interest in idiocy, an accidental offshoot of Itard's philosophical explorations with Victor of Aveyron; the centralized paternalism of the asylum movement; the development of scientific theories of evolution and degeneration, and the subsequent agitation for eugenic policies. Out of these many and disparate threads, the nineteenth-century ideas of idiocy were woven. And out of similar materials we continue to weave our own motley beliefs about intelligence, intellectual disability and the difference between them.

Bibliography

The editions quoted in the text are noted in parentheses after the sources.

Ackroyd, Peter (1990) *Dickens*, New York: HarperCollins.

Andrews, Jonathan (1996) 'Identifying and Providing for the Mentally Disabled in Early Modern London', in David Wright and Anne Digby, eds, *From Idiocy to Mental Deficiency: Historical Perspectives on People with Learning Disabilities*, Studies in the Social History of Medicine, London: Routledge, pp. 65–92.

Andrews, Jonathan (1998a) 'Begging the Question of Idiocy: The Definition and Socio-Cultural Meaning of Idiocy in Early Modern Britain: Part 1', *History of Psychiatry*, 9: 65–95.

Andrews, Jonathan (1998b) 'Begging the Question of Idiocy: The Definition and Socio-Cultural Meaning of Idiocy in Early Modern Britain: Part 2', *History of Psychiatry*, 9: 179–200.

Annan, N. G. (1955) 'The Intellectual Aristocracy', in J. H. Plumb, ed., *Studies in Social History: A Tribute to G. M. Trevelyan*, London: Longmans, Green, pp. 241–87.

Anonymous (1613) *Tarlton's Jests*, London.

Anonymous (1747) *The Case of Henry Roberts, Esq, a Gentleman, who, by unparalleled Cruelty was deprived of his Estate, under the Pretence of Idiocy*. London.

Anonymous (1858) 'Cretins and Idiots: What Has Been Done and What Can Be Done For Them', *Atlantic Monthly*, February: 410–19.

Anonymous (1865a) 'Idiot Asylums', *Edinburgh Review*, 122 (July): 37–74.

Anonymous (1865b) 'The Psychology of Idiocy', *Journal of Mental Science*, 11: 1–32.

Anonymous (1866a) 'Deterioration of Race', *The Lancet*, 23 June: 691–92.

Anonymous (1866b) 'Race Degeneration', *The Lancet*, 17 February: 181.

Anonymous (1866c) 'Idiot Asylums', *Journal of Mental Science*, 11: 607–8.

Anonymous (1876) 'Idiots and Imbeciles', *Journal of Mental Science*, 22: 503–5.

Anstie, Francis Edmund (1865) 'Insane Patients in London Workhouses', *Journal of Mental Science*, 11: 327–36.

Archer, Thomas (1865) *The Pauper, the Thief, and the Convict; Sketches of Some of Their Homes, Haunts, and Habits*. (London: Garland, 1985.)

Archer, Thomas (1870) *The Terrible Sights of London and Labours of Love in the Midst of Them*, London: Stanley Rivers.

Arieno, Marlene (1989) *Victorian Lunatics: A Social Epidemiology of Mental Illness in Nineteenth-Century England*, Selinsgrove, PA: Susquehanna University Press.

Aristotle. *The Politics.* (T. A. Sinclair, trans., Harmondsworth: Penguin, 1962.)

Armin, Robert (1600) *Foole Upon Foole.* (H. F. Lippincott, ed., Studies in English Literature, Elizabethan Studies 20, Salzburg: Institut für Englische Sprach und Literatur, 1979.)

Armin, Robert (1608) *A Nest of Ninnies.* (Incorporated within H. F. Lippincott's edition of *Foole Upon Foole*, Studies in English Literature, Elizabethan Studies 20, Salzburg: Institut für Englische Sprach und Literatur, 1979.)

Armin, Robert (1609) *The History of the Two Maids of More-Clacke.* (Alexander S. Liddie, ed., New York: Garland, 1979.)

Astell, Mary (1696) *An Essay in Defence of the Female Sex in Which Are Inserted the Characters of a Pedant, a Squire, a Beau, a Vertuoso, a Poetaster, a City-Critick, & c.: In a Letter to a Lady/Written by a Lady*, London.

Atkinson, Doris and Jan Walmsley (1999) 'Using Autobiographical Approaches with People with Learning Disabilities', *Disability and Society*, 14: 203–16.

Atkinson, Doris and F. Williams, eds (1990) *Know Me As I Am: An Anthology of Prose, Poetry and Art by People with Learning Difficulties*, Sevenoaks: Hodder and Stoughton.

Austen, Jane (1818) *Northanger Abbey.* (Harmondsworth: Penguin, 1972.)

Bakhtin, Mikhail (1984) *Rabelais and His World*, Hélène Iswolsky, trans., Bloomington, IN: Indiana University Press.

Barickman, Robert, Susan MacDonald and Myra Stark (1982) *Corrupt Relations: Dickens, Thackeray, Trollope, Collins and the Victorian Sexual System*, New York: Columbia University Press.

Barker-Benfield, G. J. (1976) *The Horrors of the Half-Known Life: Male Attitudes Toward Women and Sexuality in Nineteenth-Century America*, New York: Harper and Row.

Barker-Benfield, G. J. (1992) *The Culture of Sensibility: Sex and Society in Eighteenth-Century Britain*, Chicago, IL: University of Chicago Press.

Barr, Martin (1904) *Mental Defectives: Their History, Treatment and Training*, Philadelphia, PA: Blakiston's Son & Co.

Barrett, Michael Anthony (1986) 'From Special Education to Segregation: An Inquiry into the Changing Character of Special Provision for the Retarded in England, c. 1846–1918', PhD Dissertation, University of Lancaster.

Beach, Fletcher (1885) 'A Case of Idiocy with Well-Marked Hereditary History', *Journal of Mental Science*, 31: 198–200.

Beames, Thomas (1850) *The Rookeries of London.* (London: Frank Cass, 1970.)

Beer, Gillian (1996) *Open Fields: Science in Cultural Encounter*, Oxford: Clarendon Press.

Bell, Anne Olivier, ed. (1977) *The Diary of Virginia Woolf, Vol. I: 1915–1919*, London: Hogarth.

Bell, H. E. (1953) *An Introduction to the History and Records of the Court of Wards and Liveries*, Cambridge: Cambridge University Press.

Benedict, Barbara M. (1994) *Framing Feeling: Sentiment and Style in English Prose Fiction 1745–1800*, New York: AMS Press.

Bennett, Jennifer (1982) 'The London Democratic Association 1837–1841: A Study in London Radicalism', in James Epstein and Dorothy Thompson, eds, *The Chartist Experience: Studies in Working-Class Radicalism and Culture, 1830–1860*, London: Macmillan, pp. 87–119.

Bergson, Henri (1900) *Rire.* (Cloudesley Brereton and Fred Rothwell, trans., *Laughter: An Essay on the Meaning of the Comic*, London: Macmillan, 1911.)

Bergson, Henri (1907) *Creative Evolution*. (Arthur Mitchell, trans., Everyman Library, New York: Modern Library, 1944.)

Bérubé, Michael (1998) *Life As We Know It: A Father, a Family, and an Exceptional Child*, New York: Random House.

Bérubé, Michael (2003) 'Citizenship and Disability', *Dissent*, 48 (spring): 52–57.

Bewell, Alan (1989) *Wordsworth and the Enlightenment: Nature, Man, and Society in the Experimental Poetry*, New Haven, CT: Yale University Press.

Bigelow, Gordon (2003) *Fiction, Famine, and the Rise of Economics in Victorian Britain and Ireland*, Cambridge: Cambridge University Press.

Billington, Sandra (1984) *A Social History of the Fool*. Brighton: Harvester.

Binet, Alfred and Theodore Simon (1905) 'Méthodes nouvelles pour le diagnositic du niveau intellectuel des anormaux', *L'Année Psychologique*, 11: 191–244.

Binet, Alfred and Theodore Simon (1913) *A Method of Measuring the Development of Intelligence in Young Children*, Clara Harrison Town, trans., Chicago, IL: Chicago Medical Book Co.

Blount, Thomas (1670) *Nomolexikon: A Law-Dictionary*, London.

Bock, Martin (2002) *Joseph Conrad and Psychological Medicine*, Lubbock, TX: Texas Tech University Press.

Bogdan, Robert (1988) *Freak Show: Presenting Human Oddities for Amusement and Profit*, Chicago, IL: University of Chicago Press.

Bogdan, Robert and Steven J. Taylor (1982) *Inside Out: The Social Meaning of Mental Retardation*, Toronto: University of Toronto Press.

Bonnaterre, Pierre-Joseph (1800) *Notice Historique sur le Sauvage de l'Aveyron et sur quelques autres individus qu'on a trouvés dans les forêts, à differentes époques.* (In Thierry Gineste, *Victor de l'Aveyron, Dernier enfant sauvage, premier enfant fou*, Paris: Hachette, 2004, pp. 239–79.)

Booth, Charles (1889) *Life and Labour of the People in London*. (First Series: Poverty, Vol. I, London: Macmillan, 1904.)

Bosanquet, Helen (1914) *Social Work in London 1869–1912: A History of the Charity Organisation Society*. (Brighton: Harvester, 1973.)

Bowler, Peter (1989) *The Invention of Progress: The Victorians and the Past*, Cambridge: Basil Blackwell.

Boyle, Marjorie O'Rourke (1985) 'Fools and Schools: Scholastic Dialectic, Humanist Rhetoric; From Anselm to Erasmus', *Medievalia et Humanistica*, n.s. 13: 173–95.

Boyle, Thomas (1989) *Black Swine in the Sewers of Hampstead: Beneath the Surface of Victorian Sensationalism*, New York: Viking.

Braddon, Mary Elizabeth (1863) *Aurora Floyd*. (Oxford: Oxford University Press, 1996.)

Brain, Sir Russell (1960) *Some Reflections on Genius and Other Essays*, Philadelphia, PA: Lippincott.

Brant, Sebastian (1494) *The Ship of Fools*. (Edwin H. Zeydel, trans., New York: Dover, 1962.)

Brantlinger, Patrick (1968) 'The Case Against Trade Unions in Early Victorian Fiction', *Victorian Studies*, 13: 37–52.

Brantlinger, Patrick (2001) 'Did Dickens Have a Philosophy of History? The Case of *Barnaby Rudge*', *Dickens Studies Annual*, 30: 59–74.

Brett, R. L. and A. R. Jones, eds (1991) *Wordsworth and Coleridge. Lyrical Ballads*, London: Routledge.

Briggs, Asa (1967) 'The Language of "Class" in Early Nineteenth-Century England', in A. Briggs and J. Saville, eds, *Essays in Labour History*, London: Macmillan, pp. 43–73. (Reprinted in M. W. Flinn and T. C. Smout, eds, *Essays in Social History*, Oxford: Clarendon, 1974, pp. 154–77.)

Brontë, Charlotte (1853) *Villette*. (Oxford: Clarendon, 1984.)
Brown, William (1911) *The Essentials of Mental Measurement*, Cambridge: Cambridge University Press.
Browne, W. A. F. (1861) 'Endemic Degeneration', *Journal of Mental Science*, 7: 61–76.
Bucknill, John Charles (1873) 'Address on Idiocy', *Journal of Mental Science*, 19: 169–83.
Buffon, Comte de (George-Louis Leclerc) (1855) *Oeuvres Completes De Buffon, Vol. IV: Histoire naturelle des animaux*, Paris: Garnier Frères.
Bunyan, John (1678/84) *The Pilgrim's Progress*. (London: Oxford University Press, 1959.)
Burgoyne, Mary (2007) 'Conrad Among the Anarchists: Documents on Martial Bourdin and the Greenwich Bombing', in Allan H. Simmons and J. H. Stape, eds, *The Secret Agent: Centennial Essays*, Amsterdam: Editions Rodopi and the Joseph Conrad Society, pp. 147–85.
Burney, Frances (1796) *Camilla*. (London: Oxford University Press, 1972.)
Butler, Marilyn (1981) *Romantics, Rebels and Reactionaries: English Literature and Its Background, 1760–1830*, Oxford: Oxford University Press.
Butt, John, ed. (1963) *The Poems of Alexander Pope*, New Haven, CT: Yale University Press.
Butt, John and Kathleen Tillotson (1957) *Dickens at Work*, London: Methuen.
Cadogan, William (1748) *An Essay Upon Nursing and the Management of Children, From Their Birth to Three Years of Age*, London.
Candland, Douglas Keith (1993) *Feral Children and Clever Animals: Reflections on Human Nature*, Oxford: Oxford University Press.
Cantlie, James (1885) *Degeneration Amongst Londoners*. (New York: Garland, 1985.)
Carlyle, Thomas (1839) 'Chartism'. (In Alan Shelston, ed., *Thomas Carlyle: Selected Writings*, Harmondsworth: Penguin, 1971, pp. 149–232.)
Carnell, Geoffrey (1956) '"The Idiot Boy"', *Notes and Queries*, 201: 81–82.
Carpenter, Peter (2000a) 'The Bath Idiot and Imbecile Institution', *History of Psychiatry*, 11: 163–88.
Carpenter, Peter (2000b) 'The Victorian Small Idiot Homes Near Bath', *History of Psychiatry*, 11: 383–92.
Carpenter, Peter (2001) 'The Role of Victorian Women in the Care of "Idiots" and the "Feebleminded"', *Journal on Developmental Disabilities*, 8(2): 31–43.
Case, Alison (1990) 'Against Scott: The Antihistory of Dickens' Barnaby Rudge', *Clio*, 19: 127–45.
Chadwick, Edwin (1842) *Report on the Sanitary Condition of the Labouring Population of Great Britain*. (Edinburgh: Edinburgh University Press, 1965.)
Chaloner, Thomas, trans. (1549) Desiderius Erasmus, *The Praise of Folie*. (Early English Text Society. London: Oxford University Press, 1965.)
Chambers, Robert (1853) *Vestiges of the Natural History of Creation*, 10th edition, London: John Churchill.
Chapman, Raymond (1970) *Faith and Revolt: Studies in the Literary Influence of the Oxford Movement*, London: Weidenfeld and Nicolson.
Charon, Rita (1992) 'To Build a Case: Medical Histories as Traditions in Conflict', *Literature and Medicine*, 11: 115–32.
Chartier, Roger (1988) *Cultural History: Between Practices and Representations*, Lydia G. Cochrane, trans., Ithaca, NY: Cornell University Press.
Chesterton, G. K. (1922) *Eugenics and Other Evils*, London: Cassell.
Cheyne, George (1733) *The English Malady, or a Treatise of Nervous Diseases of All Kinds*. (London: Routledge, 1991.)

Childs, Donald (2001) *Modernism and Eugenics: Woolf, Eliot, Yeats, and the Culture of Degeneration*, Cambridge: Cambridge University Press.

Christian, Mildred (1947a) 'Carlyle's Influence Upon the Social Theory of Dickens: Part One', *The Trollopian*, 1: 27–35.

Christian, Mildred (1947b) 'Carlyle's Influence Upon the Social Theory of Dickens: Part Two', *The Trollopian*, 2: 11–26.

Clark, Sir James (1869) *A Memoir of John Conolly, M.D., D.C.L., Comprising a Sketch of the Treatment of the Insane in Europe and America*, London: John Murray.

Clark, Katherine (2007) *Daniel Defoe: The Whole Frame of Nature, Time and Providence*, Basingstoke: Palgrave Macmillan.

Clarke, Basil (1975) *Mental Disorder in Earlier Britain: Exploratory Studies*, Cardiff: University of Wales Press.

Cleland, John (1748/49) *Fanny Hill, or Memoirs of a Woman of Pleasure.* (Harmondsworth: Penguin, 1985.)

Cobb, Frances Power (1868) 'Criminals, Idiots, Women and Minors: Is the Classification Sound?' (In Barbara Dennis and David Skilton, eds, *Reform and Intellectual Debate in Victorian England*, London: Croom Helm, 1987, pp. 148–51.)

Coghill, Mrs Harry, ed. (1974) *Autobiography and Letters of Mrs. Margaret Oliphant*, Leicester: Leicester University Press.

Colby, Vineta and Robert A. Colby (1966) *The Equivocal Virtue: Mrs. Oliphant and the Victorian Literary Market Place*, Hamden, CT: Archon Books.

Collier, John Payne (1842) *Fools and Jesters, with a Reprint of Robert Armin's Nest of Ninnies (1608)*, London: Shakespeare Society.

Collins, Wilkie (1862) *No Name.* (Oxford: Oxford University Press, 1986.)

Collins, Wilkie (1875) *The Law and the Lady.* (Oxford: Oxford University Press, 1992.)

Cominos, Peter T. (1963) 'Late Victorian Sexual Respectability and the Social System', *International Review of Social History*, 8: 18–48; 216–50.

Conolly, John (1845) 'Notices of the Lunatic Asylums of Paris', *British and Foreign Medical Review*, 19: 281–98.

Conolly, John (1847) *The Construction and Government of Lunatic Asylums and Hospitals for the Insane.* (London: Dawsons of Pall Mall, 1968.)

Conolly, John (1849) 'On the Management of Hanwell Lunatic Asylum', *Journal of Psychological Medicine and Mental Pathology*, 2: 424–27.

Conrad, Jessie (1935) *Joseph Conrad and His Circle*, 2nd edition. (Port Washington, NY: Kennikat Press, 1964.)

Conrad, Joseph (1898) 'The Idiots', in *Tales of Unrest.* (New York: Doubleday, Page & Company, 1923, pp. 56–85.)

Conrad, Joseph (1907) *The Secret Agent.* (Harmondsworth: Penguin, 1990.)

Copans, Jean and Jean Jamin, eds (1978) Philippe Pinel, 'Rapport fait à la Société des Observateurs de l'Homme sur l'enfant connu sous le nom de sauvage de l'Aveyron', *Aux origines de l'anthropologie française: Les Memoires de la Société des Observateurs de l'Homme en l'an VIII*, Paris: Sycomore, pp. 87–113.

Cowell, John (1607) *The Interpreter: or Booke Containing the Signification of Words*, Cambridge.

Cox, Pamela (1996) 'Girls, Deficiency and Delinquency', in David Wright and Anne Digby, eds, *From Idiocy to Deficiency: Historical Perspectives on People with Learning Disabilities*, London: Routledge, pp. 184–206.

Craft, Michael, ed. (1979) *Tredgold's Mental Retardation*, London: Ballière Tindall.

Crawford, Iain (1991) '"Nature ... Drenched in Blood": *Barnaby Rudge* and Wordsworth's "Idiot Boy"', *Dickensian Quarterly*, 8: 38–47.

Crookshank, F. G. (1924) *The Mongol in Our Midst: A Study of Man and His Three Faces*, To-Day and To-Morrow Series, New York: E. P. Dutton.

Dale, Pamela and Joseph Melling, eds (2006) *Mental Illness and Learning Disability since 1850: Finding a Place for Mental Disorder in the United Kingdom*, London: Routledge.

Dale, Peter Allan (1985) 'George Eliot's "Brother Jacob": Fables and the Physiology of Common Life', *Philological Quarterly*, 64: 17–35.

Daly, Nicholas (1999) 'Railway Novels: Sensation Fiction and the Modernization of the Senses', *English Literary History*, 66: 461–87.

Dana, Charles (1909) 'The Zoophil-Psychosis', *Medical Record*, 6 March: 75.

Darwin Charles (1859) *On the Origin of Species by Means of Natural Selection, or the Preservation of Favoured Races in the Struggle for Life*, London: John Murray.

Darwin, Charles (1871) *The Descent of Man, and Selection in Relation to Sex*. (Princeton, NJ: Princeton University Press, 1981.)

Darwin, Leonard (1926) *The Need for Eugenic Reform*, London: John Murray.

Davey, Herbert (1914) *The Law Relating to the Mentally Defective*. (New York: Da Capo, 1981.)

David, Deirdre (1990) 'Rewriting the Male Plot in Wilkie Collins's *No Name*: Captain Wragge Orders an Omelette and Mrs. Wragge Goes into Custody', in Laura Claridge and Elizabeth Langland, eds, *Out of Bounds: Male Writers and Gender(ed) Criticism*, Amherst, MA: University of Massachusetts Press, pp. 186–96.

Davie, Neil (2005) *Tracing the Criminal: The Rise of Scientific Criminology in Britain 1860–1918*, Oxford: Bardwell.

Davis, Jana (1989) 'Sir Walter Scott and Enlightenment Theories of Imagination: Waverley and Quentin Durward', *Nineteenth-Century Literature*, 43(4): 437–64.

Davis, Lennard J. (1995) *Enforcing Normalcy: Disability, Deafness and the Body*, London: Verso.

Davis, Natalie Zemon (1975) *Society and Culture in Early Modern France*, Stanford, CA: Stanford University Press.

De Cusa, Nicholas (1440) *The Idiot in Four Books*. (John Everard, trans., London, 1650.)

De Gérando, Joseph-Marie (1800) *Considérations sur les diverses methods à suivre dans l'observation des peoples sauvages*. (F. C. T. Moore, trans., *The Observation of Savage Peoples*, Berkeley, CA: University of California Press, 1969.)

De Gérando, Joseph-Marie (1848) 'Considérations sur le sauvage de l'Aveyron', *Annales de l'éducation des sourds-muets et des aveugles*, 5: 110–18.

De la Bere, R., ed. (1970) 'Wytty and Wyttles', in *John Heywood, Entertainer*, London: Unwin, pp. 115–43.

De Selincourt, Ernest, ed. (1935) *The Early Letters of William and Dorothy Wordsworth (1787–1805)*, Oxford: Clarendon.

Defoe, Daniel (1697) *An Essay Upon Projects*. (Scholar Press Facsimile, Menston: Scolar Press, 1969.)

Dendy, Mary (1911) 'On the Training and Treatment of Feebleminded Children', in C. Paget Lapage, *Feeblemindedness in Children of School Age*, Manchester: Manchester University Press, pp. 243–96.

Dennis, Barbara (1992) *Charlotte Yonge (1823–1901): Novelist of the Oxford Movement*, Lewiston, NY: Edwin Mellen.

Dennis, Ian (1997) *Nationalism and Desire in Early Historical Fiction*, Houndmills: Macmillan.

Dewhurst, Kenneth, ed. (1980) Thomas Willis, *Willis' Oxford Lectures*, Oxford: Sanford Publications.

Dickens, Charles (1839) *Nicholas Nickleby*. (Harmondsworth: Penguin, 1999.)

Dickens, Charles (1841) *Barnaby Rudge, a Tale of the Riots of '80*. (Harmondsworth: Penguin, 1973.)

Dickens, Charles (1850) *David Copperfield*. (Harmondsworth: Penguin, 1985.)

Dickens, Charles (1857) *Little Dorrit*. (Harmondsworth: Penguin, 1985.)

Donnelly, Michael (1983) *Managing the Mind: A Study of Medical Psychology in Early Nineteenth-Century Britain*, London: Tavistock.

Douthwaite, Julia (1994/95) 'Rewriting the Savage: The Extraordinary Fictions of the "Wild Girl of Champagne"', *Eighteenth-Century Studies*, 28: 163–92.

Douthwaite, Julia (1997) 'Homo ferus: Between Monster and Model', *Eighteenth-Century Life*, 20: 176–202.

Down, John Langdon (1866) 'Observations on an Ethnic Classification of Idiots', *London Hospital Reports*, 3, 259–62; also *Journal of Mental Science*, 13 (1867): 121–23.

Down, John Langdon (1867) 'Review: *Idiocy and its Treatment by the Physiological Method*, by Edward Seguin', *Journal of Mental Science*, 13: 188–96.

Down, John Langdon (1887) *On Some of the Mental Affections of Childhood and Youth. Being the Lettsomian Lectures Delivered Before the Medical Society of London in 1887 Together with Other Papers*. (London: MacKeith Press, 1990.)

Dransfield, Scott (1998) 'Reading the Gordon Riots in 1841: Social Violence and Moral Management in *Barnaby Rudge*', *Dickens Studies Annual*, 27: 69–95.

Ducray-Duminil, François-Guillaume (1796) *Victor, L'enfant De La Forêt*, 3 vols, Paris.

Dugdale, Richard L. (1877) *The Jukes: A Study in Crime, Pauperism, Disease, and Heredity*, New York: Putnam.

Duncan, Ian (1992) *Modern Romance and Transformations of the Novel: The Gothic, Scott, and Dickens*, Cambridge: Cambridge University Press.

Duncan, P. Martin, M. B. Lond, *et al.* (1861) 'Notes on Idiocy', *Journal of Mental Science*, 7: 232–52.

Duncan, P. Martin and William Millard (1866) *A Manual for the Classification, Training and Education of the Feeble-Minded, Imbecile and Idiotic*, London: Longmans, Green & Co.

Duster, Troy (2003) *Backdoor to Eugenics*, 2nd edition, London: Routledge.

Duthie, Elizabeth (1978) 'A Fresh Comparison of "The Idiot Boy" and "The Idiot"', *Notes and Queries*, 223: 219–20.

Dybwad, Gunnar (1996) 'Setting the Stage Historically', in Gunnar Dybwad and Hank Bersani Jr, eds, *New Voices: Self-Advocacy by People with Disabilities*, Cambridge, MA: Brookline Books, pp. 1–17.

Dybwad, Gunnar and Hank Bersani Jr, eds (1996) *New Voices: Self-Advocacy by People with Disabilities*, Cambridge, MA: Brookline Books.

Eagleton, Terry (1986) *Against the Grain: Selected Essays*, London: Verso.

Easson, Angus (1979) *Elizabeth Gaskell*, London: Routledge.

Eliot, George (1860) *Brother Jacob*. (London: Virago, 1989.)

Eliot, George (1862/63) *Romola*. (Oxford: Oxford University Press, 1994.)

Ellis, Havelock (1909) 'The sterilisation of the unfit', *Eugenics Review*, 1: 203.

Ellis, Havelock (1912) *The Task of Social Hygiene*, London: Constable.

Empson, William (1966) *Some Versions of the Pastoral*, Harmondsworth: Penguin.

Engell, J. and W. J. Bate, eds (1983) *Biographia Literaria. The Collected Works of Samuel Taylor Coleridge No. 7*, Princeton, NJ: Princeton University Press.

English, James F. (1987) 'Scientist, Moralist, Humorist: A Bergsonian Reading of *The Secret Agent*', *Conradiana*, 19: 139–56.

Erasmus, Desiderius (1511) *Praise of Folly*. (Betty Radice, trans., Harmondsworth: Penguin, 1971.)

Erasmus, Desiderius (1511) *Stultitiae Laus*. (John F. Collins, ed., Bryn Mawr Latin Commentaries, Brwn Mawr, PA: Brwn Mawr College, 1991.)

Erdinast-Vulcan, Daphna (1996) '"Signifying nothing": Conrad's Idiots and the Anxiety of Modernism', *Studies in Short Fiction*, 33: 185–95.

Esquirol, Étienne (1838) *Des Maladies mentales*. (E. K. Hunt, trans., *Mental Maladies: A Treatise on Insanity*, Philadelphia, PA: Lea and Blanchard, 1845.)

Ettin, Andrew Vogel (1998) 'Will Somers', in Vicki K. Janik, ed., *Fools and Jesters in Literature, Art, and History: A Bio-Bibliographical Sourcebook*, Westport, CT: Greenwood, pp. 406–10.

Faught, C. Brad (2003) *The Oxford Movement: A Thematic History of the Tractarians and Their Times*, University Park, PA: Pennsylvania State University Press.

Felver, Charles (1961) *Robert Armin, Shakespeare's Fool*, Research Series V, Kent, OH: Kent State University Bulletin.

Ferguson, Philip (1994) *Abandoned to Their Fate: A History of Social Policy and Practice Toward Severely Retarded People in America, 1820–1920*, Philadelphia, PA: Temple University Press.

Ferris, Ina (1991) *The Achievement of Literary Authority: Gender, History, and the Waverley Novels*, Ithaca, NY: Cornell University Press.

Fitzherbert, Sir Anthony (1652) *The New Natura Brevium*, London.

Fleishman, Avrom (1967) *Conrad's Politics: Community and Anarchy in the Fiction of Joseph Conrad*, Baltimore, MD: Johns Hopkins Press.

Ford, Ford Madox (1911) *Ancient Lights and Certain New Reflections*, London: Chapman & Hall.

Ford, Ford Madox (1924) *Joseph Conrad: A Personal Remembrance*, London: Duckworth.

Ford, Ford Madox (1932) *Return to Yesterday*, New York: Horace Liveright.

Forster, John (1872) *The Life of Charles Dickens, Vol. I: 1812–1842*, Philadelphia, PA: Lippincott.

Fothergill, J. Milner (1889) *The Town Dweller: His Needs and His Wants*. (New York: Garland, 1985.)

Foucault, Michel (1961) *Madness and Civilization: A History of Insanity in the Age of Reason*. (Richard Howard, trans., New York: Vintage, 1973.)

Foucault, Michel (1969) *The Archaeology of Knowledge & the Discourse on Language*. (A. M. Sheridan Smith, trans., New York: Pantheon, 1972.)

Fraser, Derek (2003) *The Evolution of the British Welfare State*, 3rd edition, Houndmills: Palgrave Macmillan.

Fraser, John and Arthur Mitchell (1876) 'Kalmuc Idiocy: Report of a Case with Autopsy, by John Fraser, With Notes on Sixty-Two Cases, by Arthur Mitchell', *Journal of Mental Science*, 22: 169–79.

Frith, Uta (1989) *Autism: Explaining the Enigma*, Cambridge: Blackwell.

Furbank, P. N. and W. R. Owens (2006) *A Political Biography of Daniel Defoe*, London: Pickering & Chatto.

Gallagher, Catherine (1985) *The Industrial Revolution of English Fiction: Social Discourse and Narrative Form 1832–1867*, Chicago, IL: University of Chicago Press.

Gallagher, Catherine (2006) *The Body Economic: Life, Death and Sensation in Political Economy and the Victorian Novel*, Princeton, NJ: Princeton University Press.

Galt, John (1822/23) *The Entail, or the Lairds of Grippy*. (Oxford: Oxford University Press, 1984.)

Galt, John (1829) 'The Idiot', *Blackwood's Edinburgh Magazine*, October: 631–32.

Galton, Francis (1869) *Hereditary Genius*. (London: Watts, 1892.)

Galton, Francis (1883) *Inquiries into Human Faculty and Its Development*. (London: Eugenics Society, 1951.)

Gaskell, Elizabeth (1850) 'The Well at Pen-Morfa'. (In Suzanne Lewis, ed., *The Moorland Cottage and Other Stories*, Oxford: Oxford University Press, 1995, pp. 123–43.)

Gaskell, Elizabeth (1855) *Half a Life-Time Ago*. (London: Orion, 1996.)

Gaskell, Elizabeth (1857) *The Life of Charlotte Brontë*. (New York: AMS Press, 1973.)

Gaskell, Samuel (1847a) 'A Visit to the Bicêtre', *Chamber's Edinburgh Journal*, 9 January: 20–22.

Gaskell, Samuel (1847b) 'Education of Idiots at the Bicêtre', *Chamber's Edinburgh Journal*, 30 January: 71–73.

Gaskell, Samuel (1847c) 'Education of Idiots at the Bicêtre', *Chamber's Edinburgh Journal*, 13 February: 105–7.

Gelband, Spencer Hugh (1979) 'Mental Retardation and Institutional Treatment in Nineteenth Century England, 1845–1886', PhD dissertation, University of Maryland.

Gentili, Vanna (1988) '"Madmen and Fools Are a Staple Commodity": On Madness as a System in Elizabethan and Jacobean Plays', *Cahiers Élisabéthains*, 34: 11–24.

Gibson, Mary and Nicole Hahn Rafter, trans. (2006) Cesare Lombroso, *Criminal Man*, Durham: Duke University Press.

Gilbert, Sandra M. and Susan Gubar (1979) *The Madwoman in the Attic: The Woman Writer and the Nineteenth-Century Literary Imagination*. New Haven, CT: Yale University Press.

Gillie, Annis (1965) 'Serious and Fatal Illness in the Contemporary Novel', in Georgina Battiscombe and Margharita Laski, eds, *A Chaplet for Charlotte Yonge*, London: Cresset Press, pp. 98–105.

Gillies, M. A. (1988) 'Conrad's *The Secret Agent* and *Under Western Eyes* as Bergsonian Comedies', *Conradiana*, 20: 195–213.

Gineste, Thierry (2004) *Victor De L'Aveyron: Dernier enfant sauvage, premier enfant fou*, Paris: Hachette.

Gissing, George (1884) *The Unclassed*. (Brighton: Harvester, 1976.)

Gissing, George (1898) *Critical Studies of the Works of Charles Dickens*. (New York: Haskell House, 1965.)

Gladstone, David (1996) 'The Changing Dynamic of Institutional Care: The Western Counties Idiot Asylum 1864–1914', in David Wright and Anne Digby, eds, *From Idiocy to Mental Deficiency: Historical Perspectives on People with Learning Disabilities*, London: Routledge, pp. 134–60.

Gleeson, Brendan (1997) 'Disability Studies: A Historical Materialist View', *Disability and Society*, 12: 179–202.

Gleeson, Brendan (1999) *Geographies of Disability*, London: Routledge.

Goldberg, Michael (1972) *Carlyle and Dickens*, Athens, GA: University of Georgia Press.

Goodey, Chris (1994) 'John Locke's Idiots in the Natural History of the Mind', *History of Psychiatry*, 5: 215–50.

Goodey, Chris (1996) 'The Psychopolitics of Learning and Disability in Seventeenth-Century Thought', in David Wright and Anne Digby, eds, *From Idiocy to Mental Deficiency: Historical Perspectives on People with Learning Disabilities*, London: Routledge, pp. 93–117.

Goodey, Chris (2001) 'From Natural Disability to the Moral Man: Calvinism and the History of Psychology', *History of the Human Sciences*, 14(3): 1–29.

Goodey, Chris (2004) '"Foolishness" in Early Modern Medicine and the Concept of Intellectual Disability', *Medical History*, 48: 289–310.

Goodey, Chris (2008) 'Intelligence and Its Disabilities: The View From History', unpublished manuscript.

Goodey, Chris and Tim Stainton (2001) 'Intellectual Disability and the Myth of the Changeling Myth', *Journal of the History of the Behavioral Sciences*, 37: 223–40.

Goring, Charles (1913) *The English Convict: A Statistical Study*. (Montclair, NJ: Patterson Smith, 1972.)

Gould, Stephen Jay (1977) *Ontology and Phylogeny*, Cambridge, MA: Harvard University Press.

Gould, Stephen Jay (1981) *The Mismeasure of Man*, New York: Norton.

Gould, Stephen Jay (1982) 'Dr. Down's Syndrome', in *The Panda's Thumb: More Reflections on Natural History*, New York: Norton, pp. 160–68.

Greenblatt, Stephen (1980) *Renaissance Self-Fashioning From More to Shakespeare*, Chicago, IL: Chicago University Press.

Greenslade, William (1994) *Degeneration, Culture and the Novel 1880–1940*, Cambridge: Cambridge University Press.

Greenspan, Steven (2006) 'Fundamental Concepts in Mental Retardation: Finding the Natural Essence of an Artificial Category', *Exceptionality*, 14(4): 205–24.

Greenwell, Dora (1868) 'On the Education of the Imbecile', *North British Review*, 49: 73–100.

Greenwood, James (1874) *The Wilds of London*. (London: Garland, 1985.)

Greg, Willam Rathbone (1868) 'On the Failure of "Natural Selection" in the Case of Man', *Fraser's Magazine*, September: 353–62.

Gregory, Melissa Valiska (2002) 'The Unexpected Forms of Nemesis: George Eliot's "Brother Jacob," Victorian Narrative, and the Morality of Imperialism', *Dickens Studies Annual*, 31: 281–303.

Grierson, H. J. C., ed. (1932) *Letters of Sir Walter Scott, Vol. III: 1811–1814*, London: Constable.

Grove, Elizabeth (1856) *Narrative Poems; and a Beam for Mental Darkness for the Benefit of the Idiot and His Institution*, London.

Grove, Thelma (1987) 'Barnaby Rudge: A Case Study in Autism', *Dickensian*, 83: 139–48.

Hacking, Ian (1990) *The Taming of Chance*, Cambridge: Cambridge University Press.

Hacking, Ian (2000) *The Social Construction of What?*, Cambridge, MA: Harvard University Press.

Haeckel, Ernst (1866) *Generelle Morphologie der Organismen: Allgemeine Grundzüge der organischen Formen-Wissenchaft, mechanisch begründet durch die von Charles Darwin reformirte Descendenz-Theorie*, 2 volumes, Berlin: George Reimer.

Hall, Catherine (1992) *White, Male and Middle Class: Explorations in Feminism and History*, New York: Routledge.

Halliwell, Martin (2004) *Images of Idiocy: The Idiot Figure in Modern Fiction and Film*, Aldershot: Ashgate.

Harkness, Margaret (1889) *Captain Lobe* (published under the pseudonym John Law and republished as *In Darkest London* in 1891). (Victorian Series. Cambridge: Black Apollo Press, 2003.)

Hartman, Geoffrey (1987) *The Unremarkable Wordsworth*, Minneapolis, MN: University of Minneapolis Press.

Harvey, Karen (2004) *Reading Sex in the Eighteenth Century: Bodies and Gender in English Erotic Culture*, Cambridge Social and Cultural Histories, Cambridge: Cambridge University Press.

Haslam, John (1823) *A Letter to the Right Honourable the Lord Chancellor on the Nature and Interpretation of Unsoundness of Mind and Imbecility of Intellect*, London.

Hatfield Brush, Lillian M. (1935) 'A Psychological Study of Barnaby Rudge', *The Dickensian*, 31: 24–30.

Hayden, John O. (1970) *Scott: The Critical Heritage*, London: Routledge & Kegan Paul.

Hazlitt, William (1825) *The Spirit of the Age, or Contemporary Portraits*. (London: Oxford University Press, 1954.)

Helsinger, Elizabeth K., Robin Lauterbach Sheets and William Veeder (1983) *The Woman Question: Society and Literature in Britain and America, 1837–1883*, 3 vols, New York: Garland.

Henderson, Katherine Usher and Barbara McManus, eds (1985) *Half Humankind: Contexts and Texts of the Controversy About Women in England, 1540–1640*, Urbana, IL: University of Illinois Press.

Herring, Gina (1988) 'Mental Retardation and Faulkner's Ironic Vision', doctoral dissertation, Auburn University.

Hevey, David (1992) *The Creatures Time Forgot: Photography and Disability Imagery*, London: Routledge.

Hillebrand, Harold Newcomb (1922) 'The Children of the King's Revels at White-friars', *Journal of German and English Philology*, 21: 318–34.

Holdsworth, Sir William (1966) *A History of English Law*, vol. I, London: Methuen.

Hollingshead, John (1861) *Ragged London in 1861*. (London: Dent, 1986.)

Hotson, Leslie (1952) *Shakespeare's Motley*. (New York: Haskell House, 1971.)

House, Madeline and Graham Storey, eds (1969) *The Letters of Charles Dickens*. Oxford: Clarendon.

Houston, Gail Turley (1993) 'Gender Construction and the Kunsterroman: David Copperfield and Aurora Leigh', *Philological Quarterly*, 72: 213–36.

Houston, R. A. (2000) *Madness and Society in Eighteenth-Century Scotland*, Oxford: Clarendon.

Houston, R. A. (2001) 'Institutional Care for the Insane and Idiots in Scotland Before 1820', *History of Psychiatry*, 12: 3–31; 177–97.

Howe, Irving (1957) 'Conrad: Order and Anarchy', in Ian Watt, ed. (1973) *Conrad: The Secret Agent. A Selection of Critical Essays*, London: Macmillan, pp. 140–49.

Howe, Samuel Gridley (1848) *On the Causes of Idiocy*. (New York: Arno, 1972.)

Hudson, Hoyt Hopewell, trans. (1941) Desiderius Erasmus, *The Praise of Folly*, Princeton: Princeton University Press.

Huet, Marie-Hélène (1993) *Monstrous Imagination*, Cambridge, MA: Harvard University Press.

Huizinga, J. (1952) *Erasmus of Rotterdam*, London: Phaedon.

Hume, David (1739/40) *A Treatise of Human Nature*. (Oxford: Clarendon, 1978.)

Hume, David (1777) *Essays Moral, Political and Literary*. (Indianapolis, IN: Liberty Classics, 1985.)

Humphrey, Richard (1993) *Scott: Waverley*, Landmarks of World Literature, Cambridge: Cambridge University Press.

Humphreys, Robert (1995) *Sin, Organized Charity and the Poor Law in Victorian England*, New York: St Martin's Press.

Hunter, Allan (1983) *Joseph Conrad and the Ethics of Darwinism: The Challenges of Science*, London: Croom Helm.

Ireland, W. W. (1872) 'On the Classification and Prognosis of Idiocy', *Journal of Mental Science*, 18: 333–54.

Ireland, W. W. (1886) 'On the Admission of Idiotic and Imbecile Children into Lunatic Asylums', *Journal of Mental Science*, 32: 182–93.

Itard, Jean (1801) *De l'Education d'un homme sauvage ou des premiers développements physiques et moraux du jeune sauvage de l'Aveyron*. (Trans. as *An Historical Account of the Discovery and Education of a Savage Man, or of the First Developments, Physical and Moral, of the Young Savage Caught in the Woods near Aveyron in the year 1798*, London, 1802.)

Itard, Jean (1806) *Rapport fait à son Excellence le Ministre de l'Intérieur sur les Nouveaux Developpements et l'État Actuel du Sauvage de l'Aveyron*. (In Jean Itard, *Victor de l'Aveyron*, Paris: Éditions Allia, 1994, pp. 61–115.)

Iyer, Anupama (2007) 'Depiction of Intellectual Disability in Fiction', *Advances in Psychiatric Treatment*, 13: 127–33.

Jackson, Mark (2000) *The Borderland of Imbecility: Medicine, Society and the Fabrication of the Feeble Mind in Late Victorian and Edwardian Britain*. Manchester: Manchester University Press.

Jacob, Giles (1729) *A New Law Dictionary: Containing the Interpretation and Definition of Words and Terms Used in the Law; and Also the Whole Law, and the Practice Thereof….* London.

Jacobus, Mary (1970) 'The Idiot Boy', in Jonathan Wordsworth, ed., *Bicentenary Wordsworth Studies in Memory of John Alban Finch*, Ithaca, NY: Cornell University Press, pp. 238–65.

Jacques, T. Carlos (1997) 'From Savages and Barbarians to Primitives: Africa, Social Typologies, and History in Eighteenth-Century French Philosophy', *History and Theory*, 36: 190–215.

Jacyna, L. S. (1982) 'Somatic Theories of Mind and the Interests of Medicine in Britain, 1850–1879', *Medical History*, 26: 233–58.

Janik, Vicki K., ed. (1998) *Fools and Jesters in Literature, Art, and History: A Bio-Bibliographical Sourcebook*. Westport, CT: Greenwood.

Johnson, Dale A. (1999) *The Changing Shape of English Nonconformity, 1825–1925*, Oxford: Oxford University Press.

Johnson, Nora (2003) *The Actor as Playwright in Early Modern Drama*, Cambridge: Cambridge University Press.

Jones, Kathleen (1972) *A History of the Mental Health Services*, London: Routledge & Kegan Paul.

Jones, Shirley (1999) 'Motherhood and Melodrama: *Salem Chapel* and Sensation Fiction', *Women's Writing*, 6(2): 239–50.

Jordanova, Ludmilla (1989) *Sexual Visions: Images of Gender in Science and Medicine Between the Eighteenth and Twentieth Centuries*, Hemel Hempstead: Harvester Wheatsheaf.

Kaiser, Walter (1963) *Praisers of Folly: Erasmus, Rabelais, Shakespeare*, Cambridge, MA: Harvard University Press.

Kanner, Leo (1964) *A History of the Care and Study of the Mentally Retarded*, Springfield, IL: Thomas.

Kant, Immanuel (1798) *Anthropology From a Pragmatic Point of View*. (Victor Lyle Dowdell, trans., Carbondale, IL: Southern Illinois University Press, 1978.)

Karl, Frederick R. and Laurence Davies, eds (1983) *Collected Letters of Joseph Conrad, Vol. III: 1903–1907*, Cambridge: Cambridge University Press.

Kelly, Lori (2003) 'Conrad's *Secret Agent* and the Zoophil-Psychosis Diagnosis', *Conradiana*, 35(1–2): 99–103.

Kerlin, Isaac (1858) *The Mind Unveiled, or, a Brief History of Twenty-Two Imbecile Children*, Philadelphia: U. Hunt & Son.

Kiernan, V. G. (1989) *Poets, Politics and the People*. London: Verso.

King, Thomas (2004) *The Gendering of Men, 1600–1750. The English Phallus*, vol. I, Madison, WI: University of Wisconsin Press.

Kingsley, Charles (1863) *The Water-Babies*. (World's Classics, Oxford: Oxford University Press, 1995.)

Kinsman, Robert S. (1974) 'Folly, Melancholy, and Madness: A Study in Shifting Styles of Medical Analysis and Treatment, 1450–1675', in Robert S. Kinsman, ed., *The Darker Vision of the Renaissance*, Berkeley, CA: University of California Press, pp. 273–320.

Kirby, A. H. P. (1909) 'The Feeble-Minded and Voluntary Effort', *Eugenics Review*, 1: 85–96.

Kitchen, Martin (2001) *Kaspar Hauser: Europe's Child*, Houndmills: Palgrave.

Klein, Joan Larson, ed. (1992) *Daughters, Wives and Widows: Writings by Men About Women and Marriage in England, 1500–1640*, Urbana, IL: University of Illinois Press.

Kucich, John (1987) *Repression in Victorian Fiction: Charlotte Brontë, George Eliot and Charles Dickens*, Berkeley, CA: University of California Press.

Kucich, John (1990) 'Transgression and Sexual Difference in Elizabeth Gaskell's Novels', *Texas Studies in Literature and Language*, 32: 187–213.

Lane, Harlan (1976) *The Wild Boy of Aveyron*, Cambridge, MA: Harvard University Press.

Langland, William (c. 1370–90) *Piers Plowman*. (George Kane, George Russell and E. Talbot Donaldson, eds, London: Athlone Press, 1988.)

Lapage, C. Paget (1911) *Feeblemindedness in Children of School Age*, Manchester: Manchester University Press.

Laqueur, Thomas (1990) *Making Sex: Body and Gender From the Greeks to Freud*, Cambridge, MA: Harvard University Press.

Larsen, Timothy (1999) *Friends of Religious Equality: Nonconformist Politics in Mid-Victorian England*, Studies in Modern British Religious History, Woodbridge: Boydell.

Lawes, Kim (2000) *Paternalism and Politics: The Revival of Pateralism in Early Nineteenth-Century Britain*, New York: St Martin's.

Leerssen, J. Th. (1991) 'Fiction Poetics and Cultural Stereotype: Local Colour in Scott, Morgan and Maturin', *Modern Language Review*, 86: 273–84.

Liddie, Alexander S., ed. (1979) 'Introduction', Robert Armin, *A History of the Two Maids of More-Clacke*, New York: Garland.

Linnaeus (Carl Linné) (1758) *Systema Naturae*. (Facsimile reproduction of the first volume of the tenth edition, London: British Museum, 1956.)

Lippincott, H. F., ed. (1979) Robert Armin, *Foole Upon Foole*, Studies in English Literature, Elizabethan Studies 20, Salzburg: Institut für Englische Sprach und Literatur.

Locke, John (1689) *An Essay Concerning Human Understanding*. (New York: Dover, 1959.)

Locke, John (1689/90) *Two Treatises of Government*. (Everyman edition, London: Dent, 1924.)

Locke, John (1695) *The Reasonableness of Christianity, with a Discourse on Miracles, and Part of a Third Letter Concerning Toleration*. (Stanford, CA: Stanford University Press, 1958.)

Loesberg, Jonathan (1986) 'The Ideology of Narrative Form in Sensation Fiction', *Representations*, 13: 115–38.

Lohrli, Anne (1973) *Household Words: A Weekly Journal 1850–59 Conducted by Charles Dickens*, Toronto: University of Toronto Press.

Lomax, Marion (1987) *Stage Images and Traditions: Shakespeare to Ford*, Cambridge: Cambridge University Press.

Lombroso, Cesare (1876) *Criminal Man*. (Mary Gibson and Nicole Hahn Rafter, trans., Durham: Duke University Press, 2006.)

Lombroso, Cesare (1889) *The Man of Genius*. (Contemporary Science Series, Havelock Ellis, ed., 2nd edition, London: Walter Scott, 1905.)

Longstaff, George (1891) *Studies in Statistics. Social, Political, and Medical*, London: Edward Stanford.

Lovejoy, Arthur O. (1948) *Essays in the History of Ideas*. (New York: Capricorn Press, 1960.)

MacDonald, George (1864) 'The Wow o' Rivven'. (In *Works of Fancy and Imagination*, vol. X, London: Strahan, 1871, pp. 129–65.)

MacDonald, Robert H. (1967) 'The Frightful Consequences of Onanism: Notes on the History of a Delusion', *Journal of the History of Ideas*, 28: 423–31.

MacKenzie, John L. (1965) *Dictionary of the Bible*, New York: Macmillan.

Magnet, Myron (1985) *Dickens and the Social Order*, Philadelphia, PA: University of Pennsylvania Press.

Maleski, Mary A. (1998) 'Paul the Apostle', in Vicki K. Janik, ed., *Fools and Jesters in Literature, Art, and History: A Bio-Bibliographical Sourcebook*, Westport, CT: Greenwood, pp. 316–28.

Mallen, Richard D. (2001) 'George Eliot and the Precious Mettle of Trust', *Victorian Studies*, 44: 41–75.

Malson, Lucien (1964) *Wolf Children and the Problem of Human Nature*. (London: NLB, 1972, pp. 1–94; this edition combines Malson's work with Itard, *The Wild Boy of Aveyron*.)

Malthus, Thomas (1798) *An Essay on the Principle of Population*. (New York: Norton, 1976.)

Mandeville, Bernard de (1711) *Treatise of the Hypochondriak and Hysterick Diseases* (New York: Arno, 1976.)

Mangum, Teresa (1998) 'Wilkie Collins, Detection, and Deformity', *Dickens Studies Annual*, 26: 285–310.

Manheim, Leonard (1972) 'Dickens' Fools and Madmen', *Dickens Studies Annual*, 2: 69–97.

Manlove, Colin (1990) 'MacDonald and Kingsley: A Victorian Contrast', in William Raeper, ed., *The Gold Thread: Essays on George MacDonald*, Edinburgh: Edinburgh University Press, pp. 140–62.

Mann, Thomas (1926) 'Joseph Conrad's *The Secret Agent*'. (In Ian Watt, ed., *Conrad: The Secret Agent. A Selection of Critical Essays*, London: Macmillan, 1973, pp. 99–112.)

Marchbanks, Paul (2006a) 'Intimations of Intellectual Disability in Nineteenth-Century British Literature', doctoral dissertation, University of North Carolina at Chapel Hill.

Marchbanks, Paul (2006b) 'From Caricature to Character: The Intellectually Disabled in Dickens's Novels', *Dickens Quarterly*, 23: 3–14; 67–85; 169–81.

Marcus, Steven (1965) *Dickens: From Pickwick to Dombey*, New York: Basic Books.

Marshall, John (1867) 'On the Brain of a Bushwoman; And on the Brains of Two Idiots of European Descent', *Journal of Mental Science*, 12: 99–112.

Martineau, Harriet (1832) 'Ella of Garveloch'. (In *Illustrations of Political Economy*, vol. II, London: Charles Fox, 1836.)

Martineau, Harriet (1854) 'Idiots Again', *Household Words*, 15 April: 197–200.

Marx, Karl and Friedrich Engels (1848) *The Communist Manifesto*. (Samuel Moore, trans., Harmondsworth: Penguin, 1985.)

Maudsley, Henry (1862) 'The Genesis of Mind', *Journal of Mental Science*, 7: 461–94.

Maudsley, Henry (1864) 'Considerations with Regard to Hereditary Influence', *Journal of Mental Science*, 9: 506–30.

Maudsley, Henry (1867/79) *The Pathology of Mind*. (London: Julian Friedmann, 1979.)

Maudsley, Henry (1873) *Body and Mind*, London: Macmillan.

Maudsley, Henry (1874) *Responsibility in Mental Disease*. (Significant Contributions to the History of Psychology 1750–1920, vol. III, Daniel N. Robinson, ed., Washington: University Publications of America, 1977.)

Maudsley, Henry (1879) 'Materialism and Its Lessons', *Fortnightly Review*, 26 (32 old series): 244–60.

Maudsley, Henry (1895) 'A Discussion on Insanity in Relation to Criminal Responsibility', *British Medical Journal*, 28 September: 769–73.

Maunder, Andrew (2004) '"Stepchildren of Nature": *East Lynne* and the Spectre of Female Degeneracy, 1860–1861', in Andrew Maunder and Grace Moore, eds, *Victorian Crime, Madness and Sensation*, Aldershot: Ashgate, pp. 59–71.

Mayhew, Henry (1851) *London Labour and the London Poor*, 2 vols, London: George Woodfall.

Mayhew, Robert (2004) *The Female in Aristotle's Biology: Reason or Rationalization*, Chicago, IL: University of Chicago Press.

McCulloch, John Ramsay (1864) *The Principles of Political Economy*, 5th edition. (New York: Augustus M. Kelley, 1965.)

McElderry, B. R. (1955) 'Southey, and Wordsworth's "The Idiot Boy"', *Notes and Queries*, 200: 490–91.

McGann, Jerome, ed. (1980) *Lord Byron (George Gordon): The Complete Poetical Works*, 7 volumes, Oxford: Oxford University Press.

McGann, Jerome (1985) *The Beauty of Inflections: Literary Investigation in Historical Method and Theory*, Oxford: Clarendon.

McIntosh, W. Carmichael (1864) 'Stray Notes on Foreign Asylums', *Journal of Mental Science*, 10: 1–20.

McKnight, Natalie (1993) *Idiots, Madmen, and Other Prisoners in Dickens*, New York: St Martin's.

McMaster, Juliet (1984) '"Better to be Silly": From Vision to Reality in *Barnaby Rudge*', *Dickens Studies Annual*, 13: 1–17.

Melling, Joseph and Bill Forsythe (2006) *The Politics of Madness: The State, Insanity and Society in England, 1845–1914*, London: Routledge.

Mellor, Anne K. (1993) *Romanticism and Gender*, New York: Routledge.

Meredith, Isabel [Helen Rossetti and Olivia Rossetti] (1903) *A Girl Among the Anarchists*. (Lincoln, NE: University of Nebraska Press, 1992.)

Michasiw, Kim Ian (1989) '*Barnaby Rudge*: The Since of the Fathers', *English Literary History*, 56: 571–92.

Middlebro', Tom (1980) 'Burke, Dickens and the Gordon Riots', *Humanities Association Review*, 31: 87–95.

Middleton, Thomas and William Rowley (1622) *The Changeling*. (Regents Renaissance Drama, George W. Williams, ed., Lincoln, NE: University of Nebraska Press, 1966.)

Mill, John Stuart (1848) *Principles of Political Economy*, 8th edition, vol. II. (London: Longmans, Green, Reader, and Dyer, 1878.)

Miller, D. A. (1988) *The Novel and the Police*, Berkeley, CA: University of California Press.

Mitchell, David and Sharon Snyder (2000) *Narrative Prosthesis: Disability and the Dependencies of Discourse*. Ann Arbor, MI: University of Michigan Press.

Mitchison, Rosalind and Leah Leneman (1989) *Sexuality and Social Control: Scotland 1660–1780*, Oxford: Basil Blackwell.

Monboddo, Lord (James Burnet) (1774) *On the Origins and Progress of Language*, vol. I. (New York: Garland, 1970.)

More, Thomas (1516) *Utopia*. Trans. Ralph Robinson (1556). (In Susan Bruce, ed., *Three Early Modern Utopias*, Oxford: Oxford University Press, 1999, pp. 1–129.)

Morgan, John Edward (1866) *The Danger of Deterioration of Race From the Too Rapid Increase of Great Cities*. (New York: Garland, 1985.)

Morgan, Lady (Sydney Owenson) (1806) *The Wild Irish Girl*. (London: Pandora, 1986.)

Morgan, Lady (Sydney Owenson) (1827) *The O'Briens and the O'Flahertys*, 3 volumes. (London: Henry Colburn, 1833.)

Morison, Alexander (1843) *Physiognomy of Mental Disorders*, London.

Mowat, Charles Loch (1961) *The Charity Organisation Society 1869–1913: Its Ideas and Work*, London: Methuen.

Mullett, Charles F., ed. (1943) *The Letters of George Cheyne to Samuel Richardson*, Columbia, MO: University of Missouri Press.

Mulry, David (2000) 'Popular Accounts of the Greenwich Bombing and Conrad's *The Secret Agent*', *Rocky Mountain Review of Language and Literature*, 54(2): 43–64.

Neugebauer, Richard (1978) 'Treatment of the Mentally Ill in Medieval and Early Modern England: A Reappraisal', *Journal of the History of the Behavioral Sciences*, 14: 158–69.

Neugebauer, Richard (1989) 'A Doctor's Dilemma: The Case of William Harvey's Mentally Retarded Nephew', *Psychological Medicine*, 19: 568–72.

Neugebauer, Richard (1996) 'Mental Handicap in Medieval and Early Modern England', in David Wright and Anne Digby, eds, *From Idiocy to Mental Deficiency: Historical Perspectives on People with Learning Disabilities*, Studies in the Social History of Medicine, London: Routledge, pp. 22–43.

Newman, John Henry (1864) *Apologia pro vita sua*, London: Longman.

Newton, Michael (2002) *Savage Girls and Wild Boys: A History of Feral Children*, London: Faber & Faber.

Noll, Steven (1995) *Feeble-Minded in Our Midst: Institutions for the Mentally Retarded in the South, 1900–1940*, Chapel Hill, NC: University of North Carolina Press.

Nussbaum, Felicity A. (2003) *The Limits of the Human: Fictions of Anomaly, Race and Gender in the Long Eighteenth Century*, Cambridge: Cambridge University Press.

Oberhelman, David O. (1995) *Dickens in Bedlam: Madness and Restraint in His Fiction*, Fredericton, NB: York.

Oliphant, Margaret (1862) 'Sensation Novels', *Blackwood's Magazine*, 91 (May): 564–84.

Oliphant, Margaret (1863) *Salem Chapel*. (London: Virago, 1986.)

Oliphant, Margaret (1892) *The Cuckoo in the Nest*. (London: Hutchinson, 1894.)

Oliver, Michael (1990) *The Politics of Disablement*, London: Macmillan.

Oliver, Michael (1996) *Understanding Disability: From Theory to Practice*, London, Macmillan.

Ospovat, Dov (1995) *The Development of Darwin's Theory: Natural History, Natural Theology, and Natural Selection, 1838–1859*, Cambridge: Cambridge University Press.

Owen, David (1964) *English Philanthropy 1660–1960*, Cambridge, MA: Harvard University Press.

Park, Deborah Carter and John Radford (1999) 'Rhetoric and Place in the "Mental Deficiency" Asylum', in Ruth Butler and Hester Parr, eds, *Mind and Body Spaces: Geographies of Illness, Impairment and Disability*, London: Routledge, pp. 70–97.

Parkinson, J. C. (1869) 'A Day at Earlswood', London: Strahan & Co.

Pascoe, Judith, ed. (2000) *Mary Robinson: Selected Poems*. Peterborough, Ontario: Broadview.

Peakman, Julie (2003) *Mighty Lewd Books: The Development of Pornography in Eighteenth-Century England*, Houndsmills: Palgrave Macmillan.

Peele, George (c. 1593) *The Old Wives Tale*. (Patricia Binnie, ed., Manchester: Manchester University Press, 1980.)

Pelicier, Yves and Guy Thuillier (1980) *Édouard Séguin (1812–1880), 'L'instititeur des idiots'*, Paris: Economica.

Peters, Catherine (1991) *The King of Inventors: A Life of Wilkie Collins*, Princeton, NJ: Princeton University Press.

Peters, Christine (2004) *Women in Early Modern Britain, 1450–1640*, Houndmills: Palgrave Macmillan.

Pethes, Nicolas (2003) '"Victor, L'enfant de la forêt" – Experiments on the Heredity of Human Nature in Savage Children', in *Proceedings From a Cultural History of Heredity II: 18th and 19th Centuries*, Berlin: Max-Planck-Institut für Wissenschaftsgeschichte, pp. 187–209. (Available online at www.mpiwg-berlin. mpg.de/Preprints/P247.PDF.)

Pichanick, Valerie (1980) *Harriet Martineau, the Woman and Her Work 1802–1876*, Ann Arbor, MI: University of Michigan Press.

Pick, Daniel (1989) *Faces of Degeneration: A European Disorder, c. 1848–c. 1918*, Ideas in Context, Cambridge: Cambridge University Press.

Pinel, Philippe (1800) *Rapport fait à la Société des Observateurs de l'Homme sur l'enfant connu sous le nom de sauvage de l'Aveyron.* (In Thierry Gineste, *Victor de l'Aveyron, Dernier enfant sauvate, premier enfant fou*, Paris: Hachette, 2004, pp. 324–38.)

Pinel, Philippe (1801) *Deuxième partie du Rapport fait à la Société des Observateurs de l'Homme sur l'enfant connu sous le nom de sauvage de l'Aveyron.* (In Thierry Gineste, *Victor de l'Aveyron, Dernier enfant sauvate, premier enfant fou*, Paris: Hachette, 2004, pp. 351–60.)

Plasa, Carl (2005) 'George Eliot's "Confectionary Business": Sugar and Slavery in *Brother Jacob*', *Literature Interpretation Theory*, 16: 285–309.

Pollard, Arthur, ed. (1972) *Crabbe: The Critical Heritage*, London: Routledge & Kegan Paul.

Poovey, Mary (1988) *Uneven Developments: The Ideological Work of Gender in Mid-Victorian England*, Chicago, IL: University of Chicago Press.

Poster, Mark (1997) *Cultural History and Postmodernity: Disciplinary Readings and Challenges*, New York: Columbia University Press.

Prickett, Stephen (2005) *Victorian Fantasy*, 2nd edition, Waco, TX: Baylor University Press.

Rapley, Mark (2004) *The Social Construction of Intellectual Disability*, Cambridge: Cambridge University Press.

Rastell, John (1527) *Exposition of Certaine Difficulte and Obscure Words and Termes*, London.

Reed, Robert (1952) *Bedlam on the Jacobean Stage.* (New York: Octagon, 1970.)

Rice, Thomas J. (1978) '*Barnaby Rudge*: A *Vade Mecum* for the Theme of Domestic Government in Dickens', *Dickens Studies Annual*, 7: 81–102.

Rice, Thomas J. (1983) 'The Politics of *Barnaby Rudge*', in Rodert Giddings, ed., *The Changing World of Dickens*, London: Vision, pp. 51–74.

Richardson, Alan (2001) *British Romanticism and the Science of the Mind*, Cambridge: Cambridge University Press.

Richetti, John (2005) *The Life of Daniel Defoe*, Blackwell Critical Biographies, Oxford: Blackwell.

Roberts, David (1978) 'The Paterfamilias of the Victorian Governing Classes', in Anthony S. Wohl, ed., *The Victorian Family: Structures and Stresses*, London: Croom Helm, pp. 59–81.

Roberts, David (1979) *Paternalism in Early Victorian England*, New Brunswick, NJ: Rutgers University Press.

Robinson, Daniel N., ed. (1977) Philippe Pinel, *Treatise on Insanity*, D. D. Davies, trans., Significant Contributions to the History of Psychology 1750–1920, Series C: Medical Psychology, vol. III, Washington, DC: University Publications of America.

Rodstein, Susan de Sola (1991) 'Sweetness and Dark: George Eliot's *Brother Jacob*', *Modern Language Quarterly*, 52: 295–317.

Romanes, George (1888) *Mental Evolution in Man*, London: Kegan Paul.

Ronell, Avital (2002) *Stupidity*, Chicago, IL: University of Illinois Press.

Rosen, Marvin, Gerald R. Clark and Marvin S. Kivitz, eds (1976) *The History of Mental Retardation: Collected Papers*, vol. I, Baltimore, MD: University Park Press.

Rosenberg, Brian (1996) *Little Dorrit's Shadows: Character and Contradiction in Dickens*, Columbia, MO: University of Missouri Press.

Rosner, Mary (2004) 'Deviance in *The Law and the Lady*: The Uneasy Positionings of Mr. Dexter', *Victorian Newsletter*, 106: 9–14.

Rowntree, B. Seebohm (1901) *Poverty: A Study of Town Life*, London: Thomas Nelson.

Royal Commission on the Care and Control of the Feeble-Minded (1909) *The Problem of the Feeble-Minded: An Abstract of the Report of the Royal Commission on the Care and Control of the Feeble-Minded*, London.

Royce, Samuel (1878) *Deterioration and Race Education*, Boston: Lee & Shepard.

RT (1853) 'Crétins and Idiots: A Short Account of the Progress of the Institutions for Their Relief and Care'. (In Marvin Rosen, Gerald R. Clark and Marvin S. Kivitz, eds, *The History of Mental Retardation: Collected Papers*, vol. I, Baltimore, MD: University Park Press, 1976, pp. 113–40.)

Rudé, George (1956) 'The Gordon Riots: A Study of the Rioters and Their Victims', *Transactions of the Royal Historical Society* (5th Series), 6: 93–114.

Rushton, Peter (1988) 'Lunatics and Idiots: Mental Disability, the Community, and the Poor Law in Early Modern England, 1600–1800', *Medical History*, 32: 34–50.

Rushton, Peter (1996) 'Idiocy, the Family and the Community in Early Modern North-East England', in David Wright and Anne Digby, eds, *From Idiocy to Mental Deficiency: Historical Perspectives on People with Learning Disabilities*, Studies in the Social History of Medicine, London: Routledge, pp. 44–64.

Ryan, Joanna, with Frank Thomas (1987) *The Politics of Mental Handicap*, London: Free Association.

Salisbury, Joyce (1994) *The Beast Within: Animals in the Middle Ages*, New York: Routledge.

Saunders, Janet (1988) 'Quarantining the Weak-Minded: Psychiatric Definitions of Degeneracy and the Late-Victorian Asylum', in W. F. Bynum, Roy Porter and Michael Shepherd, eds, *The Anatomy of Madness, Vol. III: The Asylum and Its Psychiatry*, London: Routledge, pp. 273–96.

Saward, John (1980) *Perfect Fools: Folly for Christ's Sake in Catholic and Orthodox Spirituality*, Oxford: Oxford University Press.

Scheckner, Peter (1987/88) 'Chartism, Class, and Social Struggle: A Study of Charles Dickens', *Midwest Quarterly*, 29: 93–112.

Scheerenberger, R. C. (1983) *A History of Mental Retardation*, Baltimore, MD: Brookes.

Schmidt, Gerald (2005) 'George Gissing's Psychology of "Female Imbecility"', *Studies in the Novel*, 37(3): 329–41.

Scott, Sir Walter (1814) *Waverley, or, 'Tis Sixty Years Since*. (Harmondsworth: Penguin, 1972.)

Scull, Andrew (1979) *Museums of Madness: The Social Organization of Insanity in Nineteenth-Century England*, London: Allen Lane. (Harmondsworth: Penguin, 1982.)

Séguin, Édouard (1843) 'Hygiene et éducation des idiots'. (In Yves Pelicier and Guy Thuillier, eds, *Edouard Séguin (1812–1880), 'L'Instititeur Des Idiots'*, Paris: Economica, 1980, pp. 51–160.)

Séguin, Édouard (1846) *Traitement moral, hygiène et éducation des idiots*. (Nendeln: Klaus Reprint, 1978.)

Séguin, Édouard (1866) *Idiocy: And Its Treatment by the Physiological Method*. (New York: Gryphon, 1994.)

Séguin, Édouard (1875) *Report on Education.* (Delmar, NY: Scholars' Facsimiles & Reprints, 1976.)

Shakespeare, William (c. 1605) *Macbeth.* (Cambridge: Cambridge University Press, 2004.)

Shakespeare, William (c. 1606) *Cymbeline.* (The Arden Shakespeare. London: Methuen, 1980.)

Shattuck, Roger (1980) *The Forbidden Experiment: The Story of the Wild Boy of Aveyron,* New York: Farrar Strauss Giroux.

Shelston, Alan, ed. (1971) *Thomas Carlyle: Selected Writings,* Harmondsworth: Penguin.

Sherry, Norman (1967) 'The Greenwich Bomb Outrage and the Secret Agent', *Review of English Studies,* n.s., 18(72): 412–28.

Sherry, Norman (1971) *Conrad's Western World,* Cambridge: Cambridge University Press.

Shorter, Edward (2000) *The Kennedy Family and the Story of Mental Retardation,* Philadelphia, PA: Temple University Press.

Showalter, Elaine (1976) 'Desperate Remedies: Sensation Novels of the 1860s', *Victorian Newsletter,* 49: 1–5.

Showalter, Elaine (1979) 'Guilt, Authority, and the Shadows of *Little Dorrit*', *Nineteenth-Century Fiction,* 34: 20–40.

Showalter, Elaine (1985) *The Female Malady: Women, Madness, and English Culture, 1830–1980,* Harmondsworth: Penguin.

Shuttleworth, G. E. (1877) 'Intemperance as a Cause of Idiocy', *British Medical Journal,* 1 September: 308–9.

Shuttleworth, Sally (1996) *Charlotte Brontë and Victorian Psychology,* Cambridge: Cambridge University Press.

Silverman, Kaja (1992) *Male Subjectivity at the Margins,* New York: Routledge.

Simmons, Allan H. and J. H. Stape, eds (2007) *The Secret Agent: Centennial Essays,* Amsterdam: Editions Rodopi and the Joseph Conrad Society.

Simmons, Harvey G. (1978) 'Explaining Social Policy: The English Mental Deficiency Act of 1913', *Journal of Social History,* 11(3): 387–403.

Simpson, Murray (1999) 'The Moral Government of Idiots: Moral Treatment in Séguin', *History of Psychiatry,* 10(2): 227–43.

Sims, George R. (1889) *How the Poor Live and Horrible London.* (London: Garland, 1985.)

Slater, Michael, ed. (1999) *'Gone Astray' and Other Papers From Household Words 1851–59,* Dent Uniform Edition of Dickens' Journalism, vol. III. London: J. M. Dent.

Smiles, Samuel (1859) *Self-Help.* (London: John Murray, 1958.)

Smith, Adam (1759) *The Theory of Moral Sentiments.* (Oxford: Oxford University Press, 1976.)

Smith, Hilda (1982) *Reason's Disciples: Seventeenth-Century English Feminists,* Chicago, IL: University of Illinois Press.

Southey, Caroline Bowles (1824) 'Chapters on churchyards. Ch. IV', *Blackwood's Magazine,* 16: 317–21.

Southey, Robert (1798) 'The Idiot', *Morning Post,* 30 June.

Spencer, Herbert (1850) *Social Statistics.* (New York: Robert Schalkenbach Foundation, 1954.)

Spencer, Herbert (1866) *Principles of Biology.* (New York: Appleton, 1898.)

Stainton, Tim (1994) *Autonomy and Social Policy: Rights, Mental Handicap and Community Care,* Aldershot: Avebury.

Stainton, Tim (2000) 'Equal Citizens? The Discourse of Liberty and Rights in the History of Learning Disabilities', in Dorothy Atkinson, Mark Jackson and Jan

Walmsley, eds, *Crossing Boundaries: Continuity and Change in the History of Learning Disabilities*, Kidderminster: Bild Publications, pp. 87–101.

Stainton, Tim (2001) 'Medieval Charitable Institutions and Intellectual Impairment c. 1066–1600', *Journal on Developmental Disabilities*, 8(2): 19–29.

Stainton, Tim (2004) 'Reason's Other: The Emergence of the Disabled Subject in the Northern Renaissance', *Disability and Society*, 19: 225–43.

Stainton, Tim and Steve Boyce (2004) '"I Have Got My Life Back": User's Experience of Direct Payments', *Disability and Society*, 19: 443–54.

Stainton, Tim and Patrick McDonagh (2001) 'Chasing Shadows: The Historical Construction of Developmental Disability', *Journal on Developmental Disabilities*, 8: ix–xvi.

Stallman, R. W. (1975) 'Time and *The Secret Agent*', in Frederick Karl, ed., *Joseph Conrad: A Collection of Criticism*, New York: McGraw-Hill, pp. 59–81.

Stedman Jones, Gareth (1971) *Outcast London: A Study in the Relationship Between Classes in Victorian Society*. (Harmondsworth: Penguin, 1992.)

Stigant, Paul, and Peter Widdowson (1975) 'Barnaby Rudge – A Historical Novel?', *Literature and History*, 2: 2–44.

Stoddard Holmes, Martha (2007) 'Victorian Fictions of Interdependency: Gaskell, Craik, and Yonge', *Journal of Literary Disability*, 1(2): 29–41.

Stone, Harry, ed. (1968) *Charles Dickens' Uncollected Writings From Household Words 1850–1859*, Bloomington, IN: Indiana University Press.

Storr, Catherine (1965) 'Parents', in Georgina Battiscombe and Marghanita Laski, eds, *A Chaplet for Charlotte Yonge*, London: Cresset Press, pp. 106–12.

Sussman, Herbert (1995) *Victorian Masculinities: Manhood and Masculine Poetics in Early Victorian Literature and Art*, Cambridge: Cambridge University Press.

Swain, Barbara (1932) *Fools and Folly During the Middle Ages and Renaissance*. (New York: Columbia University Press, 1977.)

Talbot, Eugene S. (1898) *Degeneracy: Its Causes, Signs and Results*, Contemporary Science Series, Havelock Ellis, ed., London: Walter Scott.

Taylor, Jenny Bourne (1988) *In the Secret Theatre of Home: Wilkie Collins, Sensation Narrative, and Nineteenth-Century Psychology*, London: Routledge.

Thaden, Barbara (1997) *The Maternal Voice in Victorian Fiction*, New York: Garland.

Thomas, Keith (1984) *Man and the Natural World: Changing Attitudes in England, 1500–1800*, Harmondsworth: Penguin.

Thompson, Dorothy (1984) *The Chartists*, London: Temple Smith.

Thompson, E. P. (1967/68) 'The Political Education of Henry Mayhew', *Victorian Studies*, 11: 41–62.

Thompson, E. P. (1974) 'Patrician Society, Plebian Culture', *Journal of Social History*, 7: 382–405.

Thomson, James Bruce (1866) 'The Effects of the Present System of Prison Discipline on the Body and Mind', *Journal of Mental Science*, 12: 340–48.

Thomson, James Bruce (1869) 'The Hereditary Nature of Crime,' *Journal of Mental Science*, 15: 487–98.

Thomson, Mathew (1998) *The Problem of Mental Deficiency: Eugenics, Democracy, and Social Policy in Britain c. 1870–1959*, Oxford: Clarendon.

Tillotson, Kathleen, ed. (1953) 'Introduction', Charles Dickens, *Barnaby Rudge*, Oxford: Oxford University Press.

Tomasin, Claire (1997) *Jane Austen: A Life*, London: Viking.

Tosh, John (1999) *A Man's Place: Masculinity and the Middle-Class Home in Victorian England*, New Haven, CT: Yale University Press.

Tosh, John (2005) *Manliness and Masculinities in Nineteenth-Century Britain: Essays on Gender, Family and Empire*, London: Pearson Longman.

Tredgold, Alfred F. (1908) *Mental Deficiency (Amentia)*, New York: William Wood (2nd edition 1912).

Tredgold, Alfred F. (1909) 'The Feeble-Minded: A Social Danger', *Eugenics Review*, 1: 97–104.

Trent, James (1994) *Inventing the Feeble Mind: A History of Mental Retardation in the United States*, Berkeley, CA: University of California Press.

Turner, Trevor (1988) 'Henry Maudsley: Psychiatrist, Philosopher and Entrepreneur', in W. F. Bynum, Roy Porter and Michael Shepherd, eds, *The Anatomy of Madness: Essays in the History of Psychiatry, Vol. III: The Asylum and Its Psychiatry*, London: Routledge, pp. 151–89.

Twining, Wiliam (1843) *Some Accounts of Cretinism, And the Institution for Its Cure, on the Abendberg, Near Interlachen, in Switzerland*, London: John W. Parker.

Tyor, Peter L. and Leland V. Bell (1984) *Caring for the Retarded in America: A History*, Westport, CT: Greenwood Press.

Virey, J.-J. (1800) *Dissertation sur un jeune enfant trouvé dans les forêts du département de l'Aveyron, avec des remarques sur l'état primitif de l'homme*. (In Thierry Gineste, *Victor de l'Aveyron, Dernier enfant sauvage, premier enfant fou*, Paris: Hachette, 2004, pp. 295–324.)

Vogt, Carl (1864) *Lectures on Man: His Place in Creation, and in the History of the Earth*, James Hunt, ed., London: Longmans.

Wagner, Peter (1988) *Eros Revived: Erotica of the Enlightenment in England and America*, London: Secker & Warburg.

Wallace, Alfred Russel (1870) *Contributions to the Theory of Natural Selection: A Series of Essays*. (New York: AMS Press, 1973.)

Walmsley, Jan (2000) 'Women and the Mental Deficiency Act of 1913: Citizenship, Sexuality and Regulation', *British Journal of Learning Disabilities*, 28(2): 65–70.

Walmsley, Jan (2001) 'Normalisation, Emancipatory Research and Inclusive Research in Learning Disability', *Disability and Society*, 16(2): 187–205.

Ward, Adolphus William, ed. (1907) *George Crabbe: Poems*, 3 vols, Cambridge: Cambridge University Press.

Watt, Ian, ed. (1973) *Conrad: The Secret Agent. A Selection of Critical Essays*, London: Macmillan.

Weber, Henry, ed. (1812) *The Works of Francis Beaumont and John Fletcher*, Edinburgh: Ballantyne.

Wedgwood, C. V. (1951) *The Last of the Radicals: Josiah Wedgwood, M.P.*, London: Jonathan Cape.

Wells, H. G. (1895) *The Time Machine*. (Bloomington, IN: Indiana University Press, 1987.)

Welsford, Enid (1935) *The Fool: His Social and Literary History*. (New York: Anchor, 1961.)

White, Arnold (1886) *The Problems of a Great City*, London: Remington.

White, Arnold (1909) 'Eugenics and National Efficiency', *Eugenics Review*, 1: 105–11.

White, Gilbert (1789) *A Natural History of Selborne*. (Oxford: Oxford University Press, 1993.)

Wiles, David (1987) *Shakespeare's Clown: Actor and Text in the Elizabethan Playhouse*, Cambridge: Cambridge University Press.

Williams, Raymond (1973) *The Country and the City*, Oxford: Oxford University Press.

Willis, Thomas (1683) *Two Discourses Concerning the Soul of Brutes*. (S. Pordage, trans., Gainesville, FL: Scholars' Facsimiles and Reprints, 1971.)

Wilson, John, trans. (1688) Desiderius Erasmus, *The Praise of Folly*. (Oxford: Clarendon, 1913.)

Wohl, Anthony, ed. (1986) John Hollingshead, *Ragged London in 1861*, Everyman edition, London: Dent.

Wolfensberger, Wolf (1972) *Normalization: The Principle of Normalization in Human Services*, Toronto: National Institute on Mental Retardation.

Wolff, Robert Lee (1979) *Sensational Victorian: The Life and Fiction of Mary Elizabeth Braddon*, New York: Garland.

Wordsworth, Jonathan (1966) 'A Wordsworth Tragedy', *Times Literary Supplement*, 21 July: 642.

Wright, David (2001) *Mental Disability in Victorian England: The Earlswood Asylum, 1847–1901*, Oxford: Clarendon.

Wright, David and Anne Digby, eds (1996) *From Idiocy to Mental Deficiency: Historical Perspectives on People with Learning Disabilities*, London: Routledge.

Wright, Terence (1995) *Elizabeth Gaskell: 'We Are Not Angels': Realism, Gender, Values*, London: Macmillan.

Wrigley, E. A. (1988) *Continuity, Chance, and Change: The Character of the Industrial Revolution in England*, Cambridge: Cambridge University Press.

Wrigley, E. A. and R. S. Schofield (1981) *The Population History of England 1541–1871: A Reconstruction*, London: Edward Arnold.

Wynne, Deborah (2001) *The Sensation Novel and the Victorian Family Magazine*, Houndmills: Palgrave.

Yonge, Charlotte Mary (1860) *Hopes and Fears, or Scenes From the Life of a Spinster*, London: Macmillan.

Yonge, Charlotte Mary (1864) *The Trial*. (London: Macmillan, 1908.)

Yonge, Charlotte Mary (1873) *The Pillars of the House: Or, under Wode, under Rode*, 2 vols. (London: Macmillan, 1889.)

Young, Arthur C., ed. (1961) *The Letters of George Gissing to Eduard Bertz, 1887–1903*, London: Constable.

Young, Robert (1969) 'Malthus and the Evolutionists: The Common Context of Biological and Social Theory', *Past and Present*, 43: 109–45.

Zeydel, Edwin H. (1962) 'Introduction', Sebastian Brant, *The Ship of Fools*, New York: Dover.

Zihni, Lilian Serife (1990) 'The History of the Relationship Between the Concept and Treatment of People with Down's Syndrome in Britain and America From 1866 to 1967', PhD dissertation, University College of London.

Zijderveld, Anton (1982) *Reality in a Looking-Glass: Rationality Through an Analysis of Traditional Folly*, London: Routledge & Kegan Paul.

Index